History, Rel
British Intel

ONE WEEK LOAN

Academy Postdoctoral Fellow at Jesus College, Oxford, and is the author of *Religion and Enlightenment in Eighteenth-Century England* (1998).

History, Religion, and Culture

British Intellectual History 1750–1950

edited by

Stefan Collini

Richard Whatmore

Brian Young

CAMBRIDGE
UNIVERSITY PRESS

PUBLISHED BY THE PRESS SYNDICATE OF THE UNIVERSITY OF CAMBRIDGE
The Pitt Building, Trumpington Street, Cambridge CB2 IRP, United Kingdom

CAMBRIDGE UNIVERSITY PRESS
The Edinburgh Building, Cambridge CB2 2RU, UK http://www.cup.cam.ac.uk
40 West 20th Street, New York, NY 10011–4211, USA http://www.cup.org
10 Stamford Road, Oakleigh, Melbourne 3166, Australia
Ruiz de Alarcón 13, 28014 Madrid, Spain

First published 2000

Printed in the United Kingdom at the University Press, Cambridge

Typeface Plantin 10/12 pt   *System* QuarkXPress™   [SE]

A catalogue record for this book is available from the British Library

Library of Congress Cataloguing in Publication data

History, Religion, and Culture: British Intellectual History 1750–1950
/ edited by Stefan Collini, Richard Whatmore, Brian Young.
     p.   cm.
   Includes index.
   ISBN 0 521 62638 2 (hbk.) – ISBN 0 521 62639 0 (pbk.)
     1. Great Britain – Intellectual life – 18th century.   2. Great Britain –
Intellectual life – 19th century.   3. Great Britain – Intellectual life – 20th
century.   4. Great Britain – Civilization.   5. Great Britain – Religion.
I. Collini, Stefan, 1947–   II. Whatmore, Richard.   III. Young, Brian.
DA533.H63 2000
941 21–dc21   99-042115

ISBN 0 521 62638 2 hardback
ISBN 0 521 62639 0 paperback

Contents

Part III

Preface

Although this book has been planned and written to be read and used in its own right, *History, Religion, and Culture* and its companion volume, *Economy, Polity, and Society*, form a two-book set whose scope is signalled by their common sub-title, *British Intellectual History 1750–1950*. The primary aim of the publication of these two volumes is to bring together the work of many of the leading scholars in what has become a flourishing field in the last couple of decades. But their appearance is also intended to be a way of paying tribute to the impact on that field of the work of two individuals in particular, John Burrow and Donald Winch. Winch and Burrow were for many years the animating spirits of a small group who, at the time, all taught at the University of Sussex, a group which has, in consequence, sometimes been referred to as 'the Sussex School' (a label whose appropriateness is discussed in the 'General Introduction'). In the year 2000 both men reach the retiring-age of sixty-five, and although they will both, we may hope, long continue to be active and prominent in the practice of intellectual history, a collection of their friends and admirers did not want to let this joint landmark pass unrecognised. A pleasing consequence of this originating purpose is that all the contributors to these two volumes have some connection – personal, intellectual, or institutional – with Intellectual History at Sussex and/or with Burrow and Winch as individuals, whether as students, colleagues, or friends. A colloquium was held at Sussex in September 1998 at which draft versions of all the essays were presented and discussed, and at which there was considerable collective brooding on how best to revise and integrate the essays for publication. Throughout, Donald Winch and John Burrow have been kind enough to indulge their friends in their folly, affecting a certain superficial embarrassment (presumably as a mask for their actual deep embarrassment), but nonetheless agreeing both to be participants in the colloquium and contributors to these volumes. It is characteristic of them that they should prefer to contribute to a collaborative enterprise in this way, adding their voices to a set of continuing conversations rather than simply receiving tributes from others, and in this spirit no special indulgence has been granted them as contributors by the implacable and stony-faced (but perhaps not altogether stony-hearted) editors.

This originating purpose also dictates the arrangement of the introductory material. The 'General introduction', which discusses the field of intellectual history as a whole, and Burrow's and Winch's contributions to it in particular, is reproduced in both volumes; it is then followed by a 'Presentation' specific to each particular volume, which briefly attempts to introduce the subject-matter covered by the essays and to draw out some of their relations and common themes. Readers impatient to engage with the substantive historical material should, therefore, skip the 'General Introduction' and proceed directly to the 'Presentation of *History, Religion, and Culture*'.

General introduction

I

It may be that there is no longer any need to justify the term 'intellectual history' or the practice for which it stands. If this is so – experience can, alas, still occasionally cause one to wonder – then it is a very recent development indeed, at least in Britain. Only two or three decades ago, the label routinely encountered more than its share of misunderstanding, some of it rather wilful, especially perhaps on the part of some political and social historians. There was, to begin with, the allegation that intellectual history was largely the history of things that never really *mattered*. The long dominance of the historical profession by political historians tended to breed a kind of philistinism, an unspoken belief that power and its exercise was what 'mattered' (a term which invited but rarely received any close scrutiny). The legacy of this prejudice is still discernible in the tendency in some quarters to require ideas to have 'influenced' the political elite before they can be deemed worthy of historical attention, as though there were some reason why the history of art or of science, of philosophy or of literature, were somehow of less interest and significance than the histories of policies and parliaments. In the course of the 1960s and 1970s, the mirror-image of this philistinism became even more common, particularly in the form of the claim that ideas of any degree of systematic expression or formal sophistication did not merit detailed historical scrutiny because they were, by definition, only held by a small educated minority. The fact is, of course, that much which legitimately interests us in history was the work of minorities (not always of the same type, be it noted), and it remains true, to repeat an adaptation of a famous line of E. P. Thompson's that I have used elsewhere, that it is not only the poor and inarticulate who may stand in need of being rescued from the enormous condescension of posterity.

A further, related misconception has been the charge, which still has some currency, that intellectual history is inherently 'idealist', where that term is used pejoratively to signify the belief (or, more often, assumption) that ideas develop by a logic of their own, without reference to other human activities or to what is loosely called their 'social context'. There was possibly some truth to this as a criticism of some of the work written a couple of generations ago, particularly that originating in the history of philosophy, but it is simply false as a description of what intellectual history must be like. The intellectual historian is someone who happens to find the reflective and expressive life of the past to be of interest: it is the vulgarest kind of reductivism or ideology-spotting to presume that this betrays an unspoken belief in the superiority of one form of human activity, still less an underlying commitment to a monocausal view of history.

In some quarters, the very term 'intellectual history' itself generated unease, with the result that 'the history of ideas' has sometimes been preferred as an alternative label. However, the danger here is that the emphasis on the 'history of *ideas*' may precisely suggest that we are dealing with autonomous abstractions which, in their self-propelled journeyings through time, happened only contingently and temporarily to find anchorage in particular human minds, a suggestion encouraged by the long German tradition of *Geistesgeschichte* or *Ideengeschichte* which, revealing its Hegelian ancestry, looked to the history of philosophy to provide the pattern of human history as a whole. By contrast, the term 'intellectual history' signals more clearly that the focus is on an aspect of human activity and is in this respect no different from 'economic history', 'political history', and so forth.

One final, more local, form of resistance took the form of the suggestion – only partly facetious, one fears – that there is no need for intellectual history in the case of Britain since it, at least in the modern period, has been a society with no worthwhile or significant ideas, or, in another version, one where ideas are of no consequence, or, marginally less crass, one where the preferred idiom is that of the practical or the implicit (as though these, too, were not susceptible of historical analysis). In each of these claims, not only is the premise deeply disputable but the logic is, anyway, plainly faulty, as though one were to conclude that there could be no economic history of sub-Saharan Africa or no constitutional history of post-war Italy.

Given this still-recent history of prejudice and misunderstanding, one of the striking features of the essays in these volumes is their lack of defensiveness: they are written as contributions to an area of scholarship which is already rich and complex, and their tone does not suggest any felt need to justify the larger enterprise. And it is indeed the case that the last couple of decades have seen an impressive efflorescence of work in intellectual history understood in the broad terms sketched here. Where previously the 'history of ideas' was often, especially in the modern period, a pursuit cultivated by philosophers, political theorists, literary critics, social scientists, and others pursuing the 'pre-history' of their own disciplines, recent work in 'intellectual history' is much more likely to be done by those with a trained and cultivated interest in a particular period of the past, seeking to apply the same standards of historical evidence and judgement to the intellectual life of that period as their colleagues have traditionally displayed towards its political, social, and economic life. Instead of works which cut a 'vertical' (and often teleological) slice through the past with titles like 'The History of Sociology from Montesquieu to Weber', 'The Growth of Economic Theory from Smith to Friedman', 'The Making of Modern Historiography from Gibbon to Braudel', and so on, the tendency of recent work has been towards excavating a more 'horizontal' site, exploring the idioms and preoccupations of a past period as they manifest themselves in thought and discussion about various issues that cannot readily be assigned to current academic pigeon-holes. In other words, rather than constructing a 'history of ideas', where the emphasis is on the logical structure of certain arguments that are seen as only contingently and almost irrelevantly located in the past, the informing aspiration has been to write an 'intellectual history', which tries to recover the thought of the past in its complexity and, in a sense which is neither self-contradictory nor trivial, as far as possible in its own terms.

However, although I have been suggesting that intellectual history is now becoming an established and, on the whole, accepted sub-discipline even in Britain, it would be a disagreeable consequence of the hyper-professionalism of modern academic life were this to result in the formation of a new disciplinary trade-union, with all the characteristics of parochialism and exclusiveness, together with the attendant demarcation disputes, that threaten to characterise such bodies in their militant phase. It is surely a sign of cultural health rather than of corporate weakness that several of the contributors to these volumes would not wish to be constantly or exclusively classified as 'intellectual historians', and indeed that their institutional affiliations span several academic departments, including English, History, Politics, Law, and Religious Studies.

It will, I trust, be obvious that the brief characterisation of intellectual history offered in the preceding paragraphs is open to dispute and has in fact been vigorously disputed in recent years. The work of Michel Foucault and his followers has encouraged a rather different form of engagement with the 'discourses' dominant in past societies – one which often displaces purposive historical agents from the scene altogether – and more recently still, styles of work deriving from literary theory and cultural studies have attempted to shift attention yet further away from the meaning-laden utterances of those who can be identified as members of some kind of 'elite'. Meanwhile, detailed historical work on a broad range of aspects of the intellectual life of the past continues to be carried on in a variety of less noisy or self-advertising modes. The result of these developments has been an inevitable and largely healthy pluralism of approaches: now that the legitimacy of the activity itself no longer needs to be argued for, intellectual historians can be allowed the same luxuries of disagreement and rivalry as have long been enjoyed by the more established branches of the historian's trade. And precisely because this plurality of approaches *is* now coming into being, it may be appropriate to switch the focus of attention from these general considerations to examine at slightly greater length the specific contributions to this field made by John Burrow and Donald Winch.

II

Insofar as the activity of intellectual history *has* received institutional embodiment and cultural recognition as an academic discipline or sub-discipline in Britain in the last generation or so, it has been particularly identified with the University of Sussex. Sussex was the first British university to offer a degree programme in the subject and to establish posts explicitly defined as being in the field of 'Intellectual History'. In the course of the 1970s and 1980s, some observers, claiming to find certain shared characteristics in the work published by some of those responsible for this programme, began to refer to 'the Sussex School'. This label can, at best, only ever have served as a piece of academic shorthand or argot, while at worst it was a culpable form of exaggeration or reification. No such 'school' exists or ever existed if that term be taken to imply common adherence to an explicit and exclusive methodological programme. It would be more accurate to say that the comparatively flexible and interdisciplinary structure of Sussex in those decades provided a congenial berth for a group of like-minded scholars whose interests typically tended to fall across or between the domains of the better-established academic disciplines. (I shall return to a consideration of the nature of this 'like-mindedness' in section III below.) In any event, what most certainly *is* beyond dispute is the fact that Donald Winch and John Burrow were for many years the leading figures in this group at Sussex.

Since this is not the place to attempt to recap the entire career of either Burrow or Winch, I shall merely touch on some of the more significant stages in their respective formations as intellectual historians. It is, of course, sobering for the historian above all to be brought to realise just how hard it is to reconstitute, let alone account for, the intellectual trajectories even of one's close friends, a difficulty compounded as much as eased by the risks of relying overmuch on one's own rather randomly accumulated personal archive. And anyway, perhaps writings that are in the public domain are merely the by-product or end-result of some primal process of self-fashioning – indirect records of some now undetectable early shifts in the tectonic plates of temperament and disposition. Perhaps the ministrations of any number of careers advisers were otiose from the moment in which the young John Burrow stumbled on Figgis's *Gerson to Grotius* in his school library and was enthralled rather than baffled; perhaps all that has followed was already prefigured in the scene in which the teenage Burrow, crouched on the floor next to the family wireless, took notes, no doubt of a daunting illegibility even then, from a series of talks on 'Freedom and its Betrayal' by a speaker he had up till that point never heard of called Isaiah Berlin. And why it was that, at almost exactly the same time, the young Donald Winch was to be found rather self-consciously reading Plato's *Republic* while on holiday by the shores of the Baltic, or why it was that, though a student of economics, he chose to attend, for two years running, Michael Oakeshott's lectures on the history of political thought – these may be matters which defy further explanation, though in each case the temptations of teleology are strong (and have here not been altogether resisted).

Academically, both men were shaped in the 1950s. For John Burrow, an undergraduate at Christ's College from 1954 to 1957, the initial scholarly context was provided by the Cambridge History Tripos, and more especially its options in the history of political thought where he was particularly stimulated by the teaching of Duncan Forbes. At an early stage, Burrow had found the dominant genres of political and economic history less than wholly congenial, and after graduating he embarked, under the benign but necessarily somewhat distant supervision of Kitson Clark, on an ambitious Ph.D. on Victorian theories of social evolution, which was submitted in 1961. More broadly, his mentor at this time in the ways of the world, no less than in the duties and opportunities of being a historian, was J. H. Plumb, an academic talent-spotter and trainer with an unmatchably successful record. A research fellowship at Christ's was followed by a college lectureship at Downing, but by the time the revised version of his thesis appeared as a book in 1966, Burrow had moved to a lectureship at the recently founded University of East Anglia.

Evolution and Society: A Study in Victorian Social Theory was an extraordinarily assured debut. The book decisively challenged the assumption that the source of mid-Victorian ideas of social evolution was to be found in the application of Darwin's biological theories, and instead traced the attempts of figures such as Spencer, Maine, and Tylor to address questions of cultural variety within the framework of a (sometimes profoundly troubled) belief in progress. As a result, the book immediately established itself as a pioneering contribution to the history of anthropology as well as a provocative exploration of a central aspect of Victorian culture. That the argument of *Evolution and Society* certainly did not reflect any lack of appreciation on Burrow's part of the intellectual change that Darwin *had* wrought was demonstrated by his introduction to the Penguin *Origin of Species* in 1968, while his familiarity with European, and especially German, sources in the Romantic period was evident in his substantial introduction to his new translation of Wilhelm von Humboldt's *The Limits of State Action*, published in 1969.

In Donald Winch's intellectual formation, the LSE and the discipline of Economics occupied something of the same place that Cambridge and History did for John Burrow. An undergraduate between 1953 and 1956, Winch opted to specialise in international economics under the tutelage of James Meade, but he was already revealing himself as being at least as interested in Popper's teaching on scientific method or, as mentioned earlier, Oakeshott's on the history of political thought. Moving to Princeton for graduate study, he fell under the influence of Jacob Viner, of whom he later wrote a perceptive and affectionate memoir, and began to specialise in the history of economic thought. On returning to Britain after a year's teaching at Berkeley, a post at Edinburgh was followed in 1963 by a lectureship at Sussex, which soon led to rapid promotion, and he became Reader and then, in 1969, Professor of the History of Economics.

His first book, *Classical Political Economy and Colonies*, published in 1965, already displayed what were to become trademark qualities: the substance combined a quiet mastery of the technicalities of the history of economic theory with a sure grasp of the historical embeddedness of such ideas, while the manner exhibited a seemingly unforced alliance between clarity and argumentative vigour. The book compelled the historians of government policy in the period to learn their economic letters, while at the same time infiltrating some awkward complexities into the standard chronicles of 'the rise of political economy'. A certain distance from his initial disciplinary formation was already manifest in his declared intention to 'steer clear of the history of economic analysis for its own sake in order to remain close to the issues as seen by the participants' (*Classical Political Economy and Colonies*, p. 3). In other ways, too, Winch was already contesting that canonical account of early political economy which confined itself to the Holy Trinity of Smith the Father, Ricardo the Son, and Mill the Holy Ghost, one fruit of his historical attentiveness to less fashionable figures being the substantial editorial labour of his edition of James Mill's *Selected Economic Writings* which was published in 1966.

Both men, therefore, began by initially pursuing a somewhat under-favoured branch of a powerful discipline (respectively History and Economics) and then progressively reacting against the coerciveness and complacency of representatives of mainstream traditions of those disciplines. Both had encountered the constraints of orthodox 'discipline' history as written by present practitioners of a given discipline, especially the 'pre-history of anthropology' in Burrow's case and the 'pre-history of economics' in Winch's. By the late 1960s, partly as a result of this experience, their respective scholarly interests were, quite independently of each other, moving closer together under the broad rubric of the history of social thought or of the social sciences. From his arrival at Sussex, Donald Winch had been closely involved in teaching a 'contextual' course, compulsory for all final-year students in the School of Social Sciences, called 'Concepts, methods, and values in the social sciences' (always known, not always affectionately, as CMV). In the mid-1960s he was instrumental in adding an option in 'The historical development of the social sciences' to the existing course which had previously been confined to philosophical and methodological issues. In those expansionary days, it was possible to think of making appointments to match such academic initiatives, and it was Winch, in his role as (a notably young) Dean of the School of Social Sciences, who first invited John Burrow, by then Reader in History at East Anglia, to Sussex, initially to lecture for the new course, and eventually to take up a post teaching it. (The first exchange of letters – 'Dear Mr Burrow'/'Dear Mr Winch' – has, in retrospect, something of an *84 Charing Cross Road* feel about it.) As a result, in 1969 Burrow was appointed to a post principally responsible for teaching the historical part of CMV; a few years later he transferred to the School of English and American Studies.

The University of Sussex had been founded in 1961 with the deliberate aim of 're-drawing the map of learning', and institutional expression had been given to this ideal by not establishing conventional academic departments, but instead grouping scholars with related interests into schools of study, usually with an area basis such as the School of European Studies or the School of English and American Studies. Within and across these schools, 'majors' were taught in particular subjects, while students had also to spend approximately half their time on school 'contextual' courses (such as CMV). 'Subject groups' were responsible for these majors and these were the nearest Sussex came in those days to having orthodox departments. Both the ethos and the structure of Sussex in the late 1960s and early 1970s were favourable to innovation, and it was this supportive setting that permitted the establishment initially of an MA and then, in 1969, of a undergraduate 'major' in Intellectual History, the first such degree programme to be set up at a British university. These early initiatives were undertaken by members of staff who had initially been appointed to more traditionally defined posts, such as Peter Burke in History and Michael Moran in Philosophy; crucial support was provided by James Shiel from Classical Studies and the then recently retired Helmut Pappé. A new lectureship in Intellectual History, the first to be formally designated as such, was established in 1972 and initially held by Larry Siedentop, and then, from 1974, by Stefan Collini (to whom I shall, for the sake of narrative propriety, sometimes have to refer, as here, in the third person).

The years during which these institutional arrangements were being established and consolidated – roughly the late 1960s to the mid-1970s – also saw shifts, or perhaps just modulations, in the intellectual interests of both Donald Winch and John Burrow. Winch's interest in the interaction between economic expertise and political exigency was for some time principally focused on the twentieth century, and his *Economics and Policy: A Historical Study* (1969) broke what was then new ground in its exploration of the ways in which Keynesian arguments came to penetrate the policy-making establishments of both Britain and the United States. In terms of both chronology and of sources, the book's range was impressive, moving from Alfred Marshall's attempts to accommodate the challenge of 'the social problem' within the absorbent framework of his *Principles of Economics* in the 1890s to the measures undertaken by the Kennedy–Johnson administrations of the 1960s. The interest in the role of economic advisers was sustained, and supported by a daunting display of expertise in the official and archival sources, in a study of the Economic Advisory Council of the 1930s, which was jointly written with Susan Howson and published in 1976. But, as already indicated, his earliest work had been on the foundations of political economy in the late eighteenth and early nineteenth centuries, an area of research which he never entirely deserted, as evidenced by his substantial introduction to the Penguin edition of books IV and V of Mill's *Principles of Political Economy* in 1970 and his Everyman edition of Ricardo's *Principles of Political Economy and Taxation* in 1973. Moreover, by the mid-1970s, Winch had begun to read widely in recent work by early-modern intellectual historians on the roles played by the languages of 'civic humanism' and 'natural jurisprudence' in the development of political thought during that period, and he brought the fruits of this reading to bear on the interpretation of the most canonical of all figures in the history of economic thought in his *Adam Smith's Politics: An Essay in Historiographic Revision,* which was published in 1978. This characteristically combative book sought to rescue Smith from the retrospective teleologies of the historians of economics, and to restore him to his eighteenth-century context, principally but by no means exclusively his Scottish context. This relatively short, tightly argued book was to have considerable impact both within and beyond the confines of the history of political economy, not least through its firm insistence on the distinction between the goal of recovering the historicity of a past writer and that of using the name of that writer to legitimate a variety of political or academic enterprises in the present.

During these same years, the focus of John Burrow's scholarly work also underwent some change, essentially away from its initial concentration on the history of social and political thought towards a broader engagement with Victorian culture and historiography. His essay for J. H. Plumb's *Festschrift*, published in 1974, '"The Village Community" and the Uses of History in Late-Nineteenth-Century England', signalled an early step in this direction by focusing on the historical writings of figures such as Maine, Freeman, and Maitland. At the same time, partly through the structure of teaching at Sussex (especially after his move into the School of English and American Studies), Burrow was drawn more deeply into the relations between history and literature in nineteenth-century Britain; some incidental fruits of this experience may be found in his contributions to *The Victorians*, edited by Laurence Lerner, a volume in the 'Context of English Literature' series which appeared in 1978. This phase of Burrow's work culminated triumphantly in *A Liberal Descent: Victorian Historians and the English Past*, which was published in 1981 and was joint winner of the Wolfson Prize for History for that year. The book's principal sections discuss the vast, sprawling narrative histories of Macaulay, Stubbs, Freeman, and Froude and the intellectual and historiographical traditions within which they worked, but this flat inventory signally fails to do justice to the book's widely ramifying explorations of Victorian cultural sensibility. There is now abundant evidence of how its account of the nineteenth-century Whig tradition of historical writing has left its mark on scholarship across a wide range of topics, some far removed from the confines of the history of historiography. Yet for many readers, the book's distinctiveness and charm lie in the ways in which the writing allows a cultivated sensibility to direct, inform, and give appropriately modulated expression to its historical analysis, simultaneously catching and doing justice to the idiosyncrasy of his chosen historians while placing them within intellectual and literary traditions which are characterised with great richness and subtlety.

In the early 1980s, Collini, Winch, and Burrow collaborated in writing *That Noble Science of Politics: A Study in Nineteenth-Century Intellectual*

History, whose publication in 1983 marked, both practically and symboli-
cally, the high point of their collaborative endeavour. Perhaps the least
awkward way to provide some characterisation of the book here is to
quote from the preface which was specially written (in 1996) for the
Japanese translation.

In the nature of things, a book that sets out to challenge or repudiate accepted disciplinary boundaries is likely to run the risk of baffling some of its readers. As one
reviewer sympathetically put it: 'This is going to be a perplexing book for many.
Librarians will wonder how to classify it. Specialists in politics and economics will
be embarrassed at its demonstration of how what they thought sewn up can be
unstitched. Tutors will wonder what passages their pupils can be trusted not to
misunderstand.' As the Prologue to the book was intended to make clear, some of
the intellectual energy that fuelled its writing came from our shared negative reaction to certain prevailing disciplinary dispensations. Most obviously, we repudiated those forms of 'the history of the social sciences' which consisted in finding
'precursors' and 'founding fathers' for contemporary social scientific specialisms
from among past writers the specificity and integrity of whose concerns thereby
came in for some very rough treatment indeed . . . We also repudiated the coerciveness of the priorities encouraged by 'the history of political theory', an enterprise which has enjoyed such a strong institutional position in the
Anglo-American scholarly world that political, economic, and social historians all
too easily take it to *be* intellectual history. And, more obviously, we took our distance from those kinds of approaches which are united in little else than in assuming that intellectual activity is best understood as a reflection or by-product of
some allegedly more fundamental social or economic process . . . Without wishing
to set up a new meta-discipline or to propose a panacea for wider cultural ail-
ments, we continue to regard intellectual history of the kind exhibited in this book
as a flexible and responsible approach to the intellectual life of the past. In certain
respects, intellectual history pursued in this manner may itself be regarded as
having a kind of 'anti-specialist' identity, both because it cannot be equated with
the history of one subject-matter or discipline and because it cannot be reduced to
one methodology or vocabulary.

Although there has been no further attempt at direct collaboration, it is
clear from the prefaces and acknowledgements in their subsequent works
(to cite only evidence that is in the public domain) that the ties of friendship and intellectual exchange between the three authors remain close.
However, the partly parallel and partly divergent trajectories followed by
Winch and Burrow since that period must also be noted here.

John Burrow's stylish 'Past Masters' volume on Gibbon was published
in 1985, and in the same year he gave the Carlyle Lectures at Oxford,
which were then published in 1988 under the title *Whigs and Liberals:
Continuity and Change in English Political Thought*. This slim volume
testified, as its preface acknowledged, to Burrow's 'long-standing interest
in the impact of historicist ways of thinking on European, and above all

British, culture in the post-Romantic period' (*Whigs and Liberals*, p. viii). It set some of the familiar ideas of nineteenth-century liberalism in a new perspective by tracing continuities and discontinuities with that broadly Whig tradition of political thinking whose richness and longevity have only become fully apparent with the scholarship of the last generation, and the book gracefully sketched some of the ways in which conceptions of variety or diversity were seen as essential to social and individual energy and vitality. The attempt to establish some perspectival balance in understanding the ceaseless gavotte of continuity and change is, of course, the stock-in-trade of all historians, but it is in a deeper sense at the heart of Burrow's scholarly sensibility and informs his recurring preoccupation with the mutations of intellectual traditions. As he put it in his speech accepting an honorary degree at the University of Bologna in 1988: 'Our relations to the past, or to what we conceive it to be, are, it seems to me, full of ambiguity and fascination; at once indispensable and civilising and also, as perhaps all worthwhile relations are, perilous. We may derive from them both confidence and complacency, nourishment of identity and the bigotry of exclusiveness.'

Winch's contributions to *That Noble Science* signalled what were to be his principal preoccupations during the ensuing decade: on the one hand, the question of the fate of Smith's ambitious programme in the hands of various putative successors, and, on the other, what was to prove a long engagement with the work and reputation of Robert Malthus. The former issued in a stream of essays in the 1980s and early 1990s – essays often couched in revisionist terms in an attempt to counter the later appropriation of some eighteenth- or nineteenth-century figure. His carefully crafted 'Past Masters' volume on Malthus in 1987 was the chief expression of the latter concern, but Winch was also closely involved in enabling the Royal Economic Society edition of *An Essay on the Principle of Population* finally to see the light of day, and this was later followed by his own edition in the Cambridge Texts in the History of Political Thought series in 1992. The invitation to deliver the Carlyle Lectures at Oxford for 1995 provided the opportunity to present the outlines of the synthesis of many years of work in these related areas, the full version of which was to be published in 1996 as *Riches and Poverty: An Intellectual History of Political Economy in Britain, 1750–1834*.

Even in what has thus far been an exceptionally productive writing life, *Riches and Poverty* stands out as a remarkable achievement. The book provides a learned, thickly textured account of the ways in which arguments over economic matters (in the broadest sense of the term) in this crucial period were bound up with and expressive of wider political and social identities. Its command of the purely *theoretical* complexities of classical political economy is evident yet never foregrounded: instead, the main strands of the period's attempts to grapple analytically with a new range of issues about wealth and poverty are threaded into a thickly peopled narrative tapestry, and the book is studded with intellectual vignettes that are as impressive for their concision as for their scholarship, whether it be in discussing the differences between Smith and Ferguson on the appropriateness of taking a 'philosophic' view of the rebellion of the American colonies, or in discriminating shades of unfairness in the treatment of Malthus by the leading 'Lake poets'. The book may only now be starting to make its presence felt, but it will in time surely do what all outstanding works of historical scholarship do, namely, to make it harder, or at the very least less excusable, to write the kind of shoddy, simplistic accounts of 'classical political economy' or 'the 1790s' that are regularly to be found in treatments of this period written by economists and literary scholars as well as by some historians.

As their new essays in these two volumes suggest, the stream of outstanding publications by these two authors shows no signs of drying up: at the time of writing, John Burrow is just on the point of completing a large study of European intellectual history between 1848 and 1914, while Donald Winch is organising a major British Academy project on the peculiarities of British economic experience since the Industrial Revolution. However, the last decade or so has seen some significant changes in the institutional bases from which the activities chronicled here have been carried on, changes which may make 'the Sussex School' less appropriate than ever as a collective label. In 1986 Stefan Collini left Sussex to take up a post in the Faculty of English in Cambridge, a move reflecting and encouraging a shift in his interests away from the early focus on the history of social and political thought to a concern with literary and cultural criticism, as well as a move from the nineteenth to the twentieth century. In 1995 John Burrow became the first holder of the newly established Chair of European Thought at Oxford, resuming an engagement with nineteenth-century European thinkers and writers that had been largely in the background of his intellectual activities since the late 1960s, though it had never been wholly absent. The personnel of the group at Sussex changed in other ways, too. Following Collini's departure, Anna Bryson held a lectureship there from 1986 to 1992 and Richard Whatmore and Brian Young have been lecturers in Intellectual History since 1993. Martin van Gelderen succeeded John Burrow as Professor of Intellectual History in 1995, and the appointment of Blair Worden to a Chair of History in the following year further strengthened Sussex's standing in the early-modern period. Structural reorganisation within the university led in 1997 to proposals for the establishment of the

Centre for Literary and Intellectual History, an arrangement which would give institutional expression to the close collaborative links already existing with colleagues such as Norman Vance in English, and Donald Winch formally moved into this Centre in 1998. In institutional terms, there have, therefore, been both dispersals and continuities, and at this point it is proper to leave others to take up the story, or stories, in other ways in the future.

III

The term 'the Sussex School' has, as I have already emphasised, never been more than a piece of academic shorthand, but insofar as any reality lay behind the label, it would have to be found in a series of works published from the late 1970s onwards. These in no sense constituted a coordinated programme, but they perhaps evinced certain common qualities of approach and manner, and they all focused on a series of interconnecting themes and figures in British intellectual history from roughly the mid-eighteenth to the mid-twentieth centuries. The principal titles, in chronological order, were probably the following:

> *Adam Smith's Politics: An Essay in Historiographic Revision* (1978);
> *Liberalism and Sociology: L. T. Hobhouse and Political Argument in Britain 1880–1914* (1979);
> *A Liberal Descent: Victorian Historians and the English Past* (1981);
> *That Noble Science of Politics: An Essay in Nineteenth-Century Intellectual History* (1983);
> *Whigs and Liberals: Change and Continuity in English Political Thought* (1988);
> *Public Moralists: Political Thought and Intellectual Life in Britain 1850–1930* (1991);
> *Riches and Poverty: An Intellectual History of Political Economy in Britain 1750–1834* (1996).

All three authors also published volumes in the Oxford 'Past Masters' series at much the same time: John Burrow's *Gibbon* (1985), Donald Winch's *Malthus* (1987), and Stefan Collini's *Arnold* (1988). It was no doubt characteristic that these three books should have dealt with figures normally seen as the intellectual property of three very different modern disciplines – respectively, History, Economics, and English. Over these two decades, these books were, of course, accompanied by numerous articles, essays, and reviews, some of which occasionally took a more polemical or critical stance towards works by other scholars in the field. The perception of a characteristic 'Sussex' style may also have been encouraged by the fact that a number of younger scholars who had been graduate students there began to publish work in a not dissimilar vein, including two of the contributors to these volumes, Julia Stapleton and Dario Castiglione (as well as Philip Ironside who would have been a contributor but for ill health). Notable publications from this generation include Stapleton's *Englishness and the Study of Politics: The Social and Political Thought of Ernest Barker* (1994) and Ironside's *The Social and Political Thought of Bertrand Russell: The Development of an Aristocratic Liberalism* (1996).

The work of the scholars who have been regarded as at the heart of this group has thus taken the form of substantive books and essays rather than programmatic manifestos, and its characteristics can therefore not easily be encapsulated in a few sentences. But it would be reasonable to say that the informing spirit of much of this work has been the attempt to recover past ideas and re-situate them in their intellectual contexts in ways which resist the anachronistic or otherwise tendentious and selective pressures exerted by contemporary academic and political polemic. Work in this vein has also attempted to be alert to questions of style and register, to the nuances of individual voice as well as the animating presence of intellectual traditions, and to recognise the different levels of abstraction and practical engagement involved in work in different genres. The aim has been to offer a more thickly textured sense of the interplay between, say, literary, historiographical, and economic ideas in the cultural life of Britain since the Enlightenment, as well as much subtler characterisations of the relations between such ideas and the broader social and political developments of this period.

Intellectual history in this vein has, as already observed, eschewed adherence to any of the methodological programmes or tight conceptual schemes which have from time to time been elaborated and defended in general terms – the sociology of knowledge, the history of unit ideas, the mapping of *mentalités*, the study of political languages, the critique of ideologies, the recovery of authors' intentions, the archaeology of epistemes, the deconstruction of texts, and so on. The intellectual practice of both Winch and Burrow has, of course, displayed closer affinities to some of these approaches than to others, notably to those expounded in the methodological essays of John Pocock and Quentin Skinner (leaders of what, with equal imprecision and a fine disregard for geography, has sometimes been dubbed 'the Cambridge School'). But a characteristic of the work of Burrow, Winch, and their associates has been a certain deliberate eclecticism and a preference for letting substantive scholarship speak for itself (a preference which is not to be confused with the theoretical stance of 'empiricism', properly so called), and such collective distinctiveness as this work has displayed has been more a matter of tone and level of treatment, of common preoccupations and similar dispositions, than of adherence to the precepts of any one interpretive scheme. Moreover, this work has not for the most part been directly addressed to those working in the highly contentious (and only partly historical) sub-field of 'the history of political thought', and insofar as it *has* dealt with past political debate it has, especially in recent years, certainly not concentrated on relations between past political theorising and contemporary moral and political philosophy, as so much of the work in that field continues to do. As their titles indicate, the essays in these two volumes range fairly widely over aspects of cultural and intellectual life in Britain during this period, as a result of which the history of political theory as such receives only glancing or incidental treatment.

In their occasional public ruminations on their practice, both Burrow and Winch have explored the value and limitations of the metaphor of 'eavesdropping on the conversations of the past' as a way of gesturing towards the intellectual historian's characteristic role, both immediately adding the rider that what is overheard has also to be (to use another metaphor) 'translated' for the benefit of the contemporary reader. Other, similar metaphors could no doubt capture other aspects of the constant journeying between strangeness and familiarity which is the historian's task, but at the heart of this practice has been an underlying respect for the brute fact that the thoughts and feelings of the historical agents being studied are *theirs* not ours, and that a certain empathy and interpretive charity are essential if the activity of historical understanding is to involve anything more than merely confirming one's appearance in a mirror. (This, incidentally, is one reason why the historian who is seeking understanding rather than simply collecting information need never be afraid of the glib charge of antiquarianism; the past can have no capacity to surprise us if we merely visit it to provide material for *our* debates and preoccupations.) In practical terms, this rules out an excessive high-handedness in our dealings with the dead; as Winch has put it in discussing ways of 'achieving historical understanding': 'I would confess . . . to following a fairly simple rule of thumb in such matters: past authors should be treated as one would wish one's own writings and beliefs to be treated, should the positions, by some amazing twist of fate, be reversed' (*Riches and Poverty*, p. 30). The contrast with what is suggested by the revealing metaphor of 'interrogating texts' is striking: interrogators know in advance the kinds of thing they are expecting to learn, often subjecting their victims to some pretty ungentle kinds of pressure until the process yields the desired information.

Ultimately, the most appropriate as well as most effective way to indicate some of the distinctive characteristics of the work of Winch and

Burrow would be through an extended analysis of their *practice*, and this, of its nature, cannot be undertaken in the brief compass available here. Instead, a couple of more or less arbitrarily chosen passages from their work must do duty for a fuller critical account. In the case of *A Liberal Descent*, almost any sentence taken at random could be used to illustrate how a layered richness of understanding seeks and finds expression in a prose that is sinuous and complex, yet entirely free from inert, clogging abstractions. Thus, from the discussion of Macaulay:

> The *History* is much more than the vindication of a party; it is an attempt to insinuate a view of politics, pragmatic, reverent, essentially Burkean, informed by a high, even tumid, sense of the worth of public life, yet fully conscious of its interrelations with the wider progress of society; it embodies what Hallam had merely asserted, a sense of the privileged possession by Englishmen of their history, as well as of the epic dignity of government by discussion (*A Liberal Descent*, p. 93).

No-one, not even the most inveterate Jamesian, could be tempted to describe this prose style as 'spare'. And yet there is a curious form of economy of expression here, a compacting into one sentence of elements which, taken alone, could too easily become blandly propositional and, hence, exaggerated. Even the wilful disregard for the usual proprieties in the use of the semi-colon plays, I am sorry to have to acknowledge, its part. As in the treatment of each of the major historians he discusses, the sense of intimacy with Macaulay here is intense, but it is the opposite of mimetic: it 'places' Macaulay's characteristic themes, and such placing always depends upon the kind of distance engendered by reflection and comparison. The voice in this passage, as in the book as a whole, is knowledgeable, but not insinuatingly knowing; it embodies both sympathy and understanding, without in the least threatening to patronise or to recruit.

Or, for a different range of effects, one may turn to the book's discussion of Freeman's deliberate use of an archaising, 'native' style in his *Norman Conquest*:

> Like Pre-Raphaelite painting and the earnestness of Victorian Gothic, Freeman's restricted diction and syntactical austerity represent an attempt, conducted with revivalist zeal, to use archaism as a means of cleansing and renewal; as usual, the achieved effect is an almost fetidly intense, gamey Victorianism. Freeman's diction was of course not only restricted but necessarily in some measure deliberately archaic; there are times, though their preferred periods were different, when one is reminded of Rossetti's searching of old Romances for 'stunning words', though Rossetti's eclectic sensationalism was actually the reverse of Freeman's austerity: Strawberry Hill Gothick to Gilbert Scott's pedantry (*A Liberal Descent*, pp. 211–12).

Comparison and allusion rank high among Burrow's preferred literary instruments: his broad range of cultural reference yields unlooked-for similarities which simultaneously help isolate distinctiveness. His own vocabulary can be high, in more than one sense, but the manner is conversational rather than pedagogic, and in this passage the calculated off-handedness of the final clause has an aphoristic crispness, the effectiveness of which would be dissipated and perhaps even rendered doubtful in any more laboured exposition of the point. More than many historical figures, Freeman may now seem to invite mockery and even derision, and it is not the least of the achievements of the section of the book from which this passage comes that it resists this invitation, restoring intelligibility to his cultural enthusiasms and endowing his quirkiness with energy and purpose without ever merely sending him up or putting him down.

Turning to *Riches and Poverty*, one faces a different kind of difficulty in excerpting, since Winch's austerer style tends to produce its effects by means of a kind of sustained command. The following passage is simply one of dozens which display the book's incisive grasp of the choreography of intellectual alliance and antagonism as it introduces a discussion of the relations between the ideas of Smith, Burke, Paine, and Price at the end of the eighteenth century. Having remarked that Burke 'suggested the possibility of an inversion of the more familiar sequence expounded by Hume, Smith, and other Scottish historians of civil society, whereby commerce brings an improvement in manners and the arts and sciences in its train', Winch proceeds in characteristic fashion to allow historical complexity to erode the simplicities of later stereotypes:

Paine's extrapolation of the more widely accepted sequence into the future, however, and the welcome given to Smith's system of natural liberty by other contemporary opponents of Burke, has proved as useful to students of turn-of-the-century radicalism as it has to students of what later was seen as Burke's conservatism. In Paine's case, it has allowed him to be characterised as a spokesman for an upwardly mobile society of self-interested economic individualists, as the radical embodiment of all those 'bourgeois' qualities that Smith, alongside and in harmony with Locke, is supposed to represent [a footnote hauls a selection of eminent miscreants into the dock at this point]. As in the case of Burke, some of the resulting characterisations have had an homogenising effect on the diverse qualities of radicalism in this period. Including Price alongside Paine in this comparative exercise acts as a reminder that supporters of revolution did not always speak with the same voice when diagnosing the economic conditions most likely to consort with republican institutions. Price did not fully share Paine's 'Smithian' confidence in the progressive potential contained in the spread of commerce and manufacturing. Nor, as we shall see, did Smith share Paine's belief in the capacity or necessity for commerce to civilise by revolutionising government (*Riches and Poverty*, p. 131).

The passage is in some ways a promissory note, one made good by the rest of the chapter from the opening paragraphs of which it is taken. It is, typically, argumentative, and it is revisionist in the way complex, freshly seen history is always revisionist, in refusing the mind any easy resting-place in familiar modern categories. The chapter is entitled 'Contested Affinities', a phrase which is almost emblematic of the way Donald Winch writes intellectual history, with its constant attempt to do justice both to family resemblances and to family quarrels. The very structure of the prose vetoes any slack assimilation of what were subtly different positions, yet a clarity of outline survives through all attention to idiosyncrasy.

Or, for an example of how a seasoning of irony can contribute to, rather than detract from, fair-mindedness, consider his account of Arnold Toynbee's 'extraordinary lament' about the development of political economy earlier in the nineteenth century:

he regarded the failure to emancipate political economy from the influence of Ricardo's ruthless abstractions as a significant tragedy . . . As in the case of Keynes's equivalent regrets that the rigidities of Ricardian orthodoxy had vanquished Malthusian insights, the underlying belief in the importance of economic theory, whether as source of hope or betrayal, now seems almost as remarkable as the criticism. How could the mild-mannered Ricardo's theorems and parliamentary speeches be seen as so malevolent, let alone as so influential? . . . Yet Toynbee's horrified fascination with Ricardo and his own interest in political economy were not of the kind epitomised by George Eliot's character, Tom Tulliver, who was said to be fond of birds – that is, of throwing stones at them. Toynbee was earnestly seeking an accommodation between history and political economy, though his early death prevented the union from coming to fruition (*Riches and Poverty*, pp. 416–17).

By this point in the book, the reader will know how authoritative and deeply grounded are Winch's judgements about the extent of the exaggeration present in one generation's view of another; only someone so profoundly familiar with the intricacies of classical political economy *and* so well versed in the extensive literature about its alleged impact on policy could have earned the right to raise this question about Toynbee's reaction without seeming merely glib. The prose secretes a strong sense of proportion, as much by the balance of the sentences as by the quiet contrasts between 'tragedy' and 'regrets', between 'mild-mannered' and 'malevolent', and so on. Yet Toynbee's position is neither mocked nor dismissed; indeed, being placed alongside Keynes's 'equivalent regrets' almost confers an additional dignity on it. And as the passage from which this extract is taken continues, the conventional caricature of Toynbee, like the still more conventional caricature of Ricardo with which it is too easily contrasted, comes to seem exactly that.

Other passages from both authors could, of course, be cited to illustrate other traits, but there is just one general feature of the work of both Winch and Burrow which may merit separate mention here, particularly since it can lead to a misperception or undervaluing of that work in certain quarters. Neither of them has felt obliged to introduce every observation and to preface every claim with extensive lists of works by other scholars upon which they are building or against which they are reacting. Such slightly ritualised roll-calls of (not always entirely relevant) recent books and articles sometimes seem to be taken, particularly in the United States, as an indication, perhaps even a guarantee, of a work's scholarly seriousness. By contrast, although there is no lack of familiarity with the work of other scholars in the writings of Burrow and Winch – indeed, there is considerable evidence of their implicit engagement with it – both have opted for lightly carried learning in place of academic name-dropping. As Winch characteristically puts it at the end of the 'Prologue' to *Riches and Poverty*:

> Like any safety-conscious traveller to places that are new to me, I have read the work of the many *ciceroni* who have explored the territory before me. My footnotes record my debts to these sources and occasionally my opinions of those I have found less reliable as guides. As the term 'secondary sources' implies, however, none of them can ever be a satisfactory substitute for the real thing. For this reason, they will not be mentioned in the text from this point onwards (*Riches and Poverty*, p. 31).

IV

As indicated in the Preface earlier, these two volumes bring together the work of many of the leading scholars currently engaged in the field of modern British intellectual history. Needless to say, they write in their own distinctive styles, and their inclusion here should not be taken as an endorsement, and still less as any kind of imitation, of those features of the work of Burrow and Winch discussed in this introduction. Moreover, in assembling these essays, our aim has not been to try to produce a comprehensive 'intellectual history of modern Britain'; rather, each volume is devoted to a cluster of closely related themes. The contributions in *Economy, Polity, and Society* are primarily focused on the various ways in which 'economic thought' is inextricably embedded in a wider range of social and political debates, while those in *History, Religion, and Culture* particularly address the relations between historiography, religion, and conceptions of natural and social change. (The contents of each volume are summarised more fully in their respective 'Presentations'.)

In both volumes, the arrangement of essays is primarily thematic, while at the same time a rough chronological sequence from the mid-eighteenth to the mid-twentieth century is maintained. It has to be acknowledged that the second half of our stated period is dealt with somewhat less intensively than the first, and that, in particular, the years between 1900 and 1950 receive rather short shrift, apart from the essays by Winch and Stapleton (the unfortunate withdrawal of one contributor and the disabling illness of another reduced the planned coverage here). Something should also be said about the geographical or cultural limits of the terrain. Cultures are not discrete, sealed entities; ideas have scant respect for merely political boundaries, individuals belong to more than one 'culture', and the life of the mind is inherently cosmopolitan. Nonetheless, there is a certain pragmatic logic in confining attention to the intellectual life carried on within a given national culture, a unit often defined in primarily linguistic terms. Of course, a generation or two ago, these volumes might have been unselfconsciously sub-titled essays in *English* intellectual history, but both scholarly, and political develop-ments have drawn attention to the problematic nature of that traditional label. In addition, passing references to links with the American colonies in the eighteenth century or with the problems of empire in the nine-teenth are more easily accommodated under the wider term, and what one might call 'the Scotticisation of English culture' is an important theme of the first half of the nineteenth century in particular. For all these reasons, the use of the term 'British' in our sub-title can serve as no more than an approximate marker, a signal that these essays do not make the intellectual life of other societies such as France or Germany their primary focus, but equally that they do not confine themselves, rigidly and artificially, to the intellectual life of England in the strict, territorial sense.

It should also be clear that there are large areas of the intellectual history of the period in question which are, designedly, not covered in these volumes. There is, for example, little directly on the history of phi-losophy; similarly, although both Boyd Hilton's and John Burrow's essays touch on scientific topics, there is no sustained engagement with the history of scientific thought in this period; Brian Young's essay apart, there is little direct discussion of imperial themes, and so on for many other topics one might mention. These exclusions are intended to have no polemical significance; they are an incidental result of inviting contribu-tions from scholars with a particular range of overlapping interests. Still less is popular culture made the focus of attention here; the essays over-whelmingly focus on ideas which attained a certain level of elaborated expression as part of the educated culture of their day. Again, this is not the outcome of some principled hierarchisation of subject-matters; the only 'principle' it could be said to instantiate is that one must study, and be allowed to study, what one finds interesting. But perhaps that is not, after all, an entirely unimportant principle. Jacob Burckhardt spoke of historiography as the record of what one age finds of interest in another. Not the least of the achievements of Donald Winch and John Burrow has been that they have helped us to find the intellectual life of Britain in this period so interesting.

Presentation of *History, Religion, and Culture*

This volume opens with three essays which focus on aspects of eighteenth-century historical writing. Mark Phillips considers the general question of 'historical distance', that is, the ways in which a narrative situates itself and its implied reader in relation to the events it describes. 'Distance' here embraces degrees of proximity, both chronological and emotional: elements of detachment, perspective, sympathy, immediacy, and so on can be found in different proportions within the same text, and the proportions of the mixture will vary between genres and between periods. Phillips challenges the common post-Romantic assumption that only that writing which parades an explicit form of sympathetic identification qualifies as 'real history'. Taking Hume's observations on Clarendon's account of the execution of Charles I as his starting point, he explores some of the dimensions of this topic in a variety of forms of historical writing in the eighteenth and early nineteenth centuries, indicating how changes in the governing assumptions about historical distance can affect the extent to which a work of history from one period is fully legible as such in another: the rise of the Romantic protocols of sympathy and immediacy led early nineteenth-century readers, such as John Stuart Mill, to censure Hume's *History*, along with other works of Enlightenment historiography, for its want of engagement with the lives of the historical agents whose doings it describes. Phillips also brings out the ways in which attention to questions of distance can help to illuminate topics such as the early nineteenth-century's recovery, in the name of the governing values of intimacy and sentimentalism, of earlier autobiographical and memoir writing, or the ways in which in the work of Burke and Macaulay the operation of tradition should be understood as a 'sentimental construction'.

Both John Pocock and David Womersley focus on a single historian, Edward Gibbon, and more specifically on the treatment of religion in his work, (its apparent 'distance' was one of the things which made that treatment so controversial). Pocock begins with a question about the narrative structure of the *Decline and Fall*: why did Gibbon start his history of

Christianity only in the post-apostolic period rather than dealing with its earlier role? It was the implicitly sceptical treatment of Christianity in chapters 15 and 16 of that work which attracted a storm of criticism from the book's first readers, a response by which Gibbon professed himself surprised (Pocock's is one of several essays in this volume to concern itself with what might be called questions of 'reception'). Pocock addresses the 'narrative awkwardness' of the placing of the two chapters at several levels, pointing to the difficulties Gibbon faced in attempting to treat the sacred as part of secular history. He also emphasises the contrasts between the English and European contexts in which the issues were considered, contrasting the greater latitude of belief tolerated in the former with the more insistent attempts in Europe to replace Christianity with some form of 'civil religion'. Responses to Gibbon's assumed purposes in these chapters have tended to govern understanding of his work at the time and since, but Pocock concludes by considering the possibility that Gibbon may not have been wholly in control of the literary expression of his own intentions at this point.

David Womersley also addresses the vexed question of Gibbon's presumed unbelief and its relation to contemporary responses to his work. Womersley indicates the ways in which recent scholarship has moved away from the traditional emphasis on Gibbon as 'the English Voltaire', emphasising instead that he may have held, at certain periods in his career, a more nuanced position on the role of religion in history – more nuanced, certainly, than that conveyed by the notorious two chapters discussed by Pocock. Womersley, however, shifts the balance back in the Voltairean direction a little by focusing on the hitherto unknown presence in Gibbon's library of a manuscript copy of one of the most notorious works of clandestine irreligion produced by the early Enlightenment, the *Livre des trois fameux imposteurs* (i.e. Moses, Jesus, and Mahomet). This suggests a revision or complication of the established chronology of Gibbon's intellectual development, and raises in a new form the question of his own religious convictions. He later responded to criticism of the 'irreligious' tendency of his writing by adopting a more emollient and defensive posture towards Christianity: this may, or may not, have reflected shifts in his own deepest beliefs, but Womersley suggests it should be viewed in terms of what he calls 'Gibbon's successive literary personae' and the workings of his 'hunger for literary fame and his attempts to control that fame once he had acquired it'.

The four essays in part II all deal, though in different degrees and from different angles, with the place of religion in nineteenth-century British intellectual and political life. Brian Young's essay charts a shift in attitudes towards native Indian religion on the part of British historians and commentators. An Enlightenment historian such as William Robertson could adopt a broadly benign view of Hinduism (and of the French, a comparable source of irreligion in the eyes of the orthodox), and this encouraged what might be called a form of 'Scottish Orientalism', particularly propounded in the pages of the *Edinburgh Review*. But a broad sympathy for Indian religion could be shared by other late eighteenth- and early nineteenth-century writers, including scholarly churchmen such as Thomas Maurice. However, as religious earnestness and sectarian missionary zeal spread in the early decades of the nineteenth century, much more hostile denunciations of the superstitions of the Hindus became common, led by historians of the East such as the Evangelical Claudius Buchanan and the Baptist William Ward. As Young shows, a particularly significant element governing British responses was the fascination with, perhaps fixation on, the phallic cults and presumed licentiousness of eastern religions. And in an interesting twist, Young indicates how James Mill's unrelentingly rationalist history was in fact heavily indebted to the accounts of Ward and Buchanan for its hostile portrait of Hinduism. Between them, the Evangelicals and the Utilitarians played a dominant role in shaping attitudes and policy towards India in the first half of the nineteenth century, and their shared suspicion of the barbaric potential of Indian religious practices was assumed to be borne out by the atrocities of the Mutiny.

The religious sectarianism of nineteenth-century British culture is also a central theme in Blair Worden's essay on the Victorians and Oliver Cromwell. Before the early Victorian period, English attitudes towards the great revolutionary regicide were largely hostile, but in the course of the nineteenth century enthusiasm for Cromwell and his achievements became increasingly marked, culminating in the rapturous celebrations of his tercentenary in 1899, by which time he had become (according to S. R. Gardiner) 'the national hero of the nineteenth century'. Both Macaulay and, more especially, Carlyle contributed to this rehabilitation, but Worden identifies four principal reasons of a broader kind for the change. First, there was a shift in historical and political thinking that gave a new interest and respectability to the civil war period. Second, the struggles for political and social enfranchisement in the nineteenth century offered a new dimension of social aspiration and grievance to perceptions of the causes Cromwell represented. Third, the Victorian religious revival, and the more general taste for moral earnestness, gave Cromwell's Puritanism a compelling attraction, especially though not exclusively to the Nonconformists, who themselves played a more prominent part in the political and social life of this period. And finally, in the context of Gladstonian liberalism and, subsequently, imperialism, the ethical dimension of Cromwell's foreign policy and his contribution to England's expansion were re-appraised. As a result, Cromwell had by the end of the century ceased to be seen principally as a sectarian figure but was instead cherished as a national possession, though Worden indicates that his reputation and prominence declined sharply in the first few decades of the twentieth century.

In the first few decades of the nineteenth century, there was no stauncher defender of the position of the Established Church, whether against its own Tractarian tendencies or against its Catholic and Nonconformist rivals, than the *Quarterly Review*. William Thomas's essay provides an example of the ways in which the concerns of intellectual and political historians can be brought into fruitful contact. Drawing on a wealth of new material mined from the archives of John Murray, Thomas explores the ways in which the policy of the review in its first half-century responded to related shifts in the position of the Anglican Church and the Tory party. The *Quarterly* was even more of a party organ than was the *Edinburgh*, and its standing depended upon its known closeness to the counsels of the Tory leadership. Thomas documents how the literary side of the review was essentially conducted by J. G. Lockhart, leaving responsibility for the political articles in the hands of John Wilson Croker, who was Peel's confidant. When the potential tensions in this arrangement came to the surface, the priority of the review's political identity asserted itself, and, as Thomas shows, Lockhart had to back down for fear of losing the close political connection which gave the review its cachet. This connection ceased to operate after 1846, however, and Thomas suggests that the quarterlies were anyway by that point becoming too slow-moving to keep up with the pace of politics. He concludes by suggesting (the point is addressed from another angle in Boyd Hilton's essay, chapter 8) that by the middle of the nineteenth century the periodicals expressed and responded to the less sectarian character of public debate.

John Ruskin's was one of the most profoundly and pervasively religious sensibilities of the nineteenth century, albeit one which expressed itself in increasingly unorthodox forms. Noting how Ruskin, in his appreciations of art and architecture, moved between details and the whole without sufficiently attending to the organising role of the intermediate category of 'mass', John Drury explores a similar pattern in his religious responses, where his mind habitually jumped from a single blade of grass to its place in the scheme of creation without engaging with intermediate bodies of doctrine (Ruskin is also discussed from a different point of view in Jane Garnett's essay in the companion volume, *Economy, Polity, and Society*). For Ruskin, being a Christian involved knowledge of 'the beauty of creation' not of 'a system of salvation', and his energies were wholly devoted to making his readers *see* what was around them. By the same token, he regarded deeply held belief (not necessarily of a conventional or currently acceptable religious kind, but *belief* nonetheless) as the precondition of art. All the most powerful art of the past 'was in some way reverential – had awe in it'. 'All great Art is praise.' In characterising the workings of this sensibility across the huge range of subjects about which Ruskin wrote, Drury's essay blends elements all too frequently compartmentalised under the headings of 'art history', 'religious studies', and so on, as well as indicating the part to be played in intellectual history by sympathetic portraiture.

The essays in part III explore some of the relations, across a span of time running from the early nineteenth century to the middle of the twentieth, between scientific ideas about change or development and assumptions about the nature and growth of the national community. Boyd Hilton's essay attempts to bring the work of historians of science into closer contact with that of intellectual and political historians. Focusing on diverse forms of scientific writing in the second quarter of the nineteenth century, he explores a complex pattern of correlations between social status, professional role, political allegiances, religious beliefs, and scientific convictions about the nature and mechanism of change in both the natural and social world. Hilton rejects any simple distinction between 'radical' and 'establishment' scientists, just as he shows that political antagonisms and affinities were more complicated than any conventional Whig/Tory divide would suggest. But he does emphasise that there were close and unobvious links between politics and science, in the broadest sense of each term, especially in the 1820s and 1830s, and he brings out the significance of the divide between those who espoused essentially dualist explanations of the nature of mind and matter and those who propounded some form of monism. As already noted, Hilton's essay converges with William Thomas's in seeing the intellectual and cultural life of the mid-Victorian period as less violently divided and partisan than that of the years between Waterloo and the repeal of the Corn Laws; it also intersects with John Burrow's contribution in several interesting ways, not least in their differing accounts of the place of gradualist, developmental views of change in the 1830s.

Burrow's essay explores, across a wide range of genres and discourses, a shift in the representation of time and change, principally from an informing emphasis on eventfulness, even of a catastrophic, apocalyptic kind, to the subtler picturing of it as a kind of sedimentary process. This shift can be charted most strikingly in terms of changes in the governing assumptions and metaphors drawn from geology, from the Vulcanist and Neptunist theories of the early decades of the nineteenth century, chiefly derived from the work of James Hutton, to the model of the longer-term, uniformitarian operation of physical laws which was increasingly accepted following the publication of Charles Lyell's *Principles of Geology*. Burrow tracks affinities and resemblances across several cultural forms, from John Martin and the kind of theatrical spectacular known as 'the Drury Lane sublime' to Carlyle's attempt to render the disruptive, volcanic power of the French Revolution, and on to the sustainedly ironic conception of the unseen operation of unintended consequences in a mid-Victorian figure such as Walter Bagehot. In these terms, Burrow finds unremarked similarities between writers as diverse as, for example, the novelist George Eliot and the historian William Stubbs, especially in the difficulties of representing imperceptibly slow change or of narrating a 'history without heroes'.

The final two essays in the volume, by Peter Mandler and Julia Stapleton, form a natural pair as they both attempt to relate features of English social thought from the mid-nineteenth to the mid-twentieth century to questions of national identity. At first sight, it may be the contrast or differences between the two essays which seem most striking. The nub of the contrast could be exaggerated by saying that whereas Mandler is struck by the relative *absence* of thinking along nationalist lines in English social thought, Stapleton emphasises its *pervasiveness*. More specifically, Mandler's essay explores some of the reasons for the relative weakness, in comparison to other European countries at the time, of racial and nationalist thinking in Britain in the mid-Victorian decades between 1848 and 1886. He emphasises instead how the dominant framework of large-scale historical understanding was provided by what he calls the 'civilisational perspective', which blended Whiggish and social evolutionary thinking. Here the governing metaphor is that of the ladder, which different nations ascended at different speeds. England was, of course, seen as being nearer the top than most, a happy condition accounted for in different terms by different writers – some emphasised the role of geography or accidents of history, others qualities of character formed by religion or social customs, and so on. But on the whole, Mandler argues, they did not resort to a biological category of 'race' to explain such differences, and they assumed the potentially universal or least widespread operation of the mechanisms at work, not their uniquely national properties. Mandler brings out the ways in which even figures such as Bagehot or Buckle, who are sometimes taken to be proposing essentially racialist principles of historical analysis, were in fact not really doing so.

At first sight, as already noted, Julia Stapleton's essay may seem to be offering the opposite argument. She wants to emphasise how the political thought of the later nineteenth and early twentieth centuries was suffused with ideas of English national identity. The antagonism which mid-century radicalism exhibited towards the national culture tended to subside in the later decades of the century, and even the various manifes-tations of socialist critique, from William Morris to the Fabians, in prac-tice made an appeal to an assumed distinctiveness of English national character as manifested in its peculiarly fortunate political history. Stapleton brings out the smugly celebratory aspects that the appeal to 'Englishness' could take by the time we get to such diverse representatives of English political thinking in the twentieth century as Stanley Baldwin or E. M. Forster, and she sees a more distant or critical perspective only re-asserting itself after 1945. One obvious way to diminish any apparent conflict between these two essays is to remark that they focus on different periods: here it may to some extent be helpful to think of the universalist idiom of the mid-Victorian decades giving way to a more celebratory and patriotic vocabulary in the late nineteenth and early twentieth centuries. But that is clearly not the whole story, partly because these essays overlap in dealing with the period from the 1860s to the 1880s in particular, but also because it overlooks the different focus of the two essays, which, it is only a slight exaggeration to say, are concerned with issues which operate at different levels of abstraction. Mandler is chiefly attending to those the-ories or concepts which the more intellectually ambitious mid-Victorian social theorists used to *explain* social change: here he is surely right to say that biological notions of race played practically no part in such explana-tions, and that explanations in terms of some inherent *national* differences, some fundamental *Volksgeist*, or some form of geographical determinism, were less marked in England than in some of the other leading European countries. But this is, of course, compatible with such theorists having a largely positive attitude towards the achievements or characteristics which, understood purely in historical terms, could be seen as character-istically English. Thus, while the *mechanism* of social change appealed to in such theories was potentially universalist and not particularist, the political *attitudes* of these writers could, as in the case of writers as different as Bagehot or Freeman, display markedly celebratory character-istics. Stapleton, by contrast, deals with a more heterogeneous body of writing, where she is identifying the recurrence of certain attitudes or loy-alties rather than the explanatory mechanisms of social theory. In other words, universalising models of social change, positive attitudes towards features of the national history, and specific forms of political critique may have coexisted, in different mixtures, across the long period covered by these two essays, each of which principally focuses on a different ingre-dient in the mixture.

Part I

1 Historical distance and the historiography of eighteenth-century Britain

Mark Salber Phillips

I

In his essay 'Of Tragedy' David Hume offers a striking observation on Clarendon's *History of the Rebellion*. As Clarendon approaches the execution of King Charles, Hume writes, he

supposes, that his narration must then become infinitely disagreeable; and he hurries over the king's death, without giving us one circumstance of it. He considers it as too horrid a scene to be contemplated with any satisfaction, or even without the utmost pain and aversion. He himself, as well as the readers of that age, were too deeply concerned in the events, and felt a pain from subjects, which an historian and a reader of another age would regard as the most pathetic and most interesting, and, by consequence, the most agreeable.[1]

Hume's sympathetic understanding of Clarendon's reticence, combined with the clear sense that the spectacle that had been most painful to an earlier generation had become most interesting to his own, highlights the issue I want to address in this essay: the question of historical distance, both as a general problem for historiographical narrative and as a specific issue in the historical writing of Hume's century. Hume clearly accepts the fact that both Clarendon and his audience found themselves in a kind of proximity to the regicide that ruled out many potential representations of that event, especially (we surmise) the kind of detailed, pathetic treatment that Hume himself would later offer his own readers in the *History of England*. Implicit, then, in his remarks, is an understanding that historical distance is a significant variable in historical accounts, affecting both the historian and his audience ('an historian and a reader of another age'). Implied, too, is the sense that the choice of historical distance (whatever the constraints under which the choice is made) is of fundamental

I am most grateful to Ed Hundert and Stefan Collini for their careful reading and criticism of this essay.

[1] David Hume, *Essays, Moral, Political and Literary* (Indianapolis, 1985), pp. 223–4. The present essay is a summary of a theme presented in greater detail in my forthcoming study, *Society and Sentiment; Genres of Historical Narrative in Britain, 1750–1820*.

importance in shaping the narrative and especially in governing the audience's emotional response to events.

Hume's retrospect on Clarendon points, then, to two kinds of distance. The first is the distance that separates the historian from the specific past under description. This is the sense of distance with which historians are most familiar. It refers, for example, to our present vantage on the horrors of the Holocaust or the Second World War, but its importance was already signalled in the early nineteenth century when Scott sub-titled his first great novel "'Tis Sixty Years Since'. Distance in this first sense has recently drawn a lot of attention, giving rise to a considerable literature on 'history and memory'. A second dimension of distance, however, remains largely unexplored and is my subject here. This is the sense, implicit in Hume's remarks, that historical narratives not only *reflect* distance but also *construct* it.

Temporal distance is, of course, a given in historical writing, but temporal distance may be enlarged or diminished by other kinds of distances, which we might think of as formal, conceptual, and affective. Thus historical distance, in the fuller sense I want to give it, refers to more than the passage of time that separated Hume from Clarendon or Clarendon from the regicide, just as it incorporates something more than the issue of affective engagement so prominent in Hume's essay as well as in other eighteenth-century descriptions. In this wider sense, historical distance indicates the sense of temporality constructed by every historical account as it positions its readers in relation to the past. It includes political as well as emotional engagement (or disengagement) and is the consequence of ideological choices, as well as formal and aesthetic ones. I would argue that in this enlarged and more complicated sense historical distance is an intrinsic feature of all historical accounts, though (for the very reason that it is implicit in so much of what we do when we write or read history) it is one that has been neglected by both historians and literary scholars. I want to suggest, too, that paying attention to historical distance will help to shed light on some key issues in eighteenth-century historiography – not least the reasons why the works of even the greatest historians of this period came to be neglected or misread by later generations of readers.

The problems of historical representation Hume observed in relation to the traumas of the seventeenth century have become a major preoccupation for the historical consciousness of the twentieth, and it is disturbing to think that, in relation to the atrocities of this century, we too may now be swept up in the same transition from horrified reticence to pathos and even pleasure. (It would be hard to deny that some novelists, filmmakers, and scholars currently find the Holocaust a subject 'the most pathetic and most interesting, and, by consequence, the most agreeable'.)

By the same token, it must also be true that our growing recognition of the need to establish historical perspective even on the most horrifying events of recent times will give us some help in dealing with issues of historical distance as they arose for other generations. Unfortunately, the dichotomy of history and memory which structures so much current thinking about issues of historical representation is probably too simple to be of much help in exploring the larger stakes involved in historical distance. Indeed, the presumed opposition between the elongated perspectives of history and the closeness of memory may well obscure the issue: far from disclosing the potential variability of historical distance, as was suggested by Hume's remarks on Clarendon, such a dichotomy decides the issue before we have even begun.

I see two sorts of reasons why attention to questions of distance should be of particular interest to students of historiography. First, I want to argue that historical distance is a neglected, but important variable in historical accounts that is closely connected to both the politics and the poetics of historical writing. Consequently, attention to distance may give us ways of connecting a formal analysis of literary structures to an ideological discussion that seeks to place narrative in a world inhabited by active readers and their complex social and political interests. Second, I want to suggest that in the absence of critical attention to this dimension of historiographical practice, we have found it too easy to issue pronouncements on the nature of history that implicitly erect a single standard of distance as a norm for all historical work. In fact, norms of historical distance are themselves products of history and they have changed markedly over time. For this reason dogmatic constructions of distance are especially evident when historians and critics of one age set themselves in judgement on the works of another, a point which I will illustrate at the end of this essay by looking at some vicissitudes in Hume's reputation as a historian.

II

I began by suggesting that every historical account must position its audience in some relationship of closeness or distance to the events and experiences it recounts. Historical distance, in other words, is an issue that confronts everyone who writes in the historical genres and one that is registered in every reading of a historiographical text. But we must also recognise that there is no single stance that is proper for all works of history. Rather, appropriate distance can be highly variable and will shift markedly even within the confines of a single text. Moreover, the textual strategies that establish distance can range from ones that place events at a considerable conceptual or emotional remove to those that demand immediate response. What I am calling distance, in other words, necessarily incorporates the full range of positionings, both near and far. Distance refers to the possibility of making past moments close and pressing – in order to intensify, for example, the affective, ideological, or commemorative impact of an event – as well as that of stepping back from the historical scene – perhaps to emphasise the objectivity, irony, or philosophical sweep of the historian's vision. At the same time, we need to recognise that a desire to evoke the closeness of the past does not necessarily lead to commemoration; as Nietzsche and Foucault both demonstrate, a keen sense of the presence of history can serve as the prelude to a repudiation of the past rather than its preservation. Equally, though the long view is often invoked for purposes of ironic detachment, it can also serve to ground a profession of faith, whether in the power of Reason (as in Hegel or Marx) or the endurance of the nation (as in Burke or Braudel).

In practice, the determination of historical distance is a matter of balance or tension between these opposing impulses, and, as I have said, even within a single work the balance will shift and adjust. These variations may register different emotional or ideological responses to events; they may also reflect the ways in which the historian constructs an authorial voice, or chooses to vary the rhythms of a narrative. Unfortunately we lack a vocabulary for describing these choices and tensions. For want of better English words, I will label the opposing impulses *approximative* and *distanciating*; what matters, however, is not the terms we use, but rather the recognition that the concept of historical distance must be capable of incorporating *both* the desire to figure the past as close or present and (in the more normal sense of distance) the opposing impulse to seek detachment or removal.

This observation that historical distance is the product of a dialectic intrinsic to the way in which historical accounts work has a number of implications for the study of historiography. Some of these have to do with the dynamics of the individual work, some with questions of genre, and some with periodic changes in assumptions about historical thought and composition. For each of these levels of discussion – text, genre, period-style – I will begin by outlining some ways in which the question of distance can be approached. Later, I will return to each of these dimensions of the problem and offer some illustrations drawn from the historiography of the eighteenth and early nineteenth centuries.

Let me begin at the level of the study of individual texts. Here recognition of the dialectics of historical distance points towards a broad inquiry concerned with identifying the variety of features of historical accounts that shape the reader's relationship to past events. Stated so abstractly, however, the question may give the misleading sense that I am speaking of universal features of historical writing that uniformly produce effects of proximity or distanciation in some equally universalised reader. On the contrary, questions of distance should be addressed to the specific vocabularies of historical thought in a given time, as well as to all the particular conditions of literature and social life that shape the expectations of historically specific reading publics.

Considering distance in the way I am suggesting calls for attention to matters of audience as well as of authorship. The consequence will be an added degree of complexity, since we will need both a social and a narratological analysis in order to comprehend the ways in which a history mediates the relationship between its intended readership and a chosen past. As a point of departure, however, this combination of formal and social concerns seems more hopeful than the usual habit of grouping histories under the flag of rival philosophical or political schools. Historical writing, it still seems necessary to say, is not simply an extension of politics by other means. Party labels serve a purpose, of course, but they encourage us to focus attention on the biographical circumstances of historians or their abstract intellectual programmes at the expense of pursuing genuine textual analysis.

On another level, distance is also an important feature of history considered as a genre, or as I prefer to think of it, as a family of related genres and sub-genres. (For the eighteenth century, this family would include not only the familiar narratives of national history such as Hume's, but also local histories, histories of manners, conjectural histories, and literary histories, as well as a good deal of writing in such closely related genres as biography, memoir, and travel.) This approach to history as a family of closely related genres is important to my argument for reasons I need to explain very briefly. First, all genres are defined by relationships of contrast and competition with other related and rival literatures.[2] Accordingly, genre study needs to be especially alert to those features that articulate this competition for audiences and differentiate one group of texts from another. Over time, as new audiences and new questions arise, these differentiating features will tend to change. Accordingly, genre study is closely involved in tracing intellectual histories, of which it becomes a key instrument. Second, when thinking about genre, it is important to think about history's location on a larger map of literatures

---

[2] On genre, see Alastair Fowler, *Kinds of Literature; An Introduction to the Theory of Genres and Modes* (Oxford, 1982). I have discussed the usefulness of genre study for historiography in a critique of the 'tropology' of Hayden White, in my 'Historiography and Genre: A More Modest Proposal', *Storia della storiografia/Histoire de l'historiographie*, 24 (1993), pp. 119–32.

and disciplines. In the period I am considering, the historical genres occupied a key mediating position: on the one side, history was flanked by the rising new genre of the novel, on the other it was touched by the key new discipline of political economy. This mediating position meant that history was an important foil in the formation of new genres; reciprocally, it also meant that history absorbed into its own repertoire many of the practices of surrounding disciplines and genres. As a result, neighbouring literatures often provide us with the clearest indications of the direction of change in historical thought and practice.

Variations in distance – whether formal, conceptual, or affective – appear to be an important part of the way in which readers distinguish between competing genres of historical writing, or differentiate history from its nearer neighbours. The eighteenth century's taste for biography and memoir, for example, clearly owes a great deal to a sentimentalist desire to endow the past with strong evocative presence. But conceptual distance also had a strong appeal in this period: the philosophical and conjectural histories that were such a marked feature of the Enlightenment were generally thought to promise a deeper understanding of the past than conventional narratives of statecraft, a claim that was principally based on the longer perspectives opened up by philosophical judgement.

Variation in historical distance affects period-style as well as genre. I do not mean to suggest that each period possesses one invariable norm of historical distance. But it has gone largely unnoticed that such norms do change over time and that changes of distance may have considerable impact on the way in which readers in one period respond to the writing of another. Clearly there was a notable shift in the predominant sense of distance between the generation of Hume and Robertson and that of Macaulay and Carlyle (though not one that was unprepared for in the earlier writers). In the interval, historical accounts lost some of the aloof philosophical generality that eighteenth-century readers associated with 'the dignity of history' and sought to capture some of the evocative closeness that in the earlier period belonged primarily to the 'minor genres' of biography and memoir. It would be a mistake, however, to characterise the changes too narrowly as a literary-aesthetic movement; rather what is commonly labelled 'romantic historiography' belongs to a much broader reconfiguration of historical thought that manifests itself in a desire for a new sense of immediacy or historical presence.

Since distance has not been recognised as an important variable in historical accounts, such shifts either go unnoticed or are given partial and misleading labels. (The so-called 'revival of narrative', widely discussed in the 1980s, is a recent example of this kind of insufficient characterisation.[3]) Early nineteenth-century interest in historical evocation is usually labelled without much differentiation as 'romantic', though one could argue that its roots were in eighteenth-century sentimentalism and that its strength in the nineteenth century had a great deal to do with the politics of Burkean tradition. An investigation of historical distance will not, of course, automatically supply a key to the relations between these aesthetic and ideological movements; nonetheless, distance may be a useful tool for thinking about their relatedness.

III

To this point, I have given a brief outline of some ways in which historical distance might be a useful point of departure for examining both the politics and poetics of historical writing. For the sake of clarity, I have divided the question into three levels of discussion: first, those issues that concern analysis of individual accounts; second, those that are directed to the characteristics of the various historical genres (and especially to the way these genres are differentiated and compete for readership); and third, those that concern periodic changes in styles of thought and writing. For each of these three levels of discussion, I would like now to offer some brief illustrations of the kinds of texts and problems where identifying distance as a dimension of historiography may be useful.

I will begin with Hume's *History of England* as an example of the ways in which distanciating and approximative impulses combine in a single text. Historians have long regarded Hume's work as a history strongly marked by irony. This assessment is largely a response to Hume's authorial voice, whose tone is often heavily ironic, especially when commenting on the follies of religious and political enthusiasts. More recently, however, students of English literature, who tend to be less literal minded in their reading of texts, have looked at aspects of Hume's literary practice and found some highly wrought scenes of virtue in distress.[4] Hume's staging of the death of Mary Queen of Scots, for example, or his picture of the last days of Charles I, far from being ironic, are clearly a product of eighteenth-century sentimentalism.

In short, we have been given two very different views of Hume's narratorial stance, with little sense of the need to reconcile the two or to coordinate both with other aspects of Hume's politics and aesthetics. From the perspective I have indicated above, however, it is clear that irony and

---

[3] See Lawrence Stone, 'The Revival of Narrative; Reflections on a New Old History', in *The Past and the Present* (London, 1981).

[4] See J. C. Hilson, 'Hume: The Historian as Man of Feeling', in J.C. Hilson *et al.*, eds., *Augustan Worlds: Essays in Honour of A. R. Humphreys* (Leicester, 1978).

sentiment are, in fact, two of the principal dimensions of historical distance in the *History of England*. Neither can really be understood in its own terms, since (along with a number of other formal and conceptual vocabularies) both irony and sentiment help to establish the dialectic of distance in the work as a whole. In fact, these two positionings are not as far apart as we generally think. Many of Hume's most sentimental moments involve not only innocent sufferers but also their tormentors, who are the same religious and political bigots that provoke his irony. Thus the evident sentimentalism of the scene of the execution of Mary Queen of Scots, for example, is intensified by the brutality of the behaviour of the Bishop of Peterborough, who continually harasses her to abandon her Catholic faith. The sentimental nature of this passage has everything to do with the fact that the spotlight rests on the suffering woman; turn it on her clerical tormentor and the same scene would be transformed by ironic distance.[5]

But it is not in the individual scene or event that we can see the full extent to which Hume's irony and his sentimentalism are inter-related; as his comments on Clarendon implied, there is a deeper level on which Hume recognised that the pleasures of historical sympathy were available only because of the conceptual distanciation that (in part) manifests itself as irony. Ultimately the lesson of Hume's narrative of the seventeenth century is that Hanoverian Britain could look back on the Revolution as a phase of history now properly over, its tragic and pathetic scenes no longer to be confined by the partisan debates of earlier generations of historians and politicians. It was only because this distance had finally been achieved (so Hume believed, though his critics made him wonder) that it was possible to move beyond the pained reticence of Clarendon's generation to the sympathies of his own; only in this politically distanciated perspective could a murdered king be represented as a suffering father and a loving husband.

Before I leave the question of the structures of individual texts, I want to return briefly to the matter of authorial voice. Until now I have spoken of irony only as a form of distanciation because the focus has been on the way in which an ironic stance removes both writer and reader from a simple or direct relation to the past. From another perspective, however, the reader may well register the ironic voice primarily as an invitation to recognise the shared perspectives linking reader and writer. In this sense, irony may well contribute to a sense of intimacy, more than one of aloofness or detachment.

Rather than illustrating this point by returning to Hume, let me offer an

---

[5] Hume, *History of England*, 6 vols. (Indianapolis, 1983), IV, pp. 247–51.

illustration from a younger writer who was also a master of the ironic voice. Here is a brief summary of the reign of Henry VIII:

The Crimes and Cruelties of this Prince, were too numerous to be mentioned, (as this history I trust has fully shown) and nothing can be said in his vindication, but that his abolishing Religious Houses, and leaving them to the ruinous depredations of time has been of infinite use to the landscape of England in general, which probably was a principal motive for his doing it, since otherwise why should a Man who was of no Religion himself be at so much trouble to abolish one which had for ages been established in the Kingdom.[6]

This (and much else in the same delicious vein) is the work of the sixteen-year-old Jane Austen, who wrote this solemn spoof for the entertainment of her family. Clearly, we would be misjudging very severely if we thought that in this little circle of readers (or really auditors), the ironic voice added up to simple distanciation.

Let me turn now to the second part of my discussion, which is the question of genre. The works of Lucy Hutchinson, John Evelyn, and Samuel Pepys were all published for the first time in the early decades of the nineteenth century. These memoirs have long been appreciated as prime witnesses to English life in the time of the Revolution and Restoration, but we are less apt to recognise their significance for the historiography of the early *nineteenth* century. Contemporary reviewers made it clear, however, that the belated appearance of these eye-witness accounts responded to a widely felt desire for more immediate access to a dramatic period of English history. Francis Jeffrey summarised this spirit in commenting on a lesser memoir of the period, one that he had to admit did not live up to his highest expectations for the genre. Nonetheless, he wrote:

it still gives us a peep at a scene of surpassing interest from a new quarter; and at all events adds one other item to the great and growing store of those contemporary notices which are every day familiarising us more and more with the living character of by-gone ages; and without which we begin, at last, to be sensible, that we can neither enter into their spirit, nor even understand their public transactions.[7]

As Jeffrey's words indicate, the great attractions of these historical memoirs was the sense of historical immediacy they conveyed. These belated publications, to put it another way, constituted a new, more intimate history of the seventeenth century, one achieved not by calling on the usual resources of historical narrative, but assembled by force of editorial appropriation. A prime example of this process, and the way in which it engaged with problems of distance, is Lucy Hutchinson's

---

[6] Jane Austen, *The History of England* (Chapel Hill, N.C., 1993), pp. 13–14.
[7] *Contributions to the Edinburgh Review* (1846), p. 464.

memoir of the civil war, the *History of the Life of Colonel Hutchinson* (1806). Hutchinson's life of her husband held great attractions for an early nineteenth-century audience, but in this period of post-revolutionary reaction, there could also be some nervousness about celebrating the life of this prominent Cromwellian soldier and regicide. Evidently, the work's first editor, the Reverend Julius Hutchinson, felt the embarrassment acutely. His first defence is a crude version of Hume's argument for distance. We ought not to attempt to judge the colonel's actions, Hutchinson explained, 'considering the tempest and darkness which then involved the whole political horizon'. In the end, however, it was female authorship rather than the colonel's military and civic virtues that provided the best strategy, and Hutchinson closes his preface by linking the female biographer to a female audience and a presumptively female genre:

> The ladies will feel that it carries with it all the interest of a novel strengthened with the authenticity of real history: they will no doubt feel an additional satisfaction in learning, that though the author added to the erudition of the scholar, the research of the philosopher, the politician, and even the divine, the zeal and magnanimity of a patriot; yet she descended from all these elevations to perform in the most exemplary manner the functions of a wife, mother, and mistress of a family.[8]

Evidently, Julius Hutchinson's editorial efforts (which he also pursued in footnotes to the text) were calculated to emphasise sentimental and approximative elements in the *Life*, a strategy that aimed to de-politicise the text and reposition it as a kind of family memoir. But editorial manipulation did not always aim at sentimental proximity; it was equally possible for a belated publication to move a text towards increased distanciation. A notable case in point is John Wilson Croker's edition of Boswell's *Life of Johnson* (1831) in which a famous work of contemporary biography was transformed into an historical memoir, the eighteenth-century equivalent of Pepys or Evelyn.

In its original publication, the *Life* had struck many readers as gossipy, trivialising, and intrusive. Worse yet, Wordsworth, speaking for conservative opinion, later blamed Boswell for initiating a taste for a style of biography that undermined respect for privacy and weakened the sense of reserve essential to the British character. Boswell 'had broken through the pre-existing delicacies', Wordsworth charged, 'and afforded the British public an opportunity of acquiring experience, which before it had happily wanted'.[9]

Croker was, of course, aware of these charges, and he acknowledged that it would be possible to question 'the prudence or propriety of the

---

[8] Lucy Hutchinson, *Memoirs of the Life of Colonel Hutchinson* (1806), p. xiv.
[9] 'Letter to a Friend of Burns', in *The Prose Works of William Wordsworth*, ed. J. B. Owen and J. W. Smyser (Oxford, 1974), p. 120.

original publication'. The implication of his preface, however, was not simply that the time had long since gone to question the original decision, but that with the passage of time the impropriety itself had disappeared, to be replaced by a new and unquestionably *historical* interest. As the 'interval which separates us from the actual time and scene increases', wrote Croker, 'so appear to increase the interest and delight which we feel at being introduced . . . into that distinguished society of which Dr Johnson formed the centre, of which his biographer is the historian'.[10]

Boswell, in short, would make a new appearance in the more respectable guise of historian. To do so, however, he would need the cooperation of his editor, whose labours were devoted to elaborating an apparatus of scholarship to rescue the work from 'the gradual obscurity that time throws over the persons and incidents of private life'. As the reviewer in the *Monthly* put it, in enthusiastic echo of Croker's own prologue: 'He has succeeded far beyond any hopes which we had ventured to entertain, in arresting the progress by which one of the most entertaining memoirs in our language, was making towards the regions, not indeed of oblivion but of obscurity.'[11] The reviewer went on to admit that the resulting apparatus made the text less appealing 'to those classes of readers, unhappily too numerous, who like nothing but plain sailing'. But, though the bracketed additions and corrections or the 'perpetual reference to the notes' might be troublesome, he was sure that there was no better way of doing the job. And had the work of rescue not been undertaken now, in a very few years the witnesses would have disappeared and the effort could not have succeeded at all.

In all this, Croker's sympathetic reviewer was perhaps deliberately missing the point. He saw the success of Croker's efforts without acknowledging the antecedent political and moral problem that gave his editorial labours their full value. In the moral rescue of Boswell's *Johnson*, time was more of an ally than an enemy, and if the apparatus of footnotes and brackets impeded readers who were looking for 'plain sailing', so much the better. From the start the editor's central purpose was to remove the work from the category of gossipy amusement and position it in the higher one of instruction. In serving this effort the scaffolding of scholarship was undoubtedly there to shore up the crumbling building, but it also served to emphasise its value as a historical monument.

As in the question of genre, so too in that of period-style, contrast provides indispensable help towards definition. The implicit period-norms of eighteenth-century historiographical practice are never so obvious as in their repudiation by those who came after – the writers generally

---

[10] John Wilson Croker, ed., *The Life of Samuel Johnson* (1831), pp. v–vi.
[11] *Monthly Review*, n.s. 2 (1831), pp. 453–4.

known to literary history as the romantic generation. But we also have to be careful to contextualise this evidence, since the early nineteenth-century tended to caricature eighteenth-century precedents to which, nonetheless, it inevitably owed a great deal. This caution is particularly important since the shift in distance that occurred at this time was so powerfully felt that we remain in many ways under its influence. As a result, we still tend to read eighteenth-century texts through nineteenth-century eyes and lose the opportunity to historicise this important moment in the history of historiography.

John Stuart Mill was for a time a great admirer of Carlyle, who was pleased to consider James Mill's son a disciple. The younger Mill's enthusiastic review of Carlyle's *French Revolution* speaks for Carlyle's own sense of historical distance and at the same time offers very useful evidence of the way these norms stood between nineteenth-century audiences and the historical sensibility of the previous century. It would be difficult, Mill wrote, to explain Carlyle's virtues to anyone still satisfied with the histories of an earlier day:

If there be a person who, in reading the histories of Hume, Robertson, and Gibbon (works of extraordinary talent, and the works of great writers) has never felt that this, after all, is not history – and that the lives and deeds of his fellow-creatures must be placed before him in quite another manner, if he is to know them, for them to be real beings, who once were alive, beings of his own flesh and blood, not mere shadows and dim abstractions; such a person, for whom plausible talk *about* a thing does as well as an image of the thing itself, feels no need of a book like Mr Carlyle's; the want, which it is peculiarly fitted to supply, does not consciously exist in his mind.[12]

As is evident, one of the striking things about Mill's criticism of Enlightenment historiography is that he pays full compliments to the talents of the earlier generation, while at the same time denying that their work should be considered history at all. What was lacking was a matter of sympathy and of method. 'Does Hume throw his own mind into the mind of an Anglo-Saxon, or an Anglo-Norman?' Mill asks; does any reader feel he has gained 'anything like a picture of what may actually have been passing, in the minds, say, of cavaliers or of Roundheads during the civil wars?'[13]

Anyone acquainted with the idealist tradition in historiography will recognise the tenor of Mill's criticism. In fact, his complaint that Hume

---

[12] *Essays on French History and Historians*, ed. J. M. Robson and J. C. Cairns (Toronto, 1985), p. 134. The review appeared in the *London and Westminster Review*, July 1837. Significantly, Mill supported his argument with the evidence of genre: the vast production of historical plays and historical novels, he wrote, were the best evidence that such a 'want' was generally felt.   [13] *Essays on French History*, p. 135.

had failed to 'throw his own mind' into past times has continued to shape Hume's reputation right up to the present. But before turning to twentieth-century commentary, I want to pursue a little further the evidence Mill gives us that a major shift in norms of distance had indeed taken place in the first part of his century.

Some of the most familiar pronouncements of 'romantic' historiography can be read as statements about the issue of distance. A prime example is Carlyle's definition of history as 'the essence of innumerable biographies'. This famous, but often misunderstood dictum has less to do with a preference for a particular narrative form than with the need to conceive of the historical process as something actual and experienced. As Carlyle put it, he wanted to gain 'some acquaintance with our fellow-creatures, though dead and vanished, yet dear to us; how they got along in those old days, suffering and doing'.[14] Carlyle certainly did not mean to suggest that biography offered a kind of short cut to historical understanding; on the contrary, in his view it was the political economists and other heirs of the Enlightenment ('cause and effect speculators') who gave history a false transparency by distancing it from the mysteries of experience. He contrasted his own desire to evoke history's immediate presence with the aloof philosophical style of Enlightenment and post-Enlightenment historians ('those modern Narrations of the Philosophic kind'), whose lofty generalisations he compared to the resonant emptiness of an owl hooting from a rooftop.[15]

Macaulay's early writings on history speak still more directly to the problem of distance. Writing history, he argued, has always involved a difficult effort to join reason and imagination, but recent times had witnessed a complete divorce between the two, which only the very greatest of historians might yet be able to overcome. Significantly, Macaulay posed the dilemma as a problem of genre. Much like those who today talk of history and memory, burying in each unspoken assumptions about distance, Macaulay saw modern historical understanding as having suffered a division between the distanciating rationality of analytical historians and the evocative power of the historical novel:

To make the past present, to bring the distant near, to place us in the society of a great man on an eminence which overlooks the field of a mighty battle, to invest with the reality of human flesh and blood beings whom we are too much inclined to consider as personified qualities in an allegory, to call up our ancestors before us with all their peculiarities of language, manners, and garb, to show us over their houses, to seat us at their tables, to rummage their old-fashioned wardrobes, to

---

[14] 'Biography', in *The Complete Works of Thomas Carlyle: The Centenary Edition*, 30 vols. (London, 1897–1904), XXVIII, p. 47.   [15] *Ibid.*

explain the uses of their ponderous furniture, these parts of the duty which properly belongs to the historian have been appropriated by the historical novelist.[16]

To overcome this division, Macaulay suggested, would require more than Shakespearean powers; a truly great historian would need to combine the science of Hallam with the imagination of Scott.

Macaulay's heroic conception of the great historian reworks on historiographical grounds the familiar romantic trope of divided consciousness according to which a self-conscious modernity had lost the naive unity of thought and feeling once possessed by the ancient Greeks. Consistent with this abiding mythos, Macaulay's terms of reference are to a literary history, not a political one, and nothing in these early essays suggests a conscious linking of his desire for a more evocative history with the ideological commitments that might be implied in the desire 'to call up our ancestors before us'. Nonetheless, historical evocation clearly had a politics as well as an aesthetics, which no discussion of historical distance can afford to ignore. Indeed, I want to suggest that, for all the evident importance of romanticism, Macaulay's desire 'to make the past present' owes most of all to Burke and that the most powerful influence reshaping early nineteenth-century assumptions about distance was Burke's doctrine of tradition.[17]

The reader who approaches Burke's *Reflections* looking to find a coherent view of tradition considered as a historical process of transmission will find this a frustrating text. Burke is more concerned to urge his readers to revere what is traditional than to define tradition as such. Mortmain, entail, natural growth, partnership, contract, the succession of generations – any of these ways of figuring continuity might have been made the basis for a description of the way tradition functions, but mixed together in the urgency of his polemic, the rapid play of metaphor creates the sense of a pervasive presence that nonetheless resists clear definition. In Burke, tradition is probably best understood not as a thing in itself, but as a manner of experiencing the world. Like sympathy or sublimity, it is a sentimental construction. As such, it is far from being limited to the constitution or any other institution of law or government. Rather, it enters into the whole texture of social life and is best expressed in the workings of manners and opinion, which for Burke, as for his Scottish contemporaries, constituted the most fundamental level of historical experience.

Though we do not normally think of Burke in the context of the Scottish Enlightenment, the differences as well as similarities are

---

[16] T. B. Macauley, 'Hallam', in *Miscellaneous Essays and Poems*, 2 vols. (New York, n.d.), I, p. 310. The essay was first published in the *Edinburgh Review* in September 1828.

[17] On Burke's importance for nineteenth-century historiography, see J. W. Burrow, *A Liberal Descent; Victorian Historians and the English Past* (Cambridge, 1983).

instructive. Hume looked upon the achievements of post-revolutionary Britain with a measure of confidence that allowed him to cultivate a certain detachment with respect to the revolutions of the previous century. Burke, on the other hand, wrote from what he saw as the brink of a threatened loss of that stability of manners on which Hume generally believed his polite and commercial society could rely. These differences expressed themselves in a notable shift of historical distance. As a result, in the writings of Burke and his followers the distanciation encouraged by Hume gave way to an anxious insistence on the affective power of historical presence.

To write history in the framework of tradition means, of course, to take the long view. Paradoxically, however, the long view of history may well be the path to the sort of presentism that Butterfield stigmatised as the 'whig interpretation', by which historical continuities are invoked to authorise a current creed. This, to use a more recent vocabulary than Butterfield's, amounts to marshalling history for the purposes of memory, and its stylistic signature is a rhetoric of immediacy designed to heighten history's prescriptive force. Thus, in the name of respect for a current of change that runs deep and slow, many nineteenth-century historical narratives foreshortened history in ways that are designed to endow particular episodes or experiences with a special power to shape both the present and the future. Reframed appropriately, the most remote events in history could be made emblematic of later destinies, while the manners of the earliest ages – divorced from the universalising ambitions of eighteenth-century historical anthropology – acquired new significance as evidence of deep and persisting traits that determined the character of the nation.

IV

The new norms of historical distance first initiated by sentimentalism and then given new force by the influence of both Burke and the romantics have continued to shape critical judgement on eighteenth-century historiography. Hayden White, for example, pronounces the following verdict on Hume's history and Enlightenment historiography in general:

The sceptical form which rationalism took in its reflection *on its own time* was bound to inspire a purely Ironic attitude with respect to the past when used as the principle of historical reflection. The mode in which all the *great* historical works of the age were cast is that of Irony, with the result that they all tend towards the form of Satire, the supreme achievement of the literary sensibility of that age. When Hume turned from philosophy to history, because he felt that philosophy had been rendered uninteresting by the sceptical conclusions to which he had been driven, he brought to his study of history the same sceptical sensibility. He found it increasingly difficult, however, to sustain his interest in a process which displayed to him only the eternal return of the same folly in many different forms. He viewed the historical record as little more than the *record* of human folly, which led him finally to become as bored with history as he had become with philosophy.[18]

It would be unfair to single out White's exaggerated views except that they help to clarify assumptions underlying comments that are far better informed. John Stewart, for example, in a careful study of Hume's politics, finds reason to dismiss Hume's history for reasons that in many respects are similar to White's:

The *History*, in an important sense, is antihistorical. The great stimulus to English historians, especially in the seventeenth century, had been the desire to trace up 'privilege' or 'prerogative' to the 'ancient constitution.' By demonstrating the invalidity of such a mode of argument, Hume annihilates much of the old justification for studying the past. It is notable that when he had finished his essentially negative task, he did not undertake another historical work.[19]

Stewart evidently assumes that there is only one acceptable relationship to the past, a relationship of (political) connectedness; thus seeking historical knowledge that enables a kind of *dis*engagement seems to him not simply a different sort of politics, but an illegitimate form of history. More broadly, Stewart's dismissal of a great historical narrative as essentially anti-historical depends on confidently held assumptions about what constitutes a properly historical attitude. Taking his cue from Butterfield and others, Stewart treats historiography as, by definition, a literature of recuperation, and for this reason he laments that Hume never displays 'the true historian's love for the past'.[20]

Stewart's criticisms echo what John Stuart Mill had written a century and a half before; more immediately, his views parallel those of R. G. Collingwood, though Collingwood was more explicit about the roots of his philosophy of history in the romantic and historicist legacy of the nineteenth century:

A truly historical view of human history, sees everything in that history as having its own *raison d'être* and coming into existence in order to serve the needs of the men whose minds have corporately created it. To think of any phase in history as altogether irrational is to look at it not as an historian but as a publicist, a polemical writer of tracts for the times. Thus the historical outlook of the Enlightenment was not genuinely historical; in its main motive it was polemical and anti-historical.[21]

---

[18] Hayden White, *Metahistory* (Baltimore, 1973), p. 55.
[19] John B. Stewart, *The Moral and Political Philosophy of David Hume* (New York, 1963), p. 299.   [20] *Ibid.*, p. 298.   [21] R. G. Collingwood, *Idea of History* (Oxford, 1956), p. 77.

Just as 'love of the past' serves Stewart as a way of distinguishing the polemicist from the 'true' historian, so 'sympathy' is a litmus test for Collingwood. Speaking of romanticism, Collingwood writes that when one compares the complete lack of sympathy for the Middle Ages shown by Hume to 'the intense sympathy for the same thing which is found in Sir Walter Scott, one can see how this tendency of Romanticism [i.e. sympathy] had enriched its historical outlook'.[22]

Collingwood was right, of course, about Hume's general lack of sympathy for the medieval world, but his own inability to accept the standpoint of Enlightenment historiography in its own terms seems at least as blatant a failure of sympathy as Hume's. Surely Collingwood's own philosophical programme would require us to look at eighteenth-century historiography, no less than any other practice or institution, as 'having its own *raison d'être* and coming into existence in order to serve the needs of the men whose minds have corporately created it.' In fact, as I have indicated, the criticisms offered by White, Stewart, and Collingwood stem from a conception of historical distance that only emerged as a consensus of European thought in the course of the half-century that followed Hume's histories. An uncritical application of this standard to eighteenth-century historical literatures amounts to a failure to achieve what Collingwood himself calls 'a truly historical view of human history'.

My point is making these remarks, however, is not (except indirectly) to defend Hume's reputation. Rather, by underlining the importance of unexamined assumptions about historical distance in shaping that reputation, I want simply to emphasise that these norms must themselves be understood as historically variable. It should be clear, then, that historical distance itself has a history which we will need to know more about if we are to appreciate the ways in which the historiography of any place or time has served 'the needs of the men whose minds have corporately created it'. But just because assumptions about distance lie close to the heart of what we think history's methods and purposes should be, these assumptions have seldom been brought to the surface, and have more often been the subject of dogmas than of questions.

[22] *Ibid.*, p. 87. The historian, he writes, 'must never do what Enlightenment historians were always doing, that is, regard past ages with contempt and disgust, but must look at them sympathetically and find in them the expression of genuine and valuable human achievements'.

2   Gibbon and the primitive church

J. G. A. Pocock

I

The fifteenth and sixteenth chapters of Edward Gibbon's *History of the Decline and Fall of the Roman Empire* present a number of problems to scholars. They are far from being the whole of what Gibbon has to say about the history of Christianity; indeed, I am prepared to argue both that they are no more than preliminary to that history, which for Gibbon's purposes begins with the Council of Nicaea, and that they are an unsatisfactory prelude, with the consequence that they have been read out of context and made a touchstone by which the *Decline and Fall* as a whole has been judged. But to make these claims is to leave in want of a solution the problems of how Gibbon came to write them as they are, and how his critics and adversaries came to read them as they did. We may pursue with David Womersley – whose recent edition of most of the replies to chapters 15 and 16 has added to the debt all Gibbon scholars owe him[1] – the question of the exact nature of Gibbon's unbelief and the ways in which he represented it to his public.[2] Or we may enquire into the place these chapters occupy in the structure of the *Decline and Fall* as a narrative sequence, and ask what this enquiry may tell us about the processes by which he came to write it. These alternatives cannot in fact be separated, for if the two chapters fit ill into the *Decline and Fall*, we need all the more to know why Gibbon needed to write them. In this essay I shall lean towards the second alternative enquiry, without losing sight of the first.

I shall take my departure from a question asked as early as 1776 by James Chelsum of Christ Church, Oxford. He asks – and he is not alone in asking – why it is that Gibbon begins his enquiry into Christian history

---

[1] David Womersley, ed.: (1) *Edward Gibbon: Bicentenary Essays* (with the assistance of John Burrow and John Pocock), (Oxford, 1997); (2) *Religious Scepticism: Contemporary Responses to Gibbon* (Bristol, 1997).

[2] Womersley, 'Gibbon and the "Watchmen of the Holy City": Revision and Religion in the *Decline and Fall*', in Rosamond McKitterick and Roland Quinault, eds., *Edward Gibbon and Empire* (Cambridge, 1997), pp. 190–216; 'Gibbon's *Memoirs*: Autobiography in Time of Revolution', in *Bicentenary Essays*, pp. 347–404; and his essay in the present volume.

in the post-apostolic period, and has nothing to say about the actions of the apostles themselves or even those who had known them; although – Chelsum points out – it was during this earlier period that Christian communities became so widely established as to attract the attention of the persecuting emperors and then of Constantine.[3] An account, however conceived, of the rise and progress of Christianity might have been expected to begin with this process or even with the journeys and letters of St Paul himself.

I shall suggest that Chelsum was asking a reasonable question. As we shall see, he and others thought that Gibbon had sinister motives for proceeding as he had, but we need not concur with this to find the procedure historiographically odd. Gibbon does indeed start his enquiry late, and consequences flow from this for his history of both the empire and the church. It is scarcely too much to say that the *Decline and Fall* contains not a word about Christianity until the last sentence of the fourteenth chapter, when, on the heels of a sentence about the victory of Constantine increasing the burden 'as well of the taxes as of the military establishment', we are informed that 'The foundation of Constantinople, and the establishment of the Christian religion, were the immediate and memorable consequences of this revolution'.[4] This after fourteen chapters of the *Decline and Fall*, of which the disintegration of the Antonine monarchy occupies the first seven; there ensue two chapters on the Persian and German enemies of Rome, and five more recounting the wars of the Illyrian soldier-emperors, the establishment of a new kind of monarchy by Diocletian, and the wars among his successors as far as the victory of Constantine. In all this Christianity plays no part whatever, and if – as most of us do – we take the phrase 'Decline and Fall' to refer in the first place to the disintegration of the Augustan principate, Gibbon has left us uninformed as to what, if anything, he thought Christianity had to do with it.

Yet he is known to have insisted that there was 'an inseparable connection' between the rise of Christianity and the decline of the empire;[5] and we may if we wish search for this connection in the history of the Constantinean monarchy, begun in his second volume and not accomplished till the end of his sixth, or suppose (as I do) that it is not a matter of Christianity undermining the empire, but of replacing it as a new kind of civilisation. Attempts have been made to find covert messages about

---

[3] James Chelsum, 'Remarks on the Two Last Chapters of Mr Gibbon's History . . .' [1776], in *Religious Scepticism*, pp. 2–3.

[4] Edward Gibbon, *The History of the Decline and Fall of the Roman Empire*, vol. I, ch. 14; ed. David Womersley, 3 vols. (Harmondsworth, 1994), I, p. 445.

[5] *Edward Gibbon: Memoirs of My Life*, ed. Georges A. Bonnard (New York, 1966), p. 147. Cf. the General Observations appended to chapter 38 (Womersley edn, II, p. 510).

Christianity as a cause of decline in the text of the first fourteen chapters, but I am unpersuaded by them; the causes there expressly and repeatedly given seem to me quite sufficiently elaborated to justify the belief that they are seriously intended. But the question remains unanswered by Gibbon whether Christianity played any part in the history of Rome before Constantine. Why, after all, were the Christians persecuted? Did the emperors suppose they were acting against a serious danger to the state, or were they merely engaging in a necessary piece of normal police action? The supposition that chapter 16 is intended to minimise the scale of the persecutions may support the latter reading; but history is a narrative, and it is reasonable to ask whether it is with that intention alone that these actions have been left out of it. Christianity may have been either a major threat or a minor nuisance; but in recounting a history that includes attempts to prohibit it, the historian might have accorded it a role, and there has been none. What then is the place of chapters 15 and 16 in the history of the empire?

II

Such are the first fruits of an attempt to see how chapters 15 and 16 are situated in the formation of Gibbon's historical narrative. If we next consider them as the first step in the formation of a narrative history of the church – not hitherto mentioned – we repeat the question asked by Chelsum; why does Gibbon begin in the post-apostolic age? A possible answer, which occurred to his critics, is that by that time the Christians formed a community large and diverse enough to be susceptible of his kind of historical analysis, the pursuit of secondary and secular causes; for all critics agreed that it was his aim to situate Christianity in the setting of secular, not sacred history. To have begun his narrative earlier would have involved the risk of offering a secular analysis of the actions and character of sacred personages: the apostles, even Jesus himself; and it is easy to see reasons why this would have entailed risks that Gibbon would choose not to run. Yet the decision to avoid them weakens the rhetoric of his narrative and argument. Catholic historians, such as Tillemont, had no hesitation in offering histories of the actions of Jesus, based on the four Gospels, and of the apostles, based on the Acts and Epistles and on tradition. These histories are of course orthodox; they accept the premise of their master documents that these actions were moved by sacred and divine forces. Gibbon's understanding of Jesus and the apostles was no doubt unorthodox and very likely secular; we can see why he chose not to state it; but the decision to omit it, starting his history at a later date, necessarily weakened his narrative, argument, and rhetoric in two ways. In the first

place, it obliged the reader to infer what his history of Christ and the
apostles would have been, and obliged him to insert occasional language
from which such inferences might be made. This reinforced the charge
made by his critics that he proceeded too much by way of innuendo; a
charge which, all our admiration for the magnificence of his irony should
not allow us to forget, revealed a strategic weakness in his position.

In the second place, it obliged him to leave unasked questions to which
he must have desired to give answers. The history of Christianity which
he did develop was pre-eminently a history of theology, of what happened
when the original Christian message (whatever that was) became entan-
gled with Hellenic philosophy. If there is no word of Christianity in his
first fourteen chapters, there is a significant and perhaps crucial passage
in the thirteenth which recounts the rise of neo-Platonism,[6] and the
divergences and collisions between the Jewish and Greco-Syrian intelli-
gences are centrally important in chapter 15, when the primitive church is
shown divided between Ebionites and Gnostics.[7] Yet a great actor in
history is missing from a narrative that begins after him: the Apostle to
the Gentiles,[8] who may be said to have begun Christian history by
extending it from the Jews to the Greeks, and whose writings develop a
theology of salvation and rebirth only intimated in the Gospel narrative.
Gibbon might well have begun his narrative with Paul, whose recorded
actions and writings he could have taken at face value while offering a
commentary of his own; or with the Apostle John, whose Fourth Gospel,
contending that the Logos had been made Flesh, we know he regarded as
the initial and decisive step towards constructing Christ's divinity in
Platonic terms. It was indeed this that he rejected – as did Joseph
Priestley, among the most vehement if least orthodox of his Christian
critics – and his reasons for rejection could have been incorporated in a
counter-apostolic history of apostolic times. Such a history existed in the
minds of his readers; they knew what it was, and they wanted to know why
he had not written it – as one of them, Priestley, was in the process of
doing.

What did Gibbon think about Jesus? Priestley did not deny his divinity;
he only denied the Incarnation, the Atonement and the Trinity; and it was
Gibbon who recommended Priestley to the attention of the civil magistrate, not the other way round.[9] The relations between orthodoxy, dissent
and unbelief in the eighteenth century are many-sided and complex.

---

[6] Womersley, *Decline and Fall*, I, pp. 398–9.   [7] *Decline and Fall*, I, pp. 452–9.

[8] The Apostle Paul is not to be found in the *Decline and Fall*'s original index, reprinted by
Womersley, or in that supplied by J. B. Bury to his 1909 edition. He is mentioned once in
chapter 15 (I, p. 500) and in a footnote to chapter 16 (p. 519).

[9] *Decline and Fall*, V, ch. 54, n. 42 (Womersley, III, p. 439); *Memoirs*, p. 172.

Priestley thought Jesus a man sent by God, who might very possibly be sent again; but he can be seen playing a part in bringing Thomas Jefferson and John Adams to their conviction that Jesus was nothing other than a teacher of natural morality and natural religion, who had suffered an unjust fate.[10] This was the character to which the liberal-Protestant insistence on the identity of revealed truth and social morality might reduce him in the end, as of course it is still doing; but what Gibbon objected to in Priestley was not his Unitarianism but his revolutionary messianism and his expectation of the fall of the civil powers. There is language to be found in the *Decline and Fall* which can be read as reducing Jesus to the status of a moral preacher;[11] but we come closer to the debate between Gibbon and his critics in the well-known footnote that remarks of the seer and thaumaturge Apollonius of Tyana that he

was born about the same time as Jesus Christ. His life (that of the former) is related in so fabulous a manner by his disciples, that we are at a loss to discover whether he was a sage, an impostor, or a fanatic.[12]

The crucial word is 'impostor', and Gibbon does not have to be intimating his belief that Jesus was an impostor so much as his awareness that the question whether he was one may and must be asked and cannot easily be answered by the use of human evidence. We encounter here the problem of the impostor in eighteenth-century thought – recently high-lighted by Silvia Berti's discovery of an author for the *Livre des trois imposteurs*[13] and David Womersley's discovery that Gibbon possessed a copy of this work – and it is important to keep in mind two things: first, that the issue commonly if not always turned on the pretension to work miracles; second, that the impostor was more often than not (though certainly not in the *Livre*) a benign figure, a legislator or moralist who had been tempted to claim prophetic or thaumaturgic authority by the incorrigible superstition of those to whom he preached. It was the tragedy of the legislator, wrote Anquetil-Duperron of Zoroaster, that he was obliged to choose between the hypocrisy of saying what he did not believe and the enthusiasm of believing what he said;[14] alternatively, wrote Diderot (probably) in the *Histoire des deux Indes*, that he was forced to claim a sacred authority which priests then erected into systems of power

---

[10] *The Adams–Jefferson Letters*, ed. Lester J. Cappon, 2 vols. (Chapel Hill, 1959–88); for Priestley see index.

[11] *Decline and Fall*, I, p. 520; II, pp. 933–4. The Ebionites recur in the context of an enquiry into the belief in Jesus' divinity.   [12] *Decline and Fall*, I, p. 315; cf. p. 560, n. 138.

[13] Silvia Berti, ed., *Trattato dei tre impostori: la vita e lo spirito del signor Benedetto de Spinoza* (Turin, 1994).

[14] A. H. Anquetil-Duperron, *Zend-Avesta, ouvrage de Zoroastre . . .*, 2 vols. (Paris, 1771), II, pp. 65–6.

conducted by themselves in his name.[15] But Jesus was not a legislator; if he had been an impostor, it was because he worked miracles either to strengthen the morality which he taught with the promise of eternal happiness, or to convince others that he was the Son of God redeeming mankind from their sins. And it was possible that the imposture had not been his, but that of whoever had first claimed that he had healed the sick and risen from the dead.

Gibbon's critics, we may read in their texts, made themselves the defenders of Christ's miraculous energies and Gibbon into their attacker. This he pretty certainly was; but as he had written nothing concerning Christ's life on earth, they were obliged to charge that he had attacked them indirectly. It is worth noticing that Christ the sanctifier of morality seems to play a larger part in the debate on both sides than Christ the redeemer of sins. Anglican rhetoric may have tended in that direction where Anglican theology would not; clergymen with a grasp of their own orthodoxy knew exactly where the doctrine of Atonement was situated. Gibbon, however, did not find, or did not notice, the Atonement playing so large a part in the debates of the patristic epoch as the Trinity and the Incarnation, and himself paid it little attention. It is a consequence that among the 'secondary causes' he lists for the spreading acceptance of Christianity, he does not include, as he might have, a widespread sense of sin and need for the assurance of redemption. In its place he gives emphasis to the doctrine of personal immortality; though, as both Richard Watson and Smyth Loftus pointed out, it was a concept well enough known to the ancients if not always accepted, and the true stumbling block, which it was a triumph to have overcome, was rather the resurrection of the body.[16]

In tracing the debate over Gibbon's view of Christianity, we need to pay constant attention to what he chose to attack and what his adversaries chose to defend. We have to recognise in the latter a coherent account both of what they wished to affirm and of the position and strategy they took Gibbon to be adopting. This means that we must avoid, as still to some degree programmed into our minds, the Enlightenment assumption that theology is inherently meaningless and the agnostic assumption that clerics are mere passive defenders of tradition by rote. As historians of discourse, we need to recognise two living discourses in collision; and if this does not necessarily mean that Gibbon was saying what his adversaries took him to be saying, it means both that we have to understand their reasons for interpreting him as they did, and that the questions of what he was saying and with what effect remain to be answered.

[15] G. T. Raynal, ed., *Histoire des établissements et du commerce des européens dans les deux Indes*, 4 vols. (Geneva, 1780), I, pp. 60–4.

[16] *Religious Scepticism*, pp. 53–5 (Watson); 146–8, 163 (Loftus).

They took him, then, to be launching an attack on Christianity – a statement probably true, but in need of further specification – by way of an attack on the miraculous powers vested in the church; and here several of them were able to give an answer to James Chelsum's question about Gibbon's decision to begin his enquiry late in the church's history. They supposed that he was following the strategy of Conyers Middleton thirty years previously, who had designed his *Free Inquiry* as a criticism of the persistence of miraculous powers in the church's second century – an argument not necessarily heterodox given the Protestant agreement that they had ceased at some time or other – but had left it more than doubtful whether he held that miraculous powers had existed later than the lifetimes of the apostles, or Christ himself, or even then.[17] They presented Gibbon as a disciple of Middleton – it is unclear whether they knew that Gibbon's youthful conversion to Catholicism had occurred as a revulsion against him, and that his feelings towards Middleton must have been ambivalent – and behind Middleton some of them affected to discern the figure of Bolingbroke, and behind Bolingbroke the English deists and Voltaire.[18] They situated Gibbon, then, in a context of generalised deism – I hold this term to be imprecisely used – and the succession of deists they presented was predominantly English. In the present climate of Europeanisation, it is easy to regard this as proof of insular chauvinism, and to set about replacing it by some explanatory framework with better sub-continental credentials; and Gibbon had of course lived in Lausanne and Paris. It may be, however, that the English context to which Gibbon's critics belonged does possess some explanatory force, and that the process traced by Paul Turnbull, of representing Gibbon as the English Voltaire and his irreligion as Parisian in origin[19] – this too may be imprecise – took place somewhat later than the first replies to the *Decline and Fall*.

I do not hold that Gibbon was an English deist, or perhaps even a deist at all – we know that he shared Hume's scepticism about the possibility of

[17] Conyers Middleton, *A Free Enquiry into the Miraculous Powers, which are supposed to have subsisted in the Christian Church, from the earliest ages through several successive centuries; by which it is shewn that we have no reason to believe, upon the authority of the primitive Fathers, that any such powers were continued to the Church, after the days of the Apostles* (London, 1749). For Gibbon's relation to Middleton, see most recently B. W. Young, '"Scepticism in Excess": Gibbon and Eighteenth-Century Christianity', *Historical Journal*, 41, 1 (1998), pp. 179–99.

[18] *Religious Scepticism*, pp. 53 (Watson on modern deists as Gnostics); 97–115 (Watson on deism in general); 150–3 (Loftus on Gibbon as follower of Middleton); 161, 170–1 (Gibbon as deist); 172–3 (Gibbon and Middleton – Loftus); 187 n. 5 (Davis), 216–17 (Gibbon and Bolingbroke – Milner).

[19] Paul Turnbull, '"Une marionette infidèle": The Fashioning of Edward Gibbon's Reputation as the English Voltaire', in *Bicentenary Essays*, pp. 279–308.

a natural religion,[20] though this scepticism would extend to atheism in the Lucretian-Spinozistic sense in which that term was chiefly used – but I am here interested in what his critics meant to defend when they called him one. They were concerned to defend the actuality of miracles, about which they could see that Gibbon was altogether sceptical, and it is important to understand what was at issue here. We think of a miracle as an event against the course of nature, performed by a divine being or by divine power vested in a human actor; and we know of, and adopt, the contention of Enlightened philosophers that no human testimony can demonstrate that such an event has taken place. A debate with believers therefore takes the form of a debate over the possibility or impossibility of miracles; and in pursuing it, we sometimes lose sight of the purpose with which the believer holds the miracles to have been performed. The divine being performs them in order to demonstrate that he is acting in the world; the prophet, apostle or saint demonstrates that divine powers have been conferred upon him. Here the possibility of imposture arises. The impostor pretends to miraculous or visionary powers in order to pretend that he is divinely empowered, or – far more rarely – a divine being himself; if Jesus feigned miracles in order to pretend that he was incarnate God he must have been the greatest impostor of all time. But the sceptic can leave the question of imposture open – as Gibbon did in the case of Apollonius/Jesus – while maintaining simply that human critical intelligence can never affirm that a miracle has occurred; it is too improbable for its possibility to be asserted.

How does the believer respond to the sceptic? To understand this we must accept that he understands the miracle as a sign even more than as a wonder; it is the only signification by which a divine being can unequivocally proclaim that he is present and acting in the world, and to affirm that it can never be known that a miracle has happened is to affirm that divine action in the world – as distinct from immanent in it – can never be said to have taken place. Gibbon, his critics perceived, had carried his scepticism about miracles, as he had evidently meant to do, to the point where he could not be a Christian, could not believe in any relation of sacred history at all. He might therefore be a deist, one who held that God might be deducible from the workings of the world but performed no extraordinary actions in it; and as it required a still greater comprehension of Gibbon's scepticism to recognise that he was not in fact a deist, they continued to regard him as one. Some, who knew that there were

---

[20] See his letter to J. B. Suard, dated 20 December 1776, published by Michel Baridon, 'Une lettre inédite d'Edward Gibbon à Jean-Baptiste-Antoíne Suard', *Etudes anglaises*, 24, 1 (1971), pp. 79–87. I am indebted to Patricia Craddock and David Raynor for help with this reference.

forms of unbelief going beyond deism proper, continued to use the word as a portmanteau term embracing all of them, and this is sometimes done even today.

It was not unreasonable to define Gibbon's unbelief in imprecise terms, since we are not certain whether he could have stated it as other than a generalised scepticism. The belief of his adversaries that it took the form of an unshakeable, because testimony-proof, scepticism regarding miracles carried them to the verge of questioning his acceptance of the divinity of Jesus Christ; since the miraculous darkness at the moment of the Passion, while not one of the miracles Jesus had worked as proof of his mission, had at least occurred at the end of his earthly life, and was as close as Gibbon got to considering that life's events.[21] The replies we read to the *Decline and Fall*, however, enlarge the concept of the miraculous in quite another direction, which opens up the question of Gibbon's historiography in a new way. They require, as proof of orthodoxy and conviction, a confession that the spread of Christian belief among pagans rather than Jews, in the apostolic period and beyond it, was a phenomenon so extraordinary as to defy explanation in secular terms and deserve the epithet 'miraculous'; and they see Gibbon's resort to secondary and human causes for the growth of Christianity as proof that he does not regard it as brought about by divine intervention in human history.[22] Now when the word 'miraculous' is used in this setting, it must be as a figure of speech; for a conversion is not an event superseding or suspending the ordinary operations of physical nature, and the miracles ascribed to the apostles (and on other authority to their successors), whatever their importance as signs, were seen by relatively few and were instrumental in relatively few conversions. To a Protestant mind in particular, conversion occurred when the Word was preached and was accepted by some among its hearers.

It might of course be maintained that this could not occur without some special gift or operation of grace upon both the preacher and his auditory; there may have been more of Calvinism in the minds of Gibbon's adversaries than meets the eye or we are self-programmed to recognise. An operation of grace upon the spirit, however, is not a miracle except by a perhaps questionable extension of the term. A further strategy open to those professing that the spread of Christianity had been an extraordinary event was providentialism. It could be maintained that the

---

[21] *Decline and Fall*, I, pp. 512–13; *Memoirs*, p. 147; *Religious Scepticism*, pp. 19–21 (Chelsum); 85–9 (Watson); 183–4 (Loftus).

[22] *Religious Scepticism*, pp. 2, 39 (Chelsum); Watson's emphasis is rather on the persistence of miraculous powers in the early church; 130–3 (Loftus); 159–62, 173; 208–11 (Davis); 224 (Milner); 237, 249 (Priestley).

Creator in his wisdom had so disposed the condition of mankind at the time of Christ's appearing that hearts and minds were exceptionally disposed to receive his message. This was not an assertion of the miraculous in the sense of the extraordinary, so much as an assertion that the ordinary – or rather the historical – had been extraordinarily disposed, and that the element of epiphany was supplied by the unmistakable evidence of the providence disposing it. It was an advantage of the providential argument that it permitted the Christian to make use of secular and historical causes; a disadvantage to which Gibbon could blandly reply that these were precisely the causes he himself alleged, and that he had nothing to do but bow the head to those who discerned the workings of providence in them. It would be a reiteration of Humean argument, removed from the natural level to the historical. There is evidence, however, that Gibbon had taken a further step, also Humean but carrying him beyond the anti-providential reading: evidence which may have been unknown to his adversaries but certainly would not have surprised them.

A version of the providential thesis proposed that the state of man had been unusually sinful at the time of Christ's appearing, due to the depravity of the emperors and the immoralities of polytheism, so that the time was ripe for the message of repentance and redemption. This can be found in such major historians as Mosheim and Robertson,[23] and is also glanced at in Gibbon's drafts for his first work, the *Essai sur l'étude de la Littérature* which he began composing at Lausanne in 1758. Here a good deal about the wickedness of the times occurs in conjunction with a clear statement, the last he ever wrote, that there is something extraordinary about the spread of Christianity: an unknown man belonging to a despised people is put to death, and within three centuries the cross has been erected on the ruins of the Capitol in the name of a doctrine which defies reason and subdues it.[24] However, Gibbon eliminated this passage when he revised his *Essai* in 1761, and the published text replaces it by what seem to be reflections upon religion as a natural phenomenon produced by the human mind, similar to the scheme of Hume's *Natural History of Religion*, which Gibbon could have read by that time. There are accounts of the religion of the savage and then of the polytheist.[25] This is rightly taken for a move on Gibbon's part towards the critical analysis of religion, a replacement of Christian history by the study of Christianity as

---

[23] J. L. Mosheim, *De Rebus Christianis ante Constantinum Magnum* (Helmstedt, 1753); *An Ecclesiastical History Ancient and Modern* (London, 1765); William Robertson, *The Situation of the World at the Time of Christ's Appearance, and its Connexion with the Success of his Religion, Considered* (Edinburgh, 1755).

[24] British Library Add. MSS 34880, fols. 154–5.

[25] *The Miscellaneous Works of Edward Gibbon, Esq.*, ed. Lord Sheffield, 5 vols. (London, 1814), IV, pp. 70–88.

a historical phenomenon; and this of course is precisely what his adversaries objected to in the notorious two chapters. Now if what we have here
is a project for replacing Christian faith by philosophical history – a
replacement which certainly occurred in Gibbon's own mind – it could be
said that we have one of those 'Enlightenment projects' of which there are
so many that it seems a mistake to lump them all together under the name
of 'The Enlightenment project', as is so often done on the left and on the
right. But what is a project and what conditions must be met for the word
to be used?

In a very remarkable contribution to Womersley's *Bicentenary Essays*,[26]
Girolamo Imbruglia has assembled evidence that an unmistakable
project was being mooted by *philosophes* in Paris about the time of
Gibbon's visit there in 1763. Diderot and others were convinced that the
time had come to promulgate and define a strictly philosophic civil religion, and that a necessary step in this direction was the construction of an
histoire ecclésiastique. It would seem that this plan had much in common
with Giannone's *Triregno* thirty years before, in that a general history of
religion in the human mind was to be combined with a strongly
Spinozistic statement of the religion of nature, in which mind and matter
should become one. Here we have what is certainly a project; indeed a
'regular plan' formed by a 'literary cabal' for 'the destruction of the
Christian religion', as Edmund Burke was to phrase it twenty-seven years
later.[27] The problem before the cabal, however, was to find its historian.
Voltaire would not do; his history of religion would be too deist and old-
fashioned for Diderot;[28] and their thoughts seem to have turned first to
Hume, doubtless on the strength of his *Natural History* – though a comprehensive history of religion in all its forms was about the last thing
Hume can be imagined undertaking – and then to Galiani, with whom
Diderot and Grimm entered into discussions. In the end nothing came of
it; one can easily imagine that the more Diderot talked about the idea, the
less likely it was that anyone could be found to carry it out; and
Imbruglia's narrative ends with Diderot berating Grimm for betraying
the cause of philosophy by his loss of interest in the project.

Imbruglia seems to me to make it quite clear that Gibbon in 1763 had
no hand in Diderot's project and there is no sign that he knew it was going
on. Few of the *philosophes* in that year had reason to think him a person of
any importance; it is our eye that is caught by the *Essai sur l'étude de la littérature*; and it would be a very long shot indeed to find evidence that he

[26] Girolamo Imbruglia, '"My Ecclesiastical History": Gibbon between Hume and Raynal',
in *Bicentenary Essays*, pp. 73–102.
[27] Edmund Burke, *Reflections on the Revolution in France* (Indianapolis, 1987), p. 97.
[28] Cf. his *Philosophie de l'histoire* (1765).

knew what Diderot was about in his remark in the *Memoirs*, twenty-five years later, that he found Holbach's dinner table populated by atheists who 'laughed at the scepticism of Hume'.[29] The central point, surely, is that neither Gibbon nor even Hume had reason to take part in devising a civil religion and an ecclesiastical history around which *philosophes* might rally on a ground structurally opposed to Christianity. In Erastian Protestant cultures – part-Latitudinarian England, part-Moderate Scotland – it was easier to leave Christianity to liberalise itself, hoping in America that it would arrive at some Unitarian vanishing point.[30] In such climates unbelief grew in the movement beyond Socinianism and deism to scepticism, and had no need of the plunge into a post-Spinozistic atheism. Nor was it necessary to construct a civil religion with public and non-Christian rituals of its own. Imbruglia, concluding his essay with the observation that there is much in common between Gibbon's history of Christianity and Raynal's – much of it written by Diderot – nevertheless adds that 'Gibbon had been convinced that the best defence of reason lay in the separation of the elite from the populace. Like Fréret, he was an academic in public and an atheist in private.'[31] To this I would only add that 'unbeliever' is perhaps a better word than 'atheist.' The latter was sure he knew how the universe was constituted; he believed too much and professed it too openly. His civil religion was the first step to fanaticism. Thus Burke, and thus Gibbon in his *Memoirs*.

But chapters 15 and 16 do not succeed in maintaining the separation between public and private; Gibbon made his unbelief too evident and too comprehensive, and was condemned as an enemy to Christianity. David Wootton has argued that these chapters are 'Voltairean'[32] – their first critics, in their un-European way, thought that English deism was enough to account for them – but I find this description imprecise. Voltaire in his own fashion had an 'Enlightenment project', that of creating a climate in which Catholic, Jansenist, and Calvinist theology should become forever impossible; but Gibbon, I suggest, need aim no further than rendering them harmless, and in England this could be achieved through the tolerance possible to an Erastian church whose supremacy was maintained by the state. If he had an 'Enlightenment project', which is doubtful, it was that of enquiring whether it was possible to return to the happy state of ancient religion, in which sceptically tolerant magistrates had presided over the rituals rendered necessary by the superstition of the masses.[33] But – as Hume could and may have taught Gibbon – this

---

[29] *Memoirs*, p. 127.
[30] The hope of Thomas Jefferson; see *Adams–Jefferson Letters, passim*.
[31] *Bicentenary Essays*, p. 102.   [32] *Ibid.*, p. 216, n. 50. Wootton's essay should be read in full.
[33] *Decline and Fall*, I, ch. 2; Womersley, I, pp. 56–8.

project was at risk in any era after an abstract monotheism had filtered down to the masses and made them capable of fanaticism and enthusiasm. The Enlightened insistence that they were irredeemably superstitious had an element of wishful thinking about it; that was not their most dangerous characteristic, as in England was very well known. Gibbon was in London during the Gordon riots, and remarked: 'Forty thousand Puritans, as they might be in the time of Cromwell, have started out of their graves.'[34]

For such reasons the anglophone historians were in two minds about superstition; Hume preferred Laudian ritualism to the Puritan fanaticism which had then (but not now) been necessary to the assertion of English liberty,[35] Gibbon admired the image-worship of the Italians which had made the Popes the defenders of liberty against the iconoclast emperors.[36] In Hanoverian Britain, however, such paradoxes should no longer be necessary, and it was a question whether Enlightenment called for anything more than a traditional orthodoxy for those who needed it, presided over by lay and clerical magistrates who were prepared to view it with detachment, playing the role of the Stoic and Epicurean magistrates in the world of Roman polytheism. Such might be believers or unbelievers, but they must accept the presence of philosophers who did not believe at all; the role of the latter, however, was to provide a philosophical and historical critique of religion, without necessarily replacing it by a civil religion, or alternative system of public belief, backed by a radical historiography. There was no need for anyone to play the part of Diderot, or of Toland. In England, particularly, we have to do with an Enlightenment *sans philosophes*, and *sans projets*.

III

Gibbon seemed to his adversaries to be carrying on an 'Enlightenment project', in the sense of a general undermining of Christianity, in which he was certainly not a believer. It seems fair to ask, however, whether he had any such project, in the form of a planned persuasive strategy, in mind; there are other possibilities. In pursuing this problem, we need to keep asking what it was that persuaded his adversaries that he did intend something of the sort; and here it is worth noting that it was not his attack on the authority of the clergy that had this effect. When, late in chapter 15, he contended that the authority of bishops in the primitive church had led to

---

[34] *The Letters of Edward Gibbon*, ed. J. E. Norton (London, 1956), II, p. 243.
[35] David Hume, *History of Great Britain* (1754); *The History of England*, ed. William B. Todd, 6 vols. (Indianapolis , 1983), V, pp. 459–60.
[36] *Decline and Fall*, V, ch. 49; Womersley, III, p. 101.

the rise of patriarchates and afterwards of papacy, there was no objection from his critics;[37] this was the origin of popery to which as Protestants they were accustomed to give credence. Gibbon had not said much about the apostolic succession, and the canon of his adversaries does not include high churchmen rallying to its defence, as had been the case in the seventeenth century. Gibbon's offence was that in chapter 15 he had undermined the authority of miracles and the belief that the spread of Christianity had been an extraordinary event, and in chapter 16 had undermined the authority of martyrs, those in whom faith had risen to the height of a supernatural virtue. And so of course he had; the question is why, with what intentions, and with what effects?

If we follow Girolamo Imbruglia in suggesting that Gibbon's solution lay in 'the separation of the elite from the populace', it may be worth recalling that the first volumes of the *Decline and Fall* coincide in time with the movements we imprecisely bring together under the title of Rational Dissent.[38] These aimed at relief, either from the obligation to subscribe to the Thirty-Nine Articles with their uncompromisingly Trinitarian and Athanasian clauses, or from the civil disabilities imposed upon Dissenters. The first part of this programme was at least as much Anglican as it was Dissenting; there had long been in the church of England those who, in privacy but not in secrecy, held the doctrine of the Trinity to be at least debatable, and some of these now wished to come out from their closet status and seek public recognition. When this relief was denied them, they faced the choice between leaving the Church and declaring themselves Unitarians, as some of them did, and reverting to their former status as a Socinian samizdat. The Radical Enlightenment, the Enlightenment project of the late Georgian anglophone world, consisted in some brand of revolutionary Unitarianism, but only in Jefferson's United States was this carried out as a political programme, and then with very mixed consequences. The samizdat alternative, however, was Enlightened in its own way. Gibbon, I wish to suggest, would be perfectly entitled to see, and there is some evidence that he did see, the modern equivalent of his ancient scheme of a philosophic magistracy ruling over a cultic populace in the government of a Trinitarian Establishment by a philosophic episcopate, 'subscribing', as he once put it, 'with a sigh or a smile'[39] to doctrines which among themselves they debated to the point where Socinianism gave way to scepticism: the English equivalent of the Parisian belief that Geneva was now ruled by Socinians if not deists.

[37] *Religious Scepticism*, p. 75 (Watson).
[38] Knud Haakonssen, ed., *Enlightenment and Religion: Rational Dissent in Eighteenth-Century Britain* (Cambridge, 1996).   [39] *Decline and Fall*, V, ch. 54; Womersley, III, p. 439.

But chapters 15 and 16 failed radically as the project of such an Enlightenment. When Gibbon wrote in his *Memoirs* that he had failed to realise how deeply his countrymen were still attached 'to the name, or the shadow, of Christianity',[40] he did not mean that he had wrongly supposed that English Christianity was reduced to a shadow, so much as that he had over-estimated the acceptability of the view that it was so reduced. The philosophers who had gone beyond Socinianism to scepticism were not, in his scenario, the adversaries of the Enlightened clerics on the debatable ground between Socinianism and Trinitarianism; but in the reception of the *Decline and Fall* he found himself treated as an adversary where – he would have us believe – he had not expected such treatment. David Womersley has shown that his revisions to the two chapters antedate the responses to them;[41] but this need mean no more than that he belatedly realised what was about to happen. We need not altogether reject the thesis that Gibbon had over-estimated the extent to which he was going to get away with it.

I attach importance here to the circumstance that among Gibbon's adversaries were Richard Watson and Joseph Priestley; not on the grounds that they headed the attack or that they caused Gibbon most concern – both would be false – but because by focusing attention on them we can learn something about the reception of the *Decline and Fall* available in no other way. Neither Watson nor Priestley was fully orthodox; yet Gibbon selected Watson as the most amicable of his adversaries and treated Priestley with greater venom even than that shown towards Henry Davis.[42] The latter had attacked Gibbon's scholarly integrity and he considered this an affront to his honour; but Priestley was an ideological and political enemy against whom Gibbon called for legal and political action. Richard Watson, later Bishop of Llandaff and Cambridge Professor of Divinity – not particularly active in either role – was a member of that probably Socinian circle around Edmund Law of Peterhouse, who might have benefited by some relaxation of the obligation to subscribe to the Thirty-Nine Articles.[43] His promotion to Llandaff in 1782 – 'I dare not boast the making of Dr Watson a bishop', says Gibbon[44] – may have owed something to the Duke of Grafton, one of those theologically liberal noblemen at whom Burke looked askance in

---

[40] *Memoirs*, p. 159.   [41] *Religious Scepticism*, introduction.
[42] Henry Edwards Davis, *An Examination of the Fifteenth and Sixteenth Chapters of Mr Gibbon's History* [1778], in *Religious Scepticism*, pp. 185–214; Gibbon, *A Vindication of Some Passages in the Fifteenth and Sixteenth Chapters of the History of the Decline and Fall of the Roman Empire* [1779], in Womersley ed., *Decline and Fall*, III, pp. 1106–84.
[43] J. C. D. Clark, *English Society, 1688–1832* (Cambridge, 1986), pp. 311–15; John Gascoigne, *Cambridge in the Age of the Enlightenment* (Cambridge, 1989), pp. 215–18, 239–42, 246–7.
[44] *Memoirs*, p. 160.

the *Reflections*;[45] but Burke feared the quasi-revolutionary sympathies of the Rational Dissenters, and Watson passed the rest of his days in support of the regime, defending Christianity (against Paine as well as Gibbon), the declaration of war with France in 1793, and the union with Ireland in 1801. He was in short a type of the conservatively liberal prelate and magistrate Gibbon never ceased to admire, one who would defend the public value of positions he held discussable in private, so that his liberalism and even his scepticism became means of upholding the established order, as was also the case with Gibbon and Hume.

Yet there are limits to the kinds of support which any regime can accept, and we are at the point at which Nigel Aston has quite rightly reminded us that orthodox clerics must regard as subversive the support offered them on sceptical grounds.[46] Watson was not particularly orthodox, though his bishopric committed him to the affirmation of received orthodoxy. We have to remember that this was not necessarily hypocritical, the affair of 'a sigh or a smile', but was based on a clear distinction between private conversation and public profession. As far back as 1689, when anti-Trinitarian doctrine had surfaced and the Act of Toleration had been withheld from those who denied the Trinity, it had been made clear that the doctrine might lawfully be discussed and various conclusions mooted, but that public profession and congregation on a Unitarian base did not enjoy the protection, or the leniency, of the law. This was the 'toleration' which the radical wing of Rational Dissent, led among others by Priestley, firmly rejected as insufficient. For Watson, however, it was enough, perhaps more than he needed to demand; and his reply to Gibbon, *An Apology for Christianity*, consists in a courteous, reasonable, but quite inflexible affirmation of the fabric of orthodox belief at all those points at which he held Gibbon's arguments to be indifferent or hostile. These do not include the doctrine of the Trinity, for the reason that neither the text of chapters 15 and 16, nor the history of the church at the moment where those chapters take it up, have reached the point at which that doctrine becomes the matter of disputation; we are back with the question of why Gibbon chose to begin that history where he did.

Watson, who more than once informed Gibbon of his dislike of public controversy, may be read as accusing Gibbon of launching one; of letting him know that there are positions which must be defended if they are publicly attacked, the more so when the attack is neither a direct assault nor a critical history, but a highly selective historical essay beginning at a late date and allowing the attack to become known by means of retrospect, implication, and innuendo. Like all Gibbon's critics in the first

[45] Grafton elevated Law to Carlisle and Hinchcliffe to Peterborough in 1769, Watson to Llandaff in 1782. Burke, *Reflections*, pp. 11–12.   [46] *Bicentenary Essays*, p. 262, n. 52.

wave of response to the two chapters, he charges both that they launch a general assault on Christianity and that they do not launch it; he sees the comprehensive character of Gibbon's irony as proof that his dislike of Christianity is comprehensive, and as proof that he has expressed his opposition to it in language which is neither philosophical nor historical, but merely rhetorical. To the extent to which the two chapters are not a comprehensive history of the church before Constantine – and Gibbon admired the histories of this period by Le Clerc and Mosheim, which he had before him – we must (to that extent) agree with this description. The question before us is what Gibbon meant by launching the two chapters in their present form; are they an Enlightenment project, or are they an authorial aberration?

In Watson, however, Gibbon found himself opposed not by high churchmen or partisans of orthodoxy – 'the voice of our priests was clamorous and bitter'[47] does not apply here – but by an advanced liberal churchman whom he did not find unsympathetic, but who was nevertheless telling him that he had gone too far in a public direction and had moved too indirectly. It is the problem of philosophy and public speech, with which of course Gibbon was well acquainted; in the *Memoirs* he seems to be accusing himself of failure to appreciate it adequately. The reverse of the medal appears when we consider Gibbon's collision with Joseph Priestley, though this did not come about until after 1782, when Priestley published his *History of the Corruptions of Christianity,* including some animadversions upon Gibbon in an appendix,[48] and Gibbon retorted upon him in a chapter of his fifth volume, published in 1788.[49] Though this debate does not belong to the history of the reception of chapters 15 and 16 in isolation, they are very much present in it, as they had now begun to dominate the reception of the *Decline and Fall* as a whole, and have continued to do ever since. The history of Gibbon and Priestley thus gives us our first opportunity to consider the two chapters and their reception in the context of the *Decline and Fall* as a completed work.

Priestley was a radical Unitarian, who had departed altogether from Nicene orthodoxy in either its Catholic or its Calvinist form. His *History of the Corruptions* is therefore a history of that orthodoxy, in which he condemns the growth of such false doctrines as the Trinity, the Incarnation, the Atonement, the Sacrament, and the immortality of the soul in separation from the body, all of which are depicted as the effects of the intrusion upon the Christian message of neo-Platonist and Platonist philosophy, together with what Priestley took to be its Gnostic and Egyptian

---

[47] *Memoirs*, p. 160.   [48] *Religious Scepticism*, pp. 235–49.   [49] Note 9, above.

accretions inherited from magian antiquity. The structure of the *History of the Corruptions* thus closely parallels that of the *Decline and Fall*; for, starting with its second volume, the latter traces the corruptions of Christianity and recounts them as a history of Platonist accretions and the invention of theology as a species of false philosophy. An important difference, however, is that Gibbon is interested in these events solely as civil history, or rather as means to the intrusion of ecclesiastical upon civil history, and its adoption of authority; he therefore writes a sceptical history, not like Diderot a history leading to a new philosophy and authority. For Priestley, on the other hand, the history of corruption is an intrusion upon Christian truth, a history of departure from that truth, and his history resembles that envisaged by the atheist Diderot in being a means to the truth's restoration.

Priestley was a Christian, in the sense that he thought Christ a divine being, who had come and might come again. This would probably disappoint Jefferson; it outraged Gibbon, less on account of Priestley's residual Christianity than of his millennialism. He had advanced beyond the petitions of Rational Dissent to advocacy of the complete separation of church and state, in whose false unity all the corruptions had culminated. Gibbon (and Burke) found him declaring in 1782 that for the end of religious establishments 'we must await the fall of the civil powers. Calamitous, no doubt, will that time be',[50] and indeed the separation of church and state was a revolutionary objective, to be achieved only in the foundation of the United States. Priestley was to end his days on the banks of the Susquehanna.

Gibbon knew revolutionary enthusiasm when he saw it. Priestley had gone far beyond making the private word public, as Gibbon had been reproached for doing; he had made it divine – the enthusiast's classic mistake – and had written history which was prophecy and moved its author to fulfil it. That Priestley's history of Christianity was so like Gibbon's must have increased the latter's indignation. But between Watson, for whom Gibbon had said too much, and Priestley, who had said too much for Gibbon, what was the status of chapters 15 and 16 of the *Decline and Fall*? What had they said, been intended to say, succeeded in saying? What answers to these questions are suggested by the various ways of looking at them?

---

[50] Joseph Priestley, *An History of the Corruptions of Christianity*, 2 vols. (Birmingham, 1782), II, p. 484; *Decline and Fall*, V, ch. 54, n. 42 (Womersley edn, III, p. 439); Burke, *Reflections*, p. 50.

IV

We read these two chapters as masterpieces of irony – which of course they are – and we suppose that their intended achievement is carried out by the irony they display: the expression of a generalised scepticism towards Christianity, conveyed and articulated by an ironic treatment of every aspect of Christianity covered in them. This is what is meant by calling them 'Voltairean'. Voltaire was known for his unequalled capacity to speak ironically and derisively of any and every subject that fell in his way, though his irony is often morally serious. (It is also very different from Gibbon's irony; Gibbon thought that Voltaire's irony sometimes mastered his mind, which was not what irony was meant to do.) It has to be remembered, however, that part of Gibbon's irony consists in innuendo, and that his critics were not altogether wrong in suggesting that his use of innuendo arose because, like Middleton before him, he had started his narrative at a late period and left it to be inferred that what he had to say applied to the earlier period also; this is a large part of what they mean by, and call, Gibbon's 'deism'. The irony and the innuendo begin to look different when situated in a consideration of Gibbon's use of historical narrative, and of the kinds of history in which he situates his account of Christianity. We return once more to James Chelsum's question: why did Gibbon start where he did?

The question of his narrative enlarges into the question of his project. 'What the Deuce had he to do', Hugh Blair asked Adam Smith, 'with Attacking Religion? It will both Clog his Work and is in itself Unhistorical and out of Place.'[51] A history of the Roman empire called for a history of Christianity only in so far as the latter fitted in to the narratives needed to make sense of the former. It did not call for a generalised display of unbelief, except in so far as the history of late antiquity offered the points of intersection between civil, sacred, and ecclesiastical history; and if there was a project of affirming the prior intelligibility and authority of the first of these three, it might be necessary to dismiss the second in order to discredit the third. We are on safe ground in attributing such a project to Gibbon and calling it Enlightenment. But his assault on sacred history is carried out by innuendo; he pretends to leave it intact and focus only on secondary causes; and the effect, as Chelsum and others pointed out, is that he supplies no history of the apostolic age, and his history of the age of the martyrs is isolated from narrative as a separate enquiry. Where narrative fails, innuendo is part of what is left.

I have been suggesting that, despite all their brilliance, there is some-

---

[51] Hugh Blair to Adam Smith, 3 April 1776, in *The Correspondence of Adam Smith*, ed. I. S. Ross and E. C. Mossner (Oxford, 1977), no. 151, p. 287.

thing indeterminate about chapters 15 and 16; it is unclear just what they achieve, either as Enlightenment project or as history of the Decline and Fall. Project and narrative are interwoven in their unsatisfactoriness; it is because Gibbon does not provide a full narrative of the church's history before Constantine – there are many reasons why he does not – that he is driven back on a structure so variously discursive that it indicates a highly generalised dislike of Christianity. That he felt this dislike is fairly clear; that he was read as expressing it, and therefore did express it, is obvious; to suggest that he expressed it without meaning to would be ridiculous; but it is still possible to ask what intentions he carried out by expressing it, and whether he was entirely clear what these were. A full-scale discrediting of Christianity would be a project intelligible in a Parisian milieu to which he did not belong; in the English milieu it proved unnecessary and counter-productive, and the Scottish question I have quoted was well asked. We are left with Gibbon's own verdict, that he had over-estimated the extent to which the English milieu permitted the open move beyond Socinianism to scepticism; and this, though written fifteen years later in a time of heated response to French revolution,[52] is easily made to fit the facts. But there are questions which it leaves unanswered and perhaps unasked. How, for example, do the two chapters fit into the narrative and explanatory structure of the *Decline and Fall?* The establishment of the Christian religion by Constantine has a set of immediate and necessary consequences: the outbreak of Christological dispute at Alexandria, the assembling of the Council of Nicaea, Constantine's discovery that theological dispute is serious politics, and the increase of power which such dispute brings to the Christian clergy. That Gibbon did not get around to dealing with the history of Nicaea until five chapters and five years later does not mean that its imminence was unknown to the controversialists of 1776.

But that history does not call for chapters 15 and 16, nor do they do more than a certain amount to prepare the way for chapters 20 and 21. The prospectus for the whole *Decline and Fall,* published with the first volume, has little to say about the growth of ecclesiastical power, and if Gibbon's adversaries realised where he was going next, it was because they understood the logic of church history and religious scepticism rather than because he had told them. Gibbon in these chapters was not carrying out a declared plan, and it is worth asking how far, in 1776, the plan for the ecclesiastical history he then began to write was formed in his mind. We are indebted to Peter Ghosh for his reminder that Gibbon wrote the *Decline and Fall* as he went along, and did not always know how

---

[52] Womersley, 'Gibbon's *Memoirs*: Autobiography in Time of Revolution', in *Bicentenary Essays*, pp. 347–404.

it was going to turn out.[53] I am exploring the possibility that we have an instance of that phenomenon here.

It would entail believing that in the two chapters Gibbon did more than he intended to do; not that he did not do it or that he did not want to do it or know that he was doing it, but that he was uncertain of the intentions, and therefore of the strategies, which he was carrying out in doing it. In the *Memoirs* he tells us that he found his first volume extremely difficult to write, that what became the two chapters was once long enough to form a separate volume, and that it was very hard to reduce them to their present size.[54] Every working historian has passed through such an experience, and this makes it easier to believe what he here says; but I am proposing that he found himself committed to a church history at a moment when he had not quite decided how to write it, with what Enlightenment project in mind he was going to write it, or how he was going to relate it to the history of Decline and Fall, about which his intentions were formed to a point where he could try to execute them. In consequence he found himself in a crisis of organisation, from which the two chapters emerged with the deficiencies noted by his adversaries, by Hugh Blair (an able critic), and by us. They emerged as a series of sceptical discourses about early Christian history,[55] from which it was right to infer a general antipathy to that religion on Gibbon's part; and – Gibbon being Gibbon – they are written with a rhetorical brilliance and a coherence of style that may justify readers and literary scholars in treating them as a unitary work of art. It is dangerous, however, to infer from their coherence as rhetoric a coherence of strategy and intention which, when they are considered either as Enlightenment project or as historiography, I find reason to doubt that they possess. Because they do not belong fully within any structure, they have, first, been considered in isolation from the *Decline and Fall* as a completed work, and second, been used to evaluate the intention of that work as a whole. I am arguing that they do not carry that burden, but my essay is merely a continuation of a long debate over these chapters as a problem. I explore the possibility that this problem arose, and still exists, because Gibbon was not fully in control of them as he wrote them.

[53] P. Ghosh, 'Gibbon's Dark Ages: Some Remarks on the Genesis of the *Decline and Fall*', *Journal of Roman Studies*, 73 (1983), p. 23.

[54] *Memoirs*, p. 156.

[55] It was at this point, at the colloquium held to prepare this volume, that David Womersley and I were simultaneously seized by the intuition that the two chapters (like the 'General Reflections on the Fall of the Roman Empire in the West') may have originated as a separate dissertation, which Gibbon fitted into his history, rather than written as part of a designed sequence of chapters planned as composing it. It is easier to suspect this than to demonstrate it.

3   Gibbon's religious characters

David Womersley

I

For Gibbon's contemporaries there was no debate. They knew that Gibbon was a religious sceptic in the manner of Voltaire, and they also knew that, like his notorious predecessor in disbelief, Bolingbroke, the infection had been acquired by personal contact. The greatest English historian had left Oxford in disgrace, and had instead chosen to graduate from the infidel schools of Ferney and Battersea.[1]

Even Gibbon's friends and defenders felt that there was little that could be done by way of rebuttal. For instance, while preparing the *Miscellaneous Works* for publication Sheffield drafted a long note extenuating Gibbon's irreligion:

Mr Gibbon was not, in the first instance, aware how offensive his Irony, and manner of mentioning the Christian Religion must be; and that he did not mean to outrage Society in the Degree that has been supposed . . . When the mischief and wantonness of disregard to established Opinions was mentioned, he exceeded in expression all that was said. He was so habituated to the infinitely more extravagant writings of Voltaire and others, and to the extreme levity of conversation, among the generality of those with whom he had lived, that he thought himself comparatively decent; and has often expressed great surprize that He had given so much Offence.[2]

To have presented Gibbon's religious scepticism as, as it were, a failure of table manners, picked up innocently and by accident in the wrong sort of company, might have been an effective strategy of exculpation if it could

---

I wish to record at the outset my gratitude for permission from the Athenaeum Club to refer to, and quote from, manuscript material in their possession.

[1] *The Gentleman's Magazine*, 46 (1776), p. 366.

[2] Yale University, Beinecke MS Vault, Sect. 10, Drawer 3, Section B, B 11 i. The full text of the note (which exists in two states, indicating an unusual expenditure of effort on Sheffield's part) is full of interest. The grounds for disbelieving that Gibbon was as innocent in this matter as Sheffield here presents him are set out in my 'Gibbon and the "Watchmen of the Holy City": Revision and Religion, in *The Decline and Fall*, in R. McKitterick and R. Quinault, eds., *Edward Gibbon and Empire* (Cambridge, 1997), pp. 190–216; hereafter cited as *Gibbon and Empire*.

have been brought off. However, in the event Sheffield left the note unpublished. It was a decision which we can interpret only as an acknowledgement that, in his opinion and on this count, there was nothing to be done. The stain of irreligion was indelible, and attempts at mitigation would only make matters worse.[3]

However, where Sheffield flinched, modern scholars have persevered. In the last twenty years the orthodoxy that Gibbon was a deist of Voltairean stripe has become discredited as a result of critical pressure exerted from three directions. In the first place, the contemporary identification of Gibbon as the English Voltaire now no longer seems an inevitable and natural reading of his work. Instead, it has come to be considered as an episode in English religious politics which can be narrated and understood in language and from standpoints different from those of the original participants.[4] Secondly, careful and more extensive reading of Gibbon's private papers has uncovered evidence to suggest that the historian's religious convictions were in fact more nuanced than his contemporaries were prepared to allow, be it in the direction of either an extreme scepticism which was as averse to atheism as to belief,[5] or even a complicated adherence to a kind of Christian faith.[6] Finally, since 1976 and the bicentenary celebrations of the publication of the first volume of *The Decline and Fall*, contextual readings of the history have on the one hand helped us to understand why Gibbon should have been on occasion sharply critical of and at variance with Voltaire,[7] while on the other they have also demonstrated how much more scholarly and open-minded was Gibbon's understanding of religion as an aspect of human history than was Voltaire's.[8] As this view has developed, chapters 15 and 16 of *The*

---

[3] Such, at least, was the opinion of William Hayley, who endorsed one of the MS versions of this note as follows: 'suppress the whole Note – the Ground does not admit of any very solid & satisfactory defence – a slight palliation will only provoke more Severity against the delinquent' (Beinecke MS Vault, Sect. 10, Drawer 3, Section B, B 11 i, on the verso of the second sheet).

[4] Paul Turnbull, '"Une marionette infidèle": The Fashioning of Edward Gibbon's Reputation as the English Voltaire', in David Womersley, ed., *Edward Gibbon: Bicentenary Essays* (Oxford, 1997), pp. 279–307; hereafter cited as *Bicentenary Essays*. Nigel Aston, 'A "Disorderly squadron"? A Fresh Look at Clerical Responses to *The Decline and Fall*', in *Bicentenary Essays*, pp. 253–77.

[5] B. W. Young, '"Scepticism in Excess": Gibbon and Eighteenth-Century Christianity', *The Historical Journal*, 41 (1998), pp. 179–99.

[6] Paul Turnbull, 'The "Supposed Infidelity" of Edward Gibbon', *The Historical Journal*, 5 (1982), pp. 23–41. Paul Turnbull, 'Gibbon's Exchange with Joseph Priestley', *British Journal for Eighteenth-Century Studies*, 14 (1991), 139–58. Paul Turnbull, 'Gibbon and Pastor Allamand', *The Journal of Religious History*, 16 (1991), pp. 280–91.

[7] For instance, John Robertson, 'Gibbon's Roman Empire as a Universal Monarchy: the *Decline and Fall* and the Imperial Idea in Early Modern Europe', in *Gibbon and Empire*, pp. 247–70, esp. p. 264.

[8] J. G. A. Pocock, 'Superstition and Enthusiasm in Gibbon's History of Religion', *Eighteenth-Century Life*, 8 (1982), pp. 83–94.

Decline and Fall have emerged, not as the pinnacle of English prose irony, but as a premature and misleading formulation of issues and concerns which would receive more satisfactory and less tendentious treatment later in the history.[9] The old and the new positions on chapters 15 and 16 are of course not incompatible, but the divergence between them indicates the direction in which the tides of Gibbon scholarship have been running. From being Voltaire's twin, Gibbon has become almost his antagonist.

This essay engages with these developments at a number of points, from a number of different angles, and to various effect. In the first place, it presents new information about the contents of Gibbon's library which obliges us to think afresh about Gibbon's acquaintance with the most radical works of religious heterodoxy produced by the early European enlightenment. For Gibbon's library contained a manuscript copy of a notorious work of clandestine irreligion, the *Livre des trois fameux imposteurs*. This libertine and materialist treatise exposed Moses, Jesus, and Mahomet (its three eponymous impostors) as the founders of religions which all erected and supported the power of a few on the basis of the credulity of the many. It is amongst the most exultantly bitter of all the late seventeenth- and early eighteenth-century attacks on priestcraft, and amounts to a compendium of the most striking arguments mounted against organised religion.

Although the evidence is far from unambiguous, and is particularly enigmatic when we try to arrive at hard dates, the hitherto unreported presence of this work on Gibbon's shelves invites us to postulate on the part of the younger Gibbon a phase of engagement, albeit of uncertain depth and duration, with the most heterodox religious writings of the eighteenth century. So to that extent I will be offering a measure of qualified support to the now largely discredited reading of Gibbon's religious attitudes as Voltairean. However, my ambitions in this regard extend no further than the assertion of what was in danger of being forgotten, namely that Gibbon's contemporary critics were guilty of extremity and incompleteness, but not total error, when they saw only the mark of French irreligion on Gibbon's forehead. An interest in and acquaintance with the sceptical writings of the French enlightenment in their most radical form was one element in the historian's religious outlook. It was never the most powerful element, and was probably of diminishing influence over the course of Gibbon's life.[10] But nevertheless it was there,

---

[9] J. G. A. Pocock, 'Edward Gibbon in History: Aspects of the Text in *The History of the Decline and Fall of the Roman Empire*', in *The Tanner Lectures on Human Values* (Salt Lake City, 1990), pp. 289–384.

[10] The fact that, as I infer below, Gibbon probably left his copy of the *Trois fameux imposteurs* in London when he left England for Lausanne in 1783 suggests that in his opinion it would not be wanted on the future intellectual voyages he had planned.

and it demands to be weighed rather than dismissed. Gibbon's contemporaries undoubtedly mistook the part for the whole when they saw in him the English Voltaire. But modern scholars are in danger of falling into an equal, although opposite, error when they reject that label as a thoroughly unwarranted misreading.

I will then review succinctly the religious character of Gibbon's writings – or, more accurately, the perceptible confessional characteristics of Gibbon's successive literary personae – from the *Critical Observations* of 1770 to the drafts of the *Memoirs* composed at various dates in the late 1780s and early 1790s. Although this period of course includes the whole of the composition and publication of *The Decline and Fall*, I will place the emphasis on Gibbon's lesser writings. This is partly because I wish to redress what I see as an imbalance in the contrary direction, but also because in these other writings the evidence, less conditioned by the presence of narrative, lies more open to view. In the *Vindication* Gibbon amused his fancy by imagining a 'Theological Barometer . . . of which the Cardinal [Baronius] and our countryman Dr Middleton should constitute the opposite and remote extremities, as the former sunk to the lowest degree of credulity, which was compatible with learning, and the latter rose to the highest pitch of scepticism, in any wise consistent with Religion.'[11] Gibbon's own religious pressure (to follow the logic of his conceit), at least as it found expression in his writings, varied markedly in the last twenty-five years of his life, ranging from pugnacious deism to enthusiastic support for that champion of the High Church, Bishop Horsley. I will conclude by suggesting how these fluctuations in pressure can be most satisfactorily explained.

II

The library of the Athenaeum possesses twenty-four volumes containing 403 tracts from Gibbon's library.[12] There is no certain information about how these tracts came to be deposited in the customary London habitat of the most senior clerics of the Church of England. Nor is there any way of knowing who was responsible for grouping the tracts into their present volumes (although the fact that the uniform bindings of the volumes manifestly post-date their arrival in Pall Mall should make us wary of assuming that their present groupings are the result of Gibbon's sorting of them into categories).[13] It seems likely that they were amongst that

[11] Edward Gibbon, *The History of the Decline and Fall of the Roman Empire*, ed. David Womersley, 3 vols. (Harmondsworth, 1994), III, p. 1151; hereafter cited as *DF*.
[12] They are classified as 'Edward Gibbon's Tracts', and have no further press-mark. They are not recorded in G. Keynes, ed., *Gibbon's Library* (London, 1940); hereafter cited as *K*.
[13] Each volume is stamped on the spine 'Gibbon Tracts': not a useful denotation in Gibbon's own library.

portion of his library which Gibbon decided not to take with him to Lausanne in 1784, but left in Downing Street at the town house of his friend Lord Sheffield.[14] In this way on Gibbon's death they escaped the sale of the Lausanne library to William Beckford, and its subsequent dispersal.[15]

The extremely miscellaneous nature of the collection, in terms both of subject-matter and dates of publication, suggests that they were not all purchased by one man. In the overwhelming majority of the pamphlets we can detect the tastes and interests of Gibbon's grandfather, the well-informed, diligent and, above all, prosperous government contractor.[16] A smaller but still substantial number bring to mind Gibbon's dismissive characterisation of his father's literary tastes:

The library at Buriton was my first inheritance and peculiar domain. It was stuffed with much trash of the last age, with much High-Church Divinity and politics, which have long since gone to their proper place.[17]

However, not even Gibbon at his most mischievous could have suspected that time and accident might conspire in irony, and determine that the 'proper place' for the *Trois imposteurs* should eventually be the library of the Athenaeum. And indeed the *Trois imposteurs* falls into a group of pamphlets which seem to reflect the interests of the future historian rather than those of his father. In particular, the presence in the collection of works by Charles Marie de la Condamine and the great French

---

[14] For the details of this division and storage of the remnant of Gibbon's library, see *The Letters of Edward Gibbon*, ed. J. E. Norton, 3 vols. (London, 1956) II, pp. 353–6 and 3, 53; hereafter cited as *L*.   [15] *K*, pp. 27–36.

[16] For instance (as a representative sampling only): Thomas Violet, *True Narrative of Proceedings in the Court of Admiralty* (1659), *Lettres sur le nouveau système des finances* (1720), J. Campbell, *Dangers to the Trade of Great Britain with Turkey and Italy from the Spaniards* (1734), William Carter, *The Usurpations of France upon the Trade of the Woollen Manufacture of England* (1695), Thomas Houghton, *The Alteration of the Coyn* (1695), Stephen Barbier, *An Expedient to Pay the Publik Debts* (1719), Joseph Gander, *The Palladium of England* (1703), *The State of the Navy in Relation to Victualling* (1699), J. Nalson, *The Present Interest of England* (1683), Simon Smith, *The Herring Busse Trade, Expressed in Sundry Particulars* (1641), *The State of the Copper and Brass Manufactures in Great Britain* (1721), *A Brief Essay on the Copper and Brass Manufactures of England* (1712), Joseph Trevers, *Essay to the Restoring of our Decayed Trade* (1695). Gibbon's grandfather can have purchased no pamphlet published after 1736, since he died at the end of that year.

[17] *The Autobiographies of Edward Gibbon*, ed. J. Murray (London, 1896), p. 248 (from draft 'C'); hereafter cited as *A*. For instance: William Sherlock, *The Case of the Allegiance due to Sovereign Power Stated* (1691), Thomas Wagstaffe, *Remarks on some late Sermons, especially on that of Dr Sherlock* (1695), Francis Atterbury, *Discourse on the Death of Lady Cutts* (1698) [High Church divinity]; *Relation de la reddition d'Edimbourg et de la victoire du Prince Charles Edward sur le Général Cope* (1745), Prince Charles Edward, *Extrait de son manifeste* (1745), Jonathan Swift, *The Public Spirit of the Whigs* (1714) [Jacobitism and Toryism].

geographer J. B. B. d'Anville is evidence of the priorities and enthusiasms of the younger Edward Gibbon.[18]

The physical aspect of the manuscript offers few clues as to provenance and date. It consists of 180 pages written in a neat, fluent hand which is not Gibbon's. Such slips as there are suggest the effects of copying at speed (for instance, jumping a line when reading from the copied manuscript), rather than an inability to understand what was being transcribed. We may suppose, therefore, that the copyist had a sound reading knowledge of French. I am informed that the letter formation suggests that the copyist was French.[19] I have not yet examined the paper for watermarks or other signs of date and origin.

Internal evidence is only slightly more helpful. The bibliography of the *Trois imposteurs* is excessively complicated. Manuscript traditions which have yet to be fully fathomed exist alongside an enigmatic series of printed texts published under a number of titles, and the relations within and between the two exhibit (if even such a cautiously neutral word does not imply too high a degree of definition) that higher level of uncertainty which arises from the attempt to correlate two variables.[20] However, the most recent attempts to establish a taxonomy of the manuscripts of the *Trois imposteurs* indicate that the later versions of the text are characterised by an expansion of the section dealing with Moses. The manuscript in Gibbon's library conforms to this pattern, and so it would appear to post-date 1712–18 and to be part of the manuscript tradition emanating from the library of Eugene of Savoy.[21]

---

[18] For instance, J. B. B. d'Anville, *Analyse géographique de l'Italie* (1744) and *Analyse de la carte, intitulée, les côtes de la Grèce, et l'Archipel* (1757); C. M. de la Condamine, *Supplément au journal historique du voyage à l'équateur* (1752). On the importance of d'Anville to Gibbon, see Guido Abbattista, 'Establishing the "Order of Time and Place": "Rational Geography", French Erudition and the Emplacement of History in Gibbon's Mind', in *Bicentenary Essays*, pp. 45–72. Gibbon had met Condamine in Paris during the early months of 1763 (*A*, pp. 201 and 261).

[19] Private communication from R. E. Alton.

[20] Notable recent works include: M. Jacob, *The Radical Enlightenment* (London, 1981); S. Berti *et al.*, eds., *Contexts of Imposture* (Leiden, 1991); S. Berti, 'The First Edition of the Traité des trois imposteurs and its Debt to Spinoza's Ethics', in M. Hunter and D. Wootton, eds., *Atheism from the Reformation to the Enlightenment* (Oxford, 1992), pp. 183–220; S. Berti, F. Charles-Daubert, and R. H. Popkin, eds., *Heterodoxy, Spinozism, and Freethought in Early Eighteenth-Century Europe: Studies on the Traité des Trois Imposteurs* (Klewer, 1996). Silvia Berti's Franco-Italian edition is the most useful: S. Berti, ed., *Trattato dei tre impostori* (Turin, 1994). It is a pleasure to acknowledge my indebtedness for guidance and practical assistance to Justin Champion and David Wootton.

[21] Here the work of F. Charles-Daubert is central: 'Les principales sources de l'Esprit de Spinosa', in *Groupe de recherches spinozistes. Travaux et documents 1* (Paris, 1989), pp. 61–107, 'Les Traités des trois imposteurs aux XVIIe et XVIIIe siècles', in G. Canziani, ed., *Filosofia e religione nella letteratura clandestina secoli XVII e XVIII* (Milan, 1994), pp. 291–336, and '*L'Esprit de Spinosa* et les *Traités des trois imposteurs*: rappel des différentes familles et de leurs principales caractéristiques', in *Heterodoxy, Spinozism, and Freethought*

The most tantalising clue to both date and provenance occurs at the end of the manuscript, which is annotated as follows in a different hand (although again not Gibbon's):

The following appears in a Mss Copy of this work, left for collation from M^r. Lilly of King St Covent Garden.

'Permittente Domino Barone de Hoendorf descripsi hunc Codicem ex Autographo in Bibliot: Serenissm: Princip. Eugenii in Sabaudia.

SH.[22]

Here we have what is undoubtedly an important clue to the dating of the manuscript. Allusions to the Baron de Hohendorf and Eugene of Savoy are commonly encountered in connection with the *Trois imposteurs*; it is Mr Lilly of King Street, with his taste for dangerous manuscripts, who arouses one's interest. But so far he has eluded identification.[23]

There are, I think, two possibilities concerning how this manuscript found its way into Gibbon's library. The first is that its presence is due to the 'very intimate connection' which had grown up between Gibbon's father and David Mallet.[24] Mallet, of course, was Bolingbroke's literary executor and also a near neighbour of the Gibbons in Putney. It was Mallet who had consoled Gibbon's father on the death of his first wife;[25] it was to Mallet that Gibbon's father had in 1753 taken his apostate son (and by whose philosophy Gibbon claimed to have been 'more scandalized than reclaimed');[26] and it was to Mallet that the upbringing of Gibbon's heiress cousin, Catherine Elliston, had been entrusted'.[27] Moreover, the Mallets seem also at least to have tried to inoculate Gibbon's father with Whiggism and irreligion: 'as they [David and his wife Lucy] both thought with freedom on the subjects of Religion and Government, they successfully laboured to correct the prejudices of his

---

in *Early Eighteenth-Century Europe*, pp. 131–89. I owe these references to the kindness of Justin Champion.   [22] Athenaeum MS, p. 180.

[23] A possibility may be the John Lilly who was clerk to the Stationers' Company during 1673–81; an identification which would have the problematic effect of dating the manuscript very early.

[24] *A*, p. 46 (from draft 'F'). David Mallet (originally Malloch) (1705?-65); poet, dramatist and man of letters; friend of Thomson, Bolingbroke, and Pope; under-secretary to the Prince of Wales, 1742; according to Wilkes, 'a great declaimer in all the London coffee-houses against Christianity'. The presence in the collection of tracts from Gibbon's library of Bolingbroke's *Last Will and Testament, with copy of an original letter giving reasons for leaving the Kingdom in March 1715* (1752) may also suggest the influence of Mallet.

[25] *A*, p. 218 (from draft 'C'); compare drafts 'F' (pp. 46–7) and 'E' (p. 295 and n. 6).

[26] *A*, p. 130 (from draft 'B').

[27] *A*, p. 309 n. 29 (from draft 'E'); compare draft 'A' (pp. 384–5). This occurred not without vocal misgivings on the part of the pious Hester Gibbon (Patricia B. Craddock, *Young Edward Gibbon: Gentleman of Letters* (Baltimore and London, 1982), pp. 36, 86–7; hereafter cited as *Young Edward Gibbon*).

education'.[28] As William Law put it (in a letter which apparently, but almost incredibly, was substituted for one even less tactful written by Hester Gibbon), the family of the historian were at this period 'shut among infidels, rejoicing in their friendship, and thankful for having a seat where dead Bolingbroke yet speaketh'.[29] If one looks amongst the acquaintance of Edward Gibbon senior for the source of any religious heterodoxy, then Mallet is the prime suspect.

It may therefore be a significant circumstance that, on his return from Lausanne in 1758, Gibbon seems to have boarded with the Mallets:

> The most useful of my father's friends were the Mallets; they entertained me with civility and kindness, at first on his, and afterwards on my own account; and I was soon (if I may use Lord Chesterfield's word) *domesticated* in the family. Mr Mallet himself, a name among the English poets, is praised by an unforgiving enemy (Dr Johnson) for the ease and elegance of his conversation; and his wife, whatsoever might be her faults, was not deficient in wit or knowledge. By his assistance I was introduced to Lady Hervey, the mother of the present Earl of Bristol, who had established a French house in St James's place. At an advanced period of life, she was distinguished by her taste and politeness; her dinners were select: every evening her drawing-room was filled by a succession of the best company of both sexes and all nations; nor was I displeased at her preference and even affectation of the books, the language, and manners of the Continent.[30]

Here we have a fascinating glimpse of Gibbon mingling in sophisticated, cosmopolitan circles. The best account we have of these *soirées* and of the interests of the woman around whom they revolved is that of her friend and correspondent, Horace Walpole:

> After his [Lord Hervey's] death, Lady Hervey resided at Ickworth with her father-in-law, and on his decease passed some years in France, where she was so great a favourite with Mlle de Charolois, sister of the Duke of Bourbon, that she had an apartment in each palace of the princess. She was intimate too with the Duchess dowager d'Aiguillon, the celebrated Madame Geoffrin, the Président de Lamoignon, and Monsieur Helvétius. Returning to England she built a very elegant house in the French taste in St James's Place, gave dinners, and was always at home in an evening to a select company: men of letters and *beaux esprits* and her friends of the other sex. The principal were Lord Bath, Lord Chesterfield, Lord Melcombe, Lord Mansfield, Lord Lyttelton, Lord Ilchester, Lord Holland, Mr Mallet, Ramsay the painter and author, and several others.[31]

---

[28] *A*, p. 379 (from draft 'A').

[29] Quoted in D. M. Low, *Edward Gibbon 1737–1794* (London, 1937), p. 45.

[30] *A*, pp. 245–6 (from draft 'C'; compare the slightly greater candour, and the slightly looser writing, of the equivalent passage in draft 'B', in *A*, p. 160). Lady Mary Hervey (1700–68); wife of John, Lord Hervey of Ickworth; admired by Voltaire; reputed to be of Jacobite sympathies and Catholic leanings.

[31] *Horace Walpole's Correspondence*, ed. W. S. Lewis, Robert A. Smith and Charles H. Bennett (London and New Haven, 1961), XLI, p. 416.

This potent cocktail of high birth, social polish, literary accomplishment, and religious scepticism might easily intoxicate a young man whose aspirations lay in the direction of literature.

A further circumstance to be borne in mind is that Mallet seems particularly to have influenced the young Gibbon in matters of literature. It was to Mallet that Gibbon turned for advice when seeking to 'restore the purity of my own language, which had been corrupted by the long use of a foreign Idiom'. [32] It was in part from Mallet that Gibbon took counsel when preparing his *Essai sur l'étude de la littérature* for the press in 1761.[33] On publication, Mallet seems to have been energetic in dispersing copies of the *Essai* amongst the influential.[34] And Gibbon's 'last act in town' before setting out on the Grand Tour in January 1763 was 'to applaud Mallet's new tragedy of Elvira'.[35] If the second Mrs Gibbon (herself a distant relation to Mallet) was correct when on 1 June 1755 she wrote to Hester Gibbon that 'the intimacy between Mr. Gibbon and the Mallets is at an end', the same it seems could not be said about Edward Gibbon Esq.[36]

The other possibility is that Gibbon acquired the manuscript when abroad, and brought it back with him to England. It is difficult to believe that the vigilant Pavilliard would have allowed Gibbon to encounter such libertine material, let alone to procure it for his own study, so we can pass over Gibbon's first stay in Lausanne and concentrate on his second, between May 1763 and April 1765.[37] On this trip Gibbon mixed with

---

[32] 'By the judicious advice of Mr Mallet, I was directed to the writings of Swift and Addison:'; *A*, p. 166 (from draft 'B'). The equivalent passage in draft 'C' provides once more a fascinating comparison; *A*, p. 251.

[33] *A*, p. 170 (from draft 'B'); compare drafts 'D' and 'C', where Gibbon permits himself some mild freedoms on the subject of Mallet's 'præposterous' judgement; *A*, pp. 255 and 402. The parallel passage in draft 'E' is, in keeping with the general Burkean character of that draft, more censorious in its comments on the notorious deist Mallet, whom (recalling perhaps Burke's contemptuous swipe at Mallet's mentor, Bolingbroke?) Gibbon disparages as over-rated and forgotten (*A*, p. 300 and n. 16). On the subject of the character of draft 'E', see my 'Gibbon's *Memoirs*: Autobiography in Time of Revolution', in *Bicentenary Essays*, pp. 347–404.

[34] Mallet's acquaintances received a substantial portion of the author's copies of the *Essai*: *Gibbon's Journal to January 28th. 1763*, ed. D. M. Low (London, 1929), p. 27; hereafter cited as *J1*. See also the letter of 1761 from Mallet to Gibbon, where he asks for 'one of your books, well bound, for myself: all the other copies I gave away, as Duke Desenany drunk out ten dozen of Lord Bolingbroke's Champagne in his absence – to your honour and glory' (Edward Gibbon, *Miscellaneous Works*, ed. Lord Sheffield, 2 vols. (1796), I, p. 422; hereafter cited as *MW 1796*).   [35] *A*, p. 198 (from draft 'B').

[36] Quoted in Craddock, *Young Edward Gibbon*, p. 86. Notwithstanding this apparent estrangement (which Dorothea Gibbon may have exaggerated in order to please her new sister-in-law), Mrs Mallet came down into Hampshire during September and October 1759 and stayed with the Gibbons at Buriton (*ibid.*, p. 142).

[37] The dates as given in draft 'E' of the *Memoirs* (*A*, p. 301).

those who might have found little to shock or surprise them in the *Trois imposteurs*. Moreover, Gibbon also now met John Baker Holroyd, later Lord Sheffield, whose own Grand Tour writings evoke a robust irreligion.[38] It would be misleading to imply that Gibbon turned the Grand Tour into an education in religious scepticism, since so much of his time while abroad was passed in serious antiquarian and scholarly study, as his Lausanne journal testifies. But it would be equally misleading to doubt that Gibbon's tour of the continent included encounters with irreligion, in much the way that such tours were commonly supposed to do.[39]

III

Whenever it was that this manuscript entered the Gibbon family library, and by whatever route, it is nevertheless the case that the personae Gibbon created for himself in two works he wrote after returning to England from the Grand Tour in June 1765 – the *Critical Observations on the Design of the Sixth Book of the Æneid* (1770) attacking Warburton, and the long letter he wrote in answer to Hurd's *An Introduction to the Study of the Prophecies concerning the Christian Church* (1772) – were both in part characterised by religious scepticism.

In draft 'E' of his *Memoirs* Gibbon described the gestation and argument of his *Critical Observations on the Design of the Sixth Book of the Æneid*, and passed judgement:

> In the year 1770 I sent to the press some *Critical Observations on the Sixth Book of the Æneid*. This anonymous pamphlet was pointed against Bishop Warburton, who demonstrates that the descent of Æneas to the shades is an Allegory of his initiation to the Eleusinian mysteries. The love of Virgil, the hatred of a Dictator, and the example of Lowth, awakened me to arms. The coldness of the public has been amply compensated by the esteem of Heyne, of Hayley, and of Parr; but the acrimony of my style has been justly blamed by the Professor of Gottingen. Warburton was *not* an object of contempt.[40]

Warburton's stock might well have risen in Gibbon's estimation during the 1790s, when the Bishop of Gloucester's views on Church and State must have seemed consolingly robust.[41] Twenty years earlier, however,

---

[38] The first meeting with Holroyd occurred on 1 September 1763, *Le Journal de Gibbon à Lausanne* , ed. G. A. Bonnard (Lausanne, 1945), p. 21; hereafter cited as *J2*. By 6 April of the following year Gibbon noted that he had conceived 'une veritable amitié' for Holroyd (*J2*, p. 259). A selection of Holroyd's Grand Tour correspondence is published, with a linking commentary by Georges Bonnard, as 'John Holroyd in Italy', *Etudes de lettres: bulletin de la Faculté des Lettres de l'Université de Lausanne*, part II, 2 (3) (1959), pp. 122–35.

[39] Bruce Redford, *Venice and the Grand Tour* (New Haven and London, 1996), esp. ch. 1 (pp. 5–25).   [40] *A*, pp. 304–5.

[41] See A. W. Evans, *Warburton and the Warburtonians: A Study in Some Eighteenth-Century Controversies* (London, 1932), p. 44.

when the pressure to find and build alliances against the contagion of revolution had not existed, Gibbon had frankly despised Warburton's *Divine Legation of Moses Demonstrated*. And his contempt found partial expression in the accents of deism, and a sardonic celebration of 'the Antient Alliance between the Avarice of the Priest and the Credulity of the People'.[42]

Towards the end of his life Warburton founded a series of lectures of which the purpose was to expound and defend the Biblical prophecies concerning the Christian Church. The first series of these lectures had been delivered in 1768 by Warburton's ally, lieutenant, and factotum, the Archdeacon of Gloucester Richard Hurd. When in 1772 these lectures were published as *An Introduction to the Study of the Prophecies concerning the Christian Church*, Gibbon wrote pseudonymously to Hurd (asking for any answer to be addressed to '*Daniel Freeman, Esq. at the Cocoa Tree, Pall Mall*') posing the question '*Whether, there is sufficient evidence that the Book of Daniel is really as ancient as it pretends to be.*'[43] The point was crucial to Hurd's overall argument, for as Gibbon reminded him, 'from this point the Golden Chain of Prophecy, which you have let down from Heaven to earth, is partly suspended'.[44]

Gibbon had written once before against Hurd in 1762, albeit for his own satisfaction. Having read Hurd's edition of Horace, he composed an essay of thirty pages disputing Hurd's interpretation of these two epistles, and deplored, in passing, Hurd's 'excessive praises (not to give them a harsher name)' of Warburton.[45] Although the letter of 1772 shared the earlier essay's distaste for 'Warburton and his bloodhounds', it was at once more succinct and more rhetorically elaborate than its predecessor, reading at certain points like a first attempt at phrases and textual

---

[42] *The English Essays of Edward Gibbon*, ed. P. B. Craddock (Oxford, 1972), p. 136; hereafter cited as *EE*.   [43] *L*, I, pp. 338 and 328.

[44] *L*, I, p. 328. Hurd first became aware of the identity of the author of this letter when he saw his reply published without his permission in Gibbon's *Miscellaneous Works*, I, pp. 455–63. He had evidently therefore not accepted Gibbon's offer to disclose his identity: 'if you have any scruple of engaging with a mask, I am ready, by the same channel, to disclose my real name and place of abode' (*L*, I, pp. 338–9). He then published Gibbon's original letter, together with his reply (in a version which differs slightly from that published in the *Miscellaneous Works*) in the *Works of Richard Hurd, DD, Lord Bishop of Worcester*, 8 vols. (1811), V, p. 363. This is the only text we possess of this work of Gibbon's. He seems either not to have made, or to have destroyed, any copy for his later personal use, and Sheffield did not choose to print a text in either the five-volume octavo second edition of the *Miscellaneous Works* (1814), or the supplementary third quarto volume of the *Miscellaneous Works* (1815).

[45] *Q. Horatii Flacci Epistolæ, ad Pisones et Augustum*, 2nd edn (Cambridge, 1757). *MW 1796*, II, pp. 27–50; II, p. 27. In his journal Gibbon marked the importance to his own intellectual life of this engagement with Hurd when in the entry for 18 March 1762 he commented that it had 'started a new train of ideas upon many curious points of Criticism' (*J1*, p. 49).

manoeuvres which would later be executed with more precision in *The Decline and Fall*.[46] However, like the *Critical Observations* of two years before, the letter to Hurd on the Book of Daniel was written from within a milieu of Tory deism.[47] It was a persona well calculated to affront the (then strongly Whiggish) clergyman Hurd.[48] In 1772 the name of his persona – 'Daniel Freeman' – recalled the Tory appropriation of what had been originally an Old Whig language, while the address at which 'Daniel Freeman' might be found – 'the Cocoa Tree' – reeked of old Toryism.[49]

[46] *A*, p. 304 n. 21. For phrases which read like first attempts at topics which would preoccupy Gibbon in *The Decline and Fall*, consider the following: 'This age indeed, to whom the gift of miracles has been refused, is apt to wonder at the indifference with which they were received by the ancient world' (*L*, I, p. 333) anticipates 'When the law was given in thunder from Mount Sinai; when the tides of the ocean, and the course of the planets were suspended for the convenience of the Israelites; and when temporal rewards and punishments were the immediate consequences of their piety or disobedience, they perpetually relapsed into rebellion against the visible majesty of their Divine King' and 'But how shall we excuse the supine inattention of the Pagan and philosophic world, to those evidences which were presented by the hand of Omnipotence, not to their reason, but to their senses?' (*DF*, I, pp. 449 and 512); 'An irreligious prince may be indiscreet enough to treat with ridicule whatever is held sacred by his subjects; but he will entertain too great a contempt both for the people, and for popular superstition, ever to think of forcibly separating them from each other' (*L*, I, p. 335) looks forward to 'We may be well assured, that a writer, conversant with the world, would never have ventured to expose the gods of his country to public ridicule, had they not already been the objects of secret contempt among the polished and enlightened orders of society' (*DF*, I, p. 58).

[47] Gibbon's father exposed his son to Tory and even Jacobite influences, such as that of Crop, the mayor of Southampton and simulacrum of Fielding's Squire Western, who 'drinks hard, rails against all ministers and keeps alive the small remains of Jacobitism at Southampton' (*J1*, p. 144).

[48] Hurd's *Moral and Political Dialogues* (1759) were on publication regarded as Whig, but in his *Tracts by Warburton and a Warburtonian* (1789) Samuel Parr noticed in later editions of this work 'clippings and filings, the softening and varnishings, of sundry constitutional doctrines' as Hurd became steadily more Tory in outlook: Warren Derry, *Dr Parr: A Portrait of the Whig Dr Johnson* (Oxford, 1966), pp. 81–6.

[49] For the best available survey of the mutations of the languages of Whiggery, see J. G. A. Pocock, 'The Varieties of Whiggism from Exclusion to Reform', in his *Virtue, Commerce, and History* (Cambridge, 1985), pp. 215–310. For the political connotations of the Cocoa Tree, the coffee-house in Pall Mall at which the Tory society, Edward Harley's Board, had met every Thursday during the parliamentary session since 1727, and of which Gibbon's father had long been a member, see Linda Colley, *In Defiance of Oligarchy: The Tory Party 1714–60* (Cambridge, 1982), pp. 71–5, 137, 140, 165, 206, 211 and 280. Gibbon's retrospective account of his listless town life between 1758 and 1760 confirms the political associations of the club; he was 'reduced to some dull family parties, to some old Tories of the Cocoa-tree, and to some casual connections, such as my taste and esteem would never have selected' (from draft 'C', *A*, p. 245; cf. also *L*, I, p. 204 and n. 2). At the time, however, he had been more enthusiastic: 'We ... returned to the Cocoa-tree. That respectable body, of which I have the honor to be a member, affords every evening a sight truly English. Twenty or thirty, perhaps, of the first men in the kingdom, in point of fashion and fortune, supping at little tables covered with a napkin, in the middle of a Coffee-room, upon a bit of cold meat, or a Sandwich, & drinking a glass of punch. At present, we are full of Privy Counsellors and Lords of the Bedchamber;' (*J1*, p. 185: cf. also pp. 186 and 200).

Furthermore, the analysis 'Daniel Freeman' places before Hurd is couched in deist language, and draws upon the general account of the psychology of religion and of the wiles of priestcraft promulgated in works such as the *Trois imposteurs*:

The eager trembling curiosity of mankind has ever wished to penetrate into futurity; nor is there perhaps any country, where enthusiasm and knavery have not pretended to satisfy this anxious craving of the human heart.

Such an extraordinary interdict [Darius's forbidding of religious worship for thirty days], by depriving the people of the comforts, and the priests of the profits of religion, must have diffused a general discontent throughout his empire.[50]

What is more, the recurrent idiom of the letter is that of elaborate irony, which after 1776 would have been easily recognisable as Gibbonian, but which in 1772 must have seemed the signature of an unusually urbane deist:

Since you have undertaken the care and defence of this extensive province [of Biblical prophecy], I may be allowed, less as an opponent than as a disciple, to propose to you a few difficulties; about which I have sought more conviction than I have hitherto obtained.

To the first of these incidents I am so far from forming any objection, that it seems to me, in the true style of the oriental customs in war and government. But the two last are embarrassed with difficulties, from which I have not been able to extricate myself.

. . . the hopes I still entertain, that you may be able and willing to dispell the mist, that hangs, either over my eyes, or over the subject itself.[51]

Finally, 'Daniel Freeman's' credentials are put beyond doubt when we note that the criterion for belief in matters of religion which he proposes for Hurd's endorsement is substantially that of Hume in 'Of Miracles':

May I not assume as a principle equally consonant to experience, to reason, and even to true religion; 'That we ought not to admit any thing as the immediate work of God, which can possibly be the work of man; and that whatever is said to deviate from the ordinary course of nature, should be ascribed to accident, to fraud, or to fiction; till we are fully satisfied, that it lies beyond the reach of those causes?' If we cast away this buckler, the blind fury of superstition, from every age of the world, and from every corner of the globe, will invade us naked and unarmed.[52]

In both these jousting engagements with prominent Christian apologists we can see Gibbon writing in evident familiarity with the tones and

---

[50] *L*, I, pp. 329 and 335. The prophecies of the Book of Daniel had earlier been a focus of deist controversy, and awareness of that lineage permeates this encounter between Gibbon and Hurd on both sides (cf. Leslie Stephen, *English Thought in the Eighteenth Century*, 2 vols. (1876), I, p. 228).   [51] *L*, I, pp. 327, 332, and 338.

[52] *L*, I, pp. 328–9.

strategies of religious scepticism; a familiarity to which the manuscript of the *Trois imposteurs* concealed in his library had, we may suppose, contributed.

IV

Gibbon's interest in deistical literary personae extended at least until 1777, for it is traceable in the Voltairean moments in chapter 15 of *The Decline and Fall*, as well as in his revisions to the final two chapters of volume I of the history.[53] However, when it came to meeting his detractors in the open field of the *Vindication*, rather than sniping at them from the cover of the footnotes to *The Decline and Fall*, a different character was called for. Gibbon's critics had in attacking him donned the mantle of Bentley, that flail of the early eighteenth-century deists whose personal example and whose reply to Anthony Collins were such important templates for the orthodox polemicists of the later eighteenth century.[54] Gibbon retorted by assuming Bentleian characteristics himself, including an imitation of Bentley's churchmanship.[55]

Bentley had been appointed Master of Trinity as a result of the influence of latitudinarian Whigs such as Tenison. Always an object of suspicion to High Churchmen such as Atterbury (who had suggested that Bentley's critical methods would lead to Biblical scepticism), in 1702 Bentley had showed his opposition to High Church moves in convoca-

[53] For the contemporary perception of such Voltairean moments, see e.g. Henry Davis, *An Examination of the Fifteenth and Sixteenth Chapters of Mr. Gibbon's History* (1778), p. iii (hereafter cited as *Examination*), and his *A Reply to Mr. Gibbon's Vindication* (1779), pp. 162–3 (hereafter cited as *Reply*). For the significance of the revisions, see my 'Gibbon and the "Watchmen of the Holy City"', pp. 190–216.

[54] I shall discuss in fuller detail than constraints of space make possible here exactly how Gibbon and his adversaries engaged each other over the meaning and possession of Bentley's legacy, rather as Odysseus and Ajax contended for the armour of Achilles, in my forthcoming *Gibbon and 'The Watchmen of the Holy City': The Historian and his Reputation, 1776–1815*.

[55] The closeness between Gibbon's writing in the *Vindication* and the polemical style of Bentley was remarked on by near contemporaries. Robert Tyrwhitt annotated his complutensian edition of Bentley's *Dissertation Upon the Epistles of Phalaris* in two places with markings indicating his awareness of how Gibbon had echoed Bentley (Tyrwhitt's copy of Bentley's *Dissertation* is held at the Bodleian Library, press-mark 29981 e.1: see pp. cxii and 487). A copy of *MW 1796* in the possession of the author containing many marginalia (which internal evidence suggests were written in 1834) includes the following corroborative annotation at the foot of I, p. 155, keyed to Dr Edwards' admiration of Gibbon as one 'Proud and elated by the weakness of his antagonists, he condescends not to handle the sword of controversy': 'which resembles a passage by M^r. Tyrwhitt on D^r. *Bentley*. "Sed ille adversarios velut fulmine porstravisse contentus, à pugnâ impari recepit indignabundus."'

tion by obtaining Cambridge doctorates for Nicolson, Kennett, and Gibson, who had all been denied Oxford doctorates because of their opposition to Atterbury.[56] Gibbon, whose Tory allegiances seem to have weakened after the death of his father, would later admire the 'latitudinarians of Cambridge' as the most recent practitioners of 'rational theology', so Bentley's Whiggish latitudinarianism may have been genuinely congenial to him by 1779.[57] Be that as it may, in the *Vindication* Gibbon went out of his way to display his closeness to Bentley's politics and churchmanship. He claimed to be 'a firm friend to civil and ecclesiastical freedom', a celebrant of 'English freedom', a champion of the 'free inquiries of the present age'.[58] Davis had suspected Gibbon of being 'secretly inclined to the interest of the Pope', in what he called 'this strange and unnatural alliance of infidelity and superstition'.[59] To show how wide this was of the mark, Gibbon heaped praise on radical Whigs such as Walter Moyle ('a bold and ingenious critic'), and on latitudinarians such as his old comrade in arms against Warburton, John Jortin ('learned and ingenuous').[60] He scorned Francis Eyre's religious opinions by noting that as they were 'principally founded on the infallibility of the Church, they are not calculated to make a very deep impression on the mind of an English reader'.[61] Even Richard Watson (whose attack on *The Decline and Fall* Gibbon was ready to dismiss in private as 'too dull to deserve . . . notice') was in the *Vindication* complimented on the 'liberal and philosophic cast' of his thinking.[62] As the most eminent representative in the late 1770s of the Whiggish Cambridge latitudinarianism with which Gibbon now wished to associate himself, a graceful nod towards Watson was an easy way for Gibbon to imply that less separated him

[56] J. Gascoigne, *Cambridge in the Age of the Enlightenment* (Cambridge, 1988), pp. 82–95; G. V. Bennett, *The Tory Crisis in Church and State 1688–1730: The Career of Francis Atterbury, Bishop of Rochester* (Oxford, 1975), p. 42. For the most recent extensive discussion of latitudinarianism, see Isabel Rivers, *Reason, Grace and Sentiment: A Study of the Language of Religion and Ethics in England, 1660–1780*, vol. I: *Whichcote to Wesley* (Cambridge, 1991), pp. 25–88.

[57] *DF*, III, pp. 438 n. 38. But even in the early 1760s Gibbon's preferences in churchmanship were of this kind, as his praise of Limborch as 'moderate and judicious, the general character of the Arminian Divines', and his approving statement of Erasmus's stance on theology, that 'he was always persuaded, that any speculative truths were dearly purchased at the expence of practical virtue and publick peace' indicate (*J1*, pp. 87 and 148–9).   [58] *DF*, III, pp. 1158, 1124 and 1182.

[59] *Ibid.*, p. 1142. Davis, *Examination*, pp. 87, 122 and 158. Although perhaps 'strange and unnatural', the fear of a secret alliance between Catholics and atheists or freethinkers is nevertheless commonly found in late seventeenth-century and eighteenth-century members of the Church of England: e.g. Francis Fullwood, *A Parallel: Wherein it Appears that the Socinian agrees with the Papist* (1693).

[60] *DF*, III, pp. 1167 and 1169. In his *Reply* Davis noted the strenuous 'talk against popery' in the *Vindication* (p. 49).   [61] *DF*, III, p. 1182.   [62] *L*, II, p. 129. *DF*, III, p. 1156.

from Watson than separated Watson from Chelsum, Davis, and Randolph.[63]

The corollary to Gibbon's claim that he and Bentley had values in common is his demonstration that Davis, Chelsum, and Randolph had few points of contact with the man whose successor they had implicitly claimed to be. The *Vindication* thus managed to reconfigure the conflict between Gibbon and his adversaries. They had presented it as another battle in the long-standing war between Christianity and irreligion. Gibbon re-presents it as a mirror of factional tension within the Anglican Church. Bentley himself had noted when replying to Collins that religious scepticism and Protestantism were easily confusable:

Free-thinking here for many Pages together is put for Common use of Reason and Judgment, a lawful Liberty of Examining, and in a word, good *Protestantism*. Then whip about, and it stands for Scepticism, for Infidelity, for bare *Atheism*.[64]

In paying homage to Jortin and gracious compliments to Watson, Gibbon availed himself of this proximity to present himself in the *Vindication* as a 'good protestant'.[65] The language he used of Davis, Randolph, and Chelsum, however, carried very different connotations. After 1776 the revival of revealed theology within the Church of England had dislodged latitudinarianism from the position it had occupied since the early years of the century, that of the natural outcome and extension of reformation.[66] Gibbon's praise of the Latitude men in 1788 at the end of the fifty-fourth chapter of *The Decline and Fall* must thus have struck a rather anachronistic note as an almost nostalgic gesture for a threatened and unfashionable, if not entirely departed, style of churchmanship.[67] Davis, Chelsum, and Randolph, however, were squarely within the resurgent High Churchmanship of the later eighteenth-century Church of England. Randolph had assisted Chelsum in writing his remarks, and

---

[63] The implication is further reinforced by passages such as the following, in which there exists at least an equality of rank between Gibbon and Watson, but no sort of community with Chelsum and Randolph: 'it would be inconsistent enough, if I should have refused to draw my sword in honourable combat against the keen and well-tempered weapon of Dr. Watson, for the sole purpose of encountering the rustic cudgel of two staunch and sturdy Polemics [i.e. Chelsum and Randolph]' (*DF*, III, p. 1160).

[64] Bentley, *Remarks Upon a Late Discourse of Free-thinking* (1713), p. 13. He also insisted that freethinking was a bastard child of reformation: ''Twas by the price and purchase of Their [the Reformers] Blood, that this Author and his Sect have at this day, not only the Liberty, but the Power, Means, and Method of Thinking' (p. 23).

[65] It was with this phrase that Gibbon announced to Catherine Porten his re-conversion from Catholicism in 1755: *L*, I, p. 3.

[66] Gascoigne, *Cambridge in the Age of Enlightenment*, p. 238; Peter B. Nockles, *The Oxford Movement in Context* (Cambridge, 1994), pp. 44–103; Nigel Aston, 'Horne and Heterodoxy: The Defence of Anglican Beliefs in the Late Enlightenment', *English Historical Review*, 108 (1993), pp. 895–919.   [67] *DF*, III, p. 438 n. 38.

Gibbon turned the circumstance of 'the confederate Doctors' to polemical advantage:

The two friends are indeed so happily united by art and nature, that if the author of the Remarks had not pointed out the valuable communications of the Margaret Professor, it would have been impossible to separate their respective property. Writers who possess any freedom of mind, may be known from each other by the peculiar character of their style and sentiments; but the champions who are inlisted in the service of Authority, commonly wear the uniform of the regiment. Oppressed with the same yoke, covered with the same trappings, they heavily move along, perhaps not with an equal pace, in the same beaten track of prejudice and preferment.[68]

Towards the end of the *Vindication* a very similar blow is aimed at Eyre, the Catholic cast of whose thought is brought forward to emphasise once more how badly Davis had misread the confessional dimension to the quarrel:

It is not my wish or my intention to prosecute with this Gentleman a literary altercation. There lies between us a broad and unfathomable gulph; and the heavy mist of prejudice and superstition, which has in a great measure been dispelled by the free inquiries of the present age, still continues to involve the mind of my Adversary. He fondly embraces those phantoms . . . which can scarcely find a shelter in the gloom of an Italian convent; and the resentment which he points against me, might frequently be extended to the most enlightened of the PROTESTANT, or, in his opinion, of the HERETICAL critics.[69]

It is easy to see how the terms of these oppositions ('freedom of mind', 'the most enlightened of the PROTESTANT . . . critics' and literary authenticity on one side; 'Authority', 'prejudice and preferment', 'prejudice and superstition', and oppressed uniformity on the other) hint at an opposition in churchmanship, between latitudinarian and High: a hint amplified when Gibbon referred to the '*dogmatical* part of their [i.e. Chelsum and Randolph's] work, which in every sense of the word deserves that appellation', and commented tartly on 'the force of his [i.e. Chelsum's] dogmatic style'.[70]

V

The second instalment of *The Decline and Fall*, published in 1781, conformed to the latitudinarian persona Gibbon had created for himself two years earlier in the *Vindication*. The paired portraits of Athanasius and Julian – the one a theologian who had shown the foresight of a statesman in inventing a creed which, while itself an affront to human rationality,

---

[68] *Ibid.*, III, pp. 1160 and 1159.   [69] *Ibid.*, III, p. 1182.   [70] *Ibid.*, III, pp. 1160 and 1173.

nevertheless played a benign role in the important business of softening the northern barbarians who had overrun the provinces of the empire; the other a statesman who had neutralised his personal virtues through his adherence to a fanatical theology – stand at the centre of this instalment. Together they impart to volumes II and III what we might call an implied Arianism. The Athanasian creed was a wonderful, although man-made, expedient created to meet an emergency, but it was unhelpful in an age awakened to the benefits of an undogmatic 'rational theology'.[71]

The phrase 'rational theology' comes from the middle of the third, 1788, instalment of *The Decline and Fall*. It occurs at the end of chapter 54, the account of the minor sect of the Paulicians which Gibbon transforms into an account of the religious genealogy of the reformed northern European nations. The father of rational theology was Erasmus, and after 'a slumber of an hundred years, it was revived . . . in England by Chillingworth, the latitudinarians of Cambridge . . . Tillotson, Clarke, Hoadley, &c.'[72] However, the outcome was an unstable compound of realised benefits and menacing dangers:

> The liberty of conscience has been claimed as a common benefit, an inalienable right: the free governments of Holland and England introduced the practice of toleration; and the narrow allowance of the laws has been enlarged by the prudence and humanity of the times. In the exercise, the mind has understood the limits of its powers, and the words and shadows that might amuse the child can no longer satisfy his manly reason. The volumes of controversy are overspread with cobwebs: the doctrine of a Protestant church is far removed from the knowledge or belief of its private members; and the forms of orthodoxy, the articles of faith, are subscribed with a sigh or a smile by the modern clergy. Yet the friends of Christianity are alarmed at the boundless impulse of enquiry and scepticism. The predictions of the Catholics are accomplished: the web of mystery is unravelled by the Arminians, Arians, and Socinians, whose numbers must not be computed from their separate congregations. And the pillars of revelation are shaken by those men who preserve the name without the substance of religion, who indulge the licence without the temper of philosophy.[73]

The final allusion, as a footnote makes clear, is to Priestley, at the 'ultimate tendency' of whose opinions Gibbon says the priest and magistrate may both 'tremble'.

This is a complicated moment in both the analysis of religion which Gibbon pursues in *The Decline and Fall*[74] and the evolution of his own religious personae. Gibbon's hostility to Priestley originated in December 1782 with the latter's attempt to involve Gibbon in a public debate on the

[71] *Ibid.*, III, p. 438 n. 38.   [72] *Ibid.*, III, p. 438 n. 38.   [73] *Ibid.*, III, pp. 438–9.
[74] On which, see J. G. A. Pocock, 'Gibbon's *Decline and Fall* and the World View of the Late Enlightenment' in his *Virtue, Commerce, and History* (Cambridge, 1985), pp. 143–56, esp. pp. 154–5.

history of the early Church.[75] In casting an anxious eye towards the possibly malign consequences of 'enquiry and scepticism', Gibbon inflects his own persona in the direction of the friendship towards Christianity and even the Catholicism which his prose acknowledges as positions from which the coming danger had been most accurately foreseen. We have moved a long way from the *Critical Observations* and the revisions for the third edition of volume I of *The Decline and Fall.*

The end of chapter 54 was written from within a 'world view' (to use John Pocock's phrase) conscious of its precarious position at the edge of a precipice. It was a precipice over which Europe duly tumbled in the year following its publication. Burke's analysis of the origins and significance of the French Revolution, to which Gibbon promptly subscribed, nevertheless demanded of him some delicate footwork. Burke's indictment of the French *philosophes* as fomenters of revolution must have seemed to implicate Gibbon, whose intellectual and even personal connections with those writers, and the *salons* in which they moved, was well known. The historian responded with, we may think, more ingenuity than persuasiveness when he tried to present his ironies at the expense of the early Christians as Burkean reverence for the customary: 'The primitive Church, which I have treated with some freedom, was itself at that time, an innovation, and *I* was attached to the old Pagan establishment.'[76] Such sophistry aside, the Revolution also prompted Gibbon to re-imagine his own life from a number of standpoints in the various drafts of his *Memoirs*, and it is striking that here we find him experimenting with sharply opposed personae. On the one hand, we have the admirer of 'the mighty Horsley', by whose spear the 'Socinian shield' of Priestley has been, so Gibbon says, 'repeatedly . . . pierced'.[77] On the other, we have a rather feline character, estranged from such enthusiasms, who deftly refuses to be drawn on his inward convictions: 'on Christmas Day 1754, I received the sacrament in the Church of Lausanne. It was here that I suspended my Religious enquiries, acquiescing with implicit belief in the tenets and mysteries which are adopted by the general consent of Catholics and Protestants.'[78]

Such positions, while not incompatible, are in mood and posture hardly contiguous. To return to Gibbon's conceit of the 'Theological Barometer'; we seem to have here two different readings at virtually the

---

[75] Paul Turnbull, 'Gibbon's Exchange with Joseph Priestley', *British Journal for Eighteenth-Century Studies,* 14 (1991), pp. 139–58.

[76] *L*, III, p. 216. For a mapping of Gibbon's responses to events in France onto the composition of the *Memoirs*, see my 'Gibbon's *Memoirs*: Autobiography in Time of Revolution', in *Bicentenary Essays*, pp. 347–404.   [77] *A*, p. 318 n. 38 (from draft 'E').

[78] *A*, p. 137 (from draft 'B').

same time. They can hardly both be expressions of Gibbon's innermost beliefs, and the probability must be that neither of them is; that they are both in fact flags of religious convenience, under which Gibbon sailed when it suited him. But when was this not the case? Was there ever a time after that fateful visit in June 1753 to the chaplain of the Sardinian ambassador[79] when Gibbon acted out of simple religious conviction? It is tempting to postulate that Gibbon's return to the Church of England in 1754 coincided with the beginnings of an underlying religious scepticism, which after 1776 was dissembled and camouflaged but never really abandoned.

A more interesting alternative, however, may be to note that Gibbon's successive religious personae fall into two camps: initially they are all provocative, subsequently they are all defensive. Religion for Gibbon is at first a goad, which he uses to attract attention; thereafter, it is a shield behind which he shelters when that attention proves to be hostile. We may do better, then, to follow Gibbon's example. We might suspend our enquiries after his religious beliefs, and ponder instead the striking fact that after 1754 his religious personae, or characters, seem to have been all shaped by the imperatives of that much more fundamental element in his identity than the need for religious consolation: namely, his hunger for literary fame, and his attempts to control that fame once he had acquired it. In this perspective, the conclusion of draft 'E' of the *Memoirs* offers us a striking juxtaposition:

In old age, the consolation of hope is reserved for the tenderness of parents, who commence a new life in their children; the faith of enthusiasts who sing Hallelujahs above the clouds, and the vanity of authors who presume the immortality of their name and writings.[80]

The life of writing and the life of religious faith are parallel, but separate. For Gibbon, perhaps, they were also mutually exclusive.

[79] *A*, pp. 87–8 and n. §   [80] *A*, p. 349.

Part II

4   'The Lust of Empire and Religious Hate':
       Christianity, history, and India, 1790–1820

Brian Young

> And have the purveyors of imperial lust
> Torn from their parents' arms again
> The virgin beauties of the land?
>
> Robert Southey, *Thalaba the Destroyer*[1]

I

On 18 June 1822, the Sixteenth, the Queen's Light Dragoons, set sail for Calcutta on board *The Marchioness of Ely*. The officers of the regiment discovered a favoured book during the voyage, the recently published *Ivanhoe*, for sometime either in December 1822 or January 1823 an Ivanhoe party was held in their honour at Calcutta. One of the party, a Captain Luard, with all the attainments expected of a young officer of the day, not only played his part in the arrangements, but also completed a sketch of the assembled dignitaries and their ladies, dressed as the leading figures in the novel.[2] It should not come as too much of a surprise that imaginative literature played so strong a role in the formation of the minds of those obliged to make the long journey to India. Aside from a slowly emerging literature on India, there was little for such people, soldiers, civil servants, or clergy, to draw upon in addressing this forbiddingly 'other' culture. When confronted by the ululations of Hindu women at the shrine of Juggernaut in Orissa in 1806, Claudius Buchanan, the evangelical vice-president of Fort William College at Calcutta, similarly took refuge behind Milton's depiction of Pandemonium in attempting to convey his extreme sense of religious disorientation.[3] It was, then, to comfortingly familiar literature that the British in India, like the

---

I would like to thank Mishtooni Bose, Colin Kidd, Partha Mitter, Heather Montgomery and John Walsh for their comments on earlier drafts of this essay.

[1] 2 vols., (1801), I, p. 119.
[2] Henry Graham, *The History of the Sixteenth, the Queen's Light Dragoons (Lancers) 1759 to 1812* (Devizes, 1912), pp. 70–2. I am indebted to Dr Elizabeth Armstrong for this reference, and for details of the Calcutta Ivanhoe party.
[3] Claudius Buchanan, *Christian Researches in Asia* (Cambridge, 1811), pp. 136, 140.

Spanish in America, were obliged to return when trying to make sense of this new old world.[4] A similar question likewise confronted the British to that which had earlier exercised the Spanish colonial imagination: how much respect could a proto-imperial power show to indigenous religions? Hinduism was particularly problematic in this connection, and it is the reactions to that religion of various historians writing between 1790 and 1820, all of whom were Christian clergy, which this essay will examine.

The essay, therefore, largely complements P. J. Marshall's important study, *The British Discovery of Hinduism in the Eighteenth Century* (1970), which concerned itself with the researches of a specifically secular community of scholars in British India. One of the major themes of Marshall's work was the congruence which these writers discovered between their considered views of Hinduism and their own varying ideals of a natural religion which was sometimes akin to deism, and sometimes closer to a non-dogmatic conception of Christianity.[5] As was the case with Marshall's work, this essay will not be concerned with Islam, the other major religion of India, although it is frequently a marked presence in eighteenth-century discussions of the sub-continent. One of the most interesting, if eccentric, historians of India, Thomas Maurice, even went so far as to write an execrable play, *The Fall of the Great Mogul* (1806), concerning the fall of Muslim power in India, complete with Hindu priests acting as a somewhat shambolic Greek chorus. When attempting to win a prize instituted at Cambridge by Claudius Buchanan in 1805, Francis Wrangham likewise lamented the decline of Hindu learning under the supposedly oppressive rule of the Muslim princes. Declaring against what he asserted to be the defining features of the Muslim presence in India, Wrangham denounced 'The Lust of Empire and Religious Hate' before celebrating the liberating effects of a new, more genial presence in India, whose presiding genius was Sir William Jones.[6] Such optimism effaced an incipient problem which would grow ever more luxuriantly over the course of the nineteenth century: it would be the Christian British, rather more than the Muslim princes, who would betray their own compromising tendencies to the 'Lust of Empire and Religious Hate', a process in

---

[4] On the analogous European experience of the Americas, see Anthony Grafton, *New Worlds, Ancient Texts: The Power of Tradition and the Shock of Discovery* (Cambridge, Mass., 1992).

[5] P. J. Marshall, 'Introduction' to *The British Discovery of Hinduism in the Eighteenth Century* (Cambridge, 1970), pp. 1–44.

[6] Thomas Maurice, *The Fall of the Mogul, A Tragedy, Founded on an Interesting Portion of Indian History* (1806); Francis Wrangham, *A Poem on the Restoration of Learning in the East* (Cambridge, 1805), pp. 5, 9–10. On the background to Buchanan's prizes, see Allan K. Davidson, *Evangelicals and Attitudes to India 1786–1813: Missionary Activity and Claudius Buchanan* (Abingdon, 1990), pp. 113–31.

which Wrangham himself played his part when extolling plans for the thorough Christianisation of India.[7]

This was a complex process, and not all Christian commentators were as readily drawn into it as others. Nor yet, moreover, was it only Islamic princelings whom the British distrusted; an imperial rival, France, also developed its own 'Lust of Empire', and Christian writers in Britain showed themselves always ready to denounce the French as a continuing source of 'Religious Hate', be it as a centre of Catholic imperialism, Enlightenment infidelity, revolutionary rationalism, or Napoleonic egoism. Intellectual rivalries likewise grew up between these European powers, not least in the attempt at understanding India's indigenous religions. The nature and standing of Hinduism came under increasingly heated discussion by Christians as the eighteenth turned into the nineteenth century. Attitudes began to shift as the politically turbulent 1790s turned into the more conservative 1800s, a transition which can be seen in the differing nature of the work on India undertaken by the clerical historian William Robertson and that of his fellow Scot, the decidedly anticlerical James Mill. Robertson's last published work, *A Historical Disquisition Concerning the Knowledge which the Ancients had of India* (1791), is considered by many as the major founding text of what has been called 'Scottish Orientalism', a notably varied tradition which would culminate in Mill's *History of British India* (1817).[8]

The guiding principle of Robertson's liberal and cosmopolitan work was a simple one, although it would grow increasingly contentious in the decades ahead: 'In our reasonings concerning religious opinions and practices which differ widely from our own, we are extremely apt to err.'[9] Nevertheless, much of Robertson's discussion encompassed what would become familiar clichés of a British understanding of India, although he had a direct interest in the country, and some local knowledge of it, through his two sons, who served in the army there.[10] So it was that

---

[7] Wrangham, *A Dissertation on the Best Means of Civilising the Subjects of the British Empire in India, and of Diffusing the Light of the Christian Religion through the Eastern World* (1805); Wrangham, *A Sermon on the Translation of the Scriptures into the Oriental Languages* (Cambridge, 1807).

[8] Jane Rendall, 'Scottish Orientalism: from Robertson to James Mill', *Historical Journal* 25 (1982), pp. 43–69; Geoffrey Carnall, 'Robertson and Contemporary Images of India', in Stewart J. Brown, ed., *William Robertson and the Expansion of Empire* (Cambridge, 1997), pp. 210–30. More generally, see Marilyn Butler, 'Orientalism', in David Pirie, ed., *The Romantic Period* (Harmondsworth, 1994), pp. 395–447.

[9] William Robertson, *A Historical Disquisition Concerning the Knowledge which the Ancients had of India* (1791), pp. 320–1. For a sensitive reading of this text, see Karen O'Brien, *Narratives of Enlightenment: Cosmopolitan History from Voltaire to Gibbon* (Cambridge, 1997), pp. 163–6.

[10] Stewart J. Brown, 'Robertson and the Scottish Enlightenment', and Jeffrey Smitten, 'Robertson's Letters and the Life of Writing', in *William Robertson*, at pp. 33, 52–3.

Robertson emphasised the permanence of Indian manners, unchanged since the days of Alexander the Great, when they appeared 'a gentle effeminate people'. Likewise, India's Islamic conquerors, with the notable exception of Akber the Great, were condemned in conventional terms; their rule was enforced by 'ferocious violence and illiberal fanaticism'.[11] More unusually, as a stadialist, Robertson praised its distribution of ranks and separation of professions as 'one of the most undoubted proofs of a society considerably advanced in its progress'.[12] Such a benign view of the caste system was not widely shared by many of his contemporaries, nor would it be taken up by many of his intellectual successors.

Indeed, Robertson's notably sympathetic portrayal of the Hindus was far too benign for the tastes of many of the commentators and historians who would follow in the wake of his explorations of India's religious culture. He praised Hindu laws as 'the jurisprudence of an enlightened and commercial people'; Hindu literature was held to have presented the doctrine of the separation of matter and spirit with suitable dignity: Brahminical speculations were frequently of a quality commensurate with the interest taken in them by the ancient Greeks.[13] In contrast with later writers, Robertson traced elements of providentialism in their thought, allowing him to draw parallels with those Stoic doctrines which he seemed increasingly to favour in his own later years. Similarly, he insisted that the Brahmins were worshippers of one God, and their advocacy of a whole pantheon of deities was but another instance of the priestly deployment of the double-doctrine of truth for the initiated few and comforting fables for the uninitiated many.[14] One should not, however, conclude that he was uncritical of Hinduism, which he also described as a 'vast and complicated system of superstition' which had been effected by the 'craft of priests' on the 'credulity of the people'. This description prefaced an account of the 'progress of superstition and false religion' of which Hinduism was but a prime, if occasionally exalted example.[15]

Of a piece with this more critical reflection was his denunciation of the supposed sensuality of Hindu worship, an accusation which would become typical among British observers of Indian mores. He condemned the presence of bands of female prostitutes employed to dance and sing in Hindu temples; the gestures of these dances and the words of their songs were held by Robertson to 'trespass' against 'delicacy' – likewise, he was scandalised by the 'indelicate' paintings which covered the pagodas.

[11] *Historical Disquisition*, pp. 20, 154, 261–2, 272.   [12] *Ibid.*, p. 258.
[13] *Ibid.*, pp. 275, 296–8.
[14] *Ibid.*, pp. 300–1, 324–8, 332–4; Nicholas Phillipson, 'Providence and Progress: An Introduction to the Historical Thought of William Robertson', in Brown, *William Robertson*, pp. 55–73.   [15] *Historical Disquisition*, pp. 312–34.

Above all, Robertson was offended by an object which would become something of an obsession amongst British commentators (and which would be viewed, predictably perhaps, rather differently by French scholars): the lingam. Placed within the inmost recesses of the temple, it was declared by Robertson, with a periphrastic delicacy which would become equally typical amongst British observers, to be 'an emblem of productive power too gross to be explained'.[16] Heinrich Zimmer, an Indologist, defined the lingam, an attribute of the creator god Shiva, more simply and less pruriently as the divine phallus, which 'denotes the male creative energy of Shiva'. In Indian art it frequently occurs in combination with the yoni, 'the primary symbol of female creative energy'.[17] Once more demonstrating a distinction from his more xenophobic and anti-Gallic contemporaries, Robertson, who had expressed some sympathy for the French Revolution, saw Britain's duties as an 'enlightened' nation as complementing those already undertaken by France. It was their duty to preserve as much of the Hindu philosophy as was left, so that 'Great Britain may have the glory of exploring fully that extensive field of unknown science, which the academicians of France had the merit of first opening to the people of Europe'.[18] Such scholarly grace would not prove typical of the rivalry which rapidly developed between the two imperially inclined nations over the interpretation of the ancient cultures of India.[19] Robertson, however, was not a marked enthusiast for empire, and he saw it as his task to warn his readers of the dangers of discriminating against native populations on the grounds of race and religion.[20]

II

Implicit in Robertson's writings on India is an engagement with Edmund Burke's conduct during the impeachment of Warren Hastings. During the course of the trial, Burke famously made himself an authority on, and something of an apologist for, Hinduism.[21] Robertson held an exalted regard for Hastings, comparing him with Akber the Great in his understanding of, and interest in, Hindu culture.[22] John Logan, like Robertson a cleric and an historian, was much more clearly bound up with these controversies as a published apologist for Hastings. A notorious drunk, as

---

[16] *Ibid.*, pp. 319–20.
[17] Henrich Zimmer, *Myths and Symbols in Indian Art and Civilization*, ed. Joseph Campbell (Princeton, 1946), pp. 26–7.   [18] *Historical Disquisition*, p. 311.
[19] On which see, Edward Said, *Orientalism: Western Conceptions of the Orient* (London, 1978), pp. 75–6.   [20] *Historical Disquisition*, pp. 335–6.
[21] *The Writings and Speeches of Edmund Burke*, ed. P. J. Marshall, vol. V: *India: Madras and Bengal, 1774–1785*, and vol. VI: *India: The Launching of the Hastings Impeachment, 1785–1788* (Oxford, 1981–91).   [22] *Historical Disquisition*, p. 273.

well as a noted poet, Logan was seen out of his parish by a righteous congregation, and he headed for London, where he ended his short life as a
hack journalist in 1788.[23] In 1787 he had published an Edinburgh lecture
detailing the supposed innateness of despotism to Asia, in which religion
was seen to have reinforced the power of the throne, thereby instituting a
theocracy which prevented progress and guaranteed India's famed
immutability.[24] A year later, this radical Whig – who had in 1783 produced *Runnamede*, a play which pointedly celebrated the liberties of the
subject against the crown – defended Hastings from his accusers in a
learned piece of polemic which cited Montesquieu and Gibbon on the
nature of despotism and empire against the claims of Burke and his colleagues.[25] Even Macaulay, Burke's adulatory admirer, a notably critical
old India hand, observed the 'great ability' of Logan's defence.[26]

Logan was an early instance of the descent into learned journalism
which accompanied the closing stages of the Scottish Enlightenment. It
was in the leading journal so produced, the *Edinburgh Review*, that much
discussion relating to India and its problems would take place, from
Sydney Smith's clerical denunciation of the projects for evangelisation
promoted by Claudius Buchanan, to the celebrated essay on Hastings by
Macaulay in which he praised Logan.[27] Much of the Scottish Oriental
enterprise can be followed in its pages; criticism of English works on India
was a marked feature of this developing discourse. A review by Alexander
Murray of Thomas Maurice's *Modern History of Hindoostan*, which
appeared in the *Edinburgh Review* in 1805, was sharply critical; his was not
a name to be listed alongside Voltaire, Robertson, or Hume. Although a
'well-meaning, virtuous man', Maurice was, Murray continued, 'totally
unqualified' to be an historian of India, 'both on account of the peculiar
difficulties of the subjects, and his ignorance of the Asiatic languages'.[28]
Maurice, an under-preferred cleric attached to the British Museum,
characteristically replied to a thirteen-page review with a pamphlet of
some eighty-eight pages, in the course of which he denounced his imagined reviewers as disciples of Hume, defending himself as a follower of
the more pious Jones against the dangerous tendencies of atheistical

[23] 'A Short Memoir of the Life and Writings of the Author' prefixed to *Sermons, by the Late
Rev. John Logan*, 6th edition, 2 vols. (Edinburgh, 1807), I, pp. xiii–xx.
[24] Logan, *A Dissertation on the Government, Manners, and Spirit of Asia* (1787).
[25] Logan, *Runnamede: A Tragedy* (1783); Logan, *A Review of the Principal Charges Against
Warren Hastings, Esquire, Late Governor General of Bengal* (1788).
[26] Thomas Babington Macaulay, 'Warren Hastings', *Edinburgh Review*, 74 (1841), pp.
160–255, at p. 250.
[27] Sydney Smith, 'Publications respecting Indian missions', *Edinburgh Review*, 12 (1808),
pp. 151–81.
[28] *Edinburgh Review*, 10 (1805), pp. 288–301, at pp. 291, 300–1.

French Orientalists. The review, he somewhat hysterically suggested, could only have been produced by 'a despicable JUNTO of that sceptical class' whose principles and opinions were founded on those of Bailly and Volney. Maurice also regretted the indifference of the Scots to an India on whose 'spoils' many Caledonians had grown rich; it was, he reminded his readers, Jones, 'an individual of South Britain', who encouraged an interest to be taken in the literature and history of India.[29]

It was the French and the Scots whom Maurice was always ready to accuse of atheism; interestingly, he mellowed considerably when defending himself from having made an undue comparison of himself with Edward Gibbon in writing about Genghis Khan. Gibbon he merely described as 'that splendid writer'; in the *History of Hindoostan* itself, while insisting that the history of Genghis was more properly his subject than that of the historian of Rome's decline, he complimented Gibbon's 'eloquent pen'. He conceded, moreover, that the field was immense, noting that, 'though we meet, we do not clash'.[30] Elsewhere in the *Decline and Fall of the Roman Empire*, however, Gibbon had referred to a matter central to Murray's criticism of Maurice's work, which Maurice silently chose to ignore. Writing about seventeenth-century antiquarians, Gibbon ridiculed them as men of 'profound learning and easy faith', to whom Noah's ark was as the Trojan horse to the Greeks, a means of conducting 'the great grandchildren of Noah from the Tower of Babel to the extremities of the globe'.[31] Gibbon knew full well that contemporary historians were also to be found following this itinerary: Maurice was himself deeply engaged in this apologetic endeavour.

Murray had sceptically adverted to this reading of the tenth book of Genesis, from which Maurice and others deduced the peopling of the gentile world by the Cuthites, who were obliged to wander across the globe when the impious tower of Babel was destroyed by God's wrath.[32] In so doing, Maurice was greatly indebted to two recent writers. In his immediate researches on Genesis and the religion of the gentiles, he drew on Jacob Bryant's *A New System, or, an Analysis of Ancient Mythology* (1775–6). This was one of the most eccentric but influential antiquarian enterprises of the later eighteenth century, a work contemporaneous with

[29] Thomas Maurice, *A Vindication of the Modern History of Hindustan, from the Gross Misrepresentations, and Illiberal Strictures of the Edinburgh Reviewers* (1805), pp. 7–9. On his indebtedness to Jones, see Thomas R. Trautmann, *Aryans and British India* (Berkeley, 1997), pp. 75, 80.

[30] Maurice, *Vindication*, p. 81; Maurice, *The Modern History of Hindoostan*, 2 vols. (1802–9), vol. I, Part ii, pp. ii–iii.

[31] Edward Gibbon, *The History of the Decline and Fall of the Roman Empire*, ed. David Womersley, 3 vols. (Harmondsworth, 1994), vol. I, pp. 233–4.

[32] *Edinburgh Review*, 10 (1805), pp. 292–3.

the opening volume of the *Decline and Fall*, but which seems to inhabit an altogether different, intellectually regressive world. In making an identification between the Hindu gods and those of the ancient world, Maurice was equally indebted to Sir William Jones, his senior at University College, Oxford, when Maurice was an ambitious young man, eager to make himself known as a poet.[33] The key works here were Jones's famous essays 'On the Origin and Families of Nations' and 'Of the Gods of Greece, Italy, and India', the scholarly products of his presidency of the Asiatic Society in Bengal.

The work of Bryant is superficially similar to that of Jones, but there are major distinctions between them, which Jones himself drew, but which Maurice failed to draw for himself. A structuralist *avant la lettre*, Bryant traced a hitherto confused memory of the deluge in the mythology of the ancient nations, finding in frequently dubious etymologies elements of a once universal vocabulary which had described the religion of the altogether purer, Noachic world. The truth of the sacred word would thus be confirmed, and ancient history placed upon a 'surer foundation'.[34] In expounding the Hindu evidence, Bryant assumed that more was yet to be found there, and that it was the duty of those living there to research these matters assiduously.[35] Although not himself resident in India, this was very much the task which Maurice assumed for himself when he justified his work against the claims of such French 'infidels' as Volney, whose mythological researches sought to compromise the standing of the Mosaic writings.[36] Jones likewise accepted the peopling of the world by the sons of Noah: his project was the creation of a suitably convincing Mosaic ethnography based on Hindu evidence. Jones critically followed Bryant's 'profound and agreeable work, which I have thrice perused with increased attention and pleasure, though not with perfect acquiescence in some other less important parts of his plausible system'. He particularly opposed Bryant's employment of 'conjectural etymology', protesting against its use in serious historical research.[37] Maurice, however, was all too happy to follow such conjectures, even using them to explain the derivation of his own surname from trace-elements of a once universal language.[38]

---

[33] On the personal details of Maurice's life, compromised throughout by an ambition which failed to secure the patronage necessary for its effective promotion, see his entertaining and revealing, *Memoirs of the Author of the Indian Antiquities*, 3 vols. (1819–22).

[34] Jacob Bryant, *A New System, or, an Analysis of Ancient Mythology*, 3 vols. (1775–6), I, pp. v–xvii, 1–127, and passim.   [35] *Ibid.*, III, pp. 212–32, 600–1.

[36] Maurice, *History of Hindoostan*, I, pp. xx–xxiii; Maurice, *Indian Antiquities*, 9 vols. (1792–1800), V, pp. 837–1091.

[37] Sir William Jones, 'On the origin and families of nations', in *The Works*, 6 vols. (1799), I, pp. 129–42, at pp. 137, 139; Trautmann, *Aryans and British India*, pp. 41–52.

[38] Maurice, *Memoirs*, I, p. 5.

It followed from the Mosaic argument that the gentiles had, in Jones's words, deviated 'from the rational adoration of the only true GOD'. Accepting Bryant's argument that the mythology of all the ancient kingdoms revealed that they had been founded by types of Noah, Jones claimed that Saturn and the Hindu law-giver, Menu, were just such Noachic types. Similarly, Zeus, Jove, and Indra were identical entities, and Jones went on to elaborate such parallels: hence Hecate/Proserpine/Kali, an example which allowed him to draw a startlingly contemporary comparison:

The wild musick of CA LI's priests at one of her festivals brought instantly to my recollection the Scythian measures of DIANA's adorers in the splendid opera of IPHIGENIA in Tauris, which GLUCK exhibited at Paris with less genius, indeed, than art, but with every advantage that an orchestra could supply.[39]

Although in his interpretation of the Hindu mythology Maurice would claim that, 'Sir William Jones afforded the clue which has directed my path throughout this dark and intricate labyrinth', he accepted the notion that the Hindu doctrines revealed an innate Trinitarianism.[40] This was a claim, however, in which Jones had earlier wondered whether 'folly, ignorance, or impiety predominates'.[41]

Maurice frequently thought the best of the Hindus, something which placed him closer to Robertson, whose work he respected, than to those of his clerical contemporaries and successors who also wrote on the subject. He admitted that, 'I have that kind of partiality which every historian possesses for the nation whose history he is probably induced by that very partiality to record': hence his Robertsonian belief that the priests veiled the truth from the multitude was easily reconciled with their belief in 'the mild, the beneficent, the uncorrupted religion of the GREAT BRAHMA'. Similarly, with a sense of propriety reminiscent of that displayed by Robertson on the question, Maurice regretted that the pagoda often acted as 'a public brothel' with the connivance of the priests. Likewise, he lamented many of the beliefs of 'the bigoted natives', whilst accepting that Hindu religion contained a balance between that which was 'mild and benevolent' and that which was also 'sanguinary and terrible'. In common with Logan, he interpreted the Indian political system as being, at heart, a theocracy; as with Robertson, so with Maurice, who saw merit in the original institution of caste, though he regretted its effects in the modern world.[42]

[39] Jones, 'On the gods of Greece, Italy, and India', in *Works*, I, pp. 229–80, at pp. 230, 237–8, 248–54, 270–1.
[40] Maurice, *History of Hindoostan*, II, p. v; Maurice, *Indian Antiquities*, IV, pp. 418–758, and V, pp. 773–836.   [41] Jones, *Works*, I, p. 277.
[42] Maurice, *Indian Antiquities*, I, pp. xxv–xxvi, xlii, xcv, 233, II, pp. 339–41, 343, V, p. 841, VII, pp. 801–2.

Indeed, Maurice seems often to have accepted rather than merely to have ritually condemned many of the necessarily different standards of the two cultures: for example, images of Bhavanee, Shiva's consort, were displayed in her temples which, 'though by no means inconsistent with *their*, are not at all consistent with *our* notions of delicacy and decorum'.[43] Maurice insisted, however, *à la* Robertson, that he would not write at great length about the lingam, a 'disgusting emblem' which he would not use to offend 'the eye of virgin innocence' among his readers. He wrote about it, he continued, in 'a theological light', concluding that the less said 'in praise or veneration of it, the better':[44] he was, however, to write about it again and again. He assumed it likely that phallic worship and its 'indecent rites' had originated with Ham, later making its way to India from Egypt; 'but too visible' in India, it was an 'outrage against decency', an 'abominable mockery of every thing sacred'. At Salsette there were to be found 'often in union, that shocks the eye of modesty, the too evident emblems of the male and female organs of generation'.[45] Not that he was always either coy or dismissive: he celebrated representations of Shiva which showed him with the scythe of time in one hand, and 'the prolific LINGAM' in the other, by drawing a religious parallel which he hoped would not incur the censure of his fellow clergy:

> but if, on so trivial an occasion, the greatest of apostles and wisest of philosophers might without impiety be quoted, St Paul, to whom the oriental philosophy of the Gnostics was well known, speaks language exactly consonant to this; for, finely retaliating upon them for their disbelief of the resurrection, he exclaims to the sceptical Corinthians, Thou fool, that which thou sowest is not *quickened* except it *die*.[46]

Maurice was also a reader of one of the more notorious works on the subject, referring his readers to Richard Payne Knight's 'curious inedited book on the Phallic worship of the ancients': he also cited another contentious work, which had in turn influenced Knight, the *Recherches sur l'origine, l'esprit et les progrès des arts de la Grèce* (1785) by the self-styled Baron d'Hancarville, a one-time pornographer turned mythologist.[47] Both Knight's *A Discourse on the Worship of Priapus* (1786) and d'Hancarville's stubbornly digressive two-volume study concentrated on the decidedly pagan elements of priapic worship. As well as opening up study of the matter through his discussion of what he considered to be the Bacchic element in Indian religion, d'Hancarville quietly celebrated a pagan

---

[43] *Ibid.*, I, p. 193.   [44] *Ibid.*, I, pp. cvi–cviii.   [45] *Ibid.*, II, pp. 257, 260, 265, 270–1, 273.
[46] *Ibid.*, III, pp. 537–8.
[47] *Ibid.*, III, pp. 474n, 499, 529; Francis Haskell, 'The Baron d'Hancarville: An Adventurer and Art Historian in Eighteenth-Century Europe', in *Past and Present in Art and Taste: Selected Essays* (New Haven, 1987), pp. 30–45.

approach to fecundity which implicitly devalued Christianity. In this sense, d'Hancarville was at one with those French scholars whom Maurice otherwise spent so much energy excoriating. Whilst plainly fascinated with d'Hancarville's intellectually liberating utilisation of Hindu material, Maurice hated the openly atheistical or, at best, deistic, use of similar sources made by men such as Volney, Dupuis, and Bailly, all of whom played their part in the ideological underpinning of the French Revolution.

Maurice attacked Bailly's hypothesis, also developed by Volney, of a Scythian race of magi who had created a basically Mithraic religion of which all other religions, from Hinduism to Christianity, were but variations.[48] Their arguments in favour of the supremely ancient Hindu chronology, which challenged the analogous standing of the Old Testament, were also questioned by Maurice, as was Volney's occasionally blasphemous use of the zodiac in making his case. Dupuis was especially despised by Maurice, who saw in his work 'the declared intention of subverting Christianity and re-erecting paganism on its ruins'.[49] Dupuis's *Origine de tous les cultes, ou religion universelle* (1794–5), could be read in such a manner, as the *idéologues* of the French Revolution sought out a means of replacing the Christianity they had abolished. Fascinatingly, Dupuis was very taken with fecundity cults, and much of his three volumes is taken up with discussion of Osiris, Bacchus, Priapus, and Hindu gods of fertility, the very concerns about which Maurice had already drawn from the no less suspect d'Hancarville in his own work.[50] In detailing the mythological understanding of the lingam promoted by these revolutionary *philosophes* and the religiously sceptical Payne Knight, Partha Mitter has rightly emphasised their inherently secularising influence on the interpretation of Indian art.[51]

For the likes of Maurice, and even more for the Christian missionaries in Bengal, the lingam was plainly a synecdoche for the supposedly unrestrained sexuality of the Oriental 'other'; the sensuality of the Hindu was a barely acknowledged, if obsessively iterated threat to the restraint of the

---

[48] Maurice, *History of Hindoostan*, I, pp. 255–71; Maurice, *Indian Antiquities*, IV, preface (unpaginated); Jean-Sylvain Bailly, *Essai sur les fables, et sur leur histoire, addressé à la citoyenne Du Bocage* (Paris, 1794); C. F. de C. Volney, *The Ruins; or, a Survey of the Revolutions of Empire* (English translation, 1792).

[49] Maurice, *Indian Antiquities*, I, pp. xvii–xviii; Maurice, *History of Hindoostan*, I, pp. 340–1, and II, pp. vi–vii.

[50] C. F. Dupuis, *Origine de tous les cultes, ou religion universelle*, 3 vols. (Paris, 1794–5), I, pp. 366–95, II (Part I), pp. 1–98, 165–95, (Part II), pp. 3–6, 66, 104–5, 188–90; Frank E. Manuel, *The Eighteenth Century Confronts the Gods* (Cambridge, Mass., 1959), pp. 263–70.

[51] Partha Mitter, *Much Maligned Monsters: A History of European Reactions to Indian Art* (Oxford, 1977), pp. 84–104.

British commentators and their imperial authority. Quite literally, it nakedly challenged their sense of propriety and of control; its much remarked upon indelicacy became an obsessive instrument of their desire to mediate between the otherness of Hindu India and the 'civilising' influence of Christian Britain. Once again, as the work of Maurice was both embellished and repudiated by the likes of the missionaries William Ward and Claudius Buchanan, the more open sexuality of the Enlightenment was to become quickly clouded over by the proprieties of evangelicalism.

III

Payne Knight was plainly a somewhat unlikely source for Maurice to use, not least because Knight's phallocentrism served as subversively irreligious a purpose as it did a privately sexual one.[52] Christian puritanism receives many slights in the argument of Knight's text, and a Gibbonian sympathy for a tolerant and gentlemanly older religion seeps through the work.[53] This is most apparent in the closing pages of the treatise as Knight eulogises the ancient Greeks, whose religious inclusiveness 'effectively excluded two of the great curses that ever afflicted the human race, Dogmatical Theology, and its consequent Religious Persecution'.[54]

Such an implicit critique of Christian exclusivity naturally challenged the basis of any sort of proselytising engagement. Both as evangelist and critic of the supposedly sensual nature of Indian religion, the Baptist William Ward was thus the very antithesis of Knight's implicit ideal of religious detachment as the major desideratum in attaining a properly scholarly understanding of the religion of other peoples. Indeed, the guiding principle of Ward's miscellaneous musings, *A View of the History, Literature and Mythology of the Hindoos* (1811), betrayed a marked antagonism to Hinduism, which he denounced as 'the most PUERILE, IMPURE, AND BLOODY OF ANY SYSTEM OF IDOLATRY THAT WAS EVER ESTABLISHED ON EARTH'.[55] Ward revealed as marked a preoccu-

---

[52] G. S. Rousseau, 'The Sorrows of Priapus: Anticlericalism, Homosocial Desire, and Richard Payne Knight', in G. S. Rousseau and Roy Porter, eds., *Sexual Underworlds of the Enlightenment* (Manchester, 1987), pp. 101–53; Randolph Trumbach, 'Erotic Fantasy and Male Libertinism in Enlightenment England', in Lynn Hunt, ed., *The Invention of Pornography: Obscenity and the Origins of Modernity, 1500–1800* (New York, 1993), pp. 253–82; Andrew Ballantyne, *Architecture, Landscape and Liberty: Richard Payne Knight and the Picturesque* (Cambridge, 1997), pp. 86–109, 134, 192–7; Giancarlo Carabelli, *In the Image of Priapus* (London, 1996).

[53] Brian Young, 'Gibbon and Sex', *Textual Practice*, 11 (1997), pp. 517–37.

[54] Richard Payne Knight, *A Discourse on the Worship of Priapus* (1786), p. 188.

[55] William Ward, *A View of the History, Literature, and Mythology of the Hindoos*, 3 vols. (1822), III, p. clxx. This work was originally produced at Serampore, the Baptist missionary centre, in 1811.

pation with the lingam as had Maurice, deploring its worship as 'an abomination', and 'a shocking violation of every thing decent'; Shivu's temples were 'polluted with filthy images', and his worship tended to inflame the mind 'with licentious ideas'. Regretting the prevalence of 'this scandalous image', Ward confessed that his attempts at fully conveying its effects were beyond him, leading him instead to extol the virtues of self-censorship. Ritual comparisons were made with Greek phallus worship, and with that of Priapus, whose story Ward held to be 'too indecent, and too well known to need recital'. Should this, nevertheless, still prove necessary, he interestingly referred his readers to Maurice's *Indian Antiquities* for further information on the matter.[56]

Sensuality was held to be the predictably besetting sin of Hindu worship, its peculiarly pervasive variety of Brahminical priestcraft calculated to delude from the very outset of maturity. Ward was preoccupied with the dangers of dancing, especially when naked, and of singing, especially sexually provocative sacred songs; the songs and dances of the Durga festival would, he felt sure, have disgraced a 'house of ill-fame'. Ward's censoriousness often conveyed a vicarious prurience to his no doubt properly appreciative readers, as when he evoked a moment of great familial concern:

> The author himself one year saw, from his own window at Serampore, in a procession on the river Ganges of the images of Doorga, sights so shockingly detestable, that he ran and closed his windows, and in a state of agony sought his children, that they might be removed to a distance from the scene.[57]

This sense of the moral duty of the European censor is strongly present in Ward, as when he typically remarks that 'The manifest effect of idolatry in this country, as held up to thousands of Christian spectators, is an immersion into the greatest moral darkness, and a universal corruption of manners.' It was not, then, devotion that led the Hindu to the temple, but 'a licentious appetite': crowds assembled at the temples in order to 'enter upon orgies which destroy every vestige of moral feeling, and excite to every outrage upon virtue'.[58]

In the time-honoured tradition of a Protestant suspicion of priests, be they Catholic or Hindu (and Ward even discerned parallels between their idols and 'Popish' statuary from the twelfth century), he referred to the cupidity and sensuality of spiritual guides who abused the faith of their employers, seeking to 'violate the chastity of their wives'. As with the conventional dismissal of a Muslim heaven, so with that of the Hindus: their future joys were wholly 'sensual', disgusting 'a chaste mind by their

---

[56] *Ibid.*, I, pp. lxxix–lxxx, and III, pp. 12–13.
[57] *Ibid.*, I, pp. xxx–xxxi, xxxvii–xxxix, c.   [58] *Ibid.*, I, pp. xcix, cvi, cxi.

grossness'. Vice necessarily commingled with their worship; a Hindu frequently left a temple 'inflamed with concupiscence', an idea which afforded Ward opportunities provocatively to hint at the lasciviousness he habitually condemned. He even gave an unintentional hint as to where best to find out about such matters when he remarked that, 'to know the Hindoo idolatry, AS IT IS, a person must wade through the filth of the thirty-six pooranus and other popular books': like Buchanan at the temple of Juggernaut, Ward, confronted by such singularly testing images, took refuge in stereotypically describing Hinduism as 'this temple of Moloch'.[59] A taste for the latest literature was also revealed by the erstwhile poet, when Ward cautiously recommended to his readers Southey's depiction of the suicidal worship of Juggernaut at Orissa in *The Curse of Kehama*. This account, while not being literally correct, 'conveys to the mind much of the horror which a Christian spectator of the car cannot but feel'.[60] Local experience colluded with literary imagination in reinforcing an image of India as a haven of superstitious excess.

Vice came from the nature of the gods themselves, and, again, veiled hints obscurely rehearsed the full horror Ward so frequently noted that he could not bring himself directly to describe. So it was that he somewhat paradoxically portrayed the goddess Durga standing upon two other deities, 'in an attitude so obviously indecent that it cannot be described', while the goddess Kali's stance towards her husband Shivu, 'has a secret meaning, well known to a Hindoo, but which is so indecent, that even they, licentious as they are, dare not make it according to the genuine meaning of the fable to which it belongs'. One goddess was described as 'a celestial courtezan', while another was humourlessly 'charged with an adulterous intercourse with Urjuna, the wife of Keohunee, a monkey'; prostitutes were noted worshippers of Saraswati, the goddess of learning, whose male devotees danced naked at her festival; priests in one sect behaved towards a woman, during an initiation ceremony, 'in a manner which decency forbids to be mentioned'.[61]

Ward's thorough rejection of the world of Payne Knight was honestly made, as he noted the favouring of pagan religions made by modern scep-

[59] *Ibid.*, I, pp. cxii, cxv, cxxii, cxxv, cxxxviii, cxl.
[60] *Ibid.*, I, p. xci; Southey, *The Curse of Kehama* (1810), pp. 147–9, where he also refers to the presence in the temple of 'A harlot-band'. Southey cited Maurice's *Indian Antiquities* as his source on this latter matter: *ibid.*, pp. 352–3. On evangelical readings of *Kehama*, see Nigel Leask, *British Romantic Writers and the East: Anxieties of Empire* (Cambridge, 1991), pp. 26, 96. On Southey's Orientalism, see Marilyn Butler, 'Repossessing the Past: The Case for an Open Literary History', in Marjorie Levinson, ed., *Rethinking Historicism: Critical Readings in Romantic History* (Oxford, 1989), pp. 64–84. For a suggestive reading of *The Curse of Kehama*, see Balachandra Rajan, *Under Western Eyes: India from Milton to Macaulay* (Durham, N.C., 1999), ch. 7.
[61] Ward, *A View*, I, pp. xcvii–xcviii, lxxv, and III, pp. 48, 133–4, 195.

tics, naming in this connection Voltaire, Gibbon, and Hume.[62] Buchanan had likewise noted a tendency on the part of the *philosophes* to admire what he thought of as the inherent syncretism of Hinduism; infidelity, he asserted, looked on Hindu rites with 'all the coldness and apathy of Voltaire'.[63] More intriguingly still, Ward also condemned a man who had notoriously relied on the work of Payne Knight, and one who, he felt, ought to have known better. It is worth citing this condemnation in full, not least as it so fully conveys the strong distaste which Ward felt for Hinduism, which he viewed with such everyday contempt, and which he equally felt armchair antiquarians safely at home had treated all too lightly:

The Reverend Mr Maurice has attempted to describe the Hindoo ceremonies, which he never saw, in the most captivating terms, and has presented these 'abominable idolatries' in the most florid colours. It might have been expected (idolatry being in itself an act so degrading to man, and so dishonourable to God), that a Christian divine would have been shocked when writing in this manner. If Mr Maurice thinks there is something in Hindoostan to excite the most sublime ideas, let him come and join in the dance before the idol; – or assist the bramhuns in crying *Hiree bul! Hiree bul!* while the fire is seizing the limbs of the young and unfortunate Hindoo widow; – or let him attend at the sacrificing of animals before the images of Kalee and Doorga; – or come and join in the dance, stark naked, in the public street, in open day, before the image of Doorga, in the presence of thousands of spectators, young and old, male and female. He will find, that the sight will never make these holy brahmuns, these mild and innocent Hindoos, blush for a moment. – Seriously, should sights like these raise the ardour of enthusiasm, or chill the blood of a Christian minister? Say, ye blush for human nature sunk in shame. As a clergyman, Mr. Maurice should have known, that antiquity sanctifies nothing: – 'the sinner, being a hundred years old, shall be accursed.'[64]

In this testy vein of ridicule the attitudes of an older generation stood condemned by those of an evangelical new wave; antiquarians were denounced by missionaries, and those who stayed at home were dismissed by those who ministered in the empire thrown up by a Providence which had overseen the destruction, first of revolutionary, and then of Napoleonic France.

Providence, Ward believed, was the means of Britain's acquiring an Indian empire, its primary purpose being the accomplishment of 'some

---

[62] *Ibid.*, I, p. cxliii.
[63] Buchanan, *Memoir of the Expediency of an Ecclesiastical Establishment for British India* (1805), p. 27; Buchanan, *Christian Researches*, p. 350. On the immediate influence of Buchanan's texts, see Davidson, *Evangelicals and Attitudes to India*, pp. 139–50, 219–26.
[64] Ward, *A View*, I, p. clxvi. Raymond Schwab was, then, quite mistaken in identifying Maurice as a denigrator of Hinduism and a fellow-exponent of Ward's missionary-position: *The Oriental Renaissance: Europe's Rediscovery of India and the East, 1680–1880*, trans. Gene Patterson-Black and Victor Reinking (New York, 1984), p. 339.

very important change in the Eastern world'; the ever 'blacker' ages of India were finally to be enlightened and evangelised by a supremely Christian power.[65] Providentialism also accounted for Buchanan's view that British India would be the means of evangelising the whole of Asia; he was to wonder forcefully if Britain's preservation from Napoleon's ambitions had been designed to allow her empire to undertake the Christianisation of her territories.[66] Significantly, Ward lamented that it was one of the major errors of the Hindu system that it 'never recognizes God under the Christian idea of Providence'. Providence had formerly allowed the Hindus to suffer under the consequences of their religion of 'darkness', and then under the despotic rule of Islamic rulers; now, 'a gracious Providence has remembered mercy, and placed them under the fostering care of a Christian government, that they may enjoy a happiness to which they have been hitherto strangers'.[67] A thriving British commercial empire would thus have a different series of effects from the mutually civilising influences William Robertson had celebrated in the commerce with India once prevalent in the ancient world. For Ward, British commerce would be the providentially chosen means of converting the whole of Asia from superstition to salvific faith:

But let Hindoost'han receive that higher civilization she needs, that cultivation of which she is capable; let European literature be transfused into all her languages, and then the ocean, from the ports of Britain to India, will be covered with our merchant vessels; and from the centre of India moral culture and science will be extended all over Asia, to the Burman empire and Siam, to China, with all her millions, to Persia, and even to Arabia; and the whole Eastern hemisphere will be gilded with the rays of the Luminary, whose beams are the sole source of all the life and moral beauty found in our world.[68]

This 'theology of empire' was shared by Buchanan, who firmly desired that 'the chief purpose and avowed Object' of British commerce ought to be 'THE MERCHANDISE OF THE GOSPEL.'[69] In common with Ward, Buchanan set himself securely against such Hindu excesses as suti and the alleged sacrifice of children to alligators at Sanjar Island; he dramatically contrasted the worship of Juggernaut at Serampore with the missionary work of the Baptists taking place alongside it.[70] Buchanan

---

[65] Ward, *A View*, I, pp. xvii–xxviii, liv.
[66] Buchanan, *Memoir*, pp. xii, 39; Buchanan, *The Star in the East* (1809), pp. 40–1.
[67] Ward, *A View*, I, pp. xlv, cxlii.   [68] *Ibid.*, I, p. liii.
[69] Buchanan, *A Sermon Preached before the Society for Missions to Africa and the East* (Cambridge, 1811), p. 92. For a similar view, see Richard Ely, 'From Church to Sect: James Stephen's Theology of Empire', *Journal of Religious History* 19 (1995), pp. 75–91, and on the future fortune of such ideas, see Andrew Porter, "Commerce and Christianity": The Rise and Fall of a Nineteenth-Century Missionary Slogan', *Historical Journal*, 28 (1985), pp. 597–621.
[70] Ward, *A View*, I, pp. xl, xli, xliv–xlv; Buchanan, *Christian Researches*, pp. 147–54.

similarly imputed the twin elements of 'Cruelty and Lasciviousness; – Blood and Impurity' to Hindu worship; again, like Ward, he sought to censor his own experience, declaring of his visit to the Orissa festival, 'I felt a consciousness of doing wrong in witnessing it.'[71] A product of the Cambridge evangelicalism which had developed, at least in part, as a reaction against the liberalism for which that university had formerly been noted, Buchanan, a Scot who had previously studied at Glasgow, was initially well disposed to the Baptists (from whom he finally separated following a quarrel over translating the Bible in 1807), but equally, and rather unexpectedly, he was happy to advert to the support for his Cambridge prizes given by Richard Watson, one of the most liberal of the Cambridge generation ahead of him.[72] Such a transition had largely become possible as a result of the ideological consequences of the French Revolution. As Buchanan noted in 1805, 'The French Revolution has imposed on us the duty of imposing new means for extending and establishing Christian principles.'[73] France, he went on to observe in 1809, had been the kingdom 'which first seduced others by its own infidelity', and which had then become 'the instrument of their punishment'.[74]

An opponent of what he dismissed as merely 'rational' Christianity, Buchanan thought a 'corrupt Theology' potentially even more dangerous than infidelity, a theme he made central to the evangelising sermons which he delivered at Cambridge in 1810.[75] Most corrupt of all, in his opinion, was Catholicism, whose practice in southern India, under the aegis of the French and the Portuguese, he strongly condemned as constituting 'the darkness of the ROMISH superstition in Pagan Lands'. He claimed to have witnessed forms of syncretistic worship in regions under Portuguese control, whereby 'the Ceremonies and Rites of Moloch are blended with the Worship of Christ!' Buchanan further opined that Catholic priests in India were 'better acquainted with the veda of Brahma than with the Gospel of Christ'.[76] There were, Buchanan argued, two

---

[71] Buchanan, *A Sermon*, p. 88; Buchanan, *Christian Researches*, p. 138.

[72] Buchanan, *Christian Researches*, pp. 362–7; Richard Watson, *Anecdotes of the Life of Richard Watson* (1817), pp. 431–5. Unusually for a theological liberal, Watson had adverted to the ideal of a Christian mission to India as early as 1784: *A Sermon Preached before the Lords Spiritual and Temporal* (1784), pp. 18–20. On Buchanan's separation from the Baptists, see Roger H. Martin, 'Anglicans and Baptists in Conflict: The Bible Society, Bengal and the Baptizo Controversy', *Journal of Ecclesiastical History* 49 (1998), pp. 293–316. Buchanan was at least as much a late product of the Cambuslang revival as he was of evangelical Cambridge, on which see Hugh Pearson, *Memoirs of the Life and Writings of the Rev. Claudius Buchanan, D.D. Late Vice-Provost of Fort William in Bengal*, 2 vols. (Oxford, 1817).   [73] Buchanan, *A Memoir*, p. 22.

[74] Buchanan, *The Star in the East*, p. 38.

[75] Buchanan, 'Sermon I', in *Two Discourses Preached Before the University of Cambridge, on Commencement Sunday, July 1, 1810* (Cambridge, 1811), pp. 12n, 59.

[76] Buchanan, *A Sermon*, pp. 88–9; Buchanan, *Christian Researches*, p. 238.

models of governing conquered territories: the Roman model, which was eventually to be adopted by the 'infidel' French, was to allow the native peoples to continue unmolested in their religious traditions; and the Christian model (which he hoped the British would finally adopt), was 'to improve the mind of the native in *religious* knowledge, as soon as the practicability of the attempt shall appear obvious'. Analysing the deprivations of the lowest caste, Buchanan dismissed such hoary Enlightenment notions as that of the 'noble savage' with a neat glance at Rousseau: 'The philosopher of Geneva himself would not have contested for the civilization of the Sooders.'[77] Equally, Buchanan was sensitive to the presence in India of Islam, a faith whose 'bigotry and intemperate zeal' he somewhat richly denounced, regretting that Islam was nursed 'in the peaceful lap of Christian liberality'. He also praised it for having once coerced the rites of Hindu 'superstition' at Orissa; it had been, in this particular, 'friendly to humanity'. In this instance, however, Islam was merely being used as a stick with which to beat the allegedly un-Christian stance of the East India Company for collecting taxes from the pilgrims, and thereby profiting from the 'worship of Moloch'.[78]

Buchanan gladly reproached the *philosophes* for having been taken in by the absurdly ancient chronology proposed by Hindu texts. His amusement at the expense of the 'credulous infidel' could, however, have been turned against him also, since he accepted Wilford's findings, later discovered to be forgeries imposed on him by unscrupulous pundits, that the Hindus had had testimonies of Christ.[79] This was a notorious blunder on Wilford's part, and was gloried in by Thomas Maurice in his critique of the Brahminical forgeries concerning a Messiah, which he felt could only have been used to promote the anti-Christian claims of French infidels.[80] Ward, who was unconvinced of anything but the deeply and irredeemably idolatrous nature of Hindu worship, also denounced the 'absurd' chronology claimed for the Hindus, noting that they lacked any real knowledge of their own history, preferring the fabulous to the true. Their chronology was merely 'inexplicable', whilst that of Moses had been properly and satisfactorily explicated by the work of Richard Bentley and other scholars of his standing.[81] The Hindu was, then, 'changeless', the caste system serving, like the Chinese shoe, both to make 'the whole nation cripples', and, consequently, to rivet 'the chains of superstition'.[82] Buchanan likewise noted that, 'They are less tenacious of opinion than of custom.'[83]

---

[77] Buchanan, *Memoir*, pp. 38, 28–9, 110.
[78] *Ibid.*, pp. 30–1; Buchanan, *Christian Researches*, p. 143n.
[79] Buchanan, *Memoir*, pp. 43–6; Buchanan, *The Star in the East*, pp. 10–13.
[80] Maurice, *Brahminical Fraud Detected* (1812).
[81] Ward, *A View*, I, pp. i, 40–1.   [82] *Ibid.*, I, pp. xiv, li, 64.   [83] Buchanan, *Memoir*, p. 26.

With such views, it is unsurprising that Buchanan should have been as critical of Robertson as Ward was of Maurice. Buchanan emphasised, against Robertson, that the primary need facing students of Hinduism was the improvement of the Indian in the modern world, and not the celebration of the intellectual improvements of the Hindu past. One discovers here the evangelical celebration of empire triumphing over the elegiac strains of a historian whose chronicling of European empires had left him relatively suspicious of their consequences. The customary priority was assigned by Buchanan to experience over mere learning, when he claimed that:

Such a sentiment indeed is apt to force itself on the mind, from a mere investigation of books. But to a spectator in India, the improvement alluded to will appear to be very partial; and the quality of it little understood in Europe.[84]

Although Ward would undoubtedly have shared this sentiment, it is interesting to observe that he developed a rudimentary theory of the universal origins of idolatry which was at least congruent with that earlier sketched by Robertson, and which seems to have had some impact on James Mill. His was the fairly commonplace notion that the depravity and fear common to primitive humanity led to the imagining of gods who derived their natures from such fear, but it was one which was not without its own history or its own influence.[85]

IV

Even though Ward and Buchanan placed a premium on experience, they both held out hopes for scholarship as a means of promoting their cause. Buchanan went so far as almost to contradict himself, asserting that the books on India which were written by those university men who had never been to the East, were generally the 'most sensible and authentic'; Ward called for '*a complete History of this very ancient and interesting people*'.[86] Small wonder, then, that James Mill should have derived so much comfort and inspiration from writers who were in so many other respects deeply antipathetic to him. His notoriously arrogant justification for writing about British India despite never having visited the country had something of its rationale already laid out in the pages of Buchanan and Ward.[87]

Mill's history can thus be seen as the nexus of many of the trends analysed in this essay. His indebtedness to Ward and Buchanan accounts in

[84] *Ibid.*, p. 109. The allusion is to Robertson's *Historical Disquisition*, p. 335.
[85] Ward, *A View*, I, p. lxiv.
[86] Buchanan, *Christian Researches*, p. 119n; Ward, *A View*, I, p. vii.
[87] James Mill, *The History of British India*, 3 vols. (1817), I, pp. xii–xv.

part for what has rightly been seen as a thoroughgoing critique of the defence of Hinduism made by Robertson.[88] He was also as merciless in his condemnation of Maurice as Ward had been, noting that his 'taste for Hindu miracles is not easily overcome'.[89] Mill's work is now shrouded in controversy. Duncan Forbes saw in it a socially and culturally disastrous legacy of rationalist historiography, while William Thomas has described it as a 'classic in the history of philistinism'. Thomas R. Trautmann sees it, along with a 1796 report on India penned by the evangelical Charles Grant, as one of the founding texts of what he calls 'British Indophobia'.[90] With Mill's work a new level of cultural, religious, and political engagement with India had come about, and this was to be continued in Macaulay's anglicising, anti-Oriental mission in Bengal, alongside the increased commitment of missionaries to the inculcation of Christianity against the claims of the supposed 'superstition' that was orthodox Hinduism.[91] Indeed, in tracing the influence of Mill's *History* on the emerging ideology of imperial India, it is vital to bear in mind that Buchanan and Ward, the pronouncedly evangelical critics of Hinduism, had provided Bentham's rationalist disciple with much of his local knowledge.[92] It was, for example, to Buchanan that Mill owed his knowledge of the Juggernaut ceremonies, and to Ward that he was indebted for his priggish condemnation of Hinduism's 'depravity of manners', complete with a ritual repudiation of the lingam as an 'obscene' object of worship.[93]

Consequently, as the largely appreciative works of Robertson, Maurice, and their like declined in importance, the altogether more censorious work of Ward continued to enjoy a high reputation, be it as a conduit for Mill's prejudices or, according to Ward's mid-nineteenth-century biographer, for its own sake. Writing in the late 1850s, John Clark Marshman insisted that Ward's work 'continues to maintain its authority as the fullest and most accurate record of the subjects on which it treats'. Marshman's work appeared in 1859, allowing him to make a dark, if

---

[88] Carnall, 'Robertson and Contemporary Images of India', pp. 221–2, 226.
[89] Mill, *History*, I, p. 364n.
[90] Duncan Forbes, 'James Mill and India', *The Cambridge Journal*, 5 (1951), pp. 19–33; William Thomas, *Mill* (Oxford, 1985), p. 68; Trautmann, *Aryans and British India*, pp. 101–24; Ronald Inden, *Imagining India* (Oxford, 1990), pp. 45–6, 89–93, 166–72; Rajan, *Under Western Eyes*, ch. 4. For a rather different view, see Javed Majeed, *Ungovernable Imaginings: James Mill's The History of British India and Orientalism* (Oxford, 1992).
[91] Forbes, 'James Mill and India', pp. 22–3, 33; Eric Stokes, *The English Utilitarians and India* (Oxford, 1959); J. W. Burrow, *Evolution and Society: A Study in Victorian Social Theory* (Cambridge, 1966), pp. 28–9, 42–9, 52. For analysis of Macaulay's perspective on India, see Rajan, *Under Western Eyes*, ch. 9.
[92] William Thomas, *The Philosophic Radicals: Nine Studies in Theory and Practice* (Oxford, 1979), pp. 98–119.   [93] Mill, *History*, I, pp. 274n, 279–80.

rather dubious, defence of Ward's notably antagonistic account of Hinduism:

While these pages were passing through the press, the mutiny of a hundred thousand of our native soldiery has been announced, and Mr Ward's view of the genuine character of Hindoostan has been laudably verified by the wanton and unparalleled atrocities committed on suffering women and helpless babes, by the mild and humane Hindoos, when released from all restraint, and at liberty to indulge their passions.[94]

In Marshman's anti-Oriental sarcasm, directed at least as much at sympathetic East India men as at tolerant antiquarians and disinterested scholars, one hears the authentic accents of religious hate, accents which had been sharpened by Ward. With the unexpected triumph of utilitarianism and evangelicalism a new period in Anglo-Indian history had dawned; and it was one in which the 'Lust of Empire and Religious Hate' would command a fuller and more relentless sway.

[94] John Clark Marshman, *The Life and Times of Carey, Marshman, and Ward: Embracing the History of the Serampore Mission*, 2 vols. (1859), I, pp. 443–4.

5   The Victorians and Oliver Cromwell

Blair Worden

I

From time to time the anniversary of a historical episode, or of the birth or death of a historical figure, touches a nation's nerve. It answers to perceptions of national identity; or it prompts the invocation of the past for present causes. One such event is the Shakespeare bicentenary of 1764. Another is the centenary of the Glorious Revolution in 1788. No English centenary, however, has produced a more prodigious intensity of sentiment than the three-hundredth anniversary, in April 1899, of the birth of Oliver Cromwell. Across the country there were fervent gatherings of his admirers. In the City Temple in Holborn, which held more than 3,000 people, a series of meetings, from which hundreds had to be turned away, lasted from noon till night. The tercentenary prompted a succession of biographies, most of them deeply felt. There was extensive commentary and debate in the press. The building of a statue of Cromwell at Westminster, which had been demanded and opposed for more than half a century, was finally accomplished.[1]

The years around the tercentenary are the climax of a movement of enthusiasm for Cromwell, even of a cult of him. The movement is essentially a Victorian one. It becomes pronounced at the beginning of

[1] While, in writing this essay, I have mainly gone my own way, I am heavily indebted to the findings of others in a field that has produced some fine work. The late Colin Matthew very kindly enabled me to use his collection of material from the archive of the collaborative research project of the 1960s on 'Nineteenth-Century Cromwell' which was led by the late Tim Mason. I have asterisked references to material taken from transcripts or photocopies in the archive, but my debt to the project is much more substantial than that system of acknowledgement indicates. I have drawn too on excellent published studies, especially: Peter Karsten, *Patriot-Heroes in England and America* (Madison, Wis., 1978); Ralph Samuel, 'The Discovery of Puritanism, 1820–1914: A Preliminary Sketch', in Jane Garnett and Colin Matthew, eds., *Revival and Religion since 1700. Essays for John Walsh* (London, 1993), pp. 201–47; Timothy Lang, *The Victorians and the Stuart Heritage: Interpretations of a Discordant Past* (Cambridge, 1995); and R. C. Richardson, ed., *Images of Oliver Cromwell. Essays by and for Roger Howell* (Manchester, 1993).

Victoria's reign and declines after its end. With its emergence the verdict of previous times was reversed. The eighteenth and early nineteenth centuries, it can be broadly said, were hostile to Cromwell. They vilified him on account both of his revolutionary deeds – the regicide, the establishment of a republic, military and sectarian rule – and of his character, which was generally held to have been one of ruthless cunning and ambition and hypocrisy. The prevailing picture of Cromwell, it is true, was far from uniform. He had always had his defenders, even his devotees, while even his critics often acknowledged that his power, however evil in origin, had been put to some good uses, both at home and abroad. Nonetheless, tribute was heavily outweighed by condemnation.

Only in the early nineteenth century did what was termed a more 'kindly' attitude to him[2] begin to influence the run of historical commentary. In the 1820s and 1830s a growing number of writers were prepared to challenge the traditional allegations of ambition and hypocrisy, and to acknowledge, albeit hesitantly and with qualifications, the sincerity of his religious beliefs and their central place in his life.[3] Across the nineteenth century the allegations would gradually recede. In the middle third of the century, speakers on Cromwell found that in their audiences the balance between the old and the new perception was finely struck, and that an imposing weight of traditional opinion had to be countered.[4] By the time of the tercentenary, the cause had been fought and won. The old charges against Cromwell, it was now widely agreed, had been refuted.[5] 'It is a sign of the modern boldness in dealing with the memory of Cromwell', a devotee accurately remarked in 1899, 'that we are able to claim him fearlessly as a saint.'[6] While respect for the goodness of his character commanded ever wider and deeper respect over the nineteenth century, assessments of his greatness became ever more awestruck. Awe of Cromwell was far from new. It had been a predominant response to him from his own time. His courage and resolution and decisiveness and artfulness, his military and political dexterity, his human insight, were keenly recognised. Before the nineteenth century, however, most commentators

---

[2] Karsten, *Patriot-Heroes*, p. 142.

[3] Thomas Cromwell, *Oliver Cromwell and his Times* (1821), pp. vi–viii; *Eclectic Review* September 1824, p. 205; *Political Penny Magazine*, 3 September 1836, pp. 1–2; Thomas Price, *The History of Protestant Nonconformity in England*, 2 vols. (1836–8), II, pp. 628ff.; *London and Westminster Review*, 24 (1839), pp. 236–8 (anonymous article by John Robertson).

[4] *Oxford Chronicle*, 14 February 1852, p. 8; A. J. Bray, *The Life of Oliver Cromwell* (1869), p. 3.

[5] Frederic Harrison, *Memories and Thoughts* (1906), p. 61; *The Daily News*, 20 April 1899, p. 6, 25 April 1899, p. 8; cf. Samuel's account, in 'Discovery of Puritanism', p. 207, of a meeting at Hackney in 1876.

[6] C. S. Horne, 'The Cromwell Tercentenary', *London Quarterly Review*, n.s. 2 (1899), p. 126.

had charged him with deploying those gifts to sinister personal ends. To his nineteenth-century admirers, the same talents had served virtuous ends. The protectorate was now widely hailed as one of the best periods of rule, and Cromwell himself as the greatest or one of the greatest men in England's history, even in the world's.

In the early nineteenth century two writers did most to promote the movement of sympathy for Cromwell. Macaulay's early essays paid tribute to the figure whom his *History of England* would call 'the greatest prince that has ever ruled England'.[7] William Godwin's *History of the Commonwealth*, published in 1825–8, though endorsing the traditional republican revulsion at Cromwell's usurpation, presented the ambition which provoked that coup as a tragic flaw, akin to Macbeth's,[8] which had ruined a noble mind. In the decades ahead Godwin's recognition of 'the elevation of his soul' would supply as much nourishment for pro- as for anti-Cromwellian feeling.[9] In the 1830s vigorous hatred of Cromwell is still widespread.[10] Yet at the same time we can see pro-Cromwellian sentiment gathering into a current.

In the 1840s it is a torrent. There is an extraordinary range of publications – some of it hostile, but a growing proportion of it admiring – on Cromwell: biographies, essays, novels, poems, songs,[11] at least two plays,[12] even a phrenological study.[13] In 1845 the press, national and provincial, was animated by a demand that a statue of Cromwell be included among the royal monuments that were being planned for the new Palace of Westminster.[14]

In the Cromwellianism of the 1840s one influence is to the fore: Thomas Carlyle. First through his lecture on Cromwell published in 1841 in *Of Heroes and Hero-Worship*, and then, more substantially, through the

---

[7] T. B. Macaulay, *History of England*, 4 vols. (Everyman edn, repr. 1972), I, pp. 116–7.

[8] William Godwin, *History of the Commonwealth*, 4 vols. (1825–8), II, p. 201, IV, p. 384; cf. Robert Southey, *Cromwell and Bunyan* (1844), p. 81.

[9] Godwin, *History of the Commonwealth*, IV, p. 586. The impact of Godwin's study seems to have been only gradual: see John Morrow, 'Republicanism and Public Virtue: William Godwin's *History of the Commonwealth*', *Historical Journal* 34 (1991), pp. 647–8.

[10] Dale Trela, *'Cromwell' in Context: The Conception, Writing and Reception of Carlyle's Second History* (Edinburgh, 1986; published by the Carlyle Newsletter), p. 7.

[11] Karsten, *Patriot-Heroes*, p. 144.

[12] *The Collected Letters of Thomas and Jane Welsh Carlyle*, ed. C. de L. Ryals and K. J. Fielding (Durham, N.C., 1970–), XVII (1990), pp. 139–40; John Watkins, *Oliver Cromwell. The Lord Protector* (1848). Another play on Cromwell had been written in the late 1830s but not performed: *London and Westminster Review*, 27 (1837), pp. 247–70; cf. Edward Bulwer-Lytton, *Richelieu* (1839), pp. 124–32. Victor Hugo's play of 1827, *Cromwell*, seems to have aroused only limited interest in England.

[13] C. Donavan, 'On the Reputed Head of Oliver Cromwell', *Phrenological Journal*, 7 (1844), pp. 365–79 (a reference I owe to the kindness of Laura Clymer).

[14] I am writing about the Cromwell statue elsewhere.

edition of Cromwell's *Letters and Speeches* first published in 1845, Carlyle was the galvanising force of Victorian Cromwellianism. He brought Oliver alive for the century and made his character vivid and immediate. Most previous interpreters had presented Cromwell from the outside. Carlyle aimed, far more successfully than earlier enthusiasts had done, to recover the inner thread of religious conviction which had given meaning and consistency to Cromwell's own life. The impact of the *Letters and Speeches* was sudden and dramatic. Readers hitherto hostile to Cromwell were abruptly converted to him. Books and lectures on him, echoing Carlyle's views, appeared with startling rapidity. The *Letters and Speeches* was frequently reprinted across the century and voraciously quoted. At the tercentenary the debt of Cromwell's reputation to it was widely and fulsomely recorded.[15]

Carlyle was astonished by the reception of his work. He had sensed, but underestimated, the movement of Cromwellianism which he set alight. A number of reasons for the rise and durability of that movement can be suggested. In this essay we shall explore four principal ones.[16] First, there is a change in historical and political thinking which gave a new interest and respectability to the civil war period. Second, there are the struggles fought in the nineteenth century for political and electoral enfranchisement, a contest which offered a dimension of social aspiration and grievance to perceptions of the civil war and especially of Cromwell. Third, there is the Victorian religious revival, which, together with the age's taste for moral earnestness, gave Cromwell's Puritanism a compelling attraction, especially though not exclusively to Nonconformists. Fourth, there is the rise of imperialism, of which Cromwell was seen as the precursor or originator. Amid those various (if frequently overlapping) impulses it is no surprise to find that the Cromwell admired by Victorians has various faces.

II

If the Cromwell tercentenary is the great political anniversary of the late nineteenth century, its eighteenth-century equivalent is the commemoration in 1788 of the Revolution of 1688. The eighteenth century, except on the radical fringe which annually recalled the regicide, did not think to celebrate the Puritan revolt. That revolt, after all, had not only lurched into excess. It had ended in failure, with the return of Charles II. By

---

[15] I explore the impact of Carlyle's interpretation in 'Thomas Carlyle and Oliver Cromwell', *Proceedings of the British Academy*, forthcoming.

[16] For other aspects of the subject – including for the populist and anti-establishment elements of Cromwellianism – see *ibid.*

contrast the Glorious Revolution, a peaceful and conservative aristocratic coup, had brought decisive and lasting success. From it there had derived those pillars of eighteenth-century stability, the Bill of Rights, the Toleration Act, the Act of Settlement.

In the late eighteenth century Tom Paine and other radicals turned against the Revolution of 1688. Only in the second decade of the nineteenth century, however, were the rival claims of the earlier revolution to attention asserted. In 1812 Francis Maseres, whose publications stimulated that process, claimed that if the resistance to James II in 1688 had been justifiable, that of the Long Parliament to Charles I had been no less so.[17] In the following decade the young Macaulay made the same point. At that stage Macaulay, whose great work would centre on 1688, found more to warm to in the earlier and, as it seemed to him, more manly revolt, whose leaders had braved the king themselves rather than bringing in a foreign ruler to do their work.[18] At the same time Godwin's *History of the Commonwealth* brought new standards and new insights to the study of Puritan rule. Other writers of the earlier decades of the century were drawn from the later to the earlier struggle.[19] John Forster, whose own writings on the Puritan revolt commanded a wide readership, pronounced it 'a grave reproach to English political biography, that the attention so richly due to the statesmen who opposed Charles I, in themselves the most remarkable men of any age or nation, should have been suffered to be borne away by the poorer imitators of their memorable deeds, the authors of the imperfect settlement of 1688'.[20] Over the century, in spite of Macaulay's *History*, the Puritan Revolution would overtake the Glorious one in public esteem. In 1888 the bicentenary of 1688 made little impression. School textbooks reflected the shift in favour of 1640–60.[21] So did J. R. Green's hugely influential *History of the English People*. It was the earlier upheaval that summoned the scholarly and moral engagement of Masson and Gardiner and Firth.

The recovery of the Puritan revolt in the earlier nineteenth century derived from two sources. First there was a shift in political thought, which had consequences for historical thought. For all the vigour of the

---

[17] Francis Maseres, ed., *Three Tracts ... under the name of Edmund Ludlow* (1812), pp. x–xi.

[18] T. B. Macaulay, *Critical and Historical Essays*, 2 vols. (Everyman edn, 1907), I, pp. 141–2, 172–6.

[19] Cromwell, *Oliver Cromwell*, p. vii; Lord Nugent, *Some Memorials of John Hampden*, 2 vols (1832), I, pp. xi–xii; Lang, *Victorians and the Stuart Heritage*, p. 115. Cf. *Eclectic Review* September 1824, p. 194; Thomas Carlyle, ed., *The Letters and Speeches of Oliver Cromwell*, ed. S. C. Lomas. 3 vols. (1904 edn), III, p. 219; John Milton, *Paradise Lost*, ed. Robert Vaughan (1866), p. liii.

[20] John Forster, *Statesmen of the English Commonwealth*, 5 vols. (1840), I, p. lxxviii.

[21] Samuel, 'Discovery of Puritanism', p. 206.

Tory reaction early in the century, Toryism had become a thoroughly parliamentary creed. Though Tories and their clerical allies would encourage that sentimental personal affection for Charles I which would persist so widely across the century, they had abandoned his political cause. Almost everyone now agreed that John Hampden had been right to oppose ship money. Down to the summer of 1641, at least, the Long Parliament's course was generally judged to have been necessary, while the raising of arms in 1642 was increasingly agreed to have been the only available means of thwarting the triumph of tyranny. The twenty or thirty years after the end of the Napoleonic wars are the period of English historiography when condemnations of Charles I's tyranny are most widespread and intense. Whig or Whiggish writers who grew up in that time agreed that Charles's reign had set the 'friends of liberty' against its 'enemies'.[22] The personal rule, that calculated attempt 'to trample into the dust . . . the laws and liberties of England',[23] had been 'the most vexatious and intolerable tyranny that ever tortured body and soul at once'.[24] It had been defeated only by 'the gallantest fight for liberty that had ever been fought by any nation in the world'.[25]. It was to key moments in the years before the civil wars – Charles I's suicidal decision to impose an Anglican Prayer Book on Scotland; the passage, by so narrow a vote, of the Grand Remonstrance through the Commons – that England 'owes her freedom'.[26] Had Charles prevailed, England would have followed the path of continental monarchies to despotism.[27] That conviction was to persist down the century.[28] But for Charles's defeat, argued Victorian after Victorian, England would now be like nineteenth-century Spain or Russia.[29]

To vindicate the parliamentary resistance to Charles I in 1640–2 was one thing. To applaud the regicide and the rule of the republic was another. In the later eighteenth century Catharine Macaulay had taken that step. William Godwin did the same in the early nineteenth. Through

---

[22] Macaulay, *Essays*, I, pp. 20, 43, 141.   [23] Forster, *Statesmen*, II, p. 380.

[24] John Forster, *The Debates on the Grand Remonstrance* (1860), p. 420. Cf. *A Sketch of the Life of John Hampden* (Nottingham, 1817); *Sketch of the Life and Character of John Hampden* (1819); *Political Penny Magazine*, 3 September 1836, pp. 1–2; Macaulay, *Essays*, I, p. 174; Dale Trela, *A History of Thomas Carlyle's Oliver Cromwell's 'Letters and Speeches'* (Lewiston, N.Y., 1992), p. 163.   [25] Forster, *Statesmen*, V, p. 305.

[26] Macaulay, *History of England*, i. 71; Forster, *Debates on the Grand Remonstrance*, p. 327.

[27] Macaulay, *Essays*, I, pp. 30–1; Macaulay, *History*, I, p. 62; cf. John Millar, *An Historical View of the English Government*, 4 vols. (1803), III, p. 318.

[28] *Morning Herald*, 16 September 1845; Milton, *Paradise Lost*, ed. Vaughan, p. liii; Peter Bayne, *The Chief Actors of the Puritan Revolution* (1878), p. 165.

[29] Daniel Wilson, *Oliver Cromwell and the Protectorate* (1848), p. 237; R. F. Horton, *Oliver Cromwell. A Study in Personal Religion* (1897), p. 7; *Daily News*, 25 April 1899, p. 8, and 26 April 1899, p. 8; *Methodist Times*, 27 April 1899, p. 265. Cf. W. Q. East, *The Last Days of Great Men* (1903), p. 79; G. M. Trevelyan, *An Autobiography* (1949), p. 159.

the nineteenth century, many devotees of Cromwell would praise, or at least vindicate, the regicide, a position which, though always a minority view, became less contentious as the century wore on. By the late-Victorian era it was widely said that Charles I's execution had put a stop to absolutist aspirations in England, that it had supplied a grim but essential 'object-lesson' to kings, who have 'sat differently on their thrones ever since'.[30] From that perspective, Cromwell's responsibility for the regicide was commendable or at least warrantable. Even so, most early nineteenth-century spokesmen for the Roundhead cause, T. B. Macaulay among them, were more cautious. They found the regicide an intelligible step, but thought it a fatal error of judgement which had wrenched the revolution from its course of constitutional propriety.

Cromwell's standing, however, did not necessarily suffer from that judgement. Two arguments were advanced in his favour, both of which distanced him from the radical fervour of his time. First, the nineteenth century frequently commended him, as the eighteenth century had occasionally done, for saving the nation from anarchy, an achievement that became more conspicuous when set beside the chaos that followed his death. Somehow he had held the forces of order together, after the regicide, after the two coups of 1653, after the failure of his parliament of 1654. The 'order' created by Cromwell, far from being an enemy to 'freedom' or 'liberty', had been its necessary partner and balance.

Second, it was maintained that Cromwell had been instinctively a friend of constitutional government: that only the exceptional pressures of revolution, or the wickedness or irresponsibility of his adversaries, had 'driven' him to 'arbitrary measures'. The regicide, the two armed coups of 1653, and the rule of the Major-Generals, were explained in such terms. At heart, it was maintained, Cromwell was enamoured of those principles of parliamentary government which the nineteenth century would make its own. There was particular admiration for the protectoral constitution which he negotiated with his parliament of 1657, the Humble Petition and Advice. With the parliamentary Nineteen Propositions of 1642, and with the Cromwellian Heads of the Proposals of 1647, the Humble Petition was deemed to have precisely anticipated the nineteenth century's own principles of parliamentary government.[31] Equally the scheme for the redistribution of parliamentary constituencies worked out by the Long Parliament and effected by Cromwell's Instrument of

---

[30] F. W. Aveling, *Cromwell and Puritans* (1899), p. 26; H. G. Groser, *Oliver Cromwell. The Hero of Puritan England* (1899), p. 89; *Daily News*, 25 April 1899, p. 8; *Proceedings of the Fourth National Council of the Evangelical Free Churches* (1899), p. 221.

[31] Macaulay, *Essays*, I, pp. 52, 182–3; Macaulay, *History*, I, pp. 100–1; Forster, *Statesmen*, III, p. 289; Forster, *Debates on the Grand Remonstrance*, p. 420; Edmund Clarke, *Lectures on . . . Oliver Cromwell* (1847), pp. 202–3; Bayne, *Chief Actors*, p. 195.

Government was urged as a model for modern parliamentary reformers.[32] When Cromwell's constitutional or parliamentary stances had found sympathy in the eighteenth century, they had been regarded as challenges to those bugbears of Hanoverian backbenchers, 'corruption and ministerial influence'.[33] In the nineteenth century that country-party perspective was adjusted to accommodate more assertive principles of parliamentary control over supply and over the executive.[34]

III

The second main strand in the earlier nineteenth-century's rediscovery of the Puritan revolt was the growing conviction that the civil wars had been the product of social developments which mirrored those of the present. The conflict had had its origin, it was maintained, in the weakening of the aristocracy under the Tudors, in the rise of the commercial classes in its wake, and in a consequent movement for civic and moral independence among groups hitherto denied political enfranchisement.[35] In 1845 one observer, rejoicing in the weakening of traditional hostile images of the Puritan revolt, attributed it to the recent spread of 'enlightened' opinion among 'the bulk of the community', to the meanest cottager and artisan.[36] The parliamentary cause was held to have reflected a comparable enlightenment. It had been a 'popular' cause, devoted to 'popular progress' and 'popular rights',[37] to political emancipation beyond Westminster and beyond the ruling class. Again the Revolution of 1688 suffered by comparison. It was a nation reprehensibly 'ashamed' of Cromwell, asserted the popular lecturer George Dawson in 1849, that had 'magnified' the 'small affair of 1688' and undervalued the 'mighty business of 1642'.[38] In the 1860s Goldwin Smith, who thought of 1688 as a merely 'aristocratic revolution', explained that 'there were other interests for which men had given their lives at Marston and Naseby, and with

---

[32] See esp. Forster, *Statesmen*, II, pp. 158–60, III, pp. 287–9; Horton, *Cromwell*, pp. 206–7.

[33] John Banks, *A Short Critical Review of . . . Oliver Cromwell* (1763 edn), p. 158. Cf. *Gentleman's Magazine*, 17 (1747), pp. 329–31; James Burgh, *Political Disquisitions*, 3 vols. (Philadelphia, 1775), I, p. 59.

[34] Macaulay, *Essays*, I, pp. 52, 182–3; Macaulay, *History*, I, pp. 100–1; Clarke, *Lectures*, pp. 2–3, 72. Cf. J. R. Green, *History of the English People*, 4 vols. (1877–80), III, pp. 193–4; S. R. Gardiner, *Cromwell's Place in History* (1897), p. 113.

[35] Macaulay, *Essays*, I, p. 144; Macaulay, *History*, I, pp. 17–19; Clarke, *Lectures*, pp. 8–9; Forster, *Statesmen*, I, p. 6; Forster, *Debates*, pp. 70–2; François Guizot, *On the Causes of the English Revolution of 1640–1688* (1850), pp. 13–14.

[36] *Buckinghamshire Gazette*, 27 September 1845.

[37] Macaulay, *Essays*, I, p. 123; Price, *History of Protestant Nonconformity*, II, pp. 165, 219; Forster, *Statesmen*, I, pp. vff., III, p. 287, V, pp. 305–6; Forster, *Debates*, p. 346; Clarke, *Lectures*, p. vi.   [38] George Dawson, *Biographical Lectures* (1886), p. 71.

which, when Cromwell died . . . all was over for many a day'.[39] Smith's words incorporate the supposition, which seems to have been widespread in the nineteenth century, that the protectorate had been a time of popular prosperity which the Restoration had cruelly terminated.[40]

In the eighteenth century, before populist interpretations of the civil wars had emerged, Cromwell, the breaker of parliaments, had been seen by republicans as the betrayer of the parliamentary cause. In the earlier and mid-nineteenth century he was occasionally seen, again because of his treatment of the nation's representatives at Westminster, as the betrayer of the popular cause. Much more often, however, he came to seem its champion. He had 'belonged to the people', from whom he had 'sprung' and for whose 'drift' he had 'an unerring instinct'.[41] In the Restoration and the eighteenth century, writers had often been dazzled by the rise of Cromwell, a commoner, to sovereignty, but they could not approve of it. Frequently they derided his lowly origins, mocked the alleged connection of his family with the brewing trade. To his nineteenth-century admirers, that affiliation became a matter of indifference where not of pride.[42] In recruiting and inspiring his troops, it was observed, he had set the claims of 'conscience', which crossed and challenged social frontiers, against the 'delusive' aristocratic values of 'honour' and 'chivalry'.[43] His encouragement of the Self-Denying Ordinance, the measure which forbade members of the Long Parliament to hold command in its armies and which removed a number of tepid military leaders from them, had been described in the eighteenth century as a 'corruption bill', an assault on placemen.[44] In the nineteenth century it was hailed as an attack on 'titled incapables' who had feared that, if the king lost battles, 'aristocracy would be in peril'.[45]

Many nineteenth-century admirers of Cromwell saw his virtues as middle-class ones. To Macaulay, he embodied 'the best qualities of the middling orders'.[46] Sometimes social images of him were rural and static.

---

[39] Goldwin Smith, *Three English Statesmen* (1867), p. 142.

[40] J. P. D. Dunbabin, 'Oliver Cromwell's Popular Image in Nineteenth-Century Britain', in J. S. Bromley and E. Kossman, eds., *Britain and the Netherlands*, 5 (1975), p. 148; Richardson, *Images of Oliver Cromwell*, p. 99; Ryals and Fielding, *Collected Letters of . . . Carlyle*, XVII, pp. 50, 68.

[41] *London and Westminster Review*, 33 (1839), p. 184; Samuel, 'Discovery of Puritanism', p. 220; John Forster, *Historical and Biographical Essays*, 2 vols. (London, 1858), I, p. 302.

[42] *London and Westminster Review*, 33 (1839), p. 233; Forster, *Statesmen*, IV, pp. 7–8; *The Nonconformist*, 19 February 1862, p. 161; Bray, *Life of Oliver Cromwell*, pp. 9–10; Andrew Fairbairn, *The New Sacerdotalism and the New Puritanism* (1885), pp. 6–7; Horne, 'Cromwell Tercentenary', p. 124; J. K. McConachie, *Oliver Cromwell. Christian and Patriot* (1899), pp. 4–5; cf. Forster, *Statesmen*, IV, pp. 7–8.

[43] Wilson, *Oliver Cromwell*, p. 79; Clarke, *Lectures*, pp. 207–8 (cf. pp. 130–1).

[44] *Gentleman's Magazine*, 2 (1732), p. 645.   [45] Dawson, *Lectures*, pp. 76, 81.

[46] Macaulay, *Essays*, I, p. 52.

To Carlyle he was a 'solid farmer'.[47] Sometimes he was portrayed as a self-made man, a witness to the merits of self-help and social improvement.[48] The readiness of the protectorate to recruit its leaders and advisers from a wide range of talent and opinion, which had earlier been seen as a mark of political magnanimity or wisdom or dexterity,[49] now answered to the Victorian demand for the appointment of the state's servants on grounds of merit rather than social rank.[50]

Writers who emphasised Cromwell's middle-class credentials tended to think of the middle class, in the seventeenth and nineteenth century alike, as the ally or senior partner of the working class[51] (or at least of its more respectable or aspirational elements[52]). Against 'the tripartite league of the king, the noble, and the priest',[53] the Roundheads had stood for 'popular privilege', for 'the people of England', for 'the despised yeomanry and mechanics'.[54] In 1846 the popular lecturer Edmund Clarke, adopting that perspective, declared that Cromwell had 'infused the loftiest energy into the common people, and showed that there was a soul in the plebeian, and a might in his arm, before which the aristocrat and his retainer were as dry twigs before the blast'.[55] Clarke's audience belonged to a great movement of middle-class and working-class discussion of Cromwell which arose in the 1840s and persisted in the ensuing decades. Debating societies and Mechanics Institutes and Mutual Improvement Societies gathered to re-live the Puritan Revolution and to assess the protector's character and stature and motives and achievements. In 1852 the Watlington Mutual Improvement Society, after a debate which had lasted seven evenings and produced, according to the *Oxford Chronicle*, speeches of 'great research, power and eloquence', resolved that 'a better Christian' than Cromwell, 'a more noble-minded spirit, a greater warrior, a more constant man has scarcely ever appeared on the face of the earth'.[56] Comparable meetings have been noticed in many parts of the

---

[47] Carlyle, *Letters and Speeches*, I, p. 114; Samuel, 'Discovery of Puritanism', pp. 213–14. Cf. Dawson, *Lectures*, p. 76; Karsten, *Patriot-Heroes*, p. 147.

[48] Richardson, *Images of Oliver Cromwell*, p. 102.

[49] William Harris, *An Historical and Critical Account of . . . Oliver Cromwell* (1763), pp. 421–5; Isaac Mann, *Twelve Lectures on Ecclesiastical History and Nonconformity* (1829), pp. 400, 422n.; cf. Macaulay, *Essays*, I, p. 52.

[50] J. M. W., *The Coming Cromwell* (1871), p. 39; Smith, *Three English Statesmen*, p. 89. Cf. Godwin, *History of the Commonwealth*, III, p. 442; S. R. Gardiner, *Oliver Cromwell* (1901), p. 282.

[51] Wilson, *Oliver Cromwell*, p. 178; Karsten, *Patriot-Heroes*, p. 143; cf. Alessandro Gavazi, *Justice to Oliver Cromwell* (1859), p. 14.   [52] Cf. *The Congregationalist*, 2 (1873), p. 49.

[53] Clark, *Lectures*, p. vii. Cf. *London and Westminster Review*, 28 (1837), p. 224; *The Free Church Chronicle* (1899), p. 153.

[54] Clarke, *Lectures*, p. vi; Cromwell, *Oliver Cromwell*, pp. 86–7; cf. *London and Westminster Review*, 33 (1839), p. 184.   [55] Clarke, *Lectures*, p. 3.

[56] *Oxford Chronicle*, 14 February 1852, p. 8.

country, but above all in northern towns and cities.[57] It was in the north
that the heavy demand for library books on the Cromwellian period was
recorded,[58] and in the north too that a touring exhibition of a painting of
Cromwell refusing parliament's offer of the crown in 1657 caused a sensa-
tion in 1859–61.[59]

IV

In the first half or so of the nineteenth century, Cromwellianism was predominantly secular. Cromwell was admired less often because of his
Puritanism than in spite of it. The religious element of the Roundhead
cause was sometimes commended as a stimulus to the pursuit of civic
virtue or civil liberty,[60] but not for itself, still less for what its eighteenth-
and early nineteenth-century critics called its 'enthusiasm'. To the debat-
ers at Watlington in 1852, Cromwell's 'enthusiasm' remained an obstacle
to admiration for him.[61] But the mood was changing. By the end of the
century his 'enthusiasm' seemed a virtue. High and late Victorian
Cromwellianism is largely, perhaps mainly, a movement of religious
Nonconformity, the heir of Puritanism. Over the first half of the century,
while individual Nonconformists – Thomas Price, Charles Mann,
William Jones, Robert Vaughan – contributed significantly (if also tenta-
tively) to the favourable reappraisal of Cromwell's character, there was no
collective enterprise of Dissent on his behalf. Nonconformists played
little part in the agitation for a statue in 1845, a movement which seems to
have caught them unawares.[62] The contrast with the tercentenary celebrations of April 1899, which Nonconformists appropriated for themselves, measures the change.

Cromwell spoke to two Nonconformist denominations above all. He
was 'the hero saint of all true Baptists and Congregationalists'.[63] Since
the Restoration, those had been the sects most grateful for the toleration
he had provided for the range of Puritan belief. Yet they had been wary of
invoking his name. In the early nineteenth century they remained so.
They knew how gravely the cause of liberty of conscience had been
damaged since 1660, and could be damaged now, by memories of his
radical politics. Since the civil wars, the weight of Tory and Anglican

---

[57] The 'Nineteenth-Century Cromwell' archive is the best source for that movement; and
see Samuel, 'Discovery of Puritanism', p. 207.

[58] Karsten, *Patriot-Heroes*, p. 145; *'Evidence taken before the Select Committee on Public
Libraries 15 May 1849' (material contributed by Edward Royle to the 'Nineteenth-
Century Cromwell' archive).   [59] Samuel, 'Discovery of Puritanism', p. 214.

[60] Godwin, *History of the Commonwealth*, III, pp. 443–4, IV, p. 584; cf. Macaulay, *History*, I,
p. 17.   [61] *Oxford Chronicle*, 14 February 1852, p. 8.

[62] *The Nonconformist*, 15 October 1845, p. 709.   [63] *The Baptist*, 4 May 1877.

historiography had equated Dissent with regicide and republicanism, which were blamed on its 'enthusiasm' and 'fanaticism'. Early nineteenth-century Congregationalist historians, William Orme at their head, strove to break that link: to show that Congregationalism (or Independency) had been hijacked by Charles I's judges, for whose deed the Congregationalist principle bore no responsibility.[64] Nonconformists who committed themselves to political causes in the decades around 1800 encountered widespread opposition from their fellows, both on spiritual and on prudential grounds, to the mixing of religion with politics.[65]

Though such disapproval persisted across the nineteenth century, its base became ever narrower. Gradually Dissent was politicised, by the struggle for, and by the advances of, political enfranchisement and religious and educational emancipation. In 1873 *The Congregationalist* declared that 'the least active and satisfactory members of the Church are, for the most part, those who have a pious horror of strong political views and decided political action'.[66] The swelling of Nonconformist political radicalism brought a reassessment of Dissent's political past. Nonconformity, its more militant adherers decided, had dwelled too much on its history since 1660, too little on its period of Cromwellian triumph. It had been too proud of its endurance under persecution during the Restoration, too grateful for the limited gains won for Dissent in 1689 by the Toleration Act of 1689 and by Whig patronage thereafter. *The Congregationalist*, calling in 1873 for an end to two centuries of humiliating subordination, looked behind them 'to those sublime days when our forefathers held sway in England. If we have served under Somers, Walpole, Fox, Grey, and Russell, we have reigned with Cromwell.'[67] Where early nineteenth-century Independents had disowned the contribution of their denomination to Puritan rule, late nineteenth-century

[64] *Works of John Owen*, ed. T. Russell, 21 vols. (1826) I, memoir by Orme, pp. 66–7, 71; Robert Vaughan, *Memorials of the Stuart Dynasty*, 2 vols. (1831), II, pp. 183–4, 258–60; Robert Vaughan, *Religious Parties in England* (1839), p. 71; *Congregational Magazine*, 15 (1832), pp. 756–8. On the same theme see *Select Tracts relating to the Civil Wars*, ed. Francis Maseres, 2 vols. (1815), I, pp. xvii–xviii; Cromwell, *Oliver Cromwell*, p. 202n.; *London and Westminster Review*, 8 (1827), pp. 334–5, 339; Mann, *Twelve Lectures*, p. 395; Thomas Lathbury, *Oliver Cromwell or The Old and New Dissenters* (1862), pp. 2, 10; Lang, *Victorians and the Stuart Heritage*, pp. 16–17, 78, 95; Samuel, 'Discovery of Puritanism', p. 204.

[65] On Nonconformity and politics see especially G. I. T. Machin, *Politics and the Churches in Great Britain 1832 to 1868* (Oxford, 1977); Richard Helmstadter, 'The Nonconformist Conscience', in Peter Marsh, ed., *The Conscience of the Victorian State* (New York, 1979), pp. 135–72; D. W. Bebbington, *The Nonconformist Conscience. Chapel and Politics, 1870–1914* (London, 1982). There is invaluable material on the same subject in the contributions by Clyde Binfield and K. R. M. Short to the 'Nineteenth-Century Cromwell' archive. (A glimpse of nineteenth-century Nonconformist Cromwellianism from an unusual angle is supplied by Hilaire Belloc, *Oliver Cromwell* (1927), p. 77.)

[66] *The Congregationalist*, 2 (1873), p. 112.   [67] *Ibid.*, p. 50.

ones were glad to remember the era when Independency 'ruled the destinies of England'.[68]

In and around the tercentenary year it was mainly political militants who wrote biographies and studies of Cromwell. It was they who paid warmest tribute to the protector's 'clear recognition of our fundamental principles'.[69] At the tercentenary, one ardent Cromwellian maintained that Christianity was 'worthless, unless it led to practical religion on this earth'. He condemned the 'miserable', 'selfish' idea, which 'finds no support in the Bible', that 'religion only consists in ensuring the safe passage to heaven of your own soul, leaving the world to welter in the mire'.[70] At the commemoration of the tercentenary at the City Temple, that 'Nonconformist cathedral', an event organised by the National Council of the Evangelical Free Churches, allusions to contemporary political evils produced crescendos of acclamation. No-one could remember such excitement in the building. The principal preacher, Joseph Parker (soon to become chairman of the Congregational Union), was 'renowned for his strong language', which he now applied, in a manner 'worthy of the Cromwellian Puritans', 'to men who sit in high places'. He electrified the congregation by calling, in a house of God, for the return of the Liberals to power.[71]

Other speakers and writers used the commemoration to address a range of contemporary evils: drink, gambling, prostitution, poverty. Most of all there was the fresh wave of 'Puseyism' that had gathered strength in recent years. Anti-popery and anti-tractarianism had always been potent forces within Victorian Cromwellianism, but never stronger than in the celebrations of 1899, of which Cromwell's 'anti-Ritualism', and the sinister influence (in the seventeenth and nineteenth centuries alike) of 'priestcraft', supplied the most persistent theme. For if Cromwell had saved the nation from civil tyranny, so had he 'rescued the English race from popery'.[72] Fierce applause greeted comparisons between his resistance to the 'persecuting sacerdotalism' of Archbishop Laud and the present-day struggle of 'imperilled Protestantism' against 'the threatened return of Romanism'.[73]

---

[68] Fairbairn, *New Sacerdotalism*, p. 6; cf. W. B. Selbie, *The Life of Andrew Martin Fairbairn* (1914), p. 169.

[69] *Proceedings of the Fourth National Council*, p. 220; cf. *Daily News*, 26 April 1899, p. 8.

[70] Aveling, *Cromwell and Puritans*, pp. 27, 30–2. Cf. *Proceedings of the Fourth National Council*, p. 278; Bebbington, *Nonconformist Conscience*, p. 12 (on the Cromwellian C. S. Horne).

[71] *Daily News*, 26 April 1899, p. 8; *The Times*, 26 April 1899, p. 12; William Adamson, *The Life of the Reverend Joseph Parker* (1902), pp. 301–3.

[72] *The Times*, 26 April 1899, p. 12.

[73] *Daily News*, 20 April 1899, p. 6; 26 April 1899, p. 8; 28 April 1899, p. 7; *Methodist Times*, 4 May 1899, p. 307; *Free Church Chronicle*, 1 (1899), p. 154. Cf. *The Congregationalist*, 2

Late nineteenth-century Nonconformist admirers of Cromwell, recognising their duty to 'work for England and the world precisely as he did', urged each other to 'awake' to meet that challenge. They told themselves that Cromwell was 'the man of the hour', that in spirit he was 'alive' or 'living now', or that 'living Cromwells' were needed now.[74] In 1902 the National Council of the Evangelical Free Churches, outraged by the Anglican bias of the Education Bill of that year, heard its leaders warn the government to expect 'noble instances of stubborn and heroic resistance', even a readiness to 'die', from men whose 'proud boast' was to be 'descendants of men like Oliver Cromwell'.[75]

The Cromwellianism of militant Nonconformity was confrontational and divisive. 'There are two Englands', commemorators of the tercentenary in Cromwell's native Huntingdon were told, 'the England of Ethelred Unready, William Rufus, Bloody Mary and Charles II' and 'the England of Alfred, Harold, good Queen Bess, and Oliver Cromwell. To which do you belong?' 'Ringing cheers answered "Oliver's! Cromwell's!"'[76] Nonconformist Cromwellians claimed to speak for 'the biggest half of the nation', for 'the great bulk of the people'.[77] The demand for a statue of Cromwell, of 'the Puritan king', of England's 'uncrowned king',[78] was a call for the recognition of a body of the population which had hitherto been oppressed but which was now ready to insist that 'the boot is on the other leg'.[79]

Yet within the stridency of Nonconformist Cromwellianism of and around 1899 there are hints of unease. By 1880 the battles for the emancipation of Dissent had been almost wholly won. Thereafter Dissent began to lose something of its momentum, of its sense of direction, even of its distinctive culture. There is a sense, as the Nonconformist Cromwellians of the late Victorian period seek the attention of young hearers and readers,[80] that tomorrow's audience is being offered yesterday's message. To the dismay of militants, much of Nonconformity was being

---

(1873), p. 51; F. A. Inderwick, *The Interregnum* (1891), p. 1; William Willis, *Cromwell and the Vaudois* (1895), p. 31; Aveling, *Cromwell and Puritans*, pp. 56, 59; *Proceedings of the Fourth National Council*, p. 11.

[74] Horton, *Oliver Cromwell*, ep. ded.; *Proceedings of the Fourth National Council*, pp. 222, 277, 278; *The Times*, 26 April 1899, p. 12; *Methodist Times*, 4 May 1899, p. 307; Adamson, *Life of Parker*, p. 302.

[75] *National Conference of Free Church Councils on the Education Bill* (1902), pp. 6–7.

[76] *Methodist Times*, 4 May 1899, p. 307.

[77] *Proceedings of the Fourth National Council*, p. 278.

[78] For those phrases see Carlyle, *Letters and Speeches*, III, p. 219; Wilson, *Oliver Cromwell*, preface; Bayne, *Chief Actors*, p. 331; Aveling, *Cromwell and Puritans*, p. 31; *Free Church Chronicle*, 1 (1899), p. 154; C. H. Spurgeon's *Autobiography . . . by his Wife*, 4 vols. (1897–1900), III, pp. 189–90.   [79] *Proceedings of the Fourth National Council*, p. 278.

[80] Horton, *Oliver Cromwell*, ep. ded.

assimilated into conventional society. The Nonconformist commemorators of the tercentenary attacked enemies not only without but within. In particular they condemned prosperous Nonconformist businessmen and politicians, 'milk-and-water men',[81] who had distanced themselves from distinctively Nonconformist causes.

Other grounds of unease are visible too. For all its fervour, the commemoration in the City Temple, as Nonconformists themselves noticed, was 'too much a middle-class affair'.[82] In the Cromwellianism of the mid-century – most conspicuously perhaps in that of Edward Miall – Dissenting aspirations had occasionally merged with egalitarian ones. By the late nineteenth century, for all the populist language of militant Nonconformity, and for all the presence of socialists in Nonconformist ranks, barriers of class and purpose divided the two movements.[83] Now that the bourgeoisie, rather than the aristocracy, was seen as the principal enemy of the working man, socialists looked elsewhere for seventeenth-century heroes. They found them in the Levellers, whom Cromwell had ruthlessly crushed. Cromwell, Carlyle's 'solid farmer', was now deemed to have been a 'capitalist farmer'.[84] At the tercentenary, Nonconformists remembered that Cromwell had defended 'the rights of the people'.[85] Socialists mocked that perspective, deriding men who 'take as their hero the bourgeois and narrow-minded Cromwell', that political instrument of 'the powerful profiteering class'. Socialist antagonism to Cromwell was antagonism to Nonconformity too. The 'pious, prayerful Cromwell', socialists alleged, had represented at once 'the chapel' and 'the till', those twin bases of Nonconformist power and sanctimony. He had stood for 'the Nonconformist conscience', for 'highly respectable' and 'hypocritically ascetic Puritans'. He had pulled down maypoles, an offensive initiative in the eyes of socialists critical of the 'municipal Puritanism' that was suppressing popular pleasures in their own time.[86] He had introduced the wretched 'British Sunday', an institution which, during the tercentenary commemorations, Nonconformists took occasion to defend from its decadent assailants.[87] At those commemorations, socialist organisations were conspicuous by their absence.

---

[81] *The Times*, 26 April 1899, p. 12.   [82] *Methodist Times*, 4 May 1899, p. 307.

[83] Helmstadter, 'Nonconformist Conscience', pp. 152, 167.

[84] Henry Hyndman, *The Historical Basis of English Socialism* (1883), p. 66.

[85] *Free Church Chronicle*, 1 (1899), p. 153.

[86] *The People's Press*, 5 July 1890; Samuel, 'Discovery of Puritanism', p. 223. Cromwell was nonetheless remembered as the champion of common rights in the Fens: Gardiner, *Oliver Cromwell*, pp. 11–12; C. H. Firth, *Oliver Cromwell and the Rule of the Puritans in England* (Oxford, repr. 1968), p. 34; G. M. Trevelyan, *England under the Stuarts* (1904), p. 251n.

[87] *Daily News*, 26 April 1999, p. 8. For the socialist complaints see J. Morison Davidson, *Annals of Toil*, 4 vols. (1899–8), II, pp. 206–7, 213, 222, 275; *The People's Press* 5 July 1890;

The Cromwellianism of militant Nonconformists, challenged from the Left, was also questioned and modified to their Right. There was a side of Victorian Cromwellianism which, far from being confrontational, was consensual, and which spoke not of 'two Englands' but of one. Sometimes those competing tendencies can be found at odds within a single Nonconformist mind. Sometimes they set Nonconformists against each other. When they did so, the more conciliatory Nonconformists could share more ground with Cromwellians outside the Nonconformist fold than within it.

The eighteenth century had for the most part repudiated the nation's Puritan past. The nineteenth century gradually, and with growing confidence, reclaimed it. Nonconformity led that movement of recovery but could not contain it. Over the later nineteenth century the Puritan inheritance became not merely a sectarian and radical property but – in the words of the great late-Victorian historian, Cromwell's biographer S. R. Gardiner, himself a man with a Nonconformist past – 'the most precious possession of the nation'.[88] Nonconformists revered Cromwell's 'earnestness' and his 'moral' sense, and rejoiced to think that those qualities had once been found in a ruler of England. Yet the same virtues won Cromwell admirers across the range of upright opinion in high and late Victorian England. Not much had been said about Cromwell's moral earnestness during the campaign for a statue of him in the 1840s. By the 1860s and 1870s it was widely and fondly commended. His blameless private life, his habits of prayer and private devotion, his godliness on his death-bed, had, it is true, long been acknowledged. To earlier generations, however, those merits had been hard to square with the ruthless energy of his public career. Now, outside as well as inside Nonconformity, they seemed of a piece with his life and character. Outside the Nonconformist fold, Cromwellians hoped for a modernised Puritanism, which in countering the evils of 'this sensual and avaricious age' would retain the 'high seriousness' of its seventeenth-century predecessor but avoid its 'narrowness'.[89] Within Nonconformity there were many who, stung by Matthew Arnold's charge of philistinism, were concerned to deny that the Puritan movement, past or present, was narrow. With other Victorians, Nonconformists emphasised Cromwell's 'largeness' of mind

---

Writings and Speeches of Oliver Cromwell, ed. W. C. Abbott, 4 vols. (Cambridge, Mass., 1937–47), IV, p. 896; Blair Worden, 'The Levellers in History and Memory, *c.* 1660–1960', in Michael Mendle, ed., *The Putney Debates 1647–1997* (Cambridge, forthcoming).

[88] Gardiner, *Cromwell's Place*, p. 106. Lang, *Victorians and the Stuart Heritage*, ch. 4, writes most interestingly on Gardiner and 'the search for a national consensus'. The Victorian appreciation of the Puritan inheritance is luminously described by Samuel, 'Discovery of Puritanism'.   [89] *★Daily Chronicle*, 14, 15 November 1899.

or heart or soul, which separated him from his less enlightened or more 'narrow' contemporaries. They underlined – indeed overstated – his love of music and his interest in the arts.

Alongside, and sometimes in conflict with, the Cromwellianism of militant Nonconformity, there grew up what was called a 'moderating' approach to Cromwell.[90] S. R. Gardiner was a key figure in that movement. Other leading contributors – though their emphases were sometimes different – were J. R. Green and the Liberal cabinet minister John Morley, another biographer of Cromwell. Those men applauded Cromwell's ethical and religious aspirations. They admired, even revered him as a man of action and courage and resolution. It was his sword, they agreed, that had saved England from political and spiritual tyranny.[91] But unlike militant Nonconformists they could not take pleasure in the violent radicalism of the revolution. Gardiner believed, as Macaulay had done, that Cromwell had always preferred 'to walk in the ways of legality'.[92] But with Macaulay too he maintained that Cromwell's departures from those methods had been counter-productive where not disastrous.[93] Gardiner concluded that Cromwell's practical achievements, astounding and often indispensable as they were, had been essentially negative and destructive.[94] Over the nineteenth century the protector's admirers had insisted that the course of English history since the seventeenth century would have been incomparably healthier had he lived another ten or twenty years or been succeeded by an equal spirit, and if the calamity of the Restoration had thus been averted.[95] The 'moderating' historians, by contrast, questioned the durability of the protectoral regime. They also pointed to the presence of moral weaknesses alongside its virtues.[96]

Where radical Nonconformists steered memories away from the Restoration towards the Puritan rule that had preceded it, Green and Gardiner and Morley maintained that Puritanism had proved (in Gardiner's words) 'of better service when it was relegated from the exercise of power to the employment of influence'.[97] Power, they thought, had

[90] *Daily News*, 15 September 1900, p. 8, and 19 October 1900, p. 6.
[91] See too Firth, *Oliver Cromwell*, p. 478.   [92] Gardiner, *Oliver Cromwell*, pp. 69–70.
[93] Gardiner, *Cromwell's Place*, p. 4.
[94] *Ibid.*, pp. 47, 78, 104; John Morley, *Oliver Cromwell* (1901), pp. 3–4; cf. *Daily News*, 26 April 1899, p. 8.
[95] Godwin, *History of the Commonwealth*, IV, p. 342; Macaulay, *Essays*, I, pp. 53, 183; Forster, *Historical and Biographical Essays*, I, pp. 335–6; Goldwin Smith, *The United Kingdom*, 2 vols. (1899), I, p. 641; Bayne, *Chief Actors*, p. 429; *Daily News* 16 March 1900, p. 6; William Arthur, *Heroes* (1902), p. 145; Harrison, *Memories and Thoughts*, p. 74.
[96] Gardiner, *Cromwell's Place*, p. 101; Morley, *Oliver Cromwell*, p. 457; cf. Lang, *Victorians and the Stuart Heritage*, p. 191.
[97] Green, *History of the English People*, III, pp. 313–14; Gardiner, *Cromwell's Place*, p. 112; Morley, *Oliver Cromwell*, p. 6.

given too much encouragement to the narrow and fanatical side of the movement. The effort to impose a strenuousness of conduct beyond the nation's moral means had obliged Cromwell to rule without the concurrence of national feeling, that essential basis of lasting and improving statesmanship. But after 1660, Gardiner judged, Puritanism, which had previously been the creed of a party, had permeated the moral sensibility of the country at large, 'penetrating and informing its conquerors'.[98] Out of it there had emerged that earnestness of principle which, when the English remembered it, remained their finest quality.

From that standpoint, Cromwell's heroism in action was but one face of a seventeenth-century movement of the human spirit which had also borne a number of other, gentler aspects. As the respect of Victorians for seventeenth-century Puritanism became more ample and secure, so Puritanism came to seem to have had many parts, spiritual, literary, pastoral, theological, political, each making its own contribution to a legacy of rich diversity. While some militant Cromwellians liked to think of their hero in lonely eminence, towering above his contemporaries, it became more common to place and assess him in the company of other Puritans, sometimes divines such as John Howe and Thomas Goodwin, sometimes the writers Milton and Bunyan.[99] What he shared with those men was the Puritan character, an attribute which was judged to have been of more durable and uplifting influence than his achievements. As Gardiner put it, 'the man – it is ever so with the noblest – was greater than his work'.[100]

Gardiner observed that Cromwell had become 'the national hero of the nineteenth century'.[101] There was some resentment at the success of the militant Nonconformists in turning the tercentenary celebrations, which ought to have been a 'national' movement, into a 'sectarian' one. It was 'petty and pitiable', complained an Anglican clergyman, 'for an extreme section of the Protestant party to identify the memory of the great Cromwell with itself'.[102] The response of Nonconformists to the broadening of Cromwell's popularity was divided. Should they cling to their vision of him as 'the typical free-churchman'? Or should they 'admit that they have no monopoly of the Lord Protector', and portray him as a

---

[98] Gardiner, *Cromwell's Place*, p. 106.
[99] See e.g. Dawson, *Biographical Lectures*, p. 68; John Tulloch, *English Puritanism and its Leaders* (1861); George Gilfillan, *Modern Christian Heroes* (1869); *Congregational Year Book 1863*, p. 202; Fairbairn, *New Sacerdotalism*, pp. 6–8; Morley, *Oliver Cromwell*, p. 6; and the Edwardian groups of stained-glass portraits of Puritans in the chapel of Mansfield College, Oxford (chosen by Fairbairn: a subject on which I am grateful for the advice of Elaine Kaye, the historian of Mansfield College); in Emmanuel United Reform Church in Cambridge; and in Fairhaven (Lytham St Annes) United Reform Church.   [100] Gardiner, *Oliver Cromwell*, p. 315.
[101] Karsten, *Patriot-Heroes*, p. 152.   [102] *The Times*, 28 April 1899, p. 8.

'typical patriot' or – with Gardiner and with a broad range of opinion – a 'typical Englishman'?[103]

There was one point, at least, on which Cromwellians inside and outside Nonconformity could easily agree. Cromwell had been tolerant in religion. This was the principal subject on which nineteenth-century admirers of Cromwell's domestic administration saw reflections of their own values and preoccupations. It was not the only one. There is the attention given to the attempts by him and his colleagues to reform the Court of Chancery and the laws governing imprisonment for debt.[104] There is the somewhat strained conviction that he hastened the advance of modern communications by improving roads and the postal service.[105] There is the equally questionable supposition that he was wedded to the ideal of free trade (though late in the nineteenth century, as politicians and thinkers came to terms with new ideas of state intervention, he became 'the first statesman who formed the concept of colonisation as an organised effort by the state'[106]). But it was in relation to his achievement of religious liberty that he looked most like an enlightened Victorian.

Admittedly Cromwell, in Victorian eyes, had not been tolerant enough. Even Nonconformists acknowledged (for the most part) that he ought to have extended toleration to Roman Catholics.[107] For though Nonconformity was anti-popish, it often saw English Catholicism as a fellow-victim both of the spirit of persecution and of the Anglican monopoly. There was some embarrassment, too, at Cromwell's proscription of Anglicanism. His instrument of proscription, the system of Triers and Ejectors, though it fascinated the Victorians as an early experiment in boards and commissions, and though it commanded widespread nineteenth-century respect as an attempt to improve the quality of the ministry, caused unease on two counts. Nonconformists who favoured the separation of church and state were sometimes troubled by the Erastianism of Cromwell's system. At the same time the Triers and Ejectors' ill treatment of Anglican divines offered a counter-weapon to modern apologists for the Church of England. Anglicans found the Cromwellian system a particularly useful point of reference during the

[103] For that dilemma see *Free Church Chronicle* (1899), p. 153; *Methodist Times*, 4 May 1899, p. 307; Horne, 'Cromwell Tercentenary', p. 129; *Daily News*, 26 April 1899, p. 6. Cf. Horton, *Oliver Cromwell*, ep. ded. and pp. 3–4.

[104] See. e.g. John Lingard, *A History of England*, 8 vols. (1819–30), VII, p. 278; Cromwell, *Oliver Cromwell*, pp. 358–9; Forster, *Statesmen*, III, pp. 294–5; V, pp. 204–8; Clarke, *Lectures*, pp. 177–98; Smith, *Three English Statesmen*, pp. 111–12.

[105] Inderwick, *Interregnum*, p. 317; J. A. Picton, *Oliver Cromwell* (1882), pp. 2, 411. Cf. Godwin, *History of the Commonwealth*, III, p. 489; *Macaulay, *History*, I, pp. 24–5.

[106] *Daily News*, 15 September 1900, p. 8.

[107] Vaughan, *Memorials of the Stuart Dynasty*, II, pp. 244–5; Benjamin Evans, *The Early English Baptists*, 2 vols. (1862–4), II, pp. 193–4; cf. Macaulay, *Essays*, I, p. 37.

controversy between Church and Dissent in 1862, when Nonconformists commemorated the bicentenary of the Great Ejection, that high point of Anglican intolerance.

It was not difficult to find explanations of the limits of Cromwell's tolerance. He had shared, it was decided, the limitations of his age. Or (more commonly) he had been ahead of that age, an age which had not understood the principles of religious toleration or perceived the inevitable limits of doctrinal certainty. Victorians often supposed Cromwell to have been in favour of universal toleration but to have been unable to carry the nation or his followers with him; or to have been thwarted by political circumstances or by the obstinate political disloyalties of worshippers outside the Puritan fold. What was overlooked was Cromwell's Calvinist theology and his insistence on its observance. He tolerated diversity in Puritan worship and ecclesiology, but not in faith.[108] Victorian Dissent, retreating from the creed of Calvinism towards a religion of conduct, sought the emancipation of denominations rather than of doctrines, and thus dwelt on Cromwell's denominational tolerance. Outside Nonconformity, Victorians were still readier to overlook his doctrinal rigour. In that as in other respects he became less a Calvinist than a Victorian liberal.

Yet if Cromwell's tolerance was widely accepted and admired, there was also a broad perception, particularly outside Nonconformity, that too few Puritans had shared that instinct. It was the superiority of Cromwell's position on toleration to that of other Puritans that drew most comment. Across the century, and especially near its end, there were voices ready to ask whether Puritanism had really contributed more to the principles of toleration than the latitudinarian wing of seventeenth-century Anglicanism. And while Cromwell's admirers instinctively thought of the religious liberty he had sought as the natural partner of civil liberty, there were liberals prepared to suggest that modern principles of civil liberty owed more to Locke or Jefferson or even Walpole than to Cromwell or his cause.

V

The variety of the sentiments that attached themselves to Cromwellianism in the late Victorian period is a sign of the strength and breadth of the movement. Yet anti-Cromwellianism persisted too. It came to the surface after the government's decision in 1899 to allow, without

[108] Blair Worden, 'Toleration and the Cromwellian Protectorate', *Studies in Church History*, 21 (1984), pp. 199–233.

formal parliamentary approval, the building of the statue at Westminster. There were protests from Tories in the Lords and Commons, while petitions against the statue attracted thousands of signatures across the land.[109] Demonological images of Cromwell continued to flourish, especially in some rural areas. It was easy enough, in 1899, to raise the old charge of ruthless hypocrisy against the 'military dictator' who had 'murdered his sovereign'.[110] The charge has often been raised since. During the twentieth century, various proposals to name roads or colleges after Cromwell were thwarted by irate local resistance.[111] Yet before that century's beginning, anti-Cromwellianism had generally been abandoned by thinking opinion. It had become, as it would remain, a fringe cause. 'All but a few fanatics', remarked *The Spectator* in 1899, 'regard' Cromwell 'as a great and noble Englishman'.[112] For two centuries the civil war divide had been kept alive by Tories and Whigs (or Liberals), by Anglicans and Dissenters. Now, at least across the broad middle ground of public opinion, it was fading.

The change is registered by the attitude of the Tory leadership to the erection of the statue at Westminster, which had been proposed four years earlier by the Liberal prime minister, Lord Rosebery. On taking power in 1895 the Tories agreed to the building of the statue, provided that Rosebery, rather than parliament, paid for it. In the subsequent debates on the statue, Salisbury and Balfour, while distancing themselves from the scheme and gently mocking it, supported it when it counted. Earlier, Cromwell had seemed to his detractors a dangerous force of destruction. His name had symbolised the threat that civil war or insurrection might come again. By the end of the century, when such anxieties had far receded, he no longer represented, to thinking opinion, anything to fear.[113] One MP was reminded by the parliamentary arguments over the statue in 1899 of the proceedings of a youthful debating society. It was, he thought, 'a blessed thing that this country can now devote itself to these abstract questions'.[114] Cromwell had been safely assimilated within a politically ecumenical conspectus of the nation's past, which was ready to honour 'great' men even when their goodness remained contested.[115] In 1844 the historian Henry Hallam, who, with Macaulay, was playing a critical role in the planning of the decoration of the new Houses of

---

[109] *Hansard*, 4th ser. 75, col. 1150; 77, cols. 749, 752, 756.

[110] *Ibid.*, 4th ser. 77, col. 750; 79, col. 950.

[111] Alan Smith, 'The Image of Cromwell in Folklore and Tradition', *Folk Lore*, 79 (1968), is the best source on the demonic Cromwell of the nineteenth and twentieth centuries.

[112] **Spectator*, 29 April 1899.   [113] Dunbabin, 'Oliver Cromwell's Popular Image', p. 158.

[114] *Hansard*, 4th ser. 79, col. 978; cf. T. H. Green, *Four Lectures on the English Revolution* (1912 edn), p. 50.   [115] *Hansard*, 4th ser. 34, cols. 1187, 1190; 79, cols. 964, 967.

Parliament,[116] hoped that the historical statues and paintings in the Palace would commemorate statesmen 'whose memory, now hallowed by time, we cherish with a more unanimous respect than contemporary passions always afford'.[117] In the 1840s no such consensus could have been secured for the commemoration of Cromwell. In 1845 the argument that Cromwell's greatness should be acknowledged even by his adversaries fell on deaf ears.[118] Yet in 1899 Balfour could successfully maintain that to reject the statue would be to 'carry ancient feuds very much too far'.[119]

Balfour's own attitude to Victorian Cromwellianism was tolerant rather than enthusiastic. Enthusiasm had nonetheless spread wide. It extended well beyond the chapels, and well beyond the earnest sentiment to be found outside Nonconformity. When Gardiner called Cromwell 'the national hero of the nineteenth century' he feared that it was not the protector's religion or morality that had won him that status. It was his achievements abroad. 'In recent years', Gardiner regretted to observe, 'it has become customary to extol Cromwell's foreign policy at the expense of his domestic.'[120] Gardiner did warm, with most Victorian commentators, to the ethical dimension of Cromwell's diplomacy, and particularly to the protector's intervention on behalf of the persecuted Vaudois in 1655. That episode was widely held, as was the broader Protestant thrust of his foreign policy, to have represented 'the highest impulses of the nation'.[121] Nonconformists, who liked to think of Cromwell's patriotism as the natural partner of his Puritanism,[122] were especially proud of his assistance to the Vaudois, a triumph of moral interventionism which they held up for imitation during the the debates over the Bulgarian atrocities of the 1870s and the Armenian ones of the 1890s.[123]

Yet if Nonconformists and 'moderate' Cromwellians could agree in praising the moral dimension of Cromwell's foreign policy, they were less comfortable when they detected an aggrandising element in his diplomacy. Here, thought Gardiner, Cromwell had deceived himself into

---

[116] House of Lords Sessional Papers, 'Fourth Report of the Commission on Fine Arts' (1845); 'Twelfth Report' (1861) (p. 8). [117] *Ibid.*, 'Third Report' (1844).

[118] *The Times*, 13 September 1845, p. 7, and 17 September 1845, p. 5; *Hampshire Telegraph*, 27 September 1845.

[119] *Hansard*, 4th ser. 79, col. 970; cf. *Hansard*, 4th ser. 34, col. 1187.

[120] Gardiner, *Cromwell's Place*, p. 100.

[121] Vaughan, *Memorials of the Stuart Dynasty*, II, pp. 228, 240ff.; J. H. Merle d'Aubigné, *The Protector* (Edinburgh, 1847), p. 26; Wilson, *Oliver Cromwell*, pp. 238–9; Smith, *Three English Statesmen*, pp. 132–4; F. W. Cornish, *The Life of Oliver Cromwell* (1882), pp. 348–50; Morley, *Oliver Cromwell*, p. 463.

[122] E.g. McConachie, *Oliver Cromwell. Christian and Patriot.*

[123] *Methodist Times*, 27 April 1899, p. 265, and 4 May 1999, p. 307; *The Times*, 28 April 1899, p. 8; *Congregational Year Book 1877*, p. 122; Richardson, *Images of Oliver Cromwell*, pp. 101–2; Samuel, 'Discovery of Puritanism', pp. 220–1.

regarding his own motives, which were essentially material, as moral. Yet, as Gardiner understood, the aggrandisement had become an essential aspect of his late-Victorian appeal. 'Even those who refuse to waste a thought on his spiritual aims', Gardiner complained, 'remember with gratitude his constancy of effort to make England great by land and sea; and it would be well for them also to be reminded of his no less constant efforts to make England worthy of greatness.'[124]

In the late nineteenth century, as so often in previous times, Cromwell's foreign triumphs won support across the party lines. Indeed in the age of Imperialism they were at least as likely to appeal to the Right as to the Left. 'There is scarcely a fossil Tory extant', observed the *Daily News* in 1900, 'who feels no pride in Cromwell, the soldier and statesman, whose patriotism was as deep as his religion.'[125] Cromwell's 'imperial purpose' and 'colonial policy', it was explained, had laid the foundations of the British Empire, while 'the spirit' which he 'engendered' had 'carried the British flag to the four corners of the earth'.[126] The late Victorian military campaigns, and especially the Boer War, produced a new fund of admiration for Cromwell. In earlier generations, few writers on him had shown an intense interest in the military campaigns of the 1640s, which seemed primitive or small-scale when set beside modern warfare.[127] Now his military stature and tactics commanded wide interest.[128] Nonconformists and other religious enthusiasts, eager for the moral and religious improvement of the British army, had their own reasons to commend the fighting qualities of Cromwell's godly soldiers.[129] Not only had Cromwell shaped the Empire. In its embryonic form he had preserved it. Above all he had preserved, through his campaigns in Scotland and Ireland, the unity (which Victorians sometimes exaggerated) of seventeenth-century Britain. His policy of union with Scotland and Ireland touched the concerns of the age of Unionism. It was thanks to Cromwell, explained

[124] Gardiner, *Cromwell's Place*, pp. 94–5; Gardiner, *Oliver Cromwell*, p. 318; Lang, *Victorians and the Stuart Heritage*, pp. 204–5.

[125] *Daily News*, 16 March 1900, p. 6.

[126] Firth, *Oliver Cromwell*, p. 386; T. S. Baldock, *Cromwell as a Soldier* (1899), p. 524. Cf. Clyde Binfield, *So Down To Prayers. Studies in English Nonconformity 1780–1920* (London, 1977), p. 233.

[127] Macaulay, *Essays*, I, p. 145; Nugent, *Hampden*, II, p. 171; cf. Morley, *Oliver Cromwell*, p. 184.

[128] W. G. Ross, *Oliver Cromwell and his 'Ironsides'* (1889); William Douglas, *Cromwell's Scotch Campaigns* (1898); Baldock, *Cromwell*; Horne, 'Cromwell Tercentenary', p. 132; S. Wilkinson, ed., *Cromwell to Wellington: Twelve Soldiers* (1899); Valerie Chancellor, *History for their Masters. Opinion in the English History Textbook* (Bath, 1970), pp. 73–4.

[129] Aveling, *Cromwell and Puritans*, p. 71; Samuel, 'Discovery of Puritanism', pp. 206, 219–20; cf. John Morley, 'Oliver Cromwell', *The Century Magazine*, 38 (1900), p. 892. Cromwell was hailed too as 'the true architect of our English navy' (Horne, 'Cromwell Tercentenary', p. 138).

C. H. Firth in 1900, that Britain had 'emerged from the chaos of the civil wars one strong state instead of three separate and hostile communities'.[130]

VI

Cromwellianism, having peaked at the end of the nineteenth century, thereafter entered a decline which, though uneven in pace and never complete, was soon conspicuous. Nonconformist enthusiasm shrank, or at least learned to keep its head down, during the first decade of the twentieth century, as Dissent predominantly retreated from political engagement and resumed its earlier spiritual priorities.[131] Though Nonconformist admiration for Cromwell would long persist, it had become essentially a preservative, even a nostalgic, rather than a proselytising or confrontational impulse. Meanwhile the gradual impact of academic history, which in the work of Gardiner and Firth brought to the Cromwellian period standards of scholarship that had reached medieval studies decades earlier, produced an insistence on contextual and chronological complexity before which moral simplicities and injunctions retreated. In 1929 W. C. Abbott's *Bibliography of Oliver Cromwell* was conceived almost as an epitaph, so sharp, and seemingly so final, had been the recent decline in the number of publications on Cromwell.[132] Five years later, principal writings on the Cromwellian era, Carlyle's *Letters and Speeches* among them, had reportedly gone out of print or become scarce.[133] Though modern parallels with Cromwell could still strike home, most notably in the age of dictators in the 1930s,[134] the passions of the previous century were rarely reignited. Over the twentieth century the English past often spoke to the present, but never as loudly or insistently as in the Victorians' relationship with Oliver Cromwell.

---

[130] Firth, *Oliver Cromwell*, p. 478. Cf. *The Liberal Unionist Scotsman*, 15 November 1899; Morley, *Oliver Cromwell*, p. 287; Lang, *Victorians and the Stuart Heritage*, p. 190; Trevelyan, *England under the Stuarts*, p. 320.
[131] Bebbington, *Nonconformist Conscience*, pp. 78ff.
[132] W. C. Abbott, *A Bibliography of Oliver Cromwell* (Cambridge, 1929), p. vii.
[133] F. H. Hayward, *The Unknown Cromwell* (London, 1934), p. 15.
[134] Richardson, *Images of Oliver Cromwell*, pp. 108–23.

6   Religion and politics in the *Quarterly Review*, 1809–1853

William Thomas

I

Everyone knows that the great nineteenth-century reviews offer the historian a rich source for studying the issues which agitated the educated classes in Victorian England, and most historians now know that in the *Wellesley Index* we have an unrivalled guide to the identity of their anonymous authors.[1] But their impact on the political process is still little explored. The old Namierite scepticism about the impact of theory and the theorists on politics has latterly been reinforced by an academic division of labour. Historians of politics and government already enjoy an unmanageably large range of sources. It seems quite reasonable to leave the conduct and influence of the higher journalism to students of literature. If you can study in detail the motives of men in power, why bother with those who, for all their eloquence and skill, can only comment after policy has been determined?

The answer, for the early and midnineteenth century at least, is that if one assumes such a division of functions, one is liable to miss a good deal. Politicians and men of letters mingled in the same clubs, the same salons, and the same country house parties. The reading public was small, the manipulation of opinion was still rudimentary, and a naive faith in the power of argument, and even in the effect of individual example, was widespread. Political office and its responsibilities were shouldered, broadly speaking, by the same class that read and wrote the reviews, and the 'classic gladiatorship' which marked its parliamentary eloquence had its counterpart in a literary convention that reviewers were custodians of a classical canon of literary taste who wrote with a patrician disdain for the hacks of Grub Street. High politics and reviewing were intimately related, and in this essay I want to illustrate that relationship in the case of the two great reviews, the *Edinburgh* and the *Quarterly;* more especially the latter.

Though they were rivals, their origins and hence their editorial tradi-

---

[1] Walter E Houghton, ed., and others, *The Wellesley Index to Victorian Periodicals, 1824–1900.* 5 vols. (Toronto and London, 1966–89).

tions were different. The *Edinburgh* was founded by four clever young men (three briefless barristers and an unbeneficed clergyman) primarily as a work of wide-ranging criticism, without political affiliation.[2] Of course the *literati* of Edinburgh patronised a culture which one must call whiggish, and Bagehot was right in a famous essay to say that the new review was the expression of the 'general, diversified, omnipresent information of the north' in which Scottish historians and philosophers were a dominant influence.[3] The *Edinburgh* distilled this Scottish culture. But it was an established literary and commercial success before it was associated with the Whig party in parliament, and even after 1808 when it may be said to have joined the opposition and the Edinburgh reviewers were in demand at Holland House, it was never slavishly the organ of the politicians. Jeffrey, its editor for its first twenty-seven years, was too conscious of the poor prospects of the Whig party, and he took care to recruit his writers from a wide range of talent; Tory, Whig and radical. In 1809 he lost the Tory contributors when the *Edinburgh* carried articles critical of the government's conduct of the war, but this did not much alter his conviction that it was literary merit, good writing, intelligent criticism, and a buoyant wit, and not politics which sold the review. One could say that the Whig party's long period in the wilderness from 1807 to 1830 reinforced this policy. The *Edinburgh* did not, before 1830, owe its authority to its proximity to ministerial circles or even to a reputation for enjoying the confidence of Whig leaders. This was in part because Whig leadership was weak and divided; but while Jeffrey was editor, his tact and firmness did not even allow Brougham, his most prolific contributor as well as the most vigorous opposition politician, to dictate the political line of the review. The *Edinburgh* was a Whig organ undoubtedly, but it was so by spontaneous agreement, not political self-interest; its loyalty was never suborned or uncritical. This is why, on Jeffrey's retirement from the editorship in 1829, his successor Macvey Napier was able, after a struggle, to resist Brougham's flagrant attempt to make the review the voice of the Whig government. Napier (supported by Macaulay and Empson) was able to call on an established editorial tradition of political independence which even a Whig Lord Chancellor could not break. Brougham's fall

---

[2] For its early years, John Clive, *Scotch Reviewers* (London, 1957) is still highly readable. For the editorship of Napier and the struggle with Brougham, Joanne Shattock, *Politics and Reviewers: the Edinburgh and the Quarterly in the Early Victorian Age* (London, 1989), pp. 24–37; for the philosophical ambience, Stefan Collini, Donald Winch, and John Burrow, *That Noble Science of Politics* (Cambridge, 1983), ch. 2. For political economy see Biancamaria Fontana, *Rethinking the Politics of Commercial Society, The Edinburgh Review 1802–32* (Cambridge, 1985), which supplies what Clive conspicuously lacks, the economic context.

[3] 'The First Edinburgh Reviewers', in *Literary Studies*, 2 vols. (Everyman edn) I, p. 22.

from power was in fact a sort of indirect victory for Napier and the *Edinburgh Review*. Napier might lose Brougham's literary facility, but in retaining (after a brief secession) Macaulay's contribution, he kept the greatest asset of the review for the next two decades.

The *Quarterly* by contrast was founded by friends of the government in 1809, to support the war in the Peninsula which was going badly. It was edited by an ardent Tory, William Gifford, who took his political direction from George Canning.[4] During his editorship it defended the actions of the government against its critics, radical as well as Whig. It is from Gifford's editorship that most of the *Quarterly*'s editorial traditions stem. The defence of the ancient constitution against subversion overflowed into literary criticism; since so many critics were rationalists and radicals, they were treated not as creative writers and artists but as enemies of order and morality. The critic's duty was to act as a kind of 'literary police', and this tradition was continued into the peace, the battle against French republicans and atheists being continued against their supposed sympathisers at home.[5] The tradition is captured by Byron's lines:

> Who killed John Keats?
> 'I', said the Quarterly,
> So savage and Tartarly;
> ''Twas one of my feats'.

The lines refer to Croker's notorious review of Keats' *Endymion*, and though the criticism is short and bland and did not kill the poet, they do illustrate a public perception of the review.[6] On Gifford's retirement in 1823, finding an editor to succeed him was a matter with a greater political resonance than was ever the case with the *Edinburgh*. Jeffrey retired not from ill-health, but because his judicial duties were incompatible with the editorship. Some such consideration also affected J. T. Coleridge, Gifford's successor, whose short tenure was partly due to concern for his own professional reputation. But his successor, J. G. Lockhart, was promoted by the *Quarterly*'s most distinguished contributor, Sir Walter Scott, his father-in-law, and his credentials were as much political as literary. Lockhart's problems, even more than Napier's, illustrate the close association of politics with literature.

Lockhart lived all his adult life in Scott's shadow, and his most famous work was his biography of Scott. Biographers have found it hard to detach

---

[4] For Gifford, see M. F. Brightfield, *John Wilson Croker* (London, 1940), ch. vi. But his editorship is covered not in the *Wellesley Index* but in Hill and Helen Shine, *The Quarterly Review under Gifford: Identification of Contributors 1809–1824* (Chapel Hill 1949).

[5] *Q[uarterly] R[eview]*, 2 no. 3 (August 1809), review of Maria Edgeworth's *Tales of Fashionable Life*, p. 146 by Gifford and H. J. Stephen.

[6] *Ibid.*, 19, no. 37 (April 1818), pp. 204–8

him from the antiquarian bric-a-brac of Abbotsford and treat him as an author in his own right.[7] He was the son of a presbyterian minister in Scotland and his family had connections with the border gentry which he may have idealised in his autobiographical novel *Reginald Dalton*.[8] The novel also draws on his period as an Oxford undergraduate, where he had a firsthand experience of the social divisions of English life. Whether, like his hero, he had claims to a landed estate which were realised only in the novel, I do not know. He certainly identified with the outlook of the border gentry and in 1820 he did duty with the Midlothian yeomanry to repress an outbreak of industrial unrest in Lanarkshire.[9] His mixture of pride in the Scottish system of parochial education and his fear of popular revolt is well expressed in a letter of December 1821 where he boasts of the high literacy of the lowland shepherds but adds that among the weavers of Glasgow reading has brought 'demoralisation, disloyalty and infidelity'. 'There Tom Paine is still the apostle of light and unshorn artificers presume to chuckle over the jokes of Candide and the Philosophical Dictionary.'[10] His early literary forays suggest another division of his allegiance. He could not decide whether as the son of a humble clergyman he should earn his living by writing, or aspire to higher status as befitted 'a member of one of the oldest families' in Lanarkshire.[11] The editorship of the *Quarterly* combined both aspirations. It was the organ *par excellence* of Church and State conservatism, but its political connections raised it above the newspapers and mere magazines. Lockhart had written for the rollicking Tory monthly *Blackwood's Magazine*. As editor of the *Quarterly* he had to disavow that brand of political scurrility. But he was never at ease in the aristocratic society of which it aspired to be the mouthpiece. He remained more in sympathy with the struggling literary hack than with the landed aristocrat. A good expression of this is his moving essay on the life and death of the novelist Theodore Hook.[12]

It was Lockhart's misfortune that the *Quarterly* needed a link with the leading politicians if it was to retain its position. His own talent would have been better suited to a more exclusively literary review, in which his alertness to literary trends, his acute appreciation of good writers whatever their politics, and his cosmopolitan interests would have given him

---

[7] Andrew Lang, *Life of J. G. Lockhart*, 2 vols. (1897) is still the best. Marion Lochhead's *John Gibson Lockhart* (London, 1954) is superficial. Lang confessed that he had not used the two volumes of Croker's letters to Lockhart now in the National Library of Scotland (NLS) or Lockhart's replies (*Life*, I, p. ix). These are in the Croker MSS in the Clements Library, Ann Arbor. The correspondence contains the bulk of my evidence in this essay, and I am grateful to Mr John Murray for allowing me to supplement it from his own MSS.   [8] 1823.   [9] Clements Lib., Croker MSS. Lockhart to Croker, 19 Apr. 1820.
[10] *Ibid.*, 2 December 1821.   [11] *Ibid.*, 13 January 1822.
[12] *QR*, 72 (May 1843), pp. 53–108.

great authority.[13] But the two great quarterlies were not read only or even primarily for their opinions on literature. What gave them their prestige was their traditional association with the two great parties in the state, to which the anonymity of their writers added a mystique, an impression that the writers' names were withheld because they were privy to the councils of the most eminent in the land. 'Your talkers of the first flight', Lockhart once wrote, 'are subservient to the hints of their political oracles. A word of Ld Lansdowne is reechoed by all the Sydneys and even Hallams and if I wished to get every Tory wit to praise a particular paper I should ask nothing but that the Duke or Peel should give it a smile and a whisper.'[14] The mystique was helped by the snobbery of the publishers, who were prepared to pay very generous fees to contributors, despite their anonymity, if the effect was to give their respective houses the cachet of noble or at least notable patronage. So the prestige was self-perpetuating. Editors who could extract from their publishers such generous payments could be choosy about contributors, and these could accept the money knowing that their anonymity would save them from losing caste as mere writers for the press. Not surprisingly, professional journalists like Hazlitt and Leigh Hunt longed to be enrolled as regular contributors to a quarterly, where they could earn a generous and regular income which would help them escape the tyranny of newspaper deadlines. The regular reviewers, on the other hand, knew that anonymity need not mean obscurity, but only that their authorship would circulate as an open secret among those readers whose esteem was worth having. It was an arrangement which presupposed a limited readership 'in the know' or anxious to seem so, and it suited a small political class and a restricted franchise. There were certainly signs that a reading public was emerging which was less exclusively political in its interests, but this was just beginning. The old system in its main features lasted Lockhart's lifetime.

II

In the first few years of Lockhart's editorship the lack of a firm political guide was apparent. On Canning's becoming premier, the old coalition which had held power under the leadership of Liverpool split, and even after Canning's death in August 1827 the disagreements were bitter. Canning's Tory opponents thought he would favour Catholic emancipa-

---

[13] I agree with Lang's judgement: 'Lockhart leaves, on a mind long and closely occupied with him, an impression as of thwarted force, of a genius that never completely found its proper path'. *Life of J. G. Lockhart*, I, p. 383.

[14] Murray MSS, John Murray, London: Lockhart to John Murray II 30 August 1838 partly quoted, but without a date, by George Paston [Emily Morse Symonds], *At John Murray's 1843–1892* (London, 1932), pp. 28–9.

tion and followed the Duke of Wellington and Peel; but when the Duke came to power and found himself forced to grant emancipation, the *Quarterly* found itself out of step. It had already expressed its opposition to the Catholic claims in a powerful article by Southey, and to repudiate Southey was to risk losing one of its best contributors.[15] But to follow him was to forfeit official help. It was only when the Whig government of Grey succeeded Wellington's and proposed parliamentary reform that the Tories united in opposition, and it was at this point that Lockhart acquired the political guide he needed. John Wilson Croker was an Irish Protestant, who had been Secretary to the Admiralty since 1809. He had served under five prime ministers and been the confidant of three. He supported Canning but was a close friend of Wellington and Peel. Lockhart later gave Croker a grateful acknowledgement of his help.

From the accession of J. T. Coleridge, Southey began to put in his wedge: and I let him drive it home because I had taken up a wrong view of what was to be the line through life of the Duke of Wellington and Peel, and saw in them the only Tories likely to keep the party together. Your secession [in 1827] left me to my own poor lights. I did not then understand the nature of official men at all as I still do very imperfectly and had you been by us at the decisive moment to interpret the talk of Downing Street in the dialect of Albemarle Street, neither Murray nor I would have allowed Southey to overrule us.[16]

So Croker from the start supplied Lockhart with the political experience he needed. An experienced observer of the political scene and a clear-headed administrator, he had been a regular contributor to the *Quarterly* since its foundation. He refused to sit in the new parliament after vehemently opposing its reform, and retirement gave him more time to write. His tally of 270 articles made him the *Quarterly*'s most prolific contributor.

The two men had at first a wary relationship which over the years ripened into close friendship. Lockhart looked after the literary side of the review, Croker the political. Lockhart knew the literary world and how to maintain the *Quarterly*'s status in it. He was aware of rising talent and, more importantly, growing reputations, and was anxious to keep the review from committing critical errors like condemning a bestseller. He was widely read, conversant with German and French literature, and very conscious of the philosophical and cultural forces which threatened the established order. He went as near as he dared to treating literature as politically neutral. Croker, on the other hand, harked back to the Gifford era, when all literature was judged for its political effects, and he was constantly itching to attack writers he considered dangerous. He was by

---

[15] *QR* 38 (October 1828), pp. 535–98; Shattock, *Politics and Reviewers*, p. 53; Lang, *Life*, II, 32.   [16] Croker MSS, Lockhart to Croker, 26 May 1845.

temperament a pessimist, disposed to suspect most social changes as changes for the worse, but he was also realist enough to grant that Lockhart was in a better position to judge. 'My life', he once admitted, 'has been spent between high politics and the most retired domesticity. I never was in literary society and have fewer literary acquaintances or associations than anyone would believe.' So despite his prejudice against contemporary taste, he admitted 'the public is now the best patron'.[17] In most cases therefore Lockhart could get his way. Exceptions were Croker's two historical interests, the French Revolution and eighteenth-century English memoirs, and contemporary politics. There were others who could review books in the first two, but in the last Croker was unrivalled. When visiting Peel at Drayton or the Duke of Wellington at Stratfield Saye, Croker was received as a familiar visitor, not as a journalist, and it was in these circles that the articles were concocted which gave the *Quarterly* its political authority.

The review's owner and publisher John Murray II took a subordinate role in determining policy. Lockhart and Croker ran the review between them and they claimed the freedom to censure even authors Murray himself published. Lockhart watched sales and tried to ensure there was no loss, but 'puffing' would reduce the *Quarterly* to the status of a mere booksellers' monthly (like *Blackwood's* or *Bentley's Miscellany*) and that, it was thought, would damage Murray in the long term.[18] Croker characteristically compared him to a constitutional monarch.

I acknowledge fully Murray's sovereignty over the Review, but 'tis a constitutional sovereignty and must be exercised thro' his ministers. He has a perfect right to change them as he thinks proper, but not to dictate to them what they shall think or say, and above all not to do so offensively.[19]

Policy was therefore not Murray's concern, even though, ultimately, he held the pursestrings. There was a political aspect to this independence. Lockhart had been appointed by Murray at a time when the publisher had also considered him for the editorship of a newspaper projected and vehemently urged on by the young Disraeli. The paper failed. Disraeli was exposed as an irresponsible speculator. Murray lost £26,000 on the fiasco, but he did not lose trust in Lockhart as editor of the *Quarterly*.[20]

Lockhart was a stranger to English politics. Croker was not. Indeed his prominence as the leading conservative critic of the Reform Bill raised his

---

[17] NLS, Lockhart MS 928, ff. 20–3, 23 January 1835.

[18] *Ibid.*, ff. 23–40, Croker to Lockhart, 10 June 1835.

[19] *Ibid.*, ff. 32–4, 'Sunday' January or February 1836.

[20] Whitwell Elwin told Brougham in 1854 that after the failure of the newspaper Murray 'had Lockhart then on his hands' and, as Coleridge was not a very good editor, offered the *Quarterly* to Lockhart. Brougham MSS, University College, London, 13 December 1854.

reputation higher than ever. Murray made a separate agreement with him that he should be paid for up to four sheets (a sheet being sixteen pages) in every quarter.[21] There was no suggestion that the *Quarterly* should represent the backbencher or any party organisation. Croker told Peel that it was 'a kind of *direction post* to a large body of people, particularly in the country and its chief use is to keep our friends in a right course and to furnish them with arguments in support of their opinions'. He added, 'I do not suppose that it makes converts, but it rallies friends.'[22] Peel made no formal agreement with its editor: Croker offered his services spontaneously to help the cause, but it was Murray's money that made it profitable. There is no direct evidence that Peel suggested topics. Sometimes Croker would tell Peel that Lockhart wanted a political article, and ask him for some leads. One such request reads: 'So, if you will pitch the keynote and give me a few bars of the melody, I will endeavour to work out my own variations on the original air.'[23] At other times Lockhart would be told that 'our political friends' had asked for an article. Peel certainly read some of the articles in proof, made comments and suggested amendments.[24] But it seems to have been in a spirit of friendly appreciation and exchange not political calculation. The articles had no official status. But they were an important part of the review's mystique. They were known to have been written by someone privy to the counsels of the Tory leadership.

This had an important bearing on Peel's troubled relationships with his party. He was at once indispensable and remote, unrivalled in mastery of official duty and parliamentary business, but cold and indifferent to people outside the circles of the politically influential. Those who knew him as a political leader were in awe of his efficiency and grasp. Croker was one of the few men who had known him since his political debut, and could give the sort of advice he would not have accepted from a political rival, but after 1832 it was advice from a man who had retired from parliament in disgust and full of prophetic foreboding of revolution. We cannot be sure how much Peel agreed with this advice, as his side of their long correspondence has been destroyed.[25] But what has survived suggests

---

[21] Brightfield, *Croker*, p. 404. Lockhart resented the fact that this arrangement was made in his absence. Murray MSS, Lockhart to J. Murray III, 28 January 1851.

[22] British Library, Add MSS 40502, ff. 326–7, 20 February 1842. Peel's reply is in L. J. Jennings, *Correspondence and Diaries of J. W. Croker*, 2 vols. (1884), II, pp. 380–1, giving advice on the line the review should take.

[23] Add MSS 40321, ff. 427–8, 25 November 1840.

[24] Jennings, *Correspondence and Diaries*, I, pp. 337–9; and Add MSS 40321, ff. 305–6, Croker to Peel, 21 December 1838.

[25] 620 letters from Peel to Croker written from 1810 to 1847 and offered in the Red Cross Sale at Christie's in July 1940, were apparently destroyed by a bomb. Jennings was probably the last to see the whole correspondence, of which he quotes about seventy-three letters.

that, allowing for the fact that Peel had a greater economic expertise and greater ambition, the two were on general principles in very close agreement.

In its political articles, Croker made the *Quarterly* Peel's mouthpiece, not the party's. Peel disliked party. He thought ministries fell from internal disagreements, not parliamentary defeats. He was more interested in finding able and reliable colleagues than a parliamentary majority. Both men thought that the Reform Act had increased the power of the Commons and weakened that of the crown. But Croker thought this meant that ministries would be driven by a parliament increasingly pledged to obey constituency opinion and that therefore Peel could do more good leading a conservative opposition than in power. Peel, less alarmist, saw that a reformed parliament called for a more united executive, one which was both more efficient and freer of the bias of party spirit. When he prepared to face the reformed Commons in his first ministry of 1834–5, the 'Hundred Days', he hoped to include two prominent Whigs, Stanley and Graham. They would not join him and he formed what he ruefully called 'only the Duke's old cabinet' and was defeated.[26] To Croker the defeat showed how far the country had moved towards a 'democratic despotism'.[27] To Peel it proved that the royal prerogative was still powerful and the management of the Commons called for a more competent team. Thereafter his aim was to keep himself free of the compromises of party so that, when the time came, he could choose his colleagues regardless of their party associations. So what historians have insisted on calling his leadership rested on a paradox: the more confident his followers became that public opinion was moving their way and that they could replace a weak Whig ministry, the more he drew away from commitment to the policies they wanted to see put into practice.[28]

The *Quarterly* was at first on Peel's side rather than that of the parliamentary party. This was partly because it thought whiggism the ally of radicalism and revolution and saw Tories as a beleaguered minority with little prospect of a return to power. It was easier to denounce the Whig government of Melbourne than to suggest alternative policies. But even when conservative forces began to rally, the review showed remarkably little inclination to encourage and exploit them. Tractarianism was an

---

[26] Jennings, *Correspondence*, I, p. 250.   [27] Add MSS 40321, f.129, to Peel, 31 March 1835.
[28] Professor Norman Gash blames the party for failing to appreciate Peel's 'governmental ethic' and following its own interest: *Sir Robert Peel* (London, 1972), p. 37. But this ignores the element of economic dogmatism to which Boyd Hilton's study of Peel ('Peel: A Reappraisal', *Historical Journal*, 22 [1979]) has called attention, and his interpretation seems to me to indicate that at the end of his second ministry Peel was inclined to substitute economic orthodoxy for parliamentary tactics.

expression of concern at Whig Erastianism and it had been growing in significance since 1833, but it was not till early 1839 that Gladstone's book on *The State in its Relations with the Church* led Lockhart to take stock of the movement. Even then the contrast with the *Edinburgh* is striking. Macaulay seized on Gladstone's book with exhilaration and in a few weeks sent Napier his famous demolition.[29] Lockhart by contrast was thrown into a dither. He was aware of the way German theological work was eroding the authority of the Bible and later in the year he read Strauss's *Life of Jesus* with mounting alarm.[30] On the other hand as he read some of the *Tracts* and Hurrell Froude's *Remains* he was repelled, though he admitted that Tractarianism might be 'a salutary counterpoise to equally baleful errors'.[31] As for Gladstone's book, he asked Croker's opinion, and then went up to Oxford to gather views on the Tracts and their authors. The visit reassured him. 'You will be glad to hear', he told Croker.

that I left Oxford with strong hopes that the Newman party may be stopped from going further. I perceived that several of their ablest friends already were of opinion that they had touched dangerous ground and that these were therefore no longer to be reckoned as of their supporters tho' they retained the highest admiration of their talents and respect for their intentions. The agitators meanwhile have done some signal services. They have stirred a new zeal for theological research, they have turned the printing of Oxford into a very useful course, producing beautiful editions of the Antenicene Fathers . . . they have excited feelings among the young men which attest their value in a very extraordinary improvement of manners and habits. Thus far well, the point is to keep them from going beyond the principles of our own Reformation and I hope the Quarterly may contribute to this by dealing w[ith] their literary history and productions in a gentle and candid vein, avoiding for the present anything like a keen controversy as to the doubtful points. The fear is that the abuse of the Enemy may urge high spirited men further than they would otherwise have dreamt of going. As to Gladstone I gave him up, he bewildered and fatigued me and I fancy he had done the like to himself before his book was done.[32]

Lockhart sent Gladstone's book to William Sewell, Fellow of Exeter College and future founder of Radley, a High Churchman whose hope was to unite Evangelical and Tractarian Anglicans. The review appeared in the *Quarterly* for December 1839, eight months after Macaulay's.[33] The following year Sewell visited Ireland and Lockhart was relieved to report that he had returned 'with his mind considerably cleared of the Pusey views by his observation of the Popish system as there reduced to Practice.'[34] Sewell

[29] *Edinburgh Review*, 69, no. 139 (April 1839), reprinted in T. B. Macaulay, *Critical and Historical Essays*, 2 vols. (Everyman edn, 1907), II, pp. 38–72.
[30] Croker MSS, 1 November 1839.   [31] *Ibid.*, 21 January 1839.
[32] *Ibid.*, 4 February 1839.   [33] *QR*, 65 (December 1839) pp. 97–153.
[34] Croker MSS, 13 October 1840.

was now encouraged to write a number of articles on Ireland which were vigorously unionist and anti-Catholic.

Croker too was learning more about the Tractarians from Samuel Wilberforce, who held his archdeaconry with a canonry of Winchester and a living at Alverstoke where Croker was building a summer residence. The two men agreed on Anglicanism as the *via media,* and Croker recommended Wilberforce to Peel for a bishopric.[35] He also became acquainted with the 'catholicising' tastes of Samuel's brother Henry and his wife's brother-in-law, Manning. Croker's Irish Protestant background made him averse to their views, and their preoccupation with whether or not the Anglican Church was apostolic struck him as absurd. But Wilberforce seems to have moderated his criticism ('Manning does *not* light his candles in the Day'[36]) and with Lockhart's help confined it to matters of ritual rather than doctrine. Lockhart had a much juster view of the position of the Tractarians in a European context. Deprecating Croker's offer of a further article on Anglo-Catholicism in May 1843 he wrote:

You dwell on the context of France and England, but what the Oxford men dwell on with equal justice is the utter infidelity of the German literature, all protestant. The reaction there has been into open Romanism. Here it is as yet only to Puseyism: but the Popish system did not lead to the Encyclopedie in Paris more directly than did the utter want of ecclesiastical authority in the north of Germany to the School of the Rationalists and Pantheists, which now includes the vast majority of the educated classes whenever German literature prevails, and has I hear gained not a few adherents here since that literature was brought into vogue among us by the imitations of Carlyle and Co.[37]

Probably Croker never read Carlyle, but the point Lockhart was making was acute: the centre of the theological revolution against Christian orthodoxy was German not French.

In so far as Tractarianism was a movement of academic clergy, impatient to be recognised and credited, and frustrated in this ambition by the authority of a Church which seemed too imbued with the lay spirit, it was bound to splinter into those who had benefited by the traditional system of preferment and those who had not. Given the *Quarterly*'s traditions, it was equally natural that it should back the Established Church against its critics, Protestant or Catholic. Lockhart's Presbyterian background made him averse to the Romanising pull, but he was too aware of the learning of the Tractarians to want (as Croker did) to abuse them. So he avoided direct assault. Ward's *Idea of a Christian Church* was reviewed by Gladstone,[38] Newman's *Essay on Development* by Milman,[39] a man of

[35] Add MSS 40501, ff. 204–7, 248–9; Croker to Peel ? January 1842, 2 February 1842.
[36] Bodleian MS Eng. Lett. d. 367 ff. 77–8, 22 April 1843.
[37] Croker MSS, 6 May 1843.   [38] *QR,* 75, no. 149 (December 1844), pp. 149–200.
[39] *Ibid.,* 77, no. 154 (March 1846), pp. 404–65.

such liberal principles that Lord John Russell made him Dean of St Paul's. The *Quarterly* was silent on the Gorham Judgement which made so many High Churchmen, including Lockhart's son-in-law Hope-Scott, go over to Rome.

Probably the disputes of Oxford divines had little interest for the bulk of the Tory party in parliament. Much more divisive were the problems of industrial unrest and the radical movements it brought. At the start of Peel's second ministry, the *Quarterly* had supported his policy of reducing tariffs on a wide range of imported goods and revising the sliding scale which governed the import of corn. Croker had been consulted and carefully briefed, and his *Quarterly* article stressed repeatedly that the agricultural interest had nothing to fear: Peel had secured the prosperity of the farmers as well as a regular supply of food for the common people. Peel revised the article and Graham, his Home Secretary, praised it as a fair statement of the government case.[40] But Lockhart was alarmed. Early in 1842, noting a fall in the *Quarterly*'s sales, he and Croker discussed what should be done. Lockhart was for less politics and some lighter articles; Croker, while admitting that his own articles might show his declining powers, said that at least in his political ones he had had 'the confidence of the leaders of our party and sometimes their actual help'. But he agreed on the need for variety and 'shorter articles and of a more general character so as to make the Review a manual of the current literature of the day, where people for 6s may find the pith and marrow of ten pounds worth of solid volumes'.[41] Lockhart wanted something more fundamental, some appeasement of what he called 'the symptoms of sulky disaffection' towards leaders of the party.[42] His own social sympathies were with the paternalism of Southey, and reading in July 1842 the *Report of the Sanitary Condition of the Labouring Population,* he called it 'a fearful volume', and told Croker it dealt with 'the one real political question – all else are vapid and worthless unless connected with it'. He suggested it be made the subject of Croker's next political article.[43] Croker, however, replied with a lecture on the distinction between the fiscal policy of the government and the social conditions of the masses. He had just written an exposition of the one which showed the *Quarterly* 'deeply in the Government's confidence'; but nothing could be done about the other. Ashley's demands were utopian. Governments could no more reduce poverty and misery than a ship's captain could control the wind and the waves. If Lockhart wanted a contributor to expound views like Ashley's he (Croker) would stop his contributions.[44]

[40] *Ibid.*, 71, no.140 (September 1842); Jennings, Correspondence, III, pp. 386–7.
[41] NLS, MS 928, no. 121, ff. 151–4, 25 January 1842.
[42] Croker MSS, 21 June 1842.   [43] *Ibid.*, 23 July 1842.
[44] Murray MSS, Croker to Lockhart, 10 September 1842.

III

Underneath the courtesies of the correspondence one can feel the growing tension between the two men. The review meant different duties for each. Croker did not need the income. For him the *Quarterly* was a link with his political friends, a pretext to be in their councils, and an occupation in retirement. He was doing some historical work, a revision of his Boswell, an edition of Hervey's memoirs, and articles on the French Revolution; but political argument was his meat, political polemic his drink. Lockhart on the other hand had to find and pay contributors to the review, for which he was in regular contact with the Murrays, father and son, and his wider literary connections made him vulnerable to the opinions of other writers and readers. Unlike Croker, he had to explain and defend the *Quarterly's* critical opinions, and he was aware of a divergence between its party politics and the public taste. He would have liked Croker, one feels, to have stuck to politics and left the rest to him. But given Croker's deal with John Murray II there was no guarantee of this. One wishes, reading his letters, that he had had more confidence in his own judgement, more tenacity. His critical instincts were usually right, but when bullied he usually gave in.

In 1842 he made a series of decisions which offended his colleague. He sent Tennyson's second volume of poems (Croker had reviewed the first rather severely in 1833) to John Sterling. When Croker asked if he could review Macaulay's *Lays of Ancient Rome*, Lockhart said he had sent the book to Milman.[45] To cope with an accumulation of articles he and Murray planned an extra number of the review and then told Croker what they had decided. The last decision reached Croker while he was staying with Peel at Drayton in late November. It was the last straw. He wrote to Lockhart resigning from the *Quarterly*. Peel had given him, he said, a mass of documents containing ample proof of the Anti-Corn Law League's complicity in the recent riots in the north. He had stayed at home, while the rest of the party went shooting, to digest all this material into a political article for the December number of the *Quarterly*, when the unexpected news came that an extra number of the review was coming out within the week. This weakened his credit with Peel: 'What will he think of me, or at least what will he think of my influence with you, or your confidence in me?' To satisfy ministers' anxiety for an early publication, he warned that the material would be published as a pamphlet.[46] Plainly Croker expected his resignation to be refused with apologies. Lockhart

---

[45] NLS, MS 928, no. 29, f. 40, Croker to Lockhart 'K[ensington P[alace] Sunday' [end October 1842]; Croker MSS, Lockhart to Croker, 2 November 1842.
[46] NLS MS 927, no. 35, ff. 47–8; copy in Croker MSS, Box 23.

and Murray were in effect being threatened with the loss of their political contacts. Lockhart replied, abjectly asking Croker to stay.[47] The extra number was dropped. The attack on the League, replete with material provided by the Prime Minister and Home Secretary, appeared in the *Quarterly* for December 1842.[48] Lockhart's capitulation, which seems to set such a limit to his editorial independence, was of course due to Murray's earlier agreement with Croker, and that in turn had a political point which could not be ignored. While a Conservative administration was in power with a huge majority, the *Quarterly* could not take the risk with its readership.

It is hard for us to appreciate now the relevance and force of its political articles, but at the time they were probably what gave each number its topical appeal. The attack on the League was powerful enough to make its leaders pull back, after the 'Plug Plot', from further attempts to incite popular demonstrations. But another reason was that Lockhart lacked, as he himself once admitted, 'the iron nerves of the man fitted for daily collision with the world'.[49] Domestic tragedy had sapped his vitality. He was not wealthy. It may have been this fact which led Peel (doubtless on Croker's prompting) to offer him the near sinecure place of Auditor of the Duchy of Lancaster the following year, and the offer led him to confide his despondency to Croker:

I am now verging on 50, have long since lost all that made life pleasant enough to be much worth caring for, and with that all the little ambition I ever had . . . Time was, when I sighed and prayed for the means of release from the eternal worry of small negotiations and explanations inseparable from the management of the Quarterly. I used to dream of being able to choose my literary tasks, then tasks no longer, for myself. I had fond dreams of doing something permanently worthy in letters. But with less idle dreams these too have flown. I am persuaded very thoroughly that I am no longer fit for anything better than the course of drudgery which has fallen hitherto to my share, and which indeed is probably less disagreeable to me than the pursuing of my [old] profession at the bar.[50]

His acceptance of the office seems to mark a turning point in his relations with Croker. Thereafter he would give occasional criticism of his articles on literary and religious issues, but he accepted the political ones without much question.

Perhaps he would have been a more effectual master of the *Quarterly*'s fortunes if he had refused the job and persevered, at least for a year or so, in his own judgement. For the backbench criticism of Peel grew, and by

---

[47] Croker MSS, 22 November 1842.   [48] *QR*, 71, no. 141 (1842), pp. 244–314.
[49] Shattock, *Politics and Reviewers*, p. 55.
[50] Croker MSS, 15 November 1843; partly quoted in Shattock, Politics and Reviewers, p. 70.

1843 even Croker grudgingly conceded that it must be addressed. As usual, however, he saw the issues in official terms. His political article for September 1843 was mostly a diatribe against O'Connell's repeal agitation, which reads like the work of a man who knew that Peel planned a showdown with the Irish leader and wanted to ensure it had a favourable response in England. But the start of the article was addressed to disaffected Tories who wanted more recognition of their economic grievances from the government. Croker assured them that the government's future was 'interwoven with the principle of agricultural protection – there has not been, in our memory, any Cabinet so largely and so exclusively connected with the landed interest'.[51] There was also a footnote warning the 'four or five young gentlemen, who are known, it seems, by the designation of *Young England*' not to sow distrust of Peel and his colleagues, 'the only statesmen in whom the great Conservative body has any confidence, or can have any hope'. He added that the public interest in their cause 'has in it more of wonder than of respect, and will certainly confer on them no permanent consideration with any party or constituency'.[52] It was a rash footnote which Lockhart would have done better to cut out, for it stirred up the leader of Young England to recall his slights at the hands of Murray and write a famous riposte. Disraeli's *Coningsby* appeared in 1844, and in it the character of Rigby was deliberately modelled on Croker. As if answering the *Quarterly*, Rigby is portrayed as the writer of articles massacring 'she-liberals' or writing about politics with 'garbled extracts from official correspondence that no one could refer to'.[53] *Coningsby* was the first salvo in Disraeli's assault on Peel, and the personal animus of the portrait of Rigby can only be explained, in a political novel about conservatism, in the light of Croker's reputation for expressing Peel's views.

Thinking he had a firm pledge of Peel's commitment to protection, Croker was still prepared to defend him against his critics after 1844; but on the issue which first clearly showed Peel had lost the support of half his party, Croker happened to agree with him. After the inconclusive prosecution of O'Connell, Peel turned to conciliation of Irish Catholic opinion with the Maynooth Grant. This ran counter to the traditional stance of the *Quarterly* in support of the Established Church, but Croker himself had always favoured Catholic emancipation, and he even held that the Union would be secure only if the State paid the Catholic priesthood. He had in 1828 stood aloof from the explosion of 'Southey's great mortar'[54] in the *Quarterly*. So when Peel proposed a Charitable Bequests Act which allowed lay endowments of the Catholic Church, and went on to increase

---

[51] *QR*, 71, no.144 (1843), p. 557.   [52] *Ibid.*, p. 554n.
[53] B. Disraeli, *Coningsby* (1844), ch. 2.   [54] Shattock, *Politics*, p. 57.

the grant to the Catholic seminary of Maynooth, Croker could quite reasonably write of 'my *old* and Peel's *new* views'[55] as if the Prime Minister had always been one step behind, in 1845 as in 1829. He realised the Maynooth Grant was highly unpopular with the party in the Commons, but he thought it less important in its implications than the legislation on bequests, and he told Peel frankly that the party would have agreed to a far larger grant for Maynooth if he had earlier made some concessions to the landed interest in his fiscal measures.[56] Their real antagonism was economic, not religious. They feared the whole prosperity of agriculture was under threat. The Maynooth debate and division were only symptoms of a deeper dissatisfaction.[57]

Croker's unease at the growing talk of corn law repeal had already led him to ask his colleagues if they wanted a change of editorial policy. The occasion was an offer from Gladstone early in 1845 of an article on Peel's economic policy, which Croker and Lockhart interpreted as a bid to acquire influence on the *Quarterly,* if not to take it over. Since John Murray II's death in 1843, the publishing firm had a new owner, his son John Murray III. It may have been this which led to the consultation. At any rate, Croker told Lockhart that the decision whether or not to abandon protection lay with him and with Murray, but particularly the latter. 'For, in truth, tho' you and I may advise and suggest, the stake is and the decision must be John Murray's. The Review is his landed interest and he should consider how it is to be most productively tilled.' They had a choice. Free-trade doctrines might prevail, in which case the *Quarterly*'s abandonment of its protectionist views would make it 'an apostate at the tail of a mob'. Or else it could keep to its old principles, formed as they had been 'in the hour that the Review was founded, in the noon of the dark eclipse with which Buonaparte over shadowed the world'. The first might be better as a mere commercial speculation, but they must decide. Croker could not resist adding that they must also consider Gladstone's worth. Could they use him? He had a reputation in the House of Commons, 'but on the other hand he is not only a heavy writer, but I have never been able to understand clearly one page that he has written not even his letters.'[58]

Lockhart and Murray evidently opted for no change. 'Our chief readers and purchasers', Lockhart was to remind Croker a few months later, 'are the Parson and the Squire'.[59] Lockhart worried a good deal about the

---

[55] NLS, MS 927, no. 42, ff. 57–8, Croker to Lockhart, 28 February 1844.
[56] Add MSS 40565, ff. 7–8, 20 April 1845.
[57] NLS MS 927, no. 50, ff. 74–5, Croker to Lockhart, 15 April 1845.
[58] NLS, MS 927, no. 47, ff. 65–7, Croker to Lockhart, 20 February 1845.
[59] Croker MSS, Lockhart to Croker, 26 February 1846.

Quarterly's consistency on the question of the Catholic claims.[60] But Croker's spirited defence of the Maynooth Grant in the June 1845 number does not seem to have alienated the parson. This was partly because Croker sought to stress that the Grant broached no new principle and hence that the outcry against it was exaggerated and came too late. But it was also the case, as Lockhart admitted with relief, that educated Anglican opinion was divided on the Grant. Bishop Phillpotts had claimed that 'all but 4' bishops were against the Maynooth Bill, but Gladstone's estimate was more favourable, sixteen for and ten against. The Tractarians were also split. 'Pusey, Newman and the Ultras of their party all for it – Hook, Palmer etc against it.'[61] Later in the month, with the vote on Maynooth impending in the Lords, Lockhart wrote justifying the *Quarterly's* earlier stance and subsequent change. If in the years 1830–41 they had been neutral on Roman Catholicism, they could not have kept their circulation.

Could really the Conservative battle have been fought with any chance of success unless on Church principles? And in that period of struggle was there any pro Catholic spirit within the Church of England except with the small section of clerical whigs Maltby, Sidney [*sic*] Smith etc? Now, in consequence mainly of the *Tractarian movement* the clergy have come to be very much divided as to the whole of this question. They know their division so well that they choose as a body to be quiescent.[62]

In the Lords the bill passed with only three bishops protesting against it.[63]

Pleasing the squire was much more controversial and difficult. For one thing, there was no *via media* to defend, as there was in religious policy. Political economy was a subject at once more recondite and more explosive. Of its technical problems and vocabulary it was still permissible (at least before 1848[64]) for an educated man to profess no view at all. But the issue of free trade versus protection in corn had been turned, by Cobden and the League, into a conflict of classes; so that advocates of the corn law (who tended to be the small freeholders and tenant farmers) were abused as rapacious landlords and advocates of corn law repeal as ferocious enemies of order. Debate had become polarised and slogan-ridden, hardly a state of things conducive to greater public agreement.

The *Quarterly* was in any case not the organ to lead any economic debate. Political economy as a body of literature was strongly whiggish in its assumptions, and the Ricardian tradition was entrenched in its rival

---

[60] *Ibid.*, 6 May 1845.   [61] *Ibid.*, 17 May 1845.   [62] *Ibid.*, 26 May 1845.

[63] G. I. T. Machin, *Politics and the Churches in Britain 1832–1868* (Oxford, 1977), p. 175.

[64] The year of J. S. Mill's *Principles of Political Economy*, which seems to me to have done more than any other work of its time to make 'the dismal science' congenial and accessible.

the *Edinburgh*. The *Quarterly*'s management was, by contrast, ill at ease with economic issues, and in the 1840s, when a contributor offered an article on an economic subject, Lockhart would refer it to Croker, who, if he did not reject it for its author's politics, passed it on to Lord Ashburton for an opinion.[65] It was easier to say the writer belonged to the other party than to consider if his arguments were valid. In effect, Croker and Lockhart thought they had secured a pledge from the government of Peel to stick by the revised sliding scale of the Act of 1842, and what served as an argument to reassure the farmer and the squire was also an excuse for not discussing an issue on its merits, except by repeating that Peel would not let them down.

Peel's 'conversion' to total repeal at the end of 1845 was therefore a double blow. It is well known that it broke the Tory party into Peelites and Protectionists and kept it out of power for a generation. But for the *Quarterly* reviewers this was a gradual development. They had not taken the side of the parliamentary party against the leadership until 1845. Believing, as they had, in a broad conservatism which defended all traditional institutions, they were late converts to the idea of the parliamentary party's unity, and by late 1846 they had given up hope of its two sections reuniting. The only course open was to become the organ of the Protectionists. But this underlined the second, more important effect of Peel's 'conversion'. It tied the review to a party with little prospect of office. Peel had taken the front bench talent with him. The *Quarterly* had little to tell the parson and the squire that they did not know already.

It took Lockhart and Croker some time to adjust to this new situation. As early as August 1846 Croker had started writing to Lord Stanley for advice on a political article in the *Quarterly*, just as he had written to Peel. But he found his correspondent nearly as pessimistic about political prospects as he was himself, while of the party's leaders in the Commons he deplored Bentinck's judgement and had a deep distrust of Disraeli.[66] He saw that the Protectionists could not form a strong government, but he could not accept the consequence that they should give up protectionism. He was an old man in poor health, and he was the last survivor of the Gifford tradition. In March 1851 he asked Stanley (shortly to become

[65] F. W. Fetter's two articles on the 'Economic Articles in the *Quarterly Review* and their Authors, 1809–52', *Journal of Political Economy*, 66 (February and April 1958), are still valuable. Croker certainly did his best to keep Whig economics out of the review, but Fetter was wrong to claim that the Whig G. P. Scrope ceased to write in *QR* after the Reform Act, and he made no mention of Lord Ashburton. Besides, being quite wedded to the idea of economics and politics as separate disciplines, Fetter assumed that *any* editorial interference in economic questions must be politically motivated.

[66] NLS MS 927, no. 64, f. 95, Croker to Lockhart, 21 August 1846 (on Bentinck); *ibid.*, no. 59, ff. 88–9, 25 January 1846 (on Disraeli).

Earl of Derby) if he wanted the connection with the *Quarterly* to continue.

Living, or rather vegetating, as I do, in a political solitude, I know *nothing* and, except yourself, *nobody* from whom I can seek information; and Mr Lockhart, tho' he lives in town and sees something of the literary and fashionable world sees little of the *interior* of politics, and indeed you may judge that he is hard pushed for a guide, when he applies to *me*.

This leads me to suggest to you whether, if you wish to preserve the *Quarterly Review* as the organ of the party, as it has so long been, you would not cultivate something of more *personal* intercourse with Mr Lockhart. I am, to all appearances and indeed feeling, as well as ever I was in my life, but I have warnings, besides my life is above three score and ten!, that prepare me for a speedy departure. My place in the *Quarterly Review* will soon be vacant, and if it is to continue the organ of the conservative party, Mr. Lockhart must be kept au courant of your views.[67]

Stanley seems to have responded by sending down his son to explore the offer. The younger Stanley went and was offered the political department of the *Quarterly* in Croker's place. Stanley 'neither accepted not declined' but his verdict was unsympathetic. 'The truth is, quarterlies are well nigh superseded by the growing influences of the daily and weekly press, which draws off the ablest writers.' He added, 'I listened to the old man without agreement or sympathy, but with a strong feeling of respect for his laborious life, acute intellect, and singleness of purpose.'[68]

Stanley was broadly right in his verdict on the quarterly review having had its day as a political journal. The political world was expanding and political events were accelerating. Even in the 1840s the *Quarterly* could hardly hope to cope with a rapidly changing political scene. In the last months of Peel's ministry its political articles were, by the time they were published, ludicrously out of date.

But the relationships between the review and the cabinet had always been onesided. The *Quarterly* derived its political authority from a personal tie: it may have been a signpost to party members, but its prestige rested on the reputation of being in Peel's confidence. If he withheld that confidence, or was (as in November and December 1845) too busy to express it, the review could only speculate in the dark. As late as December 1845, when Peel had resigned because the cabinet could not agree with his advocacy of total repeal, and *The Times* leaked his opinion, Croker denied *The Times* report, and assured the country gentlemen that

---

[67] Derby MSS, Liverpool Record Office, 13 March 1851; Stanley's reply is in Jennings, *Correspondence*, III, pp 229–31.

[68] J. R. Vincent, ed., *Disraeli, Derby and the Conservative Party: The Political Journal of Lord Stanley* (Hassocks, 1978), p. 57.

Peel would not let them down. He felt Peel would be tied by former agreements with and help to the writers of the review. Peel doubtless felt that, as they had justified his change over Maynooth, they would do the same on corn law repeal. What else was the sinecure for Lockhart supposed to serve? Their reply would probably have been that, having been in his earlier counsels, and among his most loyal supporters, he owed them at least a confidential, prior intimation of his change of mind. But that sense of a private tie rudely broken was exactly what showed how old-fashioned their assumptions had become. Peel's change had destroyed the *Quarterly*'s reputation for being *au courant* with cabinet decisions and showed his attention was on a wider constituency than the old Tory gentry it had traditionally addressed.

Lockhart retired from the editorship, disillusioned and ill, in 1853, and with him went the tradition Gifford had established. Croker's attempt to be Derby's mouthpiece did not survive Disraeli's budget of 1852. There was still a demand for long reflective and critical articles and there was obviously a large leisured readership to savour them. But these precluded a close identification with politicians and the fortunes of political parties. Whitwell Elwin, Lockhart's successor in the editorship, deliberately set himself to be non-partisan. Lockhart and Croker, no less than Jeffrey and Napier, had excluded or severely edited contributions they thought politically unorthodox. That was no longer necessary. The mid-Victorian public liked its ministries mixed and its reviews politically neutral.

7   Ruskin's way: *tout à fait comme un oiseau*

John Drury

After Mr Ruskin took his leave, Gambart asked her [the painter Rosa Bonheur's] opinion about him. 'He is a gentleman', she said, 'an educated gentleman; but he is a theorist. He sees nature with a little eye – tout à fait comme un oiseau.'[1]

I

Ruskin is weak on mass. This was pointed out to me by John Burrow on a Ruskinian enough occasion: a walk around Christ Church Meadow in Oxford. Behind us was the Meadow Building of 1862–7. Critics of it seem always to say two things about it: that it is Ruskinian and that they do not like it. There is no record in Christ Church of Ruskin's participation in its design. It went up in the reign of Ruskin's friend, Dean Liddell, who may well have taken any correspondence about it away with him when he retired – and such papers seem mainly to have vanished. Liddell was a great admirer of *Modern Painters* and *The Stones of Venice*, a capable amateur draughtsman, and a tireless builder. They fell out later, when Ruskin was Slade Professor, but in the 1860s they were getting on well enough and Thomas Deane was the chosen architect. He was the son of the surviving partner in business of Benjamin Woodward, universally loved and admired, with whom Ruskin had worked on the University Museum. Woodward died in 1861. Ruskin had insisted, during work on the museum, that one partner in the firm of Woodward and Deane was as good as another, but perhaps betrayed his real preference by getting Deane's Christian name wrong.[2] It is a preference which is likely to be shared by anyone comparing the museum with Meadow Building. The museum is graceful. Meadow Building is massive, cutting off the college from the meadow like some Great Wall of China: massive, but as a mass, charmless and oppressive. Ruskin and Oxford were lucky with

---

[1] *Reminiscences of Frederick Goodall* (1902), p. 130.
[2] Ruskin wrongly calls him 'Charles' in a letter of 1855 to Dr Furnivall, cited in the editors' introduction to *The Works of John Ruskin*, ed. E.T. Cook and Alexander Wedderburn, 39 vols. (London, 1903–12), XVI, p. xlv. All citations of Ruskin's work are to this edition.

Woodward, unlucky with Deane. And the reason for this is clear enough. Woodward could manage mass and make it both substantial and light. The younger Deane, on the other hand, was all too obediently the sort of architect of whom Ruskin approved, building large and carving boldly.[3] So he supplied a frame, or gigantic block, on which the masons and craftsmen could work in happy independence. The result is a sort of anthology of Ruskin's architectural themes, particularly from *The Seven Lamps of Architecture*, for which it would make a good visual aid: walls which are very much walls, cliff-like, imposing, and cut through by windows (none too adroitly placed) and a cavernous central arch so as to give plenty of chiaroscuro ('Rembrandtism', Ruskin had decided, ' is a noble manner in architecture, though a false one in painting'[4]); a steep roof without eaves; bold Venetian gothic windows and balconies; bands of part-coloured stone – and plenty of capitals ready for carved decoration reflecting the foliage of the adjacent meadow. Unfortunately this last feature was not carried through and the lack of ornament, along with the wearisome abundance of blank surfaces waiting for decoration which they never got, is one obvious reason for Pevsner calling the building 'joyless'. For a building so obediently under the influence of the apostle of joy in work, that is damning. But the main reason is the one which John Burrow indicated.

It is not that Ruskin was in any way opposed to mass – even if that were a conceivable attitude. It was just something which failed to claim the sustained attention of his acute and widely roving eye. If so, then some consideration of why it is so will be a good way of getting some purchase on his great achievement by following his habitual mental-cum-ocular movements. As with many prolific and energetically driven writers, some slight objection or suspicion in the face of his work can be a useful brake on its headlong career for the dazzled reader.

Ruskin mentioned mass only seldom in his whole *œuvre* – and 'mentioned' is the word; there is no discussion of it. We are not dealing with an absence but a slightness. In *The Seven Lamps of Architecture* it apparently refers to a component, such as a pillar, and is once mentioned (and no more) in the context of 'the element of decoration'.[5] These look like oddly minimising uses of the word. And this is borne out by two of his greatest descriptions of buildings in *The Stones of Venice II*. In the basilica at Torcello he is fascinated by the decoration of individual capitals and their comparative relation to each other, misinterprets the history of the pulpit completely and magnificently, and ends up with a review of the

---

[3] *The Two Paths* (1859), XVI, p. 368.
[4] *The Seven Lamps of Architecture* (1849; 1855; 1880), VIII, p. 117.
[5] *Ibid.*, VIII, p. 119.

whole building from the vantage point of the bishop's throne in the centre of the apse which treats it, not as an architectural ensemble, but as social allegory: it is a ship or ark in which the saved take their spiritual journey steered by the bishop. Looking at the outside of the apse at Murano he achieves a *tour de force* in the analysis of the balanced inter-relations of ornamental details. In both cases, he just stops short of judging mass. Elsewhere in his work it features thrice in a hexagonal diagram or 'map of the great schools', but the subject is not taken up in the text.[6] It is distinguished from space.[7] And that is about all: a very meagre gleaning from the riches of thirty-eight volumes, packed with the harvest of his wonderful eye.

Ruskin's vast literary achievement has the same drawback. All his readers feel it, sooner or later. The pleasures and rewards of reading him are enormous. Even when he is mistaken about a detail, he gets us to look. The mind is stored with images and insights. Discoveries accumulate, as on one of those ten- or twelve-mile country walks which he advocated as the perfect form of exercise and travel, or those walks in and around Venice which he described as nobody has done before or since. A walk near Chamouni can stand for them all. For once it mentions mass, even describes a couple of masses vividly, but only to say that they are too much for the easily wearied and sated eye of one 'for whom a blade of grass or a wreath of foam, was quite food enough and to spare'.

Behind me, some leagues in length, rose the jagged range of the mountains of the Réposoir; on the other side of the valley, the mass of the Aiguille de Varens, heaving its seven thousand feet of cliff into the air at a single effort, its gentle gift of waterfall, the Nant d'Arpenaz, like pillar of cloud at its feet; Mont Blanc and all its aiguilles, one silver flame, in front of me; marvellous blocks of mossy granite and dark glades of pine around me; but I could enjoy nothing, and could not for a long while make out what was the matter with me, until at last I discovered that if I confined myself to one thing, and that a little thing, – a tuft of moss or a single crag at the top of the Varens, or a wreath or two of foam of the Nant d'Arpenaz, I began to enjoy it directly, because then I had mind enough to put into the thing, and the enjoyment arose from the quantity of imaginative energy I could bring to bear upon it.[8]

As so often, the tone is confiding and it is all sustained by a lively and personal sense of companionship as he makes the reader pause and look at some little detail which speaks of so much, or, in Venice, notices a little transgression of a boundary in an inlaid design or the curl of a carved leaf: 'the expression of the power and intelligence of a companionable human soul',[9] his explanation of why pictures matter to us, applies just as well to

---

[6] *Lectures on Art* (1870), XX, p. 128.   [7] *The Seven Lamps of Architecture*, VIII, p. 118.
[8] *Modern Painters III* (1856), V, pp. 183–84.   [9] *Ibid.*, V, p. 187.

his own work – which is a sign that he is one of those writers whose criticism comes well up to the artistic level and importance of what it criticises. The *aperçus* are unforgettable. But they are irritatingly hard to retrieve, because the whole great wool-gathering exercise usually lacks, surprisingly and with the exception of *The Stones of Venice I*, architecture in the sense of clear and distinct masses. There is plenty of consistency. His ideas hang together in strong articulation. He stuck with them and developed them all his life. Despite frequent self-contradiction, they make a whole body of thought. But the absence, over long stretches of writing, of subordinate but unified and distinct masses within the whole makes retrieval of remembered passages very difficult. Finding out when or where one of his themes reaches a point of maximum definition is a constant and time-consuming problem for his readers. His disciple Proust made a masterpiece out of this commonplace pain: the difficulty of the retrieval of actuality from memory in life itself. When it comes to Ruskin's scattered treasures, Cook and Wedderburn's index comes in, thankfully, time and again. It is some comfort that Ruskin welcomed the prospect of this editorial achievement because he felt the difficulty as much as we do:

> The need of such an Index, and the hope that it might one day be supplied, were often in Ruskin's mind. On one occasion he was called upon to summarise his views upon the place of art in education. 'The principles have been stated somewhere', he said, 'in as short English as I could write. The difficulty is to find them! I can't always now myself.' 'I have left the system of my teaching widely scattered and broken', he said at another time, 'hoping always to bind it together some day.'[10]

So it is a real and pressing question as to why and how mass, or architectonic form, is so spectacularly absent from the work of such a great critic of nature, society, and art. To put it in visual terms, it is a question of why the reader of Ruskin seems to find himself in a mountain forest rather than in a cathedral. The answer to it will take in two of its likely sources in his youth: the formative influence on Ruskin's mental processes of his wide and deep knowledge of the Bible and of his polemical advocacy of Turner. Before that, though, a sense of the problem we are dealing with will be provided by some examination of how Ruskin saw and understood the world around him: the characteristic choreography of his mind as it followed his wonderful, if bird-like, eye.

II

We have to begin, unusually without any help from him, by saying what mass is. In a picture, it is something which comes between details and the

---

[10] Cited in the introduction to the editors' *General Index*, XXXIX, p. xiv.

whole. It is a substantial, intermediate wholeness, integrating a good deal of detail within itself. Both by its distinctness from other masses in the picture, and by its relation to them, it makes its contribution to the whole composition. It might, for instance, be a clump of trees and relate in both these ways to a group of buildings, a mass of cloud, or a rocky outcrop. This probably brings to mind memories of the landscapes of Claude and Poussin which Ruskin played off against Turner's – more of that later. First we need to see him characteristically at work.

Modern Painters III came out in 1856. On 27 October in the next year Charles Dodgson met its author at breakfast in the Common Room in Christ Church, where people were assembling to vote for Acland as Clinical Professor. '*Dies notabilis*', Dodgson noted in his diary. He had read *The Stones of Venice* with delight, but was disappointed by Ruskin's personal appearance and his 'general feebleness of expression'. But if nothing much came of the eagerly awaited encounter, Dodgson had stored in his mind the title at the beginning of *Modern Painters III*, 'OF MANY THINGS', and memorably gave the line to the Walrus in *Through the Looking Glass*. (He recycled Ruskin's 'true griffin' from the same book in *Alice*.[11]) 'OF MANY THINGS' was deliberate with its capital letters, and, if that is the word, strategic. Four hundred pages on in the book he notices that it has 'led me into fields of infinite inquiry'. He had announced at the start that his treatment of 'the various success of artists' in terms of their 'noble' ideas of beauty was not going to be

laboriously systematic; for the subject may, it seems to me, be more usefully treated by pursuing the different questions which arise out of it just as they occur to us, without too great scrupulousness in marking connections or insisting on sequences. Much time is wasted by human beings, in general, on establishment of systems . . . I purpose, therefore, henceforward to trouble myself little with sticks or twine, but to arrange my chapters with a view to convenient reference, rather than to any careful division of subjects, and to follow out, in any byways that may open, on right hand or left, whatever question it seems useful at any moment to settle.[12]

The 'sticks and twine' refer to the staking and tethering of plants into clumps by gardeners. So things will be left as they are and as they grow in nature. The reader is not to expect such artificial massing, but a ramble amongst by-ways and a conversation about whatever comes up at the sug-gestion of the details of the landscape. But how are these details to be arranged, and so understood, if not by massing them? Ruskin proposes a more direct way, straight to the heart: 'it is not the multiplication of details which constitutes poetry . . . but [and here the reader may still

---

[11] *Modern Painters III*, V, pp. 141–2.   [12] *Ibid.*, V, p. 18.

unwarily expect to hear something about massing them – and is disappointed] that there must be something either in the nature of the details themselves, or the method of using them, which invests them with poetical power'.[13] The matter is clinched, and organised mass excluded, by the definition of poetry which follows: 'the suggestion, by the imagination, of noble grounds for the noble emotions'. These include 'those four principal sacred passions Love, Veneration, Admiration and Joy'. This is a blow struck for romantic piety, the individual roused to worship by direct contemplation of nature, in a chapter arguing against Reynolds that 'common nature' – not least its Blakean minute particulars – is integral to great art and the noble feelings it stimulates.

Even Veronese, the master of masses which are at once imposing and light, is 'read' by Ruskin in terms of the relation of parts to the whole without intermediate masses. Veronese is discussed under the heading of 'the largest quantity of Truth in the most perfect possible harmony' – a fine summing up of his achievement. And the passage about him is altogether fine and evocative. But although mass is a topic which always seems to be about to break surface in it, it is again kept back by Ruskin's oscillation between individual components among themselves, and between each of them and the whole canvas. Veronese

chooses to represent the great relations of visible things to each other, to the heaven above, and to the earth beneath them. He holds it more important to show how a figure stands relieved from delicate air, or marble wall; how as a red, or purple, or white figure, it separates itself, in clear discernibility, from the things not red, nor purple, nor white; how infinite daylight shines round it; how innumerable veils of faint shadow invest it; how its blackness and darkness are, in the excess of their nature, just as limited and local as its intensity of light; all this, I say, he feels to be more important [sc. than Rembrandt, who has just been considered, and] than showing merely the exact *measure* of the spark of sunshine that gleams on a dagger hilt, or glows on a jewel. All this, moreover, he feels to be harmonious – capable of being joined in one great system of spacious truth.[14]

In other words, Veronese is a hero who demonstrates Ruskin's continual theme, wonderfully explored at Torcello and Murano, of parts contributing to the whole, of the part played by each contiguous but separate individual figure, 'how a figure stands relieved from delicate air, or marble wall', within 'infinite daylight' or the great society of a picture. It was a point which he liked to make by bidding his reader cover one small part of a picture with his finger, and then notice how the whole thing disintegrates in ruin as a result: 'break off the merest stem or twig of it, it all goes to pieces'.[15] He also liked to make it in terms of his doctrine of imperfection, with its marked relevance to the politics of individuals in society:

[13] *Ibid.*, V, pp. 27–8.   [14] *Ibid.*, V, p. 59.   [15] *Modern Painters II* (1846), IV, p. 240.

if therefore the combination made is to be harmonious, the artist must induce in each of its component parts . . . such imperfection as that the other shall put it right. If one of them be perfect by itself, the other will be an excrescence. Both must be faulty when separate, and each corrected by the presence of the other.[16]

This corresponded with his insistence that great painters deployed a sort of deliberate roughness or willed inadequacy which solicited the active participation of the viewer's imagination: 'piece out my imperfection with your thoughts' as the Chorus pleads in *Henry V*. So '*all* the parts of a noble work must be separately imperfect; each must imply, and ask for, all the rest'.[17] The internal social life of a picture was thus Christian, a sort of communion of individual saints held together by the forgiveness of sins, a scene of needs and supplies within the spiritual 'infinite daylight' of mutual love: the form of Christianity which George Eliot rescued from the ruins of doctrine and made into the structure of *Middlemarch*. He could also put it in more soberly negative terms which remind us of Isaiah Berlin when he notices that 'the various qualities which form greatness are partly inconsistent with each other (as some virtues are, docility and firmness for instance) and partly independent of each other'. He went so far along this proto-Berlinian line as to assert, when discussing the ideal with some suspicion, that 'there is a perfect ideal to be wrought out of every face around us – the faces of portraits can be ideal because the ideal is individual'. And it includes 'the evidences of sorrow and past sufferings'.[18]

As a final example of Ruskin's avoidance of mass, we may take his advice to a pupil faced with drawing a bank of grass, such as might form the foreground of a picture. It should not really be thought of as a foreground at all, because that would be a temptation to make it 'vigorous', 'marked', 'forcible', and so on. It would also be a lure to treat it as some sort of a mass, and that is a category which he does not even consider here except under the category of 'blots'. The obvious enough idea that it might all be sorted into a few manageable groups is spectacularly absent.

If you will lie down on your breast on the next bank that you come to (which is *close* enough, I should think, to give it all the force it is capable of), you will see, in the cluster of leaves and grass close to your face . . . a mystery of soft shadow in the depths of the grass, with indefinite forms of leaves, which you cannot trace nor count, within it, and out of that, the nearer leaves coming in every subtle gradation of tender light and flickering form, quite beyond all delicacy of pencilling to follow; and yet you will rise up from that bank (certainly not making it appear coarser by drawing a little back from it), and profess to represent it by a few blots of 'forcible' foreground colour. 'Well, but I cannot draw every leaf that I see on the bank.' No, for as . . . no human work could be finished so as to express the *delicacy*

---

[16] *Ibid.*, IV, p. 233.   [17] *Ibid.*, IV, p. 236.   [18] *Modern Painters III*, V, p. 66.

of nature, so neither can it be finished so as to express the *redundance* of nature. Accept that necessity; but do not deny it; do not call your work finished, when you have, in engraving, substituted a confusion of coarse black scratches, or in water-colour a few edgy blots, for ineffable organic beauty. Follow that beauty as far as you can, remembering that just as far as you see, know, and represent it, just so far your work is finished.[19]

This beautiful, if rather hectoringly pedagogic, passage is accompanied by an engraving of an exquisite drawing by Ruskin of grass, chervil and other foliage interlacing and floating free. It must be relevant to this inquiry that his output as a painter consisted entirely, once he was set on his literary career, of numerous watercolour studies of the highest quality, sometimes approaching Turner's. It is his eye for a study, his bird's or sketcher's eye, which can account for his lop-sided handling of Titian's *Bacchus and Ariadne*, a picture which he greatly admired. More often than not, it is the superbly drawn details of vegetation which attract his notice. Four times he refers to the aquilegia in the foreground and three times to the wonderfully rendered vine leaves; as against three references to its tone and truth of colour.

Making a definition of mass earlier in this essay evoked the landscapes of Poussin and Claude: seventeenth-century masters who got the rough side of Ruskin's advocacy of Turner. The trouble was that most people preferred them to Turner. Ruskin wanted to show such people that they were wrong. So the painters who were generally admired, even by him as a teenager, 'as perfect models of the beautiful' had to be slighted.[20] He was an advocate to the core and the approval of what is approved of never came readily to him. It got him into unnecessary difficulties with Titian and Michelangelo from time to time. Even when he had had time to collect his thoughts in *Modern Painters V*, seventeen years after *Modern Painters I*, the antipathy to classicism is still distorting. Claude and Poussin were familiar masters to the public at the time, being well repre-sented in English collections. It was natural to use them as benchmarks for getting a fix on the new phenomenon of Turner, and Ruskin was far from being as alone as he allows us to think in considering Turner a greater landscape painter than either of them, though Hazlitt refused him that distinction. Ruskin improbably considered Claude and Poussin to be atheists in the chapter on them in *Modern Painters V*, and too much given to 'peculiarly classical' restraint. Claude's 'unequalled *aerial effects*' and 'seas . . . the most beautiful in old art' are praised, but his 'dislike of all evi-dences of toil, or distress, or terror' is reprimanded and the summing up is that admiration of him is 'wholly impossible in any period of national

[19] *Ibid.*, V, pp. 164–5. [20] *The Poetry of Architecture*, I, p. 112.

vigour in art' and his influence 'over certain classes of minds . . . almost exclusively hurtful'.[21]

Presumably 'certain classes of minds' excludes the genius of Turner. Claude was a lifelong influence on him, amounting, in John Gage's view, to infatuation. Turner is reported to have wept at his first sight of a Claude landscape and Claude's 'twin models of the seaport and the lush, extensive landscape' were with him throughout his work.[22] Turner distanced himself from Ruskin's unsolicited advocacy from the first, discouraging him from publishing the essay which Ruskin wrote in Turner's defence as a nineteen-year-old. Ruskin's grudging attitude to Turner's beloved Claude was certainly a reason for this and his keeping mum about *Modern Painters* (Ruskin: 'I think he must have read my book'[23]). Ruskin's hostility to Rembrandt was probably another: Turner was so completely enthralled by him that he felt it 'a sacrilege to pierce the mystic shell of colour in search of form'.[24]

At any rate, Ruskin and Turner agreed with everyone else who has ever seen a Claude that he is a great master of the painting of air. A less celebrated aspect of Claude's work is his combination of atmosphere and mass. Huge shapes of trees and buildings are held in the circumambient air of his canvases so that they are at once distinct and integrated. Ruskin seems not to have noticed this, but it had a great effect on Turner. The transfiguration of mass is a primary cause of the excitement of his pictures. It is torn by wind and water, riddled and evaporated by light, but if it were not *there* it would not be Turner. The careful and delicate drawing with which Turner described mass gets burned away like *cire perdue* or covered over like an armature: two metaphors from sculpture which bring out the presence of sculptural mass in Turner. Dissolving mass is a dominant theme, at once compositional and narrative, of two famous Turners in the National Gallery which Ruskin loved and discussed. They were painted ten years apart and mark out what Ruskin called 'Turner's period of central power'.[25] They both depend, though Ruskin of course omits to say so, on Claude's theme of the sun over water: rising in the first, setting in the second. In *Ulysses Deriding Polyphemus* the rearing horses of Apollo's sun-chariot are just visible on the right, their exultant forms melting into the triumph of light. 'The god himself is formless, he *is* the sun',[26] victorious over vapour.[27] On the left, the sprawling limbs and head

---

[21] *Modern Painters V* (1860), VII, pp. 319–22.

[22] John Gage, *J. M. W. Turner: 'A Wonderful Range of Mind'* (New Haven, Conn., 1987), p. 110.

[23] Noted on 15 May 1843, and cited in the editors' introduction to *Modern Painters I* (1843), III, p. xli.   [24] Turner, in a lecture delivered in 1881, cited in Gage, *Turner*, p. 103.

[25] *The Turner Bequest* (1856), XIII, p. 168.   [26] *Ibid.*, XIII, p. 137.

[27] *Modern Painters V*, VII, p. 411.

of the blinded Polyphemus become transparent in anguished failure. ('I wish he were out of the way . . . that we might see the mountains better' is Ruskin's astonishing comment.[28]) So this picture turns on two kinds of dissolution, positive and negative. Between them, Ulysses' ship sails free towards us as he greets the sun with lifted arms. *'The Fighting Téméraire' Tugged to her Last Berth,* ten years on, is an integration of positive and negative dissolution into a visual *Liebestod*: red was to Ruskin the colour of sacrifice, love and death – and this picture an instance of that symbolism. The old ship's mass – 'her organized perfectness' in Ruskin's phrase[29] – is a proud and pale ghost of its former Trafalgar glory, dragged by the black and flaming little tug into the sun's firepath. Ruskin caught Turner's tragedy splendidly:

of all pictures of subjects not visibly involving human pain, this is, I believe, the most pathetic that was ever painted. The utmost pensiveness which can ordinarily be given to a landscape depends on adjuncts of ruin but no ruin was ever so affecting as this gliding of the vessel to her grave.

If he had not decided that all evidences of toil and terror were absent from Claude, he might have noticed that his *Seaport with the Embarkation of St Ursula* was a forerunner, on view in London, of *The Fighting Téméraire*. Ursula is setting out for martyrdom and there is a good deal of toil with her luggage going on.

Advocacy of Turner was a task to which Ruskin returned again and again. The character and energetic tendentiousness of his commitment to it displays, from the start and in the face of all its brilliant perceptions and intuitive sympathy, his constantly slight appreciation of mass. The 'organized perfectness' of *The Fighting Téméraire* was a rare glimpse of it. It is worth noticing that Constable's debt to Claude was the counterpart of Turner's. He took Claude's strategy with masses and made them stand up more solidly to the light, the wind and the rain – though in his later paintings the masses fray and tear under their stresses. Ruskin had, for polemical reasons which he admitted, little patience with Constable's work: 'greatcoat weather and no more'.[30]

III

An earlier source for Ruskin's neglect of mass than his defence of Turner was the Bible. 'Every fancy that I had about nature [as a child] was put into my head by some book.'[31] His father had taken as much care to nourish him on the best poetry and prose as to feed him with varied

---

[28] *The Turner Bequest*, XIII, p. 138.   [29] *Ibid.*, XIII, pp. 170–1.
[30] *Modern Painters I*, III, p. 191.   [31] *Modern Painters III*, V, p. 367.

landscapes and buildings on the formative holiday journeys. His chapters on landscape in *Modern Painters* have a way of turning out to be as much, often more, about poetry as they are about pictures. 'Classical Landscape' is Homer's. Indeed, there is a constant pull towards literature throughout his art criticism – a sufficient reason for his being studied nowadays more in English Literature faculties than in Art History. But the Book of Books was the Bible and it was his mother who methodically saturated his mind with it – daily readings and passages to be learned by heart. As a result, there is hardly a page of Ruskin without a biblical quotation or echo and the twenty-eight pages of biblical references in Cook and Wedderburn's index are by no means exhaustive. And these thousands of instances are not ornamental *jeux d'esprit*, as in, say, P. G. Wodehouse. They reflect, and even provide the structure of, all his thinking about nature.

In *Modern Painters III* he finds himself comfortably at home in 'Medieval Landscape' (part IV, chapter XIV) and its allegorical understanding, founded in the Bible, of the natural world. He considers 'the peculiar characters of the grass' more like a medieval monk than a modern botanist. Grass is one of his favourite subjects for moral reflection, and here he looks in turn at 'herb yielding seed' (Genesis 1.29) which gives food and beauty; rushes as 'the first natural carpet thrown under the human foot'; and flax which makes linen.

Observe the three virtues definitely set forth by the three families of plants; not arbitrarily or fancifully associated with them, but in all the three cases marked for us by Scriptural words:

1st.   Cheerfulness, or joyful serenity; in the grass for food and beauty. – 'Consider the lilies of the field, how they grow; they toil not, neither do they spin.'

2nd.   Humility; in the grass for rest. – 'A bruised reed shall he not break.'

3rd.   Love; in the grass for clothing (because of its swift kindling). – 'The smoking flax shall He not quench.'[32]

In *Modern Painters V* he is back on the same subject and rounds on the reader:

Do you think that I am irreverently comparing great and small things? The system of the world is entirely one; small things and great alike are part of one mighty whole. As the flower is gnawed by the frost, so every human heart is gnawed by faithlessness. And as surely, – as irrevocably, – as the fruitbud falls before the east wind, so fails the power of the kindest human heart, if you meet it with poison.[33]

---

[32] *Ibid.*, V, p. 292.   [33] *Modern Painters V*, VII, p. 452.

After which he drifts into defence of Turner and restless incoherence in pursuit of the subject of the chapter, 'Peace'. But this passage marks out clearly the points between which his mind habitually moved: the world's 'mighty whole' within which everything has its place; a detail such as a flower nipped by frost or a fruit-bud killed by the east wind (combined and related details); and, since such details are always symbolic 'hiero-glyphs' to him as well as natural actualities, the sufferings of the human heart. It is a sort of trinitarian perichoresis which is at the core of all his ramblings.

To return to where we left *Modern Painters III*. When he has got through the next (cross) chapter 'Of Modern Landscape' reprimanding its painters for dull colours, tourists for leaving litter around, and the general 'ennui and jaded intellect' deriving from 'want of faith', he is at home again in 'The Moral of Landscape'. This is one of his most genially ambulatory chapters – walking is recommended in the middle of it: 'not more than ten or twelve miles of road a day' so as to leave 'time for stopping at the stream sides or shady banks, or for any work at the end of the day'. Railways are deplored. But it is not an aimless ramble. The more the chapter goes on, the more the reader senses that the Bible is its goal.

It begins with one of his delicately gripping descriptions of the psychology of looking: how it gathers a penumbra of thought and significant association around it, but obscurely because 'If the thoughts were more distinct we should not *see so* well'[34] – the central thing, which he had earlier and most beautifully described as 'the brightness of that emotion hanging, like dew on gossamer, on a curious web of subtle fancy and imperfect knowledge'.[35] Thinking about seeing passes easily into visual autobiography:

The first thing which I remember, as an event in life, was being taken by my nurse to the brow of Friar's Crag on Derwent Water; the intense joy, mingled with awe, that I had in looking through the hollows in the mossy roots, over the crag, into the dark lake, has associated itself more or less with all twining roots of trees ever since.[36]

This is the kind of history of private perception-cum-emotion which Proust revelled in. Ruskin is being very careful here to guard the primacy, purity, and priority of sheer personal and ocular experience. 'Intense joy, mingled with awe' accompany the passage of his eye from near detail towards the dark lake, unimpeded by mass or theology. 'There was no definite religious feeling mingled with it . . . I never thought of nature as God's work, but as a separate fact of existence.' He allows for the influence of literature in general on such moments, and for their gentle

<hr />

[34] *Modern Painters III*, V, 536.   [35] *Ibid.*, V, p. 177.   [36] *Ibid.*, V, p. 365.

moral power to keep him 'good-humoured and kindly', but doctrine and positive religion are kept off. Instead, he testifies to 'a continual percep-tion of Sanctity in the whole of nature' and 'an instinctive awe' which made him 'shiver from head to foot with the joy and fear of it'.[37] This 'joy in nature seemed to me to come from a sort of heart hunger, satisfied with the presence of a Great and Holy Spirit'. This is Wordsworthian, Tintern Abbey, piety. More than that, it is the voice of an English Christian mysti-cism which can be traced back to George Herbert, 'to whom, with Dante . . . I owe more than to any other writers'.[38] 'Some book' is certainly unconsciously at work. But we should notice the pastness of it all. This is how things were until he was about eighteen or twenty, not how they are now.[39] It is a prelude, even a protoevangelium, and functions as one because it is both authentic and incomplete. Words for the experience are hard to find, though Wordsworth is some subliminal help. It awaits definition. And after digressions, which wrestle with the moral effect of vision and reach an extremity of strained relevance with praise of Molière's sincerity (not what anyone would expect in a discussion of landscape), it gets it. It is biblical and heralded:

Because it happens that, by various concurrent operations of evil, we have been led according to those words of the Greek poet already quoted, to 'dethrone the gods and crown the whirlwind', it is no reason that we should forget there was once a time when 'the Lord answered Job out of the whirlwind'.[40]

The Bible has been reached at last, synchronised with Ruskin's attaining manhood. There is no questioning of its divine authority. Now innocent nature worship and 'the sense of the presence and power of a Great Spirit . . . becomes the channel of certain truths, which by no other means can be conveyed': 'This is not a statement which any investigation is needed to prove. It comes to us at once from the highest of all authority'[41] – because that is how the Bible instructs the reader in 'two passages of God's speaking, one in the Old and one in the New Testament'. In Job 38.1 and in the Sermon on the Mount in Matthew 5–7 (one of the pas-sages which Ruskin's mother made him learn by heart) the truths of God are conveyed through nature. The Job chapters are about 'nothing else than a direction of the mind which was to be perfected to humble obser-vance of the works of God in nature'. The Sermon on the Mount incul-cates 'trusting God, through watchfulness of His dealings with His creation'. Vision, morals, nature, and God are at one: and this on the base of a quite naively devout and ready assent to the authority of the Bible – 'and no mention of any doctrinal point whatsoever'.[42]

---

[37] *Ibid.*, V, p. 367.   [38] *Ibid.*, V, p. 427.   [39] *Ibid.*, V, p. 368.   [40] *Ibid.*, V, p. 377.
[41] *Ibid.*, V, p. 378.   [42] *Ibid.*, V, p. 379.

Exclusion of doctrine concentrates attention on the Bible as the divine authority in ethics and seeing the world. This is a good enough description of its multifarious contents, at least so far as the two passages chosen from it by Ruskin are concerned. And the way in which the Bible describes the natural world, the structure of its perception, sank deep into Ruskin's mind and shaped its structure. It is simple enough. The Bible was written by scribes. One of the fundamental activities of scribes was to make lists of things. It was a workaday genre which they were able to turn to the pre-eminent Ruskinian 'direction of the mind', praise – 'All great Art is Praise'.[43] Psalm 104 is an inventory of the world's contents, from light and clouds and mountains to trees and animals and ships ('there go the ships, and there is that Leviathan' – a favourite of Ruskin). Its thirty-five verses of joyous inventory are punctuated by ejaculations of praise and end with 'Bless thou the Lord, O my soul. Praise ye the Lord.' The world is a treasury of marvellous bits and pieces, each very much itself and going its own way. Their one and only coherence transcends them all, including man: 'O Lord, how manifold are thy works! in wisdom hast thou made them all: the earth is full of thy riches'.[44] In Proverbs 30, handfuls of items are grouped together. 'Four things say not, It is enough': the grave, the barren womb, dry earth, and water. There are four little creatures which are 'exceeding wise': ants, rabbits, locusts, and spiders. Most famously: 'There be three things which are too wonderful for me, yea, four that I know not: the way of an eagle in the air; the way of a serpent upon the rock; the way of a ship in the midst of the sea; and the way of a man with a maid.'

Little groups or sublists like this are just like Ruskin's list of the three moral qualities exhibited by grass – and the many other occasions where he knocks some order into his accumulating notions by numbering them. Their purpose of exemplary moral illustration is his as well. He even shows himself capable of jumping over Newton's head and seeing the rainbow as the writer of Genesis did: it 'signifies always mercy, the spring of life'.[45] And when the sheer mystery and vivacity (why not say 'glory'?) of things escapes a moral category or any category at all, as with the 'three things which are too wonderful for me' – it evokes that most important Ruskinian attitude, admiration.

Admiration is the object of Job 38–41, in which God answers Job out of the whirlwind. The amazement caused to the human mind by looking at one natural thing after another is compounded by insistence that each of these in itself is unknowable to man. Ironically, in ramming this point

---

[43] *Modern Painters V*, VII, p. 463.   [44] Psalm 104, verse 24.
[45] *Modern Painters V*, VII, p. 419.

home time and again, God describes the ostrich and the horse, the hawk and the crocodile ('Leviathan') with the most exact sense of their outward movement and their 'instress'. Or perhaps not ironically, since He does understand them inside out, unlike Job, and has an eye for idiosyncratic detail as sharp as Ruskin's. So, as a spectator of this immense cavalcade of which he can make no coherent sense, Job learned humility. 'Now mine eye seeth thee. Wherefore I repent in dust and ashes'.[46] This was for Ruskin a paradigm of the humble mind, Wordsworth's 'wise passivity' which is the ground of accurate seeing. There can be little doubt that these Old Testament scribe–naturalists were Ruskin's tutors, and so successfully that Ruskin came to deserve the praise accorded to Solomon, the king of them all, who 'spake three thousand proverbs . . . and he spake of trees, from the cedar that is in Lebanon even unto the hyssop that springeth out of the wall'.[47]

And if they needed any help, Osborne Gordon, the Christ Church tutor, was at hand to remind Ruskin that rational Christianity was not so much a matter of doctrinal system as the performance of moral duty along with active reverence for natural beauty. For such men, the Sermon on the Mount was a summary of true religion. The lilies of the field and the birds of the air, used by Christ to inculcate a trusting life under divine providence, were all the doctrine necessary. Christianity at its least systematic, little parables and aphorisms put down one after the other to indicate the Kingdom of God, had the authority of Christ and the Bible. It told you how to look about you and what to do. You got on with it. And this includes the painter, of whom Ruskin had written at the beginning of *Modern Painters III*, characteristically imagining him engrossed in a study rather than making a composition, that: 'It does not matter whether he paint the petal of a rose, or the chasms of a precipice, so that Love and Admiration attend him as he labours.'[48]

It is entirely consistent with Ruskin's capacity to see the world as the biblical writers did that he wasted no time on the heroic attempts of his contemporaries to recast Christianity in terms more consistent with modern world-pictures. It caused him to lose his temper with the liberal F. D. Maurice when he attempted a more charitable, if bowdlerised, reading of a ferocious Old Testament passage. He supported Colenso, inconsistently but because he was being persecuted and needed an advocate. An orthodox dogmatic system was no better than modern recastings of it. Tractarianism had held no attractions to him since, as an undergraduate at Christ Church, he had seen Pusey shuffling around Tom Quad: 'only a sickly and rather ill put together English clerical gentleman, who

---

[46] Job 42.5, 6.   [47] 1 Kings 4.32, 33.   [48] *Modern Painters III*, V, p. 42.

never looked one in the face, or appeared aware of the state of the weather'.[49] Pusey's neighbour across the quad, Buckland, was far more congenial.

Ruskin was as airily negligent and contemptuous of Strauss as, more notoriously, of Darwin. Strauss's *The Life of Jesus Critically Examined* was translated by George Eliot and published in England in 1846. It proved – that is not too strong a word – that incident after incident in the Gospels were fiction spun out of Old Testament texts, treated by the evangelists as prophecy of Christ. The Gospels were full of historical myths. Ruskin was simply not interested in this: positively because he was always content to read the Bible as his mother had taught him to do, abetted by his own great powers as a sympathetic reader; negatively because historical myths were transient things beside natural myths, which were agelessly instructive about the inner nature of such things ('hieroglyphs') as rainbows and grass. He told Osborne Gordon that, as a Christian, his vital knowledge was of 'the beauty of creation' not 'a system of salvation'. The Bible was, to him, more a book of sacred nature than sacred, or salvation, history. In a sense, he was aware of Strauss's main point already and had no inclination to follow it through – which may well have something to do with his often slapdash attitude to history in general, even in *The Stones of Venice* where efforts at the evaluation of historical evidence soon get bundled off into headlong generalisations about epochs of virtue, decline, and fall.

There is no more evidence that Ruskin ever read Strauss's book than that Turner ever read *Modern Painters*. Abundant hearsay about such a *succès de scandale* probably sufficed him. Even the girls at Winnington Hall had heard about it and their headmistress wrote to Ruskin with her worries over myths. His advice to the girls was decisive:

I have always had an acute dread of this Germanism . . . so let me close . . . with this one entreaty: – that you will not any of you – until you are much older, allow yourselves to be troubled with the talk going on at present in the world of so called philosophers, respecting the typical or mythical meaning of portions of the Bible – Be assured that God will never blame you for taking His words too simply or literally: He will only blame you for not attending to them, when they are explicit – or for not obeying them, when they are imperative.[50]

His advice to adults, particularly 'simple and busy men, concerned much with art' rather than scholars, was the same. First they should spend a whole year trying to put the Sermon on the Mount into practice. Then, if successful, 'let them try the German system if they choose'.[51]

---

[49] *Praeterita* (1886–89), XXXV, p. 202.
[50] Letter to the girls at Winnington Hall, 19 May 1859, in *The Winnington Letters: John Ruskin's Correspondence with Margaret Alexis Bell and the Children at Winnington Hall*, ed., V. A. Burd (London, 1969), p. 187.   [51] *Modern Painters III*, V, p. 426.

IV

Like all conversions, Ruskin's conversion to paganism around 1858 was by no means the total change which the neophyte advertised. He had already given the public plenty of evidence of his capacity to enter into the myths of the pagans, not least when Turner painted them. It rested on his early conviction that seeing the world through the eyes of someone else was as fine a thing as seeing it though your own eyes and his acute penetrative imagination which 'gets within all fence, cuts down to the root, and drinks the vital sap'.[52] Wordsworth's sonnet 'The world is too much with us' had taught him that 'a Pagan suckled in a creed outworn' was preferable to a listless and wasted modern, if belief in his gods attuned him to their real and divine presences in sea and wind. If pagan myth conveyed an equivalent sense of the divine in nature to the Old Testament and the Sermon on the Mount, so much the better. 'Before we ask what a man worships, we have to ask whether he worships at all.'[53] This pronouncement comes at the end of the chapter on Murano in *The Stones of Venice II*. It marks a previous conversion. Ruskin's penetrative imaginative sympathy with the builders and crafts-men of medieval Venice, Catholic Christians to a man, had set him at odds with his parents' biblical Protestantism. They feared, needlessly, a tractarian-type conversion to Rome, such as Newman and others had undergone recently enough. Ruskin catered for Protestant prejudices, and shared them sincerely enough, with reprobation of the modern upholstery in the church, of the damaging treatment of the old capitals by the verger and his ladder, and of the abject mien of the worshippers. But when he confronts the great mosaic of the Madonna in the apse, this will not do. He deflects Protestant hatred of Mariolatry onto the 'fright-ful doll' below it, which attracts the modern faithful. The glorious image above, though neglected, opens his mind to the positive value of such a cult:

Let that worship be taken at its worst; let the goddess of this dome of Murano be looked upon as just in the same sense an idol as the Athene of the Acropolis, or the Syrian Queen of Heaven; and then, on this darkest assumption, balance well the difference between those who worship and those who worship not; – that difference which there is in the sight of God, in all ages between the calculating, smiling, self-sustained, self-governed man, and the believing, weeping, wonder-ing, struggling, Heaven-governed man; – between the men who say in their hearts 'there is no God,' and those who acknowledge a God at every step, 'if haply they might feel after Him and find Him.' For that is the difference which we shall find, in the end, between the builders of this day and the builders on that sand island

---

[52] *Modern Painters IV*, IV, pp. 250–1.   [53] *The Stones of Venice II* (1853), X, p. 67.

long ago. They *did* honour something out of themselves; they did believe in spiritual presence.[54]

His parents (Ruskin often has people near to him in mind as he writes – in his 'pagan' phase it would be Rose la Touche) need not worry. His conversion is to the religion of Catholics 'long ago', emphatically not to modern Romanism. They should be further reassured by the authorising role of the Bible in this passage. St Paul's oration on Mars Hill is quoted along with Psalm 14, and the whole thing is a sermon on a text from John 4.24: 'God is a spirit; and they that worship Him must worship Him in spirit and in truth.' The medieval craftsmen of Murano may, he allows, have been deficient in truth, as known by the likes of his parents, but they were strong enough on spirit and worship. We know, as neither he nor his parents knew at the time, that 'Athene of the Acropolis' was to get superbly 'penetrative' treatment as the divinity of air in *The Queen of the Air* in 1869, when his mother was still alive. The seeds of that are here. But in this passage the reference to pagan divinities is cleverly made. It takes the suspicious Protestant eye away from Roman superstition and onto a long-ago goddess, respectably enshrined in the literature of an Oxford education. More generous sentiments can be expected there – even, by association, for 'the Syrian Queen of Heaven' denounced in Old Testament prophecy (perhaps a risky reference, but prophetic of things to come in his work). For the theme of this essay, it is important to notice that Ruskin's mind works here in religion as it does elsewhere for nature. He does not compare religious system with religious system any more than he contrasted grouped mass with grouped mass in nature. That could be left to 'Germanism' and the 'so called philosophers'. He picks on a single phenomenon, meditates upon it, then invokes another. His mind is moving like the Psalmist's or that of the writer of Job. And not least because the ground and object of it all is worship: not the making of an intermediate structure of ideas but the perception, by means of the right direction of the heart set upon the God who is spirit, of single objects in the grand context of the whole.

Religion at all costs and wherever it is to be found – that seems to be Ruskin's primary demand. But it is not religion as commonly and academically understood from a detached position outside it as a coherent structure of ideas and customary rituals. It is religion from the inside, one's own inside or somebody else's, earnestly believing and looking ardently out, over the head of religious organisation, to divinity.

He speaks his mind about it most clearly, and as so often, in an unexpected place: an essay on 'Water Colour Societies' in his *Academy Notes*

---

[54] *Ibid.*, X, pp. 67–8.

for 1859. He begins by getting annoyed over the two pictures selected by the societies for special prominence. They illustrated lines from Shakespeare and from Tennyson. 'I am not going to criticise these pictures' he says, but deplores them for giving the false impression that poetry was well understood in England. This leads into a critique of vulgarity as a combination of insensibility with insincerity which results in the loss of 'animating motive' in people who still insist on tackling subjects which need it, such as poetry. The worst of all such losses is

> the loss of belief in the spiritual world. Art has never shown, in any corner of the earth, a condition of advancing strength but under this influence. I do not say, observe, influence of 'religion', but influence merely of a belief in some invisible power – god or goddess, fury or fate, saint or demon.[55]

Thus a Pythagorean who believed in 'something awful and impenetrable connected with beans', would be a stronger and better person than the kitchen-maid who sees them only as things to be boiled. Likewise an Egyptian who held hawks to be divine creatures would be better to hear on them than a taxidermist, and a Jew would paint a storm better than a modern scientist. Above all a compassionately sociable man, capable of 'love and dwelling in the spirits of other creatures', will paint a better portrait than a professor of anatomy. The message is that a sense of the spiritual significance of details is far more valuable than a utilitarian or scientific approach to them. This was the *sine qua non* of art in the past, whose 'whole temper . . . was in some way reverential – had awe in it'.[56] Illuminated Psalters were for praying with; Madonnas were painted 'to be looked up to through tears'; armour was for use in battle. Ruskin's point is the sheer and utter necessity of 'belief in the spiritual world', not necessarily believed to contain only one God but necessarily believed in, for art to be good. The fact that for once he has hit a historical nail on the head and noticed something which art historians and directors of galleries have begun to take seriously in our own time, is subsidiary – but a reminder of how penetrative he can so often be. For him, it was not a historical point that he was inculcating, but an urgent gospel for the present.

The difficulty, which contemporaries such as Carlyle and Matthew Arnold noticed, was that the gospel had to be preached at a time when, for all the crying need of it, the world view and structure of belief in which it was set was coming to pieces and rival systems were coming along, often with increasing coherence. Ruskin noticed it too and awareness of the nineteenth-century dilemma haunts most of his pages. The extraordinary thing about him is that the pages themselves are inscribed with thoughts, descriptions, and perceptions which derive directly from the heart of the

[55] *Royal Academy Notes* (1870), XIV, p. 243.   [56] *Ibid.*, XIV, pp. 244–5.

Bible, of Christendom, and of antiquity – gathered along 'the old road' as it were – and yet are not only very Victorian but vividly contemporary to people at the end of the millennium. Nobody studies intellectual history nowadays as the march of mind, but it is still quite a surprise to find how Ruskin's biblical mind, itemising and praising, speaks to the present; or how his confidence in his ability to 'enter into what a Greek's real notion of a god was', whether justified or not in a particular instance,[57] can result in a perfect description of a Harpy, or 'Snatcher':

This is a month [March] in which you may really see a small Harpy at her work almost whenever you choose. The first time that there is threatening of rain after two or three days of fine weather, leave your window well open to the street, and some books or papers on the table; and if you do not, in a little while, know what the Harpies mean; and how they snatch, and how they defile, I'll give up my Greek myths.[58]

Or again, his old-fashioned typological mode can produce a passage which works wonderfully. Treating colour as 'the type of love', the supreme element of pictorial poetry beside the chief of the Christian virtues, he says (in a vast footnote) things which reflect brilliantly both on painting and on human life – including his own happiness and tragedy:

As colour is the type of Love, it resembles it in all its modes of operation, and in practical work of human hands, it sustains changes of worthiness precisely like those of human sexual love. That love, when true, faithful, well-fixed, is eminently the sanctifying element of human life: without it, the soul cannot reach its fullest height or holiness. But if shallow, faithless, misdirected, it is also one of the strongest corrupting and degrading elements of life.

Between these base and lofty states of Love are the loveless states; some cold and horrible; others chaste, childish or ascetic, bearing to careless thinkers the semblance of purity higher than of Love.

So it is with the type of Love – colour. Followed rashly, coarsely, untruly, for the mere pleasure of it, with no reverence, it becomes a temptation, and leads to corruption. Followed faithfully, with intense but reverent passion, it is the holiest of all aspects of material things.[59]

Holy and sensual, we might say. And that would be both true to Ruskin and an indication of why he is religiously powerful a hundred years after his death to people whose sense of the sacred and the sensual has survived the collapse of theological system – and who have enjoyed the intense dedication to colour of Matisse and Bonnard. In the face of all that Ruskin gave, his weakness on mass is easily forgivable – and a way for his readers to get some idea of the way his eye and his mind moved, which is a

---

[57] *Modern Painters III*, V, p. 223.   [58] *The Queen of the Air* (1869), XIX, pp. 313–14.
[59] *Modern Painters V*, VII, p. 417n.

vindicating instance of his positive doctrine of imperfection as a social benefit: 'all the parts of a noble work must be separately imperfect; each must imply, and ask for, all the rest'.[60]

Parts imply, and ask for, all the rest throughout Ruskin's *œuvre*. They never stop doing it. It is what makes it so hard to find things in Ruskin's writings, so hard not to get diverted into other things during the search, and so hard to stop reading him. It is what structures his critical analysis of art and nature. And it is a reminder of how constantly he implies the reader in his work, soliciting and warning so personally that we can almost feel his hand on our shoulders or at our elbows. He often first sees something with our eyes (i.e. inadequately) so that we, reproved, are ready to see it with his eyes (i.e. well). Perhaps the best epitaph is a sentence from a letter to his former Oxford tutor, Brown, which is published in Dinah Birch's important contribution to the understanding of his religion, *Ruskin's Myths*: 'I find the Imperfect is the great tense of my life – quite an intense tense – but it shall not at least be aoristic any longer.'[61]

---

[60] *Modern Painters II*, IV, p. 236.
[61] Letter to W. R. Brown, 18 November 1861, cited in Dinah Birch, *Ruskin's Myths* (Oxford, 1988), p. 63.

Part III

The politics of anatomy and an anatomy of
politics *c.* 1825–1850

Boyd Hilton

I

Historians of nineteenth-century science have made remarkable
advances during the last twenty years, yet their findings have largely been
ignored by political and intellectual historians. In seeking to explain why
this should be so, it might seem unfair to scapegoat one of the few books
which, forty years ago, seriously attempted to make the necessary integration. Nevertheless, the critical success of *1859: Entering an Age of Crisis*
possibly did more harm than good. Its premise was that *On the Origin of
Species* (1859) had been a 'seminal volume'. 'The first edition was bought
up in a single day, and there followed . . . convulsions of the national mind
. . . Here, evidently, is crisis.'[1] Charles Darwin's book was shocking
because 'a great chasm seemed to have been opened between God and
Nature . . . It seemed to many . . . that God had been banished from the
world.'[2] The consequence was 'crisis' – in politics, economics, international affairs, metaphysics, and literary criticism. One of the contributors,
H. M. Jones, clearly had doubts about this premise, pointing out that the
'formation' of the Liberal Party in 1859 hardly amounted to 'crisis', and
that John Stuart Mill's *On Liberty*, published in the same year, was one of
'the great expressions of utopian hope', since it envisaged a perfect world
of amiable and rational public discussion. But having made his point,
even Jones jumped back into line. 'Still, the idea of crisis will not down . . .
In the sense that Mill looked forward to a perfection that never took
shape, one *can* regard his great essay as a gateway into crisis.'[3]

These pronouncements did not resonate with political, social, and
intellectual historians, whose response must have been: 'Crisis? What

I wish to thank David Knight, Jim Moore, Margaret Pelling, Jim Secord, and Alison
Winter for their very great help in preparing this essay.

[1] H. M. Jones, '1859 and the Idea of Crisis', in P. Appleman, W. A. Madden, and M. Wolff,
  eds., *1859: Entering an Age of Crisis* (Bloomington, 1959), p. 17.
[2] N. Annan, 'Science, Religion, and the Critical Mind', in *ibid.*, pp. 35–7.
[3] Jones, '1859', in *ibid.*, pp. 17, 24.

crisis?' Conventionally the third quarter of the century is represented as an 'age of equipoise', characterised by social harmony, orderly craft unions, consumer goods, savings banks, cooperative societies, organised philanthropy, urban regeneration, the 'great Victorian boom', and the 'golden age of English agriculture'.[4] Mill, Arnold, Fawcett, Morley, and Stephen might have had misgivings about the future, but they all adopted an eirenical tone, confident that they could draw on a basic fund of common sense among their readers. It was also a nonsense to claim that Darwinism banished God. While it helped to undermine the image of God as a retributive Jehovah obsessed with sin and judgement, that conception was fading already – indeed, one cause of the increased serenity of the 1850s and 1860s was the spread of a more comfortable theology which emphasised the love of Christ, forgiveness of sins, the unreality of Hell, the cosy domesticity of Heaven, and the eventual resurrection of the dead.[5] Whereas, during the first half of the century, disputes over baptismal regeneration, the real presence, eternal torment, the atonement, or pre-election had seemed to be matters of spiritual life and death, so that families and friends had parted for ever over Tractarianism and the Gorham Judgement, now the mood was much more detached.[6] Even *Essays and Reviews* (1860), which made a bigger splash than *Origin of Species*,[7] hardly provoked a typhoon. Heralded (mistakenly) as the long-dreaded invasion of incomprehensible German theology, it proved a pretty damp squib. In this new climate, pre-millenarians were disposed to predict a soft landing for the apocalypse, whereas formerly they had predicted 'throes and agonies' and a 'sudden and fierce convulsion'.[8] Even the 1860s' well-publicised crises of faith are beginning to be re-interpreted as relating more to personal malfunctions in family and vocational life than to some general 'intellectual and moral crisis'.[9]

Moreover, except in the most biblically literalist circles, *Origin of Species* was absorbed fairly painlessly, in sharp contrast to the anonymous *Vestiges of Creation* in 1844, whose electrical and embryological stabs at a theory of development really *had* provoked 'convulsions of the national

---

[4] W. L. Burn, *The Age of Equipoise* (London, 1964).

[5] Boyd Hilton, *The Age of Atonement, 1785–1865* (Oxford, 1988), pp. 270–6.

[6] For a striking evocation of how suddenly the mood changed *c.* 1850, see G. M. Young, 'Mr Gladstone', in *Today and Yesterday: Collected Essays and Addresses* (London, 1948), pp. 32–3.   [7] J. Atholz, *Anatomy of a Controversy, 1860–1864* (Aldershot, 1994).

[8] I. Todhunter, *William Whewell: An Account of his Writings with Selections from his Literary and Scientific Correspondence* (1876), I, p. 328.

[9] Frank M. Turner and Jeffrey von Arx in R. J. Helmstadter and B. Lightman, eds., *Victorian Faith in Crisis* (London, 1990), pp. 9–38, 262–82. The pre-1850 period suffered the most agonised crises of faith, even if their consequences – the actual comings out – were mainly deferred until the more tolerant 1850s and 1860s. P. Corsi, *Science and Religion: Baden Powell and the Anglican Debate, 1800–1860* (Cambridge, 1988).

mind'. By 1859 that mind had become attuned to evolutionary ideas, thanks to Macaulay's *History of England* (1849–61), Herbert Spencer's sociology, and corresponding advances in anthropology, etymology, and fiction. Indeed, the idea of evolution sometimes strengthened faith by attributing the existence of evil and suffering to the fact that God was only part-way through the process of creation.[10] It is therefore hardly surprising that political, social, and intellectual historians – confronting what historians of science had to say about the traumas caused by Darwin's book – should have discounted the impact of scientific disputes. Since there had *not* been any sense of national crisis during the 1860s, they naturally assumed that it was possible for life-and-death arguments to take place among scientists without them having much relevance to public and intellectual life in general.

In fact, rather than Darwinism changing the way people thought, it was more a case of the way people thought affecting their understanding of Darwinism. Thus most mid-Victorians were able to interpret natural selection in light of the progressive, 'upwards and onwards', 'finer and fitter', 'better and more beautiful' optimism prevailing in the 1860s, even though the theory itself was malevolent. In this context the re-dating of Darwin's work during the last two decades assumes particular significance. In 1975 Appel emphasised how early nineteenth-century French biology revolved around the anatomical debates between Cuvier and Geoffroy St Hilaire. At their grand set-piece debate in Paris in 1830, Geoffroy argued that human and animal anatomy could only be understood comparatively, in terms of self-organising material transmutation, with the same patterns of organic structure (unity of composition) running through the animal scale, while Cuvier argued that only a functional explanation was possible.[11] In 1981 Ospovat showed how this same polarity divided British comparative anatomists, and how Cuvier's views were reinterpreted in terms of Paley's argument from design, each creature having been specially created so that it functioned appropriately to its habitat.[12] In 1980 Kohn claimed that Darwin became a transformist as early as 1837 and formulated the theory of natural selection in 1838.[13] Finally, in 1991, Desmond and Moore suggested that, although Darwin could have published his theory of natural selection as early as 1839, he did not do so, mainly because publication would have destroyed his

[10] J. Moore, *The Post-Darwinian Controversies: A Study of the Protestant Struggle to Come to Terms with Darwin in Great Britain and America* (Cambridge, 1979).

[11] Toby A. Appel, *The Cuvier–Geoffroy Debate: French Biology in the Decades before Darwin* (New York, 1987), based on her Princeton University Ph.D. dissertation, 1975.

[12] Dov Ospovat, *The Development of Darwin's Theory* (Cambridge, 1981), pp. 33–7.

[13] David Kohn, 'Theories to Work by: Rejected Theories, Reproduction, and Charles Darwin's Path to Natural Selection', *Studies in the History of Biology*, 4 (1980), pp. 67–170.

claims to respectability, but also perhaps because he was afraid of pushing a divided society, beset by Chartism, over the edge into revolution. By the time he did publish in 1859, the 'age of crisis' had passed and it was no longer thought necessary to uphold belief in special creation and eternal torment in order to preserve social order (besides which A. R. Wallace was breathing down his neck ready to pre-empt him).[14]

By demonstrating that the battle between Cuvier's functional biology and transmutationist or 'evolutionary' biology had its origin in the 1820s and early 1830s – before fossil mammals and hermaphrodite molluscs were even a twinkle in Darwin's eye – these historians have disposed of an awkward time-lag in the older accounts between biological controversies and parallel controversies in related sciences. For example, the John Abernethy–William Lawrence debate of 1817 led to anguished conflicts throughout the 1820s. On the one hand, there was the traditional view that life was caused by an independent, God-given principle of vitality, electrical or chemical, and that nature was divided into different sets of entities, each with its own aptitudes. On the other hand, radical doctors like Lawrence and Elliotson followed Joseph Priestley in claiming that life was a function of matter in the nervous system, and that there was no basic discontinuity between living and non-living matter.[15] The partial synthesis of urea in 1828, far from indicating a link between organic and inorganic substances and so discrediting vitalism, as once was thought, might even have given vitalism 'a new lease of life'.[16] The next two decades brought Lyell's critique of providentialist and catastrophist geology, Crosse's attempts to create electrical insects from inert matter,[17] important developments in electrical affinity, chemical polarity, contagion theory, the conservation of energy, and the nebular hypothesis on the origins of the solar system. Schaffer has given the nebular hypothesis a political twist by claiming that arguments about how the cosmos was developing focused debate on whether laws of human nature could be 'established as the basis of a science of progress', and by showing how political radicals like J. S. Mill and J. P. Nichol fused their version of

[14] Adrian Desmond and James Moore, *Darwin* (London, 1991). See also the essays by David Kohn, Phillip R. Sloan, and M. J. S. Hodge in David Kohn, ed., *The Darwinian Heritage* (Princeton, N.J., 1985), pp. 71–120, 185–257.

[15] L. S. Jacyna, 'Immanence or Transcendence: Theories of Life and Organization in Britain, 1790–1835', *Isis*, 74 (1983), 311–29; Jacyna, 'The Physiology of Mind, the Unity of Nature, and the Moral Order in Victorian Thought', *British Journal for the History of Science*, 14 (1981), pp. 109–32.

[16] John H. Brooke, 'Wöhler's Urea, and its Vital Force? – A Verdict From the Chemists', *Ambix*, 15 (1968), pp. 84–114, especially 102.

[17] James A. Secord, 'Extraordinary Experiment: Electricity and the Creation of Life in Victorian England', in David Gooding, Trevor Pinch, and Simon Schaffer, eds., *The Uses of Experiment* (Cambridge, 1989), pp. 337–83.

nebular theory with political economy, phrenology, and Comtism in their efforts to buttress movements for political reform.[18] Finally, Wise and Smith have claimed, partly on the basis of developments in Cambridge mathematics, that the whole of British science underwent a cultural shift – nascent in the 1820s, becoming dominant in the 1830s, and consolidated in the 1840s – a shift whereby 'time was rediscovered'. The concept of 'economy came to mean evolution rather than balance', dynamics replaced statics, and 'temporal change became an essential feature of the economy of nature'.[19]

Pushing the focus on Darwin back to the 1830s makes sense of R. M. Young's argument that Darwin was profoundly influenced by Malthus.[20] That insight, while compelling analytically, did not fit the old chronology because the Malthusian belief in the inevitability of wars, famines, and pestilences, although very strong throughout the first half of the century, declined very rapidly after 1850. It also makes sense to locate such a portentous debate as that between functionalists and transmutationists in the first half of the century since that really *was* an 'age of crisis' – politically, socially, and intellectually – not simply because of the constant fear of revolution, but because the whole of elite culture was riven with contested notions, what Coleridge called 'polar opposite' ideas: town versus country, church versus dissent, sense versus sensibility, Augustans versus Romantics, reason versus intuition, Greeks versus Goths, masculine versus feminine, not to mention the numerous political polarities of the period over such issues as reform, Catholicism, currency, free trade, and poor relief. This was a period when there simply was no consensus, as there was in the third quarter of the century with its 'amiable and rational public discussion'.

II

Transmutationists did not wield sufficient influence to ensure that their theories were incorporated into the accepted canon of scientific texts, but comparative anatomy was being taught nevertheless. So much is clear from *The Politics of Evolution*, Adrian Desmond's wonderful *tour de force* and the most inspiring and exhilarating attempt so far to place the politics

[18] Simon Schaffer, 'The Nebular Hypothesis and the Science of Progress', in James R. Moore, ed., *History, Humanity and Evolution* (Cambridge, 1989), pp. 131–64.

[19] Norton Wise (with Crosbie Smith), 'Work and Waste: Political Economy and Natural Philosophy in Nineteenth-Century Britain', *History of Science*, 27 (1989), pp. 263–301, 391–449; 28 (1990), pp. 221–61.

[20] R. M. Young, 'Malthus and the Evolutionists: The Common Context of Biological and Social Theory', *Past and Present*, 43 (1969), pp. 109–45.

of the period in an intellectual context. By digging among radical periodicals such as the *Lancet* and the *London Medical and Surgical Journal*, and by excavating notes taken by students of lectures delivered in the medical underworld, Desmond demonstrates that a radicalised version of the French evolutionary biology of Geoffroy and Lamarck had been brought to London by Edinburgh-trained doctors such as Robert Grant and Robert Knox. He also shows how the political reform campaigns against 'old corruption' during 1829–35 had their counterpart in the attempts of middle-class radical doctors in private anatomy schools and medical unions to challenge the authority of the elite physicians and surgeons in the Royal Colleges, many of whom had been trained at Oxford or Cambridge, and most of whom ministered to the aristocracy and gentry. This in itself is unsurprising. Where Desmond excites is in his suggestion that the parties to this political struggle wielded competing zoologies and anatomies: that the medical elites adopted a functional anatomy, while radicals among the new class of urban and artisan-serving GPs promulgated 'atheistic forms of evolutionary development, materialist mental physiologies, and reductionist comparative anatomies'.[21] According to Desmond, 'Oxbridge' scholars such as William Whewell and Adam Sedgwick conceived of scientific knowledge as underwriting a mechanistic natural theology, a mode of thought which enjoyed its swan song in the 1830s with the Bridgewater Treatises. Natural theologians assumed that the natural world was fully formed, and scoured it for proofs of the power, wisdom, and goodness of God. They thought that all aspects of creation had their appropriate function and were indicative of divine design. Because humans alone possessed vitality, it followed that morbidity or corruption must be systemic, that is intrinsic to the individual organism. Most natural theologians were therefore anti-contagionists, in that they did not think that disease could be transferred from one person to another (unless by moral transmitters). Anatomically they followed Cuvier.

On the other side, radical physiologists taught a compound of antivitalism, contagionism, and above all the transmutationist anatomy of Geoffroy and Lamarck (behind whom were German philosophers largely unfamiliar to the British). According to Desmond, the reformers' theories of biological change, progress, and improvement reflected their hopes for an amelioration of the prevailing social order: 'liberals . . . saluted the new anatomists for having brought nature, man, and mind under the control of the laws of progress and development'.[22] More dangerously, however,

---

[21] Adrian Desmond, *The Politics of Evolution: Morphology, Medicine, and Reform in Radical London* (Chicago, 1989), p. 236.   [22] *Ibid.*, p. 199.

their emphasis on the operation of uniform natural laws, their belief that nature was self-regulating and not God-manipulated, their claim that ideas were a product of matter and organisation, and (in the case of Lamarckian extremists) their acceptance that acquired characteristics could be inherited, seemed cumulatively to suggest that humankind might have evolved from animals. Very skilfully Desmond shows how eventually a zoological compromise was engineered, a theory of 'punctuated progression in palaeontology, which broke the Lamarckian chain'. This was developed by Richard Owen, who ditched the old vital fluids and crude Paleyanism, and accepted a modified form of comparative anatomy based on archetypes, which required the existence of a divine law-giver and form-giver for their expression. Desmond describes this compromise as Peelite, which is apt since Peelite conservatism was founded on the need to compromise with the movement for political reform, and sought to hold the line in defensible ditches.

In distinguishing between these types of science, Desmond uses two ruling metaphors: *monarchy* and *democracy*. Elite physicians saw a regal handing down of laws by the Deity, to be interpreted to the laity by themselves as His representatives on earth. In the developmental anatomy of the reforming GPs, on the other hand, life forces were envisaged as self-fulfilling laws pushing *upwards* democratically from below. Gentlemanly scientists like Sedgwick sought to buttress Anglican power by collecting evidences for a providential superintendence of nature, whereas radicals and dissenters, seeking emancipation through knowledge, postulated a 'self-regulating nature mediated by a universal priesthood of all believers'.[23]

This distinction is beguiling but too simplistic. Desmond contends that comparative anatomists 'undercut Cuverian teleology, the mainstay of the ancient universities and corporations, and ushered in a lawfully constrained, morphologically based science, in which the capricious Paleyite monarch was ousted by a more culturally appropriate Divine legislator'.[24] Desmond seems to be suggesting that, because gentlemen scientists were natural theologians who believed in the operations of providence, they necessarily conceived of God as 'capricious'. Yet this is hardly an epithet to apply to Paley's God, a 'watchmaker' who (as Paley himself insisted) governed by 'general laws; and when a particular purpose is to be effected, it is not by making a new law nor by the suspension of the old ones, nor by making them wind and bend, and yield to the occasion'.[25] Desmond also seems to imply that one was either a providentialist or an anti-providentialist, just as one was either an elite or a radical scientist,

---

[23] *Ibid.*, p. 179.   [24] *Ibid.*, p. 199.   [25] William Paley, *Natural Theology* (London, 1802), p. 43.

either a Liberal or a Whig/Tory reactionary, but in fact it is necessary to distinguish both between different types of providentialist and different types of conservative. There *were* those (including many pre-millenarians, Ultra Tories, Ultra Protestants, and even a few Ultra Radicals) who believed in a capricious, absolutist God ruling by means of special or particular providences – and who thought that not a sparrow fell but by His say-so – but the vast majority of gentleman scientists were natural theologians and post-millenarians. They considered that God had set up the machinery of the universe expertly and only *very rarely* needed to interfere with it by a special dispensation. He had the *power* to suspend his own machinery – to ordain some personal tragedy in the hope that it would awaken an individual sinner to his or her spiritual plight, and very occasionally even to chastise an entire nation with the rods of famine, cholera, or invasion – but ninety-nine per cent of what happened was the result of *general* providence. God was a limited monarch with power to suspend the constitution in a crisis, but not a capricious one.

This exegesis might seem like an exercise in theological pedantry, but people's understandings of how providence operated was one of the most sensitive indicators of ideological difference. Take, for example, two Whig politicians, lords Althorp and Brougham. Althorp was 'engrossed' by such subjects as 'the agency of vitality', materialism, instinct, how all these phenomena relate to the doctrine of providence, whether immateriality necessarily implies immortality (in dogs, for example), the question of whether – in relation either to organised or to unorganised beings – 'vital functions do not arise from any quality impressed upon them at their creation', and whether 'the changes which have taken place in the form and surface of the earth have done so without any miraculous intervention of God'. In 1836 he wrote to Brougham regarding the operation of instinct on the actions of men and animals. Althorp felt certain that 'instinct in all cases operates by the impressions originally made by the Deity on the natural organization of his creatures and not by his special interposition in individual cases . . . My view raises I think rather higher than yours the wisdom and design which directed the divine mind in the creation, but yours is much more impressive as to the continued government of the universe and the constant dependence in which we exist on the divine will.'[26] This suggests that Brougham inclined to a theory of special and Althorp to a theory of general providence, but both were clearly providentialists and not materialists or transformationists in the radical sense.

If Desmond seems to conflate two types of functional anatomist –

---

[26] Althorp to Brougham, 8 June 1836, British Library, Althorp Papers, H14.

believers in general providence on the one hand and those who believed in the ubiquity of special providences on the other – the source of the confusion may be traced to contemporary and analogous debates in geology. Here is Desmond discussing two gentlemanly geologists, William Buckland and Adam Sedgwick:

> In paternalist Anglican society the individual . . . had no inalienable democratic rights; so the command for 'social change' could not come from below. Nature was no different. Divine intervention – outside 'Creative Interference' Buckland called it – operated whenever organic changes were needed: the abrupt appearances of fossil animals in the geological record were proof of this. For Oxbridge Anglicans nature was still an absolute monarchy. Sedgwick's Creator operated a spiritual close-borough, holding Personal control over 'natural' appointments and organic changes. God was not a 'uniform and quiescent' Legislator, but a careful meddler, 'an active and anticipating intelligence', whose immediate attention to each mollusc and man obviated any need for any self-developing species.[27]

Desmond seems to assume here that, because their science was conservative, they must have been high Tories (or 'absolutists'), but in fact Buckland was a decidedly liberal Tory, while Sedgwick was both a Whig and an 'ardent reformer' in 1831–2.[28] He especially is unlikely to have conceived of God as a spiritual borough-monger. More importantly, both men believed in 'general' providence and the rule of law. In claiming the contrary – that is that they believed in a 'special' or 'meddling' providence – Desmond is extrapolating too much from Buckland's observation that God had 'intervened' to create new fossil animals on occasions in the past. This *might have* clinched Desmond's argument *if* Buckland were someone who believed in a developmental continuum through time, but of course he did not; he believed in a succession of separate dispensations, each one internally lacking any timescale. The same distinction is evident in Sedgwick's thinking. He too said that at different epochs – such as the creation and various points in fossil history – God had interfered with the natural course of events to effect 'great changes' of organic structure. However, these were chronologically specific and not quotidian interventions. So while it was true that successive dispensations had not evolved naturally one into the other but had been *created,*

> yet, in all the instances of change, the organs, so far as we can comprehend their use, are exactly those which are best suited to the function of the being. Hence we [geologists] not only show intelligence contriving means adapted to an end, but at successive times and periods contriving a change of mechanism adapted to a change in external conditions. If this be not the operation of a powerful and active intelligence, where are we to look for it?

[27] Desmond, *Politics of Evolution,* p. 173.
[28] J. W. Clark and T. McK. Hughes, eds., *The Life and Letters of Adam Sedgwick,* 2 vols. (Cambridge, 1890), I, p. 373.

In other words, although God had 'contrived' to change the mechanism at various stages in biological and geological history, within any one epoch, and given any one set of 'external conditions', mankind was subject to a fixed mechanism. Sedgwick was adamant that, if God were ever to meddle on a day-to-day basis, he would destroy his own moral government. Even volcanoes and floods were not *necessarily* indications of arbitrary providence, since occasional 'paroxysms of internal energy', leading to the formation of mountains and seas, were 'a part of the mechanism of nature', part of its 'glorious workmanship'. All 'material things' were 'under the government of Laws', and the organisation of living matter was as 'mechanical as the works of our own hands', and differed from them 'only in complexity and perfection'.[29] The same point can be made in respect of the Tory William Whewell. Occasionally Whewell, unlike Sedgwick, suggested that God did interfere with the laws of nature, but usually he argued that the miraculous origins of organisms did not entail any breach of those laws. Historical causes might be invoked to explain past developments, but at any one time all nature is subject to the 'Final Cause' currently operating.[30] As Hodge has written,

> For Whewell, the origination of any series of events, such as a new set of species, is a matter of God's introducing new laws rather than either breaking or conforming to laws already in force ... [They were] additions made to nature. So his argument is that from the way things go, lawfully now, after these additions, one cannot arrive at an explanation of how the addition was made in the first place ... When Whewell says that God does not interpose his power, on isolated occasions, to produce a particular event, he sees that as consistent with his account of God's originating action in making these additions to the world; for such additions are not particular events, they are initiations of series, lawful series, of events, a set of organic species, for instance, a new language, or whatever.[31]

Belief in general providence and the rule of law (the 'Cuverian teleology') explains why Anglican natural philosophers, natural theologians, and political economists were individualistic rather than 'paternalistic' in their social attitudes. They believed that those in authority should not melio-

---

[29] A. Sedgwick, 'Address to the Geological Society', *Proceedings of the Geological Society of London*, 1 (1831), pp. 314–16. Moreover, even with regard to past organic changes, Sedgwick (writing in 1842) could not believe that 'these successive forms of animated nature were created and destroyed by the mere impulses of a *capricious* will: but we do believe that they were called into being, and wisely adapted to the successive conditions of our planet, during its progress from a chaotic state till it reached the perfection in which we now find it. The Author of Nature has, during all periods, formed organic beings on the same great plan.' Quoted in John Wyatt, *Wordsworth and the Geologists* (Cambridge, 1995), p. 130 (italics added).

[30] Michael Ruse, 'William Whewell: Omniscientist', in Menachem Fisch and Simon Schaffer, eds., *William Whewell: A Composite Portrait* (Oxford, 1991), pp. 112–13.

[31] Jonathan Hodge, 'The History of the Earth, Life, and Man: Whewell and Palaetiological Science', in *ibid.*, pp. 275–6.

rate man's existence by sentimental humanitarianism or social reform, for by doing so they would undo the tutelary effects of the moral machinery which God had fabricated in order to deal judicially and individually with each of his subjects. The socially deprived should 'stand on their own feet' in a competitive social market, and 'the devil take the hindmost' (or possibly the 'foremost' – in that evangelically tinged world misfortune could be regarded as a sign either of unworthiness or of grace). As Desmond points out, radical medics like Thomas Southwood Smith, a Unitarian, loathed such laissez-faire attitudes:

> Progress, melioration, and law characterized Smith's theology, just as they did his physiology . . . God's operation gave nature its strict, predetermined course, which we could interpret in terms of cause and effect. In other words, this immanent activity demanded a lawful cosmogony: since the animal and moral worlds were subject to God's ordinances, secondary causes were manifestations of His actions. There was no interfering 'outside' Deity, no arbitrary providence to give nature the appearance of whim . . . With God devoted to the reclamation of character and to an increase of happiness, social progress and the alleviation of suffering were inevitable.[32]

Yet most gentlemanly scientists were just as wedded to a cause-and-effect universe as the Unitarians. Though they believed in a transcendent rather than immanent deity, they had no truck whatever with the idea of an 'arbitrary providence' which gave 'nature the appearance of whim'. The difference was simply that Smith envisaged causes and effects taking place dynamically in a cumulative sequence, a sort of progressive creationism, whereas for natural theologians causes and effects operated repetitively in a universe that was conceived of as static.

III

The purpose of this essay is not to carp at an outstandingly fine book, but to try to render Desmond's arguments more credible to political historians by factoring the two different understandings of providence into his schema, thereby extending his two categories to four. First in this extended schema were the radical, reformist, uniformitarian, and frequently Unitarian scientists about whom he writes so compellingly and with such conviction. The other three types of scientist were all what he would call elitist, but they need to be disaggregated since they included two different types of mechanistic natural theologian and a third group which rejected natural theology completely.

There is not space to discuss at length the distinction between the two

---

[32] Desmond, *Politics of Evolution*, p. 201.

different types of mechanistic natural theologian. There were optimists who followed Paley in seeing God's clockwork machinery as working harmoniously to create happiness in the universe; and there were pessimists like Sedgwick, who followed Bishop Butler in seeing the machinery as a process of moral trial, in which human beings were repeatedly tempted and tested, with appropriate punishments brought to bear for particular crimes, thereby impressing on everyone the perfection of divine justice.[33] In the science of political economy, for example, free market policies could be seen either in a benign light, as increasing the size of the national cake to the benefit of everyone, or they could be seen in a judicial light, as rewarding persons of enterprise and punishing the lazy. In the science of anatomy, either healthy organs could be shown as contrivances to support life, or else bodily malfunctions could be explained as the outcome of intemperance. On the whole, since this was 'an age of crisis', the retributive style of interpretation was more common.[34]

There was also a fourth understanding of science which was based on revelation and which rejected natural or functional explanations of the body. In this version God's role *could* plausibly be described as 'absolutist', 'authoritarian', 'capricious', 'arbitrary', 'whimsical', 'interventionist', and 'meddling'. Some of the best work on this ultra-tory or romantic science has been written from a literary perspective. Thus De Almeida has related Keats's poetry to his ideas on the evolution of matter and mind, while Wyatt has argued that geologists in the 1830s were influenced by Wordsworth's poetry, rejecting both scientific materialism and Paleyite design-utilitarianism in their search for a rational explanation of the workings of providence. The physical laws of creation, like the moral laws elucidated in Wordsworth's *Excursion*, were 'directionalist', the product of complex interactions betrween national history, natural history, and individual history.[35] A key figure for the Romantics was Sir Humphry Davy who, as Knight has shown, combined vitalist principles with a belief in the unity of matter. His contention that 'the same ponderable matter in different electric states, or in different arrangements, may constitute substances chemically different', and conversely that two compounds could

---

[33] Hilton, *Age of Atonement*, pp. 49–55, 64–80, 163–89.

[34] Desmond frequently suggests that Sedgwick was a Paleyite, quoting C. C. Gillispie to the effect that 'Sedgwick acted as if the Anglican state would collapse if Paley's natural theology were rejected'. *Politics of Evolution*, p. 178. In fact Sedgwick hated Paley, not because of the natural theology, but because Paley offended against his evangelicalism. He disliked the fact that Paley shared the Utilitarians' facile optimism about human nature and his neglect of original sin and the need for a system of retributive justice. See A. Sedgwick, *A Discourse on the Studies of the University* (Cambridge, 1833), pp. 49–77.

[35] H. de Almeida, *Romantic Medicine and John Keats* (Oxford, 1991); Wyatt, *Wordsworth and the Geologists*.

be chemically identical and yet have very different physical properties, proved that there were 'powers' which could modify matter, and therefore that 'powers' rather than 'matter' were the main agents of order and change. Moreover, the hierarchical properties of nature were reflected in human societies, where an unequal division of property provided 'the sources of power in civilised life'. Not surprisingly, Davy's belief in hierarchy and his claim that force and not mechanism was primary in nature delighted Coleridge and other romantic philosophers.[36] Inferring the existence of 'inward powers of matter' from Davy's work in electro-chemistry ('philosophic alchemy') and from the 'dynamic geology' of the 1820s, Coleridge deliberately encouraged English scientists to adopt a dynamic rather than mechanical perspective.[37]

Work remains to be done on the ultra-tory politician Richard Vyvyan, who embarked throughout the 1830s on secret night-time experiments designed to show that nature was 'one great system of progressive development'. His aim was to forge a theory which would combine creationism, Lamarckian transmutation, animal magnetism, phrenology, psychology, and chemistry in an attempt to meet the radical anatomists on their own ground and yet, by leaving room for an active God, refute their materialism. As Secord has put it, his was 'a theory of extreme transcendentalism, commencing its view of creation with abstract geology'. By emphasising the interstices between particles, rather than the particles themselves, he developed his 'electro-chemical hypothesis', a theory of 'supreme creative energy, which is constantly engaged in promoting the automatic development of successive series of individual beings'.[38] It is unsurprising that Vyvyan should have been the prime suspect for the authorship of *Vestiges of Creation*, given that he was aiming for an intellectual synthesis between ultra-toryism and radicalism to match his politics.

Another ultra politician, though nominally a Whig, was the fourth Earl of Stanhope, who embarked with crusading vigour on the search for a medico-botanic solution to the question of health, being convinced that a benign providence would not send to any country a disease which was not capable of being treated by the extract of some indigenous vegetable

---

[36] Humphry Davy, *Elements of Chemical Philosophy* (1812), p. 488; David M. Knight, *Atoms and Elements: A Study of Theories of Matter in England in the Nineteenth Century* (London, 1967), pp. 35, 39; David Knight, *Ideas in Chemistry: A History of the Science* (London, 1992), pp. 70, 74–6; Christopher Lawrence, 'Humphry Davy and Romanticism', in Andrew Cunningham and Nicholas Jardine, eds., *Romanticism and the Sciences* (Cambridge, 1990), p. 222.

[37] Trevor H. Levere, *Poetry Realised in Nature: Samuel Taylor Coleridge and Early Nineteenth-Century Science* (Cambridge, 1981), pp. 20–35.

[38] Jim Secord, personal communication.

plant. Personally notorious for his adoption of the 'wild boy of Bavaria' in 1832, he subsequently speculated on the possibility that inferior animals might possess a reasoning and moral faculty, or in other words a mind (minds being 'necessarily immaterial').[39] Then there was the Hutchinsonian William Kirby, described by Corsi as 'the naturalist of the right-wing Hackney Phalanx'.[40] In his Bridgewater Treatise on animal creation he postulated a system of 'inter-agents' existing between God (conceived as an interventionist) and the visible material world. As Desmond puts it, these agents were depicted as a 'cherubic chain of spiritual vice-regents [whose] powers initiated every event in nature, and in society realized God's Will through His Church'.[41]

> The Deity superintends his whole creation, not only supporting the system that he has established . . . but himself, where he sees fit, in particular instances dispensing with these laws: restraining the clouds, in one instance, from shedding their treasures; and in another, permitting them to descend in blessings. Acting every where upon the atmosphere, and those secondary powers that produce atmospheric phenomena, as circumstances connected with his moral government require.[42]

It is unsurprising to discover that, as a theologian, Kirby was preoccupied with prophecy and the Second Coming. Ever agog for traces of 'the hand of God' in ordinary life, he 'watched' intently for signs of a time 'when there should be *one* great antichrist, – a single being reigning supreme, until the fiat of God should go forth to overwhelm him with a sudden confusion and destruction'.[43]

These ultra-tory scientists with their transcendental, immaterialist beliefs seem diametrically opposed to the radicals with their immanentist views. Yet in some respects the two had more in common than either had with the scientists of the liberal establishment, steeped as these were in natural law, natural theology, Newtonianism, and utilitarianism. The latter were philosophic dualists who believed in the separation of mind and matter, body and soul, good and evil, sacred and secular. They were opposed by authoritarian, ultra-tory Coleridgeans, who detested the

---

[39] Edward Binns, *The Anatomy of Sleep: or, the Art of Procuring Sound and Refreshing Slumber at Will*, 2nd edition, with annotations and additions by Philip Henry, fourth Earl Stanhope (1845), pp. 490–1.

[40] Pietro Corsi, 'A devil's chaplain's calling', *Journal of Victorian Culture*, 3 (1998), 129–37. Corsi contends that in the late 1830s evolutionary ideas were embraced by some who were neither artisans nor 'dangerous radicals' (e.g. Baden Powell, W. B. Carpenter, Robert Chambers, and Francis Newman).

[41] Desmond, *Politics of Evolution*, p. 114; Jacyna, 'Immanence and Transcendence', pp. 325–6.

[42] William Kirby, *On the Power, Wisdom, and Goodness of God as Manifested in the Creation of Animals and in their History, Habits, and Instincts*, 2 vols. (1835), I, p. xci.

[43] John Freeman, *Life of the Rev. William Kirby* (1852), pp. 46–7, 168–9.

'march-of-mind' (or 'natural law') direction in which the establishment was moving, as well as by Radicals who hated the establishment altogether. Radicals and Ultra Tories were philosophic monists, in that they saw God as being either immanent *in* his creation or else exercising day-to-day control *over* it.

This uniting of the intellectual left and right against the centre is unsurprising, since the main polarity of the day was not between Whigs and Tories, but between the liberal wings of both parties on the one hand and Ultra Tories (such as Vyvyan), high Whigs (such as Lord Morpeth), and some Radicals (non-Philosophic Radicals such as Thomas Spence) on the other.[44] Philosophically liberal Whigs and liberal Tories were not identical – *very roughly* one might describe them as Paleyite optimists and Butlerian retributionists respectively – but they had all instinctively imbibed mechanistic natural theology and philosophic dualism, as the normally unreflecting liberal Tory-turned-liberal Whig Lord Palmerston revealed in a self-defining moment in 1829 when he said, 'There is in nature no moving power but mind. All else is passive and inert.'[45] As for Ultra Tories, pre-millenarians, high Whigs, and Radicals, these groups had enough in common intellectually to explain why it was that they could all find mesmerism appealing.[46] To take another example, Klonk has shown that the most important distinction between the way in which different landscape artists perceived nature was that dividing phenomenalists and anti-phenomenalists, the latter defined as monists who believed in an 'ontological continuum between human beings and their environment'.[47]

IV

'The tide was running towards naturalism in an age rejecting Oxbridge Anglicanism for dissenting industrialism. Nature was being reformed – purged of miracles, subjected to law.'[48] Desmond's binary view of scientific debate (law against miracle) is underpinned by his sociological analysis, which pits 'upwardly mobile' bourgeois radical doctors against a monolithic upper class, including the Oxbridge scientific elite. However,

---

[44] For the way in which economic liberalism (or individualism) divided both parties throughout the 1830s and 1840s, see the powerful analysis by Peter Mandler, *Aristocratic Government in the Age of Reform* (Oxford, 1990).

[45] *Hansard's Parliamentary Debates,* 2nd ser., xxi, col. 1668.

[46] Alison Winter, *Mesmerized: Powers of Mind in Victorian Britain* (Chicago, 1998).

[47] Charlotte Klonk, *Science and the Perception of Nature: British Landscape Art in the Late Eighteenth and Early Nineteenth Centuries* (New Haven, 1996), p. 39.

[48] James Moore and Adrian Desmond, 'Transgressing Boundaries', *Journal of Victorian Culture,* 3 (1998), p. 159.

elite scientists belonged, not so much to the traditional, aristocratic ruling class, as to a Pittite or liberal-tory regime, of which the distinctive hall-marks were capital investment, banking, finance, international com-merce, office-holding, expertise, and fee-earning. Its core values derived from natural theology, Newtonian natural philosophy, and Lockean epis-temology, a heady brew which – especially in its Malthusian and spiritu-ally retributive version – was wholly appropriate for a regime based on finance capital and therefore subject to risk and contingency, profit and loss. Alienated from this regime and its values were the more traditional, authoritarian, backwoods, and often indebted sections of landed society, where Ultra Tories lurked. Their frequently high-church, high-tory, divine right, sacral, sacerdotal, paternalist, and patriarchal values were resurgent in the 1830s, but as romantic and right-wing challenges to the established late-Hanoverian regime rather than as representing the regime itself.[49] Nancy Mitford notes perceptively that during the 1830s and 1840s 'the age of reason was dying, the age of science was hardly born, and among educated people a sort of muddled mysticism began to prevail'.[50] One aspect of this anti-Newtonian backlash was a veritable welter of pre-millenarian hysteria among the well-to-do, a sense that the day of retribution was at hand. Even those Ultras who were not pre-mil-lenarians looked out for 'signs' – Robert Southey, for example, saw 'chas-tisement' and the hand of an 'overruling' or 'special' providence in the cholera contagion of 1831.[51] (Desmond is therefore right to say that ideas of 'arbitrary providence' were widespread during 1828–35, and wrong only in ascribing such ideas to the likes of establishment figures like Buckland and Sedgwick.) Other aspects of this mystical backlash were a sudden passion for the middle ages, feudalism, and a Gothic Camelot. Among its cardinal ultra-tory texts were Isaac D'Israeli's *Commentaries on the Life and Reign of Charles I* (1828–30), Robert Southey's *Thomas More* (1829), Coleridge's *On the Constitution of Church and State according to the Idea of Each* (1830), Sharon Turner's *Sacred History of the World as Displayed in the Creation and Subsequent Events to the Deluge* (1832), Oxford's *Tracts for the Times* (1834–41), William Dansey's *Horae Decanicae Rurales* (1835), A. W. Pugin's *Contrasts* (1836), W. E. Gladstone's *The State in its Relations with the Church* (1838), Thomas Carlyle's *Chartism* (1839), Joseph Nash's *Mansions of England in the Olden Time* (1839–49), and

---

[49] This is, of course, to stand on its head Professor Clark's view that the 1828–32 crisis brought about the rapid demise of high-church and high-tory values that had held sway since the seventeenth century. J. C. D. Clark, *English Society 1688–1832* (Cambridge, 1985), pp. 393–420.

[50] *The Ladies of Alderley*, ed. Nancy Mitford (1938; 2nd edn, 1967), p. xviii.

[51] *Selections from the Letters of Robert Southey*, ed. J.W. Warter, 4 vols. (1856), IV, pp. 242–9, 262, 269, 285.

Benjamin Disraeli's *Sybil* (1845). Possibly this 'high-tory' backlash served as camouflage to allow similarly monist but politically radical ideas to develop during the 1830s.

V

As noted above, Wise and Smith observed that 'time was rediscovered' during the 1830s, when the concept of 'economy came to mean evolution rather than balance'. The conflict of values this implied is nowhere better illustrated than in George Poulett Scrope's outspoken attack on Thomas Chalmers in 1832.[52] Chalmers epitomised as well as anyone the values of the ruling-class, upper bourgeois, liberal-tory establishment. Author of a Bridgewater Treatise on the science of political economy, he also sought to interpret geology and astronomy in the light of natural theology. Scrope was a radical scientist and polemicist, and an opponent of liberal-tory thought right across the board. In geology, for example, he was an early 'uniformitarian' or believer in gradual progression, the geological equivalent of developmental anatomy; in medicine he was a contagionist like Southwood Smith; in social thought a passionate anti-Malthusian (again like Southwood Smith) and very hostile to market economics, the gold standard, free trade, and the harsh New Poor Law of 1834 – all those policies, in other words, which Chalmers advocated. Private secretary to Lord John Russell and an ardent reformer, Scrope was more a radical Whig than a Tory, yet his opinions circulated in the tory *Quarterly Review*, another indication of the way in which right and left could combine against the centre.

Scrope hated Chalmers for his Malthusianism, his indifference to the material (as distinct from spiritual) state of the poor, and his opposition to social welfare policies on the grounds that these would lead to population growth and hence to Malthus's deadly trio of war, famine, and pestilence. More fundamentally, however, there were two great sources of misunderstanding between the two men. The first followed from Scrope's realisation that the discovery of deep time enabled the 'speculating geologist' to do away with those functional explanations based on floods and volcanoes which were so appealing to the evangelical or retributive version of natural theology. 'The leading idea . . . the sound of which to the ear of the student of Nature seems continually echoed from every part of her works, is – Time! – Time! – Time!'[53] Just as importantly, Scrope saw that this

[52] [G. P. Scrope], 'Dr Chalmers on Political Economy', *Quarterly Review*, 48 (1832), pp. 39–69.
[53] G. P. Scrope, *Memoir on the Geology of Central France* (1827), p. 165; Martin J. S. Rudwick, 'Poulett Scrope on the Volcanoes of Auvergne: Lyellian Time and Political Economy', *British Journal for the History of Science*, 7 (1974), p. 205.

idea of time applied forwards as well as back. So, while admitting that *eventually* the Malthusian population/food supply nightmare might catch up with the world, he pointed out that there were many uncultivated lands to be exhausted first, and objected to Chalmers writing 'as if the enemy were at the gates' already. He was baffled by the fact that Chalmers 'would starve the present race of man . . . for the comfort of his posterity in the hundredth generation', and accused him of 'assuming ultimate effects to be constantly present'. What Scrope could not see was that, for Chalmers, with his finite sense of worldly time – his dualistic belief in a sharp dichotomy between this world and eternity – his sense of the world as being in a state of mechanical motion but *not* progression – his search for a Final Cause rather than for historical causes – it made no sense to say that the food supply problem was a long-term rather than a short-term one. In Chalmers' cosmogony one could not distinguish between a present and an ultimate threat, for judgement was here and now, ubiquitous and continual.

Scrope was equally contemptuous of Chalmers' references to a 'redundant' population, his disdain for economic progress and luxury goods, and his view of humankind as a 'sober, chastened, and easily contented animal', wanting only 'shelter from the weather, and a sufficiency of wholesome food and coarse clothing', indifferent to 'art, science, literature' and 'all the pleasures of refinement, taste, and intellectual occupation'. To Scrope, all this was little better than a recipe for barbarism.

It is a constant principle of human nature, that our wants increase with the means of gratifying them . . . If there be any one desire or design more manifest than another throughout the works of nature . . . it is that there should be the utmost possible multiplication of beings endowed with life and capacity for enjoyment. We do not see that nature has contented herself with establishing little groups of organized beings in snug corners, to thrive there in security and content, through a nice adjustment of their numbers to the food within their reach . . . No! abundance, extension, multiplication, competition for room, is the order of creation.[54]

Abundance, creation, multiplication, improvement, enjoyment – Scrope was a spokesman for manufacturing as the successor to commercial society, and dismissive of Chalmers' rude and 'patriotic' civic humanism or 'Godly commonwealth ideal'.[55] He also emphasised creationist and incarnational values as opposed to Chalmers' atonement-orientated and other-worldly religion. Scrope's message and tone is similar to that of the hierarchical high Tory Humphry Davy, another proponent of producer values though in his case agrarian ones. With his enthusiasm for 'civilization' and faith in 'the progressiveness of our nature', Davy heralded

---

[54] [Scrope], 'Dr Chalmers', pp. 40, 44, 49, 61, 63–4.
[55] On which see Stewart J. Brown, *Thomas Chalmers and the Godly Commonwealth* (Oxford, 1982).

chemistry for having enabled man to satisfy his own wants and even to anticipate future enjoyments.

Science has given to him an acquaintance with the different relations of the parts of the external world; and . . . has bestowed upon him powers which may be almost called creative; which have enabled him to modify and change the beings surrounding him, and by his experiments to interrogate nature with power, not simply as a scholar, passive and seeking only to understand her operations, but rather as a master, active with his own instruments.[56]

However, it is *not* possible to reconcile the thought of either Scrope the Radical or Davy the Tory with that of the Peelite liberal-conservative establishment, that is with those who persisted in the enlightenment belief that all except mind was 'passive and inert', and who refused to admit that there were active and constituent powers in nature, or that nature might in any way be modified.

Politically liberalism had its *origins* in the 1820s, but philosophically it was rooted in the mechanistic dualism of the Lockeian–Newtonian enlightenment,[57] and began to *lose ground* in the 1820s to three different modes of thought, all of which could be described as monist. On the left there was the tradition of rational religious dissent, which in the eighteenth century had been called 'heterodoxy' but is nowadays anachronistically called 'liberal dissent'. By the 1830s rational dissent was associated particularly with Unitarianism, but it also influenced many comparative anatomists and evolutionary biologists, in whose thought it verged towards materialism. Meanwhile, on the right, the second quarter of the century saw the flowering of a type of mystical and medieval toryism, a yearning for a return to a more organic society, and belief in a God who exercised a paternalist control over the world on a day-to-day basis (rather than merely judging the world and ruling in heaven, like the God of the liberal establishment). Finally, somewhere between left and right, between Unitarianism and ultra toryism, came the type of evolutionary whiggism associated with Lord Macaulay, which was to prove intellectually more robust than either.

Politically there seems to be nothing in common between Robert Grant, S. T. Coleridge, and Lord Macaulay, but in their search for a single unifying principle whereby to explain both the natural and social worlds – and even though those unifying principles took vastly different forms – they had more in common with each other than any of them had with establishment savants of the 1830s such as Buckland, Sedgwick, or Chalmers.

---

[56] *The Collected Works of Humphry Davy*, ed. John Davy, 9 vols. (1839–40), II, pp. 318–19.
[57] Larry Stewart, 'A Meaning for Machines: Modernity, Utility, and the Eighteenth-Century British Public', *Journal of Modern History*, 70 (1998), pp. 259–94.

9 Images of time: from Carlylean Vulcanism to sedimentary gradualism

John Burrow

I

My subject is the representation of historical time: history, that is, as, for example, bounded and catastrophic or endless and, in its most profound and least perceptible ways, moving at a pace too gradual for the eye to measure directly. Also history as reassuring, as judgemental and punitive; as directional or as repetitive; as drama, plotted and portentous, or as indifferent; as governed by the same rhythms as the natural world, or as crucially distinct from it; ending with a bang; ending with a whimper; not ending.[1]

I shall be concerned here with the period and place I know best: nineteenth-century England. Even here there are limitations to be stipulated. This essay focuses essentially on the early and middle years of the century, with a glance back at the late eighteenth. It does not go on to the end of the century so there is nothing here, for example, about a major theme in that period's apprehension of time: the doom-laden scene of a dying world like that encountered by H. G. Wells' Time Traveller, which the later nineteenth century derived from the second law of thermodynamics. Of course, even within its avowed limitations, the essay is not comprehensive and all the usual caveats apply. Essentially the story I offer is a simple one, indicated by my title, from a characteristic (though far from universal) disposition to the representation of history in terms of eventfulness, even of a catastrophic, apocalyptic kind, to the subtler representation of it as a kind of sedimentary process, whose longer-term significance lay far beyond the knowledge of the actors engaged in it, for it could only be perceived retrospectively and therefore necessarily ironically, though perhaps reverentially. This combination of irony and reverence enforced by a sedimentary conception of history gives, it seems to

---

[1] In preparing this essay I have been aware of some debts too pervasive for a specific citation to be adequate. They are to Boyd Hilton, *The Age of Atonement* (Oxford, 1988); Ronald Paulson, *Representation of Revolution 1789–1820* (New Haven, Conn., 1983); and Gillian Beer, *Darwin's Plots* (London, 1983).

me, a distinctive tone to some mid-century perceptions of historic time and human agency within it. Of course it was not new: its origins lay far back, in eighteenth-century notions of unintended consequences and the aesthetics of the picturesque, as well as in Burkean political reverence touched with irony. The story is, as I have said, a simple one, and in a sense less important than its illustration. What has attracted me in it, I have to admit, is less the story itself, with its inevitable qualifications and over-simplifications, than the opportunity it offers under the rubrics of perception and representation and the shifting though never mutually exclusive metaphorical tastes of successive generations, to chart some of the themes and preoccupations of an era or generation across the boundaries of genre, so that poems, paintings, philosophies, current polemics, and works of scholarship exhibit at least partial homologies or consonances, and sometimes reciprocal influences, given to them, it seems, by their contemporaneity. In 'On History' Carlyle famously contrasted the linear character of narrative with the three-dimensionality of actual history.[2] Here I am less concerned with establishing a chronological narrative as *the* narrative, though it is certainly one, than with illustrating the one I have chosen; thickness is all.

We may begin, literally, with the spectacular. Within a month of the fall of the Bastille, in August 1789, Astley's Amphitheatre, near Westminster Bridge, was presenting, we learn from the *Times* advertisements, a display of Rope Dancing by a Signior Spinacuta and a Comic Burletta called 'The Boot Makers', followed by 'an entire new and splendid spectacle . . . The French Revolution', called 'Paris in an Uproar or the Destruction of the Bastille. One of the grandest and most extraordinary Entertainments that ever appeared, grounded on authentic facts'. It included internal and external views of the Bastille and 'a grand model of the City of Paris' and sounds good value. Incidentally, later in the advertisement, with the optimism characteristic of these months, the event was referred to as 'the late French Revolution'.[3] Boxes were three shillings, pit two shillings, gallery a shilling and side gallery sixpence, illustrating what I suppose most of us are already prepared to concede, that one's perspective on a revolution tends to vary according to one's social and financial position. The show must have been a success and provoked rivals because by October Mr Astley, fighting off the competition, had been to Paris and procured a head of de Launay, the governor of the Bastille, 'finely executed in wax to be exhibited in the same manner as . . . by the Bourgeoisie and the French

[2] Thomas Carlyle, 'On History', in *Thomas Carlyle's Works*, Ashburton edn, 17 vols. (London, 1891), XV. p. 499.
[3] *The Times Reports the French Revolution: Extracts from The Times 1789–1794*, ed. Neal Ascherson (London, 1975), pp. 19–22.

Guards'.[4] It is striking to find the Revolution turned in London so early into spectacle, even before it found its own impresario in Jacques-Louis David and deliberately staged itself in the great open air processions, festivals, ritual tree-planting and oath-swearings, which proclaimed its character as a regenerative, apocalyptic event. Revolution as theatre has become a familiar concept and it produced in England, in the early 1790s, on both sides of the polemical divide, a plethora of theatrical imagery, with each side convicting the other of imposture. Theatrical imagery became insistent in Burke's descriptions of the Jacobins: 'bombastic players, the refuse and rejected offal of strolling theatres, puffing out ill-sorted verses about virtue'.[5] Astley's and its competitors, however, provided theatre in a special sense.

In the form of popular entertainment, it stood at the confluence of a number of different genres, visual, poetic, and dramatic, and returned them again to the culture at large as a taste for the vast and the catastrophic. My point is that one of the existing categories to which the novelty of the French Revolution was most immediately assimilated in English minds was this, and it is therefore worthwhile to see a little more closely what it was. The spectacle or panorama was a particular form of entertainment in which a number of houses of entertainment specialised, though it also came to form a part of more regular theatrical performances at the larger theatres like Drury Lane and Covent Garden. It involved the interplay of lighting effects, sound, moving transparencies, and scenery, and a point was made, as we saw in the case of Astley's bill, of claims to authenticity in the representation of historic events, and in great panoramic views of cities or natural events like volcanic eruptions; above all it specialised in catastrophe.[6] It drew on an aesthetic which can be variously described as Miltonic, apocalyptic and, most generally, simply as the sublime; things murky and glowing, things vast and doomed; explosions, the crashing of rocks or buildings; destruction on a grand scale. The pioneer, in a small way, seems to have been the 'Eidophusicon' first presented, appropriately, by the artist Jean Philippe de Loutherbourg, in London in 1781. It was 'an illusionistic theatre . . . where moving and changing scenery, temporalised by mechanical means, and changing light

[4] Ascherson, *Times Reports*, p. 32.
[5] Edmund Burke, *Letters on a Regicide Peace*, in *Works*, 12 vols. (London, 1909), V, p. 317. Burke's first response to the Revolution was 'astonishment at the wonderful spectacle', 9 August 1789, quoted Paulson, *Representation of Revolution*, p. 57.
[6] The authority to whom I am most indebted here is Martin Meisel, 'The Material Sublime: John Martin, Byron, Turner and the Theatre', in Karl Kroeber and William Walling, eds., *Images of Romanticism. Verbal and Visual Affinities* (New Haven and London, 1978), pp. 211–32. See also Jack Lindsay, *J. M. W. Turner. His Life and Work* (London, 1966), esp. pp. 50–1.

supplanted entirely act and play'. Scenes from *Paradise Lost* seem to have been a speciality; such spectacles could be either illustrative or documentary. I say 'appropriately' by de Loutherbourg because in him a number of relevant themes are combined: the impresario of Pandemonium was also a Swedenborgian Illuminist and, along with Joseph Wright of Derby, famous as a painter of the early Industrial Revolution, notably the new blast furnaces at Colebrookdale.[7] In the ordinary theatres in the first half of the nineteenth century, above all Drury Lane and Covent Garden, spectacular transformation scenes were much admired: for example, the destruction of Babylon in a play on Zoroaster in 1824. Kean's production of Byron's *Sardanapalus* in 1853 concluded with a vast panoramic view of the burning and destruction of Nineveh. Archaeological accuracy was always claimed and archaeology was one inspiration. Archaeology, from the excavations of Pompeii and Herculaneum in the late eighteenth century, publicised by Sir William Hamilton, tended to draw attention to disaster and doom.[8] There were two publications on the ruins of Babylon in 1816. Babylon became, of course, a slang term for London itself: huge, growing increasingly monumental and assertive in its squares, processional ways and eventually embankments, and overhung by its perpetual pall of smoke. Mudie's guide to London, published in 1825, was entitled 'Babylon the Great'.[9] Biblical scenes, archaeological reconstructions and modern architectural developments and fantasies, Romantic and Miltonic poetry and painting, and apocalyptic imagery were welded together in what has been aptly called 'the Drury Lane sublime', to which artists like de Loutherbourg sometimes added another ingredient from the blast furnaces and vast, illuminated, never-sleeping mills of the Industrial Revolution. Artists, scene-painters, poets both established and undergraduate, inspired both by archaeology and the dramatic character of contemporary history in the Napoleonic period, walked in the glare of apocalypse, and its types in nature and history.[10] 'The End of the World, Mr Turner?' enquired one visitor to the artist's studio. 'No Ma'am, Hannibal Crossing the Alps' – itself a topical illusion to Napoleon.[11] It has been claimed that Turner was responsible for a panorama of the

---

[7] Meisel, 'Material Sublime', p. 225, For Wright of Derby in this context see Ronald Paulson, *Emblem and Expression. Meaning in English Art of the Eighteenth Century* (London, 1975).

[8] See Lindsay, *Turner*, pp. 63, 71–4 and W. Feaver, *The Art of John Martin* (Oxford, 1974), p. 11.

[9] Emerson said that 'Martin's picture of Babylon, etc. are faithful copies of the worst part of London, light, darkness, architecture and all'. Feaver, *John Martin*, p. 144.

[10] In addition to Feaver, Lindsay, Paulson, and Meisel, see also James B. Twitchell, *Romantic Horizons. Aspects of the Sublime in English Poetry and Painting 1770–1850* (Columbia, Mo., 1983). [11] Lindsay, *Turner*, p. 196.

Battle of the Nile put on in Fleet Street in 1800, with the explosion of the battleship *L'Orient* as its climax. Vesuvius contributed by unusual activity at the end of the eighteenth century.[12] Sir William Hamilton's paper on it in the *Philosophical Transactions* in 1799 was used by the painter Thomas Girtin for a disquisition on the sublime. Girtin worked on a huge panorama of London, the 'Eidometropolis' in 1802.

II

Turner, of course, like Byron and Milton is an indispensable reference point, but the acknowledged master of the apocalyptic or Drury Lane sublime in the first half of the nineteenth century was John Martin, whose large, lurid canvasses, now again fetching high prices, staged disasters, if not daily like Astley's, then almost yearly. A roll call of his paintings from 1819 until 1853 is a recital of the types of apocalypse: *The Fall of Babylon, Belshazzar's Feast, The Destruction of Herculaneum, The Seventh Plague, The Fall of Nineveh, The Deluge, The Last Man, The Eve of the Deluge, The Assuaging of the Waters, Pandemonium, The Destruction of Sodom and Gomorrah, The Great Day of His Wrath.* Apart from a pyrotechnic display of hot reds and murky blacks, the most striking features are the use of perspective to create effects of vastness, and the dwarfing of the human figure, individual or clumped in dismayed and stricken clusters, by vast, vaguely classical Babylonic buildings or huge natural rock formations. The parallel between Martin's art and the panoramic stage spectaculars focusing on disaster, and often without human figures altogether, is close.[13] The apparently endless lines of columns in Belshazzar's palace or the facade of Pandemonium allude to the continuing development of London in which Martin unsuccessfully aspired to play a part as an engineer, as well as to the grandiose architectural fantasies of Sir John Soane and J. M. Gandy.[14]

As Feaver has pointed out, Martin's stricken biblical metropolises incorporate motifs from London, Edinburgh, and Newcastle,[15] while Pandemonium seems to be along the new Thames Embankment, like Sir William Chambers' Somerset House. Life imitated art imitating life. Foreign visitors to London described it as 'Martinian',[16] while Martin's younger brother Jonathan attempted to set fire to York Minster, explaining that 'I was told by the Lord that I was to destroy the cathedral, on account of the clergy going to plays and balls, playing at cards and drink-

---

[12] *Ibid.*, pp. 71–4.
[13] The source to which the account of Martin given here is chiefly indebted is Feaver, *John Martin*. See also Meisel, 'Material Sublime'.   [14] Feaver, *John Martin*, pp. 41–3, 122–9.
[15] *Ibid.*, pp. 4, 27.   [16] *Ibid.*, p. 88.

ing wine, so fulfilling the will of God . . . that there should be signs in the heavens, blood and fire'.[17] Jonathan's escapade was turned into a stage spectacular which subsequently burnt down. Martin's *Belshazzar's Feast* was exhibited in 1821; the coronation banquet of George IV in Westminster Hall later the same year, much criticised for its lavishness, reminded one guest of Martin's picture; Martin, a radical who once hissed 'God save the King' at a concert, would not have been displeased.[18] Life seemed to imitate art, too, when the Houses of Parliament burned down in 1835, providing Turner with the perfect contemporary subject of fire and water and a doomed palace burning. Carlyle, who was also there, described how the crowd, rather pleased than otherwise, 'whewed and whistled when the breeze came, as if to encourage it', while another witness spoke of the spectators clapping like patrons in a theatre when the roof of the House of Lords fell in.[19] The patrons of Astley's and its rivals knew their manners at a disaster.

The other most striking feature of Martin's canvasses is their oppressive and hostile geology; lurid as in the early volcanic landscape of *Sadak in Search of the Waters of Oblivion* of 1812, with its shelf of red rock and fiery lake; bleak and implacable, emphasising the loneliness of the expelled Adam and Eve; or catastrophically engulfing, as in *The Deluge*. Of course anything like a full account of the sources here would involve the whole tradition of sublime landscape painting, of the volcano paintings of Claude Joseph Vernet and Wright of Derby, as well as representations of the Last Judgement. What is worth mentioning, however, are two contemporary motifs: first is the influence, as in Wright and Loutherbourg, of the man-made sublime of industrialism. Martin hailed from the coal and lead mining area of the Tyne valley. He knew the iron and glass works of the Black Country and took a practical interest in safety provisions in mine workings. As the Corn-law rhymer Ebenezer Elliot put it, 'Did Martin steal immortal hues/From London's Cloud or Carron's gloomy glare?'[20] The answer is almost certainly yes. The second contemporary influence can be illustrated in two ways; Martin was an illustrator, albeit somewhat imaginative, of the new palaeontology, depicting ferocious dragons as illustrations for the Sussex palaeontologist Gideon Mantell, and when Martin was working on *The Deluge* Cuvier visited Martin's studio and was said to have 'expressed himself pleased that he and Martin were at one over the scientific explanation of the Flood'.[21]

Actually Martin's canvasses seem more suggestive of Thomas Burnet's

---

[17] *Ibid.*, p. 59.   [18] *Ibid.*, pp. 51–2, 71.
[19] J. A. Froude, *Thomas Carlyle. A History of the First Forty Years of His Life, 1795–1835*, 2 vols. (1890), II, p. 475; cf. Lindsay, *Turner*, p. 181.   [20] Feaver, *Martin*, p. 143.
[21] *Ibid.*, p. 94.

'Sacred Theory of the Earth', which, as Marjorie Nicolson showed, exercised such an influence on the development of the sublime aesthetic, and whose description, for example, of the 'Eve of the Deluge' is so thoroughly Martinian: 'The countenance of the Heavens will be dark and gloomy, and a veil drawn over the face of the Sun. The Earth in a disposition everywhere to break into open flames. The tops of the Mountains smoking, the rivers dry, earthquakes in several places, the sea sunk and retired into its deepest channel and roaring, as against some mighty storm'.[22]

In locating one possible way of responding to the French Revolution as its immediate assimilation to Astley's menu of daily catastrophes, I was locating it, as Ronald Paulson has done, in the context of the sublime aesthetic and trying to emphasise the multi-faceted character of the latter, compounded of the poetic and pictorial fascination with earthquakes and volcanoes, of Miltonic and Piranesian traditions, of the lurid Plutonic aesthetics of early industrialism, and perhaps, what I want soon to go on to consider, of the urgent contemporary interest in geology. It was not by any means the only response or even perhaps the dominant one. The invocations by Burke and Blake and others of the imagery of the sublime were not necessarily typical even if between them they spanned the range of possible horror or enthusiasm as responses to the Revolution. Hedvah-Ben-Israel has shown that in the attempts of English historians in the first half of the nineteenth century to comprehend the Revolution, neither Burke's picture nor Carlyle's were as dominant as we might have thought; many responses were much soberer and more measured,[23] and Bianca Fontana has pointed to another, its assimilation to the Scottish genre of the history of civil society.[24] If I have dwelt on the mode of the apocalyptic as a cultural matrix for one kind of response to revolution it is not because I am claiming a typicality which I do not know how to measure, but precisely because of the contrast it affords to what I shall discuss below. What these various types of apocalypse, natural and historical, convey is a particular conception of history and historical time: abrupt, spasmodic, in a word catastrophic. It deals in shocks and endings, or types of the end, of the moments when the order of time and nature is suspended. Appropriately one of Martin's subjects was Joshua commanding the sun to stand still, and another the parting of the waters of the Red Sea, while

[22] Thomas Burnet, *The Sacred Theory of the Earth* [1691] (London, 1965), p. 301. Marjorie Hope Nicholson, *Mountain Gloom and Mountain Glory. The Development of the Aesthetics of the Infinite* (Ithaca, 1959).

[23] Hedvah Ben-Israel, *English Historians and the French Revolution* (Cambridge, 1968).

[24] Bianca Fontana, *Rethinking the Politics of Commercial Society. The Edinburgh Review 1802–32* (Cambridge, 1985), ch. 1.

Turner also chose the deluge and the destruction of Sodom, and the Angel in the Sun of the Apocalypse. For of course it is also a view of history which makes it portentous and judgemental, and must have taught people to see in contemporary events, as Burke said of the French Revolution, the 'awful drama of Providence now acting on the moral theatre of the world'.[25] It was certainly no uncommon way of seeing the Revolution, which sometimes assimilated it quite literally into the pattern of apocalypse.[26] As an interpretation of the Revolution, the apocalyptic vied with or incorporated the conspiratorial view which detected the grand design of the Freemasons and the looser and more commonsensical versions, which could still hold resonances of divine judgement or of conspiracy, which blamed it on the wickedness of the French aristocracy or the atheistic propaganda of the philosophers.

W. H. Oliver has shown that prophetic and millennialist ideas were 'significant at all social levels' and that millennialism was 'a mode of social thought [whose] images, concepts and vocabulary were relevant well beyond the limited circle of specialist writers and readers'.[27] It is needless to repeat the apocalyptic and millennial images in Blake, Coleridge, Wordsworth, and Shelley. What is important, as Boyd Hilton has shown, is the pervasiveness of images of crisis and judgement, though some millennialists prophesied a smooth rather than a violent transition.[28] But as always, among the signs were not only events of human history but natural portents, sometimes in combination. Earthquakes, traditionally a warning and type of the end, were spectacularly invoked by Richard Brothers who, in 1792, went to the House of Commons to threaten them with 'their own sudden fall into the Jaws of the Earth by a preternatural earthquake'; he also predicted that London would be destroyed by an earthquake on 4 June 1795.[29] One can only feel wistful for Martin's lost opportunity.

The most extended historiographical exploration of the mode of the apocalyptic sublime was, of course, Carlyle's *French Revolution*, published in 1837. I have been content simply to point to his book as indisputably a monument of its time, leaving open how long a shadow it cast. Again, I have not so far been dealing in any specific sense with influences on him, though I shall try to do so in a moment, but about the pervasiveness of a form of sensibility and a stock of images, deployed with varied emphasis,

---

[25] Burke, 'Regicide Peace', in *Works*, V, p. 233.
[26] Clark Garrett, R*espectable Folly. Millennialists and the French Revolution in France and England* (Baltimore and London, 1975).
[27] W. H. Oliver, *Prophets and Millennialists. The Uses of Biblical Prophecy in England from the 1790s to the 1840s* (Oxford, 1978), p. 20.   [28] Boyd Hilton, *The Age of Atonement.*
[29] Garrett, *Respectable Folly*, p. 182.

application, and literalness. Carlyle, so far as I know, took no interest in Turner or Loutherbourg or Martin, though he certainly read Byron and, one might add, Jean Paul. I do not know of any reference to him as a patron of Astley's or Drury Lane; he presumably had too much of a Puritan disapproval of such toys: he preferred the real thing. Though the millennialist Edward Irving was his closest friend and a powerful early influence, he disapproved of his millennialist literalism and became estranged from him as their views more and more diverged. In *Signs of the Times* he deplored the contemporary taste for 'vaticination' as a sign of decadence. And yet, and yet. An author one of whose earliest works is called *Signs of the Times* and a later one *Latter Day Pamphlets* is no stranger at least to the millennial vocabulary, and critics have pointed to the rhapsodic millennial ending of *Past and Present*, with its vision of England transformed. Carlyle was steeped in the culture of seventeenth-century Puritanism, if not specifically in its prophetic writings. He had something else in common too, though he seems not to have bothered to notice it, with Loutherbourg, Wright of Derby, and Martin; he was stirred by the Plutonic energy of industrialism. Approaching Glasgow in 1820, he saw an ironworks, a scene from Turner, 'smoke and yellow vapour through which pulsated an extraordinary light – a red glare that flashed up and across the skies, as if the whole world were in conflagration'. In Birmingham in 1824 he saw 'half-naked demons, pouring with sweat and besmeared with soot . . . hurrying to and fro in their red night caps and sheet-iron breeches, rolling or hammering, squeezing their glowing metal as if it had been wax or dough'.[30] That his sensibility and sense of time were, in one aspect, convulsive, spasmodic, attuned to the apocalyptic and transformative, is amply clear. The self-created veil that hides reality from us can be dispelled in an instant by an act of will or fate. The realm of unreality, Versailles at the opening of *The French Revolution*, is like the creation of a malign enchantment, an 'Armida Palace', Dubarrydom. France is seen mythologically, as plague-stricken and lying with a harlot's foot upon its neck. At the touch of the reality of death (that of Louis XV) 'Sumptuous Versailles bursts asunder like a dream.'[31]

What Carlyle could make of the notion of judgement, conflagration, and renewal, the burning up of imposture, we see of course in *The French Revolution*, and, at its most figurative, in the vision of the dying Cagliostro with which he ended the essay on the Diamond Necklace and with which he also concluded *The French Revolution*. It would alone, despite its characteristic ironic and humorous touches, be enough to establish a fundamental affinity between Carlyle and the Drury Lane sublime: 'Higher,

[30] D. A. Wilson, *Carlyle Till Marriage 1795–1826* (London, 1923), pp. 188, 342.
[31] Thomas Carlyle, *The French Revolution*, part I, bk. I, ch. 1, ch. IV, in *Works*, I, pp. 5, 19.

higher yet flames the fire sea . . . The marble images become mortar lime; the stone Mountains sulkily explode. Respectability wailing . . . leaves the Earth: not to return save under a new Avatar . . . The World is black ashes; which, ah, when will they grow green? . . . all Dwellings of men destroyed; the very mountains peeled and riven, the valleys black and dead: it is an empty World! [32] This is, of course, various things; it is a Biblical conflagration of idols; it is a type of the apocalypse in which Carlyle no longer literally believed. It is also, it has to be said, a description of a volcano in eruption; it is apocalypse and it is also geology. Volcanoes and earthquakes had been obvious images for the French Revolution ever since its inception, with their suggestion of an eruption, from the depths, of something sudden and unforeseen, yet also long prepared invisibly below the surface, and also with their traditional associations as omens of divine wrath. Carlyle's uses of them are altogether more systematic and of a different order of seriousness; they are the chief way he insinuates his conception of historical change, and we can trace their source with considerable precision. The presiding metaphor – though there are others – of Carlyle's *French Revolution* is the result of a direct, conscious, and quite specific borrowing from the geological ideas current in the Edinburgh of the early nineteenth century in which he received his education. The course he followed at Edinburgh University was a broad one in the Scottish fashion and included courses in mathematics, natural philosophy, and mineralogy, which we know he attended, under some notable teachers: mathematics under John Leslie, who thought very highly of him, natural philosophy under John Playfair, natural history under Robert Jameson, of whom he thought little;[33] it was Jameson's singular fate to be the despised teacher of both Carlyle and Darwin. We encounter, albeit in burlesque form, on the first page of *Sartor Resartus* a reference to the famous controversy between Huttonians and Wernerians in geology. We know that Carlyle's interest in learning German was first aroused not by the German Romantics whose work he did so much to popularise in Britain, but by a desire to read the geologist Abraham Gottlob Werner.[34] We are accustomed to think of Carlyle's metaphysics as essentially German inspired; undoubtedly there is some truth in this, and I do not want here to debate exactly how much. But it seems that his interest in metaphysics was first aroused

---

[32] *Ibid.*, p. 248.

[33] On Carlyle's scientific education in Edinburgh, see Wilson, *Carlyle Till Marriage*; Ian Campbell, *Thomas Carlyle* (London, 1974); and especially Carlisle Moore, 'Carlyle, Mathematics and Mathesis' in K. J. F. Fielding and Rodger L. Tarr, eds., *Carlyle Past and Present. A Collection of New Essays* (London, 1976), and by the same author, 'Carlyle and the Touch of Science' in Jeremy D. James and Charles S. Fineman, eds., *Lectures on Carlyle and his Era* (Santa Cruz, 1982).   [34] Wilson, *Carlyle Till Marriage*, p. 165.

by the classes of John Leslie, who has been spoken of as a model for Teufelsdröch.[35]

When Carlyle's stern Puritan father was shaken out of his normal stoicism by his wife's severe illness, a metaphor from geology – and one which touched on an important geological controversy – came spontaneously to Carlyle's mind; 'it was as if a rock of granite had melted and was thawing into water'.[36] The nature of granite was a critical issue in contemporary geology and it had been denied that granite was soluble. But in *The French Revolution* geological imagery is not merely illustrative; it is more like a central organising idea and it is geologically precise and even partisan. It is what was known as the 'Plutonic' theory of James Hutton, whose chief Edinburgh disciple was Carlyle's teacher, John Playfair.

I have argued at length for the specifically Huttonian nature of Carlyle's presiding geological metaphor in *The French Revolution* elsewhere and cannot repeat the argument, which depends essentially on detailed textual comparison, here.[37] Hutton's scheme for the earth is one of endless self-renewal, of a constant cycle of decay and reconstruction, as continents rise from the depths of the sea only to be eroded again.[38] At first sight this seems an implausible source for convulsive, quasi-apocalyptic imagery like Carlyle's; Hutton's geology was traditionally seen, in terms of the classification of theories now recognised as over-simplified, as belonging to the 'uniformitarian' rather than the 'catastrophist' school. This is partially misleading. Hutton's was indeed a cyclical theory which postulated a world without beginning or end, *but* while the main agent in geological decay was water its agent of renewal was heat, the central heat of the earth which fuses the rocks at great depths and raises them again above the sea to become once more a dwelling for human beings. Fire is a constructive element in the making of a world, and Hutton's 'uniformitarian' theory contains enough Plutonic energy to please any Vulcanist (as opposed to Neptunian) geologist.[39]

---

[35] *Ibid.*, pp. 84–5.   [36] Campbell, *Carlyle*. p. 54.

[37] J. W. Burrow, 'Geologia e apocalisse. Thomas Carlyle e la Rivoluzione Francese', *Intersezione*, anno IX (1989).

[38] James Hutton, *System of the Earth* (1785). See also John Playfair 'Biographical Account of the late James Hutton, FRS', *Transactions of the Royal Society of Edinburgh*, 5, part III. Both repr. in George W. White, ed., *Contributions to the History of Geology* (Darien, Conn., 1970).

[39] E.g. 'We are not to limit nature with the uniformity of an equable progression', Hutton, *System of the Earth*, p. 302. In Neptunian theory the chief agent of geological change was water. The chief advocates of the rival Neptunian (Wernerian) and Vulcanist or Plutonian (Huttonian) theories in Edinburgh in Carlyle's youth were, respectively, Jameson and Playfair. Modern accounts of Hutton's geology and its motives include, particularly, R. Grant, 'Hutton's Theory of the Earth' in L. J. Jordanova and Roy S. Porter, eds., *Images of the Earth. Essays in the History of the Environmental Sciences* (Chalfont St Giles, 1979) and Gordon L. Davis, *The Earth in Decay. A History of British Geomorphology 1578–1878* (London, 1970), esp pp. 155–96.

Carlyle reaches for the effects of the aesthetics of the sublime through lurid geological metaphors which, I want to suggest, are both more precise and more constructive than they may seem. 'Our whole being is an infinite abyss, overarched by Habit, as by a thin Earth-rind'. But let the 'Earth-rind' be once broken, 'The fountains of the great deep boil forth; fire fountains, enveloping, engulfing. Your "Earth-rind" is shattered, swallowed up; instead of a green flowery world, there is a waste wide-weltering chaos; – which has again, with tumult and struggle, to *make* itself into a world'.[40] Carlyle, it may be noted, is particularly fond of the key Huttonian term 'fusion' as a metaphor for creation of all kinds. 'A true work of art', he said 'requires to be fused in the mind of its creator'.[41] Carlyle is more catastrophic than Hutton, though the latter can be catastrophic enough too at times, if only because for Hutton most of the violent Plutonic activity he invokes takes place beneath the surface of the earth and at the bottom of the sea, which is an option hardly available to a historian. But the metaphorical structure of *The French Revolution* is, none the less, cyclical in the manner and sometimes almost in the vocabulary of Hutton's geology, not strictly apocalyptic.

Revolutionary France provokes Carlyle to Huttonian invocation to the 'stone Mountains that die daily with every rain shower, yet are not dead and levelled for ages and ages, nor born again, it seems, but with new world explosions'.[42] Like Hutton, he sees history not as directional, but as a constant interplay of destructive and constructive forces, with the latter represented above all as elemental heat: 'Remark how from amid the wrecks and dust of this universal Decay new powers are fashioning themselves adapted to the new time and its destinies'.[43] Apart from the historian's last phrase, it could be a sentence from Hutton. And if it is thought the analogy is far fetched, hear Carlyle himself on the Revolution 'as when, according to Neptuno-Plutonic Geology, the World is all decayed down into due attritus of this sort; and shall now be *exploded* and new-made!'[44] Later, France, re-making itself is a nation 'in fusion'.[45] Hutton's God and Carlyle's were very different. Hutton, as Gordon Davis explains,[46] was concerned to rescue the character of a benevolent creator from the pessimistic implications of a world apparently in terminal decay from erosion by wind and water. The permanently creative element was volcanic fire, which fused the sediment of old continents beneath the sea and thus raised up new ones in a perpetual oscillation. Carlyle's was a

[40] *The French Revolution*, part I, bk. II, ch. III. The quotations have to stand for many other possible ones. Vulcanism is omnipresent in Carlyle's book.
[41] Carlyle, *Jean Paul Richter* in *Works*, XV, p. 19. Earlier, humour is spoken of as 'the central fire' of Richter's being.   [42] *French Revolution*, part II, bk. I, ch. xii in *Works*, I, p. 303.
[43] *Ibid.*, part I, bk. I, ch. ii in *Works*, I. p. 14.
[44] *Ibid.*, part I, bk. III, ch. iv in *Works*, p. 70.
[45] *Ibid.*, part II bk. I, ch. viii in *Works*, I, p. 283.   [46] Davis, *Earth in Decay* pp. 159–60.

Calvinist God of vengeance, not the altogether politer deity of eighteenth-century natural theology of which Hutton's cyclical theory of geological change was an aspect. Carlyle's biblically phrased Vulcanism clearly enjoyed and stressed the purgative, judgemental aspect of fire, but it would be a superficial reading of *The French Revolution* that failed to recognise in it, as in Hutton's *System of the Earth*, its crucial role in renewal.

We can measure the difference by turning to his *Latter Day Pamphlets* of 1851, with its very different overt message and metaphorical structure, though geology still plays a role in the latter. It begins still in the vein of apocalyptic prophecy; in ways that suggest that not only the European revolutions three years earlier but the anti-papist scare of 1851 are at work; it is remarkable that a work of English social criticism should begin with the Pope and end with a chapter on the Jesuits. The revolutions, with the unexpected complicity of Pio Nono, have revealed monarchy and aristocracy as self-acknowledged shams; the empire of imposture, in proper apocalyptic fashion, is uncovered and overthrown, yet the new order seems powerless to be born and mere anarchy is loosed upon the world. Earthquakes and volcanoes are as usual called up to play their part as images for revolution and democracy, yet the volcano huffs and puffs and seems powerless to create the desired new world. In a metaphor which, divorced from the Huttonian context, seems curiously inappropriate, though it actually points to another moment in the Huttonian cycle, Carlyle speaks of lying in 'bottomless eddies and conflicting sea-currents . . . till once the *new* rock basis does come to light'.[47] The presiding element of *Latter Day Pamphlets* is not fire but water, and turbid, dirty water at that; it presents a world immobilised in the silt of custom and its own industrial excrement, clogged and breathless, the sediment of habit and complacent hypocrisy forming a thick, foul mud which the purifying revolutionary fires have not yet scorched and fired into the crystalline rock on which a new world can be built. The evocation of anarchy and stasis in association, the dead dog floating to and fro with the filthy Thames tide, then at its most polluted, recall Pope, as the scatological imagery of the Augean stable of bureaucracy evokes Swift. (Carlyle's resemblance to the latter had at school earned him the nickname of 'the Dean'.) That was one image of what, contrasting it with the exuberant Vulcanism or Plutonism of Carlyle's *French Revolution*, we may for short call the sedimentary, of a society choking in its own effluvia, and it has of course contemporary parallels in Dickens, Kingsley, and Engels.

---

[47] Carlyle, *Latter Day Pamphlets*, in *Works*, V, p. 9.

III

We may let that image stand for the moment as a contrast, and take, as a distant object supplying perspective, though one in need of correction, a work which saw English thought and society from the outside; incidentally its argument requires that we regard Carlyle as non-English, which of course he was. It was, it seems, another, though indirect, offshoot of 1848. It was the revolutionary experience and its failure, it is claimed, which led Jules Michelet to break off for the moment his historical work[48] and turn to those strange rhapsodic works of nature-mysticism of which, though some dealt also with the organic world, the relevant ones here are *La Mer* and *La Montagne* and particularly the latter – though it has to be said Michelet organicises them too. Michelet is, of course, the most obvious counterpart to Carlyle in nineteenth-century historiography and among historians of the French Revolution, in his orgiastic manner of composition, his evocation of elemental powers to express the role of the people in history and his metaphors of surging, boiling, overflowing energy, which he at least would not at all have minded our speaking of as sexual and visceral, though I am sure Carlyle, in his own case, would have minded very much. But it is not the comparison which is my point here, but the characterisation of English culture and history and the place in it of English geology, which he offers us in *La Montagne*. Michelet's sketch there of the history of geology, which I propose to quote in the English translation of 1878, is an early essay in what we may call the history of science as ideology, or perhaps better, as sociology of knowledge, and if one has, not surprisingly, to fault it in almost every detail Michelet might perhaps get more credit than I have noticed from its present-day practitioners for his declaration 'that our men of science, while believing that they pursue it apart from all social influences, are really affected by them unwittingly, and carry them into their very systems'.[49]

Michelet establishes a simple, obviously all too simple, correlation: continental geology is violent and cataclysmic, English is peaceful, uniform, and gradualist. Epitomising the former are the theories of the upheaving of mountain ranges by massive volcanic activity of Leopold von Buch and Elie de Beaumont. Epitomising the latter is Sir Charles Lyell and to a secondary extent Darwin, whom Michelet, presumably confusing him with his father or grandfather, calls 'Dr Darwin'. 'Men', Michelet says, 'who had been present at the terrible eruption of the revolutionary volcano, at the catastrophes of the great wars, at the national

---

[48] Linda Orr, *Nature, History and Language* (Ithaca, 1976), pp. x, 14–16.
[49] Jules Michelet, *The Mountain* (translation of *La Montagne*, 1868) (1878), p. 305.

outbursts of 1813, at the immense earthquake in which the Napoleonic empire was swallowed up – could discover nothing else but violent cataclysms in the primeval history of the globe' – hence von Buch could only detect in the mountains 'the revolutionary action of the central fire, the convulsions of the travailing earth'. Thus:

> This is what Geology accomplished on the Continent, in the region of revolutions. But immovable England, which had not experienced any great social convulsions, judged the globe from a different point of view. What had she seen in her own bosom? A progressive constitution, built up gradually without any violent change, a well-balanced government undergoing little modification; a novelty, it is true, this industrious England, which with adequate rapidity but without crisis, without struggle, step by step, has risen to her present pride of place!

Michelet seems uncertain, however, whether he wishes to see in British geology the British constitution or industrialism inscribed in the earth. In fact he sees both ('industrial' had not yet acquired its usual substantive 'Revolution'), and sees industrialism too as an image of regular process:

> they looked at Nature with eyes on whose retina was already impressed their own England, the ideal of an industrial creation. At the climax of our commotions, towards 1830, when von Buch and Elie de Beaumont seemed securely enthroned, a grave voice arose, the geology of Sir Charles Lyell. In his powerful and ingenious treatise, Earth for the first time figured as a worker who, with calm incessant and regular labour, manufactures herself . . . These then are the two schools: the school of war, the school of peace . . . The principle of 'peace at any price' which, through Cobden's exertions, prevails in the political relations of his country seems to animate Dr Darwin and Sir Charles Lyell. They suppress the revolutionary in Nature and decree that the Earth shall perform all her operations without violent excesses; that insensibly, through a vast period of years, she shall modify and transform herself.[50]

There is, of course, at the mere level of fact, a good deal about this – almost all of it in fact – that one would have to correct. 'Peace at any price' was hardly the motto either of Darwin's view of nature or of British foreign policy in the age of Palmerston. Geological uniformitarianism did not spring suddenly into existence, even though Lyell gave the impression it did, in 1830, nor can the lines of division between geological schools be simplified as Michelet and, it must be admitted, Lyell himself, suggested that they could. Theories of geological uplift from the action of heat, for example by Nicholas Desmarest, were current before the French Revolution,[51] and must therefore be a consequence, if anything, of the

[50] Michelet, *The Mountain*, pp. 116–8.
[51] See Kenneth J. Taylor, 'Nicholas Desmarest and Geology in the Eighteenth Century', in Cecil J. Schnee, ed., *Towards a History of Geology* (Cambridge, Mass., 1969). R. Hooykaas, *Natural Law and Divine Miracle. The Principle of Uniformity in Geology, Biology and Theology* (Leiden, 1963), p. 16.

American one, just as they were current in Britain as well as the continent in the early nineteenth century. They could be combined as they are in Hutton, with the notion of long-continued action over immense periods of time; Lyell's own formative years, before he published *Principles of Geology* in 1830, were years of crisis and apprehension, of Waterloo and Peterloo. And in so far as industrialism suggested analogies with natural events, regularity was only one, and perhaps not the most notable: violent Plutonic energies, fiery scenes of Vesuvian grandeur and power, were how industry, ironworks at least, struck the English imagination.

Yet I should not have mentioned Michelet only to deride him. Lyell's own culture was not, of course, the anachronistic Cobdenite one Michelet attributes to him (he was born in the 1790s), but it was not irrelevant to the way his theory was propounded. His guiding conception was, as Roy Porter has pointed out, essentially the Scottish conjectural history of the later eighteenth century, classically formulated by Dugald Stewart in his life of Adam Smith. The explanation of past geological events by causes now in operation is a form of conjectural history in this sense, and Lyell continues it with a history of geological thought which is an Enlightenment story of the overcoming of superstition by the march of mind.[52] The essentially eighteenth-century cast of Lyell's thinking, in fact, sets him significantly at odds with some of the most powerful intellectual tendencies of his time. It was, for example, at odds with evolution; Lyell's geological theory is a cyclical one, without novelty; novelty entered his account of pre-history only with successive, discontinuous, special creations of organisms. And though Lyell was fond of analogies between geology and history, acknowledging, in a sense, that history was the senior and more advanced discipline,[53] the kind of history to which his own theory is analogous was, by the nineteenth century, decidedly old-fashioned; it was that neo-classical and essentially cyclical conception of history to which some eighteenth-century historians subscribed, grounded in the notion of the uniformity of human nature.[54] To virtually all mid-nineteenth-century historians there were two cardinal truths which set them apart from such assumptions: one, the product, more than anything else, of Romanticism, above all in Germany, was the notion of the distinctive shaping of human nature by distinct cultures; the other,

---

[52] Roy Porter, 'Charles Lyell and the Principles of the History of Geology' *British Journal for the History of Science*, 9 (1976).

[53] Martin J. S. Rudwick, 'Transposed Concepts from the History of the Human Sciences in the Early Work of Charles Lyell', in Jordanova and Porter, *Images of the Earth*, pp. 68–71.

[54] E.g. Charles Lyell, *Principles of Geology. Being an Attempt to explain the former changes of the Earth's surface by reference to causes now in operation*, 2 vols. (1830), I, p. 1: 'When we study history we obtain a more profound insight into human nature by instituting a comparison between the present and former states of society.'

fostered by the revolutionary era and industrialism, was the unprecedented character of the modern history of the 'progressive' nations. Lyell's theory, of course, being geological, contradicted neither, but it was asymmetrical with both. But uniformity in Lyell was two different things, in a way he himself seems never fully to have appreciated; it meant, strictly, that explanation by secondary causes, by fixed laws of nature, eschewing the miraculous, to which increasing numbers of his contemporaries subscribed. But it also meant something Michelet correctly saw, even if it was not solely what Lyell's theory required, namely gradualism, slow, smooth process, the absence of violence. In terms of strict theory the distinction between Lyell's kind of geology and the kind loosely and inexactly called catastrophist was, as we now know, by no means absolute. Hutton, for example, who had operated with an unlimited timescale and who had proclaimed his allegiance to the idea of uniform natural causes, had spoken with considerable excitement of the vast upheavals of which nature was capable, such that Lyell, and I think also Carlyle, interpreted him as saying that new continents were formed by catastrophic upheavals. Lyell himself actually required that modern upheavals should produce impressive results so that past ones of similar magnitude could be invoked to explain, above all, the height of mountains.[55] Before the understanding of the effects of glaciation and continental movement, *all* geology was, I take it, bound to be in some sense more 'catastrophic' than it is today.

But in gauging the effects on the wider culture a good deal may be allowed to depend on the tone of the author, particularly, I suppose, among a lay public, as well as on their predispositions, and here the tone of Lyell's polemics was certainly strongly gradualist. In that sense, if we understand Michelet as speaking not so much of the influences on Lyell as on the ways he was read and understood, he may not be far wrong. Lyell was seen, and saw himself, as the apostle of gradualism, as well as of the vast timescale which through him, for the first time, impressed itself on the wider public. The central image, and indeed the frontispiece, of Lyell's *Principles* is provided by the pillars of the temple of Jupiter Serapis, on the Bay of Naples, whose columns, now above water, showed borings by marine creatures, requiring a substantial period of time to make, up to twenty-three feet above the present water table. Yet no classical account mentioned a violent inundation, which would, in any case, have overthrown the columns; the conclusion must be two very large yet gradual alterations of the water level.

It is striking how the character of geological analogies appears to

---

[55] Martin J. S, Rudwick, 'Lyell on Etna and the Antiquity of the Earth', in Schnee, *Towards a History*, pp. 288–304.

change around the mid-century in particular, and in some respects paradoxically. Igneous activity, in fact, plays a large part in Lyell's theory; heavy emphasis on the sedimentary was characteristic of the Neptunists of the earlier years of the century. Yet the wider use of geological metaphors around the mid-century, after 1848, even though it is often clearly Lyellian geology that is being appealed to because of the references to 'uniform laws', is almost invariably sedimentary. Catastrophic and volcanic analogies become less noticeable. In that sense Michelet's English came in some measure to conform to the role he writes for them. 'Strata' as a metaphor for the layering of human cultures, for example, becomes common, with the suggestion of something gradually deposited over long periods; Henry Maine uses it for law, Bagehot for society as a whole.[56] Only very occasionally does one come across references to geological unconformities as evidence of the stressful raising of lower strata.

Max Müller in the Rede Lecture of 1868 'On the Stratification of Language', uniquely to my knowledge, mentions them, but not because of their testimony to a violent past; instead they provide a perhaps not very appropriate metaphor for evidence of arrested growth in languages, which have 'remained on the surface in this primitive state'.[57] He is referring, that is, to what other scholars in this period often called 'survivals', bits of the past exposed to direct view, not to anything to do with geological violence. Indeed the fact that geology could be coupled with the history of language – as William Whewell, for example, had also done[58] – tends to show how the former was being purged of suggestions of catastrophe. The history of language itself, of course, generalised as 'the comparative method', became in turn a metaphor for other kinds of historical recovery, as Edward Freeman uses it in his *Comparative Politics* and Henry Maine in *Ancient Law*.[59] Here language becomes a metaphor for custom and for the slow, imperceptible changes by which custom transforms itself.

Concepts and metaphors from history, political economy, physiology, entomology, Darwinian ecology, and Lyellian geology criss-crossed the culture with mutual borrowings, as geologists themselves, for example,

---

[56] Henry Maine, *Ancient Law* (1861; 10th edn, 1897), p. 3. *The Collected Works of Walter Bagehot*, ed., Norman St John Stevas, 15 vols. (London, 1965–86), V, p. 208.

[57] F. Max Müller, *On the Stratification of Language*, The Rede Lecture (Cambridge, 1868), pp. 12–13.

[58] E.g. William Whewell on what he calls 'palaetiological sciences', in *Indications of the Creator* (1845), pp. 96–8, 101. Whewell's argument was unusual, however, in suggesting an early history of language of considerably accelerated change compared with the present. *Ibid.*, p. 121. Whewell was an effective critic of Lyell.

[59] See Stefan Collini, Donald Winch, and John Burrow, *That Noble Science of Politics* (Cambridge, 1983), pp. 211–12.

used historical and linguistic analogies.[60] These disciplines, I think, have two features in common. The first is the ways in which the unplanned interaction of myriads of small components – organisms or the actions of men – creates through time, collectively, something which none of them consciously intended. It was derived in part I think from the Scottish Enlightenment's conceptions of 'unintended consequences', epitomised above all in Political Economy, which made the latter in turn a metaphor for other disciplines and sciences; the biologist Milne Edwards, for example, coined the phrase 'the physiological division of labour' before Herbert Spencer borrowed it back from him for biological analogies for social science.[61] In part, again, it derives, in some cases, from the German Romantic conception of the anonymous cooperative creativity of the *Volk*, exhibited in language, myth, and legal custom.

The second element, which is to some extent itself a consequence of a belief in the significance of changes taking place insensibly, to use the eighteenth-century word, but which also places the eighteenth-century concept in a new context, is a new and in some cases intense sensitivity to the imperceptible passage of time, to the difficulty of rendering it at all adequately or of conveying different kinds of duration and the infinitesimal minuteness of the processes spoken of literally or metaphorically as sedimentation or accretion. It helped to shape mid-Victorian sensibilities in ways comparable perhaps to the influence of the microscope in the early eighteenth century, and behind it surely lies, above all, the gradualism and the unimaginable duration spoken of by geology read in the Lyellian mode, and especially, of course, after the new timescale, in the hands of pre-historic archaeologists from the late 1850s onwards, began to include man. The best-known examples, I suppose, come from George Eliot, though her metaphors tend to be physiological rather than geological. Yet it was she who spoke most explicitly of the unnoticed tragedy that lies in the fact of frequency, epitomised in the gradual process of Dorothea Brooke's disillusionment with her husband;[62] ultimately untraceable because not reducible to events and conscious awareness, but deposited grain by grain like a kind of grey sediment – not her image I hasten to say. In a melodramatic novel Dorothea would have discovered her husband's secret in a letter in a locked drawer, like the famous non-secret of Mrs Radcliffe's *Mysteries of Udolpho*. When George Eliot, speaking through her character Lydgate, looks for the antithesis of her own kind of writing, and his own microscopic science, and so for artistic inspiration of the 'vulgar and vinous' kind, she finds it in the Drury Lane

[60] Rudwick, 'Transposed Concepts', pp. 71–3.
[61] David Duncan, *The Life and Letters of Herbert Spencer* (1908) p. 542.
[62] George Eliot, *Middlemarch* (1872), bk II, ch. XX.

sublime; in Satan with wings and a tail;[63] she could be describing a picture by John Martin. The abrupt and violent had become 'vulgar'.

These, of course, are famous examples. Let us take a perhaps less familiar one, put to rather different rhetorical use, and more relevant to the way I want to conclude. There is sometimes – not invariably – in references to sedimentation as accumulation a reaching back to the aesthetics, not of the sublime, but of the picturesque, with its appreciation of such 'ornaments of time',[64] in John Gilpin's phrase, as moss and ivy and weathered stone, as well as to entirely congruous Burkean notions of accumulated experience and the unbroken yet creative sequences of precedents. Walter Bagehot uses it, for example, as a metaphor for the wisdom of the statesman. In his essay on Peel, whom he contrasts with Byron's 'volcanic mind', he says: 'Peel's opinions far more resembled the daily accumulating deposits of a rich alluvial soil. The great stream of time flows on, with all things on its surface, and slowly, grain by grain, a mould of wise experience is unconsciously left on the still extended intellect.'[65] Bagehot's essay, as a matter of fact, is rather equivocal, even condescending about Peel, yet the image can hardly seem other than grave, gentle, infinitely impressive, and Burkean. Elsewhere he uses a geological metaphor in conjunction with others – rather as in George Eliot's musings on duration, imperceptible change, and the invisible filaments of emotional attachment – to rebuke our common insensitivity, in this case to the fine grain of the past; we observe only the greater events and hence place them in a false perspective. 'There is no idea of the countless accumulation, the collision of action, the web of human feeling with which in the day of their life they were encompassed.'[66] Bagehot devoted a large part of his writing life to explaining the ways in which politics function in a day-to-day sense, dwelling sometimes with a barely sustained impatience, sometimes with an ironic connoisseurship, on the absence of events, on the quality of dullness and its political functions, on the subtle interaction of accumulated custom and prejudice with modest innovation, in what he called 'the tedium of history and the precariousness of results'.[67]

IV

Speaking of Bagehot brings us, at last, to irony – one can hardly speak of Bagehot without speaking of irony. The question I want to raise, because I

---

[63] *Ibid.*, bk. II, ch. XVI.
[64] John Gilpin, 'Observations on the River Wye' (1782) on Tintern Abbey. Quoted J. R. Watson, *Picturesque Landscape and English Romantic Poetry* (London, 1970), p. 82.
[65] *Collected Works of Walter Bagehot*, 'The Character of Sir Robert Peel', III, p. 252.
[66] *Ibid.*, p. 241.   [67] *The English Constitution*, in Bagehot, *Works*, V, p. 207.

think it raised itself for the mid-Victorians, is how one speaks of a history without heroes, almost without events, a history essentially of largely anonymous agents and unintended consequences. It is epitomised above all, in the 1860s, in Stubbs' *Constitutional History of England*, particularly in volume I, dealing with the earliest period, the period of the anonymous creativity of the folk, the work, as Darwin says in wonder of coral reefs, of 'myriads of tiny architects'.[68] Stubbs' words, in turn, in his preface, sound familiar to readers of George Eliot, though it is a decade before *Middlemarch*. The history of institutions 'has a point of view and a language of its own. It reads the character of men by a different light from that shed by the false glare of arms, and interprets in words that are voiceless to those who have only listened to the trumpet of fame. The world's heroes are no heroes to it and it has an equitable consideration to give to many whom the verdict of ignorant posterity and the condemning sentence of events have consigned to obscurity'.[69] Stubbs' first volume deals in a fashion which is both Burkean and Germanic, with changes perceptible only over centuries and with tentative beginnings, blindly made and later put to other uses in endless series of piecemeal adaptations. As he says – and this time the language sounds Lyellian as well as Burkean, though I am not imputing any specific influence – 'there are no constitutional revolutions, no violent reversals of legislation; custom is far more potent than law and custom is modified infinitesimally every day'.[70]

In contrast to the apocalyptic it was hard to represent the newer sensibility pictorially; the imperceptible is also necessarily the unpaintable. Even the frontispiece of Lyell's book is, to the eye, only an attractive engraving of ruined classical columns with their feet in still water. This is, of course, because of the difficulty of rendering time, above all infinitely slow processes, pictorially; shaggy or ruined and overgrown buildings in the picturesque tradition were about the best there was, though there is an exercise in what one might call 'peaceful geology' by William Dyce, in his *Pegwell Bay*, with its careful rendering of the layered texture of stone. But early English constitutional history was more intractable. When the Palace of Westminster was slowly rebuilt after the fire, a series of frescoes depicting English history was ordered for the House of Lords and artists were invited to submit designs. One of the successful offerings was Charles West Cope's *The First Trial by Jury*, which hardly caught the long-drawn minute and tentative processes soon to be described by constitutional historians like Kemble and Stubbs. John Martin also competed. Trying to

---

[68] Diary entry, 1836, quoted D. R. Stoddart, 'Darwin, Lyell and the Geological Significance of Coral Reefs', in Jordanova and Porter, *Images of the Earth*, p. 204.
[69] William Stubbs, *Constitutional History of England*, 3 vols. (Oxford, 1873; 2nd edn, 1875), I, preface.   [70] *Ibid.*, p. 166.

enter into the spirit of the thing, and resisting what must have been the temptation to improvise *The Wrath of God with the English Nation* or *The Last Parliamentarian*, he offered *King Canute Rebuking the Flattery of his Courtiers*, of which a watercolour version exists: the king at the edge of the sea, vainly commanding the waves. It is Martin's only picture of a miracle failing to occur, and was predictably rejected. It is not much of a picture.[71]

We need, then, to ask how one might write and make significant, as well as 'depict', a history without event, a history of gradual, all but imperceptible process, and a history apparently without a moral. The apocalyptic sublime moralises natural or supernatural events, above all, of chastisement, of justified suspensions of the natural order; the Deluge covers the world and Sodom and Gomorrah are consumed. Hutton's steady-state world was presented, by contrast, in the spirit of benign Natural Theology, as a world designed, despite some awkward appearances, for endless habitation. Lyell's world is either not moralised at all or can be so only by reference to the successive organic creations which are extraneous to his theory and incompatible with his uniformitarian notion of causality. (Tennyson recoiled from the ruthlessness of this in *In Memoriam*.) The slow Lyellian geological processes needed, for a congruous relation to organic life, to be complemented by something like an account of evolutionary process, which is of course what they received from Darwin: explaining how an order, even a progressive one, given enough time, could be produced, without presupposing an ordinance. Darwin succeeded in a sense in peopling Lyell's uniformitarian world, and in a sense, as he noted, 'moralising' it as providing a secure basis, as catastrophism did not, for the continuity of life,[72] but only at the cost of enunciating what to many of his contemporaries was a moral paradox, and one that became more monstrous when applied to the human world, that it was out of the struggle for existence, the war of nature that 'forms most beautiful and wonderful have been and are being evolved'.[73]

Carlyle, it can be argued, is, in terms of sensibility, a transitional figure. Most obviously his is the sensibility of the apocalyptic sublime, of the abrupt and convulsive, of judgement and chastisement, often figured as geological events of a catastrophic kind. Yet I have argued that he is attracted by a steady-state world, and that this, with its alternations of decay and creative convulsion, invests his historical thought with some of its controlling metaphors.[74] Moreover, Carlyle is by no means altogether

[71] Reproduced in Christopher Johnstone, *John Martin* (London, 1974), p. 94.
[72] Charles Darwin, *The Origin of Species* [1859] (Harmondsworth, 1968), p. 459.
[73] *Ibid.*, p. 460.
[74] It is, of course, consistent with another, later, influence on Carlyle, that of the Saint Simonians, with their conception of history as an alternation of 'critical' periods of dissolution and 'organic' periods of consolidation.

divorced from the gradualist, accretive sensibility we have been considering; he is even, I guess, an influence on it. The treasure of the accumulated labour of mankind, imperceptible to the eye of history because not registered as event, is one of his themes: 'the quantity of done and forgotten work that lies silent under my feet'.[75] It recalls Darwin's awe at the formation of coral reefs. For Carlyle labour goes on incessantly, unrecorded yet cumulatively significant; Breughel's peasant, as it were, continues ploughing his furrow though Icarus falls from the sky.

Yet there is a problem, and it is one which metaphors of accretion cannot address. How, in the human world, are such activities coordinated, how do they, so to say, become history? The Darwinian kind of answer, when tried out on human society in the half-century after the *Origin*, proved a disappointment; in human terms natural selection appeared to mean no more than that innovations caught on when circumstances were propitious, which hardly needed a biological analogue to carry conviction but carried little else. Carlyle would not have liked the suggestion of a Darwinian answer anyway, though Bagehot tried it out.[76] But Adam Smith had offered one a century before in terms of a softened version of the Mandevellian paradox that private vices are public benefits. Smith, before Darwin, grappled with the problem of order without an ordinance – or *perhaps* without one, given the famously enigmatic simile of an unseen hand. The paradigm case of an order generated without overall design by the unintended consequences of countless individual actions in pursuit of petty and limited motives was the market. Carlyle, of course, hated it and vehemently denied that, as he put it, 'a commonwealth' could be generated from it; perhaps Smith would have agreed. Carlyle, like all the early and mid-nineteenth-century critics of political economy, was demanding a return to a world of transparent moral relations, in which good and bad motives and actions brought their just reward. It was because he rejected the answer to the question how order is generated given in terms of unintended consequences that he resorted to heroes, courted captains of industry and what-nots, to restore morality to the collective life of human beings, just as others resorted, as George Eliot perhaps almost did, to the artificial surrogate religion of the Comtist priesthood to do the same. Comtism, like Carlyle, looked back to earlier historical ideas of organising heroes, though they were heroes of the intellect; its imagery for the accumulated treasury of mankind was the old-fashioned one of saints and heroes. George Eliot clearly responded to such examples, yet she also characteristically needed to include, like

---

[75] Carlyle, *Past and Present*, in *Works*, II, p. 113. cf. 'On History', in *Works*, XV, pp. 497–8.

[76] Bagehot, *Physics and Politics. Or Thoughts on the Application of the Principles of Natural Selection and Inheritance to Political Society*, in *Works*, VII, pp. 15–144.

Stubbs, the significance of the anonymous and barely perceptible, the choir invisible, the incalculable effects of unnumbered actions and the lives of those who made little stir in the world and rest in unvisited tombs.[77] This is, however, a highly piecemeal, as well as somewhat tentative account of progress by accretion, rather than an organising concept for explaining it. The young Bagehot in 1851 faced the question of the why and how of progress – and shrugged: 'By the sound work of old-fashioned generations – by the singular painstaking of the slumberers in the churchyard – by dull care – by stupid industry, a certain social fabric somehow exists, people continue to go out to their work, and to find work to employ them until the evening, body and soul are kept together, and this is what mankind have to show for their six thousand years of toil and trouble.'[78]

Bagehot was steeped in Adam Smith. He also quite frequently cites Carlyle and his prose has affinities with his in its humorous, but not its apocalyptic vein. It is a tantalising thought. The reference to finding work, to the market in effect, is we may say 'Smithian'; the work of the generations in the churchyard could easily be Carlylean, even Burkean; yet the ironic diction, the 'stupid industry', the shrugging 'somehow exists', is all Bagehot's own, and the 'this is all mankind has to show' turns a thought that was more usually celebratory into something very deflationary. Yet – the final irony – in the context of Bagehot's argument, it is actually an endorsement of the elemental and practical against the excitements of political oratory and journalism. French society must continue, though liberal journalists rage, and Bagehot defended Louis Napoleon's *coup d'état* at this point as necessary to its continuance. Political vice was, at this juncture, social virtue. Such paradoxes occur constantly in Bagehot, particularly, of course, in the form of the more or less benign stupidity that characterises the English.

I have suggested that the metaphor of accretion can indeed imply a kind of veneration, even awe, not least when it is applied to the concept of human labour. Yet when it went beyond labour to the more complex notion of a collective economic and social life, rather as Darwinian metaphors go beyond Lyellian ones, beyond mere accretion to the more complex notion of organisation, then the central concept of unintended consequences, the moral disjunction of motive and benefit, remains as a kind of potentiality for irony, and the greater the distance from the notion of divine providence, by whom all can be thought of as intended, the starker the irony. It is a notion with application far beyond economic life, which was in a sense too easy a target; Bagehot was far more often ironic

[77] Eliot, *Middlemarch,* the concluding words.
[78] Bagehot, 'The French Coup d'Etat', *Works,* IV, p. 36.

about politics, about the conditions of political success in an imperfect world in which merits might be disabling and limitations advantages. When it came to history he paid his tribute to unintended consequences but with, unlike Stubbs, no piety about an unseen providential hand. 'We have made, or rather stumbled upon'[79] the English constitution; a phrase which, presumably unconsciously, echoes Adam Ferguson a century earlier: 'nations stumble upon establishments which are indeed the result of human actions but not the execution of any human design'.[80] For Bagehot the constitution so stumbled upon incongruously but happily combined venerability, the product of slow growth, with efficiency, at the affordable cost only of a certain tolerance of illusion by those who knew. The price of continuity in institutions was a gradual divorce between appearance and reality, surface and function, epitomised in the monarchy and the cabinet respectively, and the price was well worth paying. To Carlyle, if he read *The English Constitution* – I know of no reference – it would have seemed as if the empire of imposture had brazenly proclaimed itself as such. It was the most outspoken of all the expressions of the sceptical, to him amoral, Whig mentality he had always despised.[81] When he spoke fifteen years earlier in *Latter Day Pamphlets* of 'the poor knowing person of this epoch' and his belief 'that lies were the rule in this earth'[82] he might almost have been judging Bagehot in advance, – 'knowing' seems exactly the right adjective. And when Carlyle wrote there that 'a solid Englishman, wholesomely digesting his pudding . . . has been used to decent forms long since divested of meaning, to plausible modes, solemnities grown ceremonial . . . all his life long',[83] he actually did anticipate, with a different emotional force but in a very similar diction, one of Bagehot's central themes.

For Bagehot, of course, the veneration which attached itself like moss or ivy to the antique but largely illusory 'dignified' elements in the constitution was irrational, but it was a mainly benign irrationality because it represented the only possible adhesive in a society whose various sections were made strangers to each other by differential intellectual progress. He pictured them in a geological metaphor, in a vocabulary borrowed from the now unfashionable Neptunists: 'Great communities are like great mountains – they have in them the primary, secondary and tertiary strata of human progress, the characteristics of the lower regions representing the old times rather than the present life of the higher regions.'[84] This was

---

[79] Bagehot, *The English Constitution*, in *Works*, V, p. 210.
[80] Adam Ferguson, *An Essay on the History of Civil Society* [1767] (Edinburgh, 1966), p. 122.
[81] 'Whiggism, I believe, is all but forever *done*. Away with Dilletanteism and Machiavellism', quoted in Campbell, *Thomas Carlyle*, p. 73.
[82] Carlyle, *Latter Day Pamphlets*, in *Works*, V, p. 13.   [83] *Ibid.*, V, p. 12.
[84] Bagehot, *The English Constitution*, in *Works*, V, p. 208.

a common nineteenth-century thought though often in other metaphors – a kind of evolutionary anthropological method applied to contemporary society. The lowest stratum was often seen as dangerous, threatening a recrudescence of savagery. But in Bagehot's metaphor here geology suggests something very different from, say, Carlyle's regenerating molten mass of elemental energy below the thin earth-rind of custom. Here the lowest stratum is itself the sediment of custom, essentially inert, while activity belongs to the higher regions. If, highly improbably, Michelet had read it, he would have felt justified in his presentation of English geology and the English mind. Apparently the last thing this Englishman expected mountains to do was to explode.

10   'Race' and 'nation' in mid-Victorian thought

Peter Mandler

I

How central were organic concepts of race and nationality to the Victorians' sense of self before the age of high imperialism at the end of the nineteenth century? Until comparatively recently intellectual historians had hardly even considered this question.[1] In dissecting English thought they had tended to focus either on the persistence of Enlightenment themes or upon the development of social-evolutionary thinking, both of a marked liberal-universalist character relatively unfissured by sharp national, still less racial distinctions.[2] But historians writing in post-colonial and post-modern modes are now making the case that even at mid-century English thought was profoundly imbued with strong concepts of race and nation, formerly associated with contemporary thought in Germany, France and Italy, but not with England.[3] This case has been made without, on the whole, engaging closely with the 'high' intellectual history of the period, partly because intellectual historians had not made explicit the racial and national implications of social-evolutionary thinking. In this essay, I want to bring out these implications

I am very grateful to Stefan Collini, David Feldman, Julia Stapleton, and Miles Taylor for comments on earlier drafts of this essay.

[1] For some early (but highly anecdotal) treatments, see Reginald Horsman, *Race and Manifest Destiny: The Origins of American Racial Anglo-Saxonism* (Cambridge, Mass., 1981), part 1; Hugh A. MacDougall, *Racial Myth in English History* (Montreal, 1982). Much better is Douglas A. Lorimer, *Colour, Class and the Victorians* (Leicester, 1978). I omit here consideration of more specialised works in the history of science, and in general the debates that took place within Victorian ethnography and anthropology, except where they touched on wider issues and audiences.

[2] J. W. Burrow, *Evolution and Society: A Study in Victorian Social Theory* (Cambridge, 1966); Stefan Collini, Donald Winch, and John Burrow, *That Noble Science of Politics: A Study in Nineteenth-Century Intellectual History* (Cambridge, 1983); John Burrow, *Whigs and Liberals: Continuity and Change in English Political Thought* (Oxford, 1988).

[3] For example, Catherine Hall, *White, Male and Middle-Class: Explorations in Feminism and History* (Oxford, 1992); Catherine Hall, '"From Greenland's Icy Mountains . . . to Afric's Golden Sand": Ethnicity, Race and Nation in Mid-Nineteenth Century England', *Gender and History*, 5 (1993), pp. 212–30; Robert J. C. Young, *Colonial Desire: Hybridity in Theory, Culture and Race* (London: Routledge, 1995). Lying behind much of this work is the inspiration of Homi Bhabha, ed., *Nation and Narration* (London, 1990).

more clearly, demonstrating how the vitality of the social-evolutionary tradition inhibited the development of biological racism and organic nationalism in England. Beyond that, I will attempt to specify where, and to what degree, nationalist views could develop in the systematic social, political, and historical thought of those crucial years between the revolutions of 1848 and the Home Rule crisis of 1886.

In the half-century before 1848, the English were already lagging well behind other Europeans in thinking seriously about 'nationality'. Without the impetus provided by new revolutionary elites seeking to mobilise a popular following or social movements seeking emancipation through national unification, they had no powerful motive to do so. The two principal political legacies of the eighteenth century – contractarianism and the Scottish Enlightenment's conjectural history – remained remarkably intact. Both assumed a fairly universal human nature and saw the great motor of history as the archetypal individual's striving for material gratification. Nations played a role in providing political institutions that catered to certain minimal collective needs, and, in the most sophisticated of Scottish Enlightenment versions, helped to ensure that the accumulation of wealth and the progress of manners proceeded hand in hand (as they normally but not inevitably would do). The latter role provided scope for the 'science of the legislator', but this science – like others of its day – was a cosmopolitan science and its lessons were theoretically applicable anywhere. The Scottish conviction that the lessons had been best learnt close to home did not impeach their potential universality. At a time when German philologists and jurisprudential thinkers were developing Herder's notion of a deeply rooted plurality of human fates, and French comparative anatomists were drawing on Lamarckian transformism to hypothesise a plurality of human origins and/or species, English thought remained determinedly universalistic and monogenetic. Its great intellectual contributions of the early nineteenth century were not in the 'racial' and 'national' spheres of philology, ethnology, or anatomy, but in the cosmopolitan science of political economy.[4] As F. W. Maitland said, looking backwards on the nineteenth century, this was 'the critical moment. Would Englishmen see and understand what was happening in Germany? Would they appreciate and emulate the work of Savigny and Grimm?' And he concluded, with some sadness for the loss of scholarship but none at all for the metaphysical implications, 'It can hardly be said that they rose to the occasion.'[5]

[4] For some of these primitive national comparisons, see George Stocking, *Victorian Anthropology* (New York, 1987), pp. 18–32.

[5] Quoted by J. W. Burrow, *A Liberal Descent: Victorian Historians and the English Past* (Cambridge, 1981), pp. 119–20. For Maitland's disapproval of the metaphysical implications of Savignian jurisprudence, see C. H. S. Fifoot, *Frederic William Maitland: A Life* (Cambridge, Mass., 1971), pp. 231–5.

It is true that the revolutionary wars, by requiring Britain to undertake its own unprecedented mobilisation against other *levées en masse*, did provide a moment of intensified national feeling and, in Edmund Burke, brought forward a potential intellectual spokesman for this feeling. Yet Burke's own liberal conformation did not allow him to travel very far down the national road. He stressed more than any other contemporary British thinker the historical uniqueness and providential greatness of British political institutions; he held that these institutions reflected 'the peculiar circumstances, occasions, tempers, dispositions, and moral, civil and social habitudes of the people';[6] but he went no further. He did remarkably little to specify what were the 'tempers, dispositions and habitudes' of the British people and certainly did not claim that they were so distinctive to the British as to disqualify other peoples from benefiting from the same kind of institutions. Furthermore, once the normality of peacetime was restored after 1815, the seeds he planted were not cultivated by English successors, but had more impact on continental ground that was already fertilised for it. As Maitland's collaborator, Sir Frederick Pollock, recognised when similarly taking stock of the century behind him, in England, Burke 'left no disciples', but continental political thought had developed 'in a spirit, and sometimes even in a form, which have more affinities with Burke than with any other Englishman'.[7]

A more decisive factor in reorientating the path of English political thought after 1815, though not in a more nationalistic direction, was its penetration by evangelical Christianity. Christian political economy, as we now appreciate better thanks to the work of Boyd Hilton, performed the same necessary task of refuting dangerous contractarianism that an organicist extension of Burke's thought might have achieved, without requiring the abandonment of commercial (and, to some extent, political) liberalism.[8] By intertwining a more powerful moral component with the material sequence of Scottish conjectural history, evangelical thought not only preserved but strengthened the presumption of a 'natural' progression from primitive to advanced states, what one might call the 'civilisational' perspective. Significantly, the progression towards civilisation was seen as 'natural' in two senses, both of which shored up earlier Scottish understandings of progress, though they also made progress seem a more arduous achievement. First, the impulse towards civilisation

---

[6] From an undelivered speech, cited by Burrow, *Liberal Descent*, pp. 105–6.

[7] Sir Frederick Pollock, *An Introduction to the History of the Science of Politics* (London, 1890), pp. 86–92, 118.

[8] Boyd Hilton, *The Age of Atonement: The Influence of Evangelicalism on Social and Economic Thought, 1795–1865* (Oxford, 1988), esp. chs. 2, 5. I say little here about what constituted civilisation, or how it was achieved, the crucial distinction being one between a universalising 'civilisation' and a diversifying 'nationality'.

was constitutionally embedded in human nature by its Maker, and then fortified by Revelation.[9] The civilisational perspective was thus not tute-lary – it gave much scope to individual conscience and action – and required only a minimum of exclusive political institutions (particularly churches, to disseminate a proper understanding of Revelation) for its smooth functioning. Second, despite the fact that the recipe for civilisa-tion had become more ethnocentric, adding to older Scottish require-ments for 'commerce' and 'manners' a narrower Protestant idea of 'character', the civilisational perspective remained potentially universal, available to all peoples. The very power of its ethnocentrism, its deliberate applicability to the whole of God's creation, limited its resort to the vocabulary or conceptual apparatus of 'race' and 'nation'.[10] It was, after all, an anglophile Frenchman, François Guizot, who was responsible for one of the most coherent and influential statements of the civilisational perspective, the *History of Civilization in Europe* (1828).

The addition of a Christian dimension might have provided more scope for nationalising English political thought, but all attempts by nationally minded Christians to move it in this direction proved abortive. In part this was due to the fact that the early nineteenth century was pre-cisely the period of religious pluralisation in Britain, with the abolition of exclusive Anglican rights in the polity in 1828–9 and attacks of mounting seriousness on the remaining privileges of the Church of England after 1832. Thus Coleridge's rather belated (and fairly gnomic) vision of an English people arranged in a social hierarchy but capped and organised by their national church, like the Burkean vision that helped to inspire it, found few English disciples, and what remained of 'Germano-Coleridgean' thinking (J. S. Mill's phrase) passed into secular, liberal hands, as we shall see later. The so-called 'Liberal Anglicans' – Thomas Arnold and his followers – formed a half-way house. But despite Duncan Forbes' attempts to portray them as full-blooded Germans in English clothing,[11] the Liberal Anglicans' thought on race and nationality looks far more English than German. They had the familiar Christian concern for moral as well as material development, but they lacked Herder's

---

[9] The most extensive and influential statement is John Bird Sumner, *A Treatise on the Records of the Creation and on the Moral Attributes of the Creator*, 5th edn, 2 vols. (1826; London, 1833), esp. part 2.

[10] In this perspective racial difference was normally taken as a comparatively superficial (and correspondingly changeable) marker of civilisational progress: see Sumner's adap-tation of Prichardian ethnology in *Records*, I, pp. 344–78.

[11] Duncan Forbes, *The Liberal Anglican Idea of History* (Cambridge, 1952). Forbes' dichot-omy between Scottish Enlightenment 'Rationalists' and Liberal Anglican 'Romantics' has already been broken down by work on the former that stresses the moral and social dimensions of Scottish thought: see, e.g., Donald Winch, *Riches and Poverty: An Intellectual History of Political Economy in Britain, 1750–1834* (Cambridge, 1996).

distinctive view that different nations had essentially different moral natures. As the Liberal Anglican H. H. Milman insisted, on the very brink of the 1848 revolutions,

Man is the same, to a great extent, in every part of the world, and in every period. Society is part of his nature, and social forms, being circumscribed in their variations, will take the same character, enact the same provisions, establish the same ranks and gradations, aim at the same objects, and attain the same ends.

And the inspiration for Milman's remarks here was not evidence of kindred institutions close to home but rather of the ancient despotism of Inca Peru.[12] The Liberal Anglicans also disdained strongly tutelary and organic functions even for the national institutions they did believe in. Such functions might be appropriate for nations in their 'youth', thought Arnold, but were less so in 'maturity' (the stage at which England had arrived). Despite some bursts of gloominess about possible degeneration, most of the Liberal Anglicans felt there was a general tendency towards maturity that would ultimately end in an apocalyptic unity of mankind.[13]

Nationality did, then, play a role in Liberal Anglican thought, but only a transitional role (out of which England was already moving); theirs was a perspective that would gain in credibility in the mid-Victorian period. In their own heyday of the 1830s and 1840s, however, even their weak idea of nationality was exceptional. At a time when intellectuals in most continental countries, especially liberals but also some conservatives, were developing an exceptionally powerful understanding of national difference, most of their English contemporaries remained indifferent or actively hostile, relying instead on the civilisational perspective for their defence of hierarchy and for their understanding of England's place in the world. Though the popular English press developed a marked interest in national history and folklore,[14] the educated press stayed aloof and, on the few occasions when it deigned to notice popular-romantic history, sniped at it. Walter Scott's novels, for instance, made for good escapism but they were not deemed serious contributions to thinking about polity or society: again, they were far more influential for these purposes in France and Germany.[15] English history was at a low ebb; it did not enter

---

[12] [H. H. Milman], 'Prescott's *Conquest of Peru*; Tschudi's *Travels in Peru*', *Quarterly Review*, 81 (1847), p. 323. Milman also takes pains to separate himself from the 'exaggerated' racial views of Thierry and of German ethnographers.

[13] As Forbes grants, *Liberal Anglican Idea*, pp. 30–8, 51–2, 56–63, 85–6, 121.

[14] Peter Mandler, '"In the Olden Time": Romantic History and English National Identity, 1820–1850', in L. Brockliss and D. Eastwood, eds., *A Union of Multiple Identities: The British Isles, c. 1750 – c. 1850* (Manchester, 1997), 78–92.

[15] For example, [Herman Merivale], 'The Pictorial History of England', *Edinburgh Review*, 74 (1841–2), pp. 430–73; 'Walter Scott – Has History Gained by His Writings?', *Fraser's Magazine*, 36 (1847), pp. 345–51.

the curricula of the ancient universities in any form until after 1848,[16] nor, with the possible exception of the work of Henry Hallam, did it have a much wider impact on the educated mind. Contemporaries were well aware of this contrast between Britain and the continent. The father of Saxonism in England, J. M. Kemble, ploughing a lonely furrow, frequently complained to his German colleagues about the lack of interest in their subject in his own country.[17] Mazzini, living in exile in England for most of this period, developed the theory that the English were simply too utilitarian a people to understand the concept of 'nationality':[18] a nationalist explanation for English cosmopolitanism that proved congenial to the odd English racist, like Robert Knox, struggling to comprehend the unpopularity of his own views.[19]

II

Those forces allegedly 'racialising' and 'nationalising' English self-consciousness after 1848 – the growth of empire, the surge of national feeling across Europe, the impact of social-evolutionary thought – must be seen against the backdrop of this flexible and adaptive civilisational perspective. What had already adapted once, under the intense pressures of the 1790s (and, more gently, in the 1830s), might well do so again. Beyond this, however, stands the possibility that post-1848 currents might well have had the effect of *reinforcing* the civilisational perspective (as the Christianising of political economy had already done), rather than of undermining it and causing a racial and/or national English consciousness to bloom.[20]

The initial response to the revolutions of 1848 among the intellectual Establishment was one of mixed horror and self-congratulation: horror at foreign foolishness, satisfaction with the comparative stability of domestic institutions. This reaction undoubtedly accentuated the sense of difference that the English felt, their feeling for the near-providential uniqueness of their own institutions, but such a reaction could hardly be

---

[16] Peter R. H. Slee, *Learning and a Liberal Education: The Study of Modern History in the Universities of Oxford, Cambridge and Manchester, 1800–1914* (Manchester, 1986).

[17] See *John Mitchell Kemble and Jakob Grimm, A Correspondence 1832–1852*, ed. Raymond A. Wiley (Leiden, 1971), passim.

[18] Neatly brought out in Miles Taylor, *The Decline of British Radicalism* (Oxford, 1995), 191–3.

[19] Robert Knox, *The Races of Men: A Fragment* (London, 1850), pp. 23–4, 169. This did not stop Knox from imagining also that his racism was gaining ground even in utilitarian England.

[20] For a telling contrast, where the impact of 1848 was decidedly to weaken the purchase that the civilisational perspective had had previously for many intellectuals, see Woodruff D. Smith, *Politics and the Sciences of Culture in Germany, 1840–1920* (New York, 1991).

couched in the very vocabulary of 'race' and 'nation' that was held responsible for continental error. Even those radicals who sympathised with the struggles of the French, German, Italian, and Slav peoples, Mazzini complained, preferred to see them as libertarian rather than national struggles, and his supposed comrades in the People's International League confirmed his suspicion by denouncing revolutions inspired by 'the principle of "nationality"' as lamentable and ludicrous failures, 'whilst those on behalf of liberty, unblended with nationality, have succeeded, have imposed upon the strongest governments'.[21] Conservative commentators, of course, identified not at all with the peoples (whether struggling for liberty or nation) but rather with the tottering multi-national empires – explicitly, with Austria – while moderate liberals might look to a stable multi-national state like Switzerland.[22]

The principal effect of 1848, then, for most of the intellectual and political Establishment was to confirm their sense that nationalism was an atavism from which England had providentially escaped and to reinforce their consciousness of England as the directive centre of a multi-national kingdom and empire, precisely the form that advanced civilisations should take. If that kingdom and empire contained peoples not yet liberated from their uncivilised clannishness – Celts, Negroes, aborigines – it was the responsibility of the English to maintain their institutional hold on such peoples in order gradually to wean them from their childishness. 'The co-existence of several nations under the same State', pronounced the future Lord Acton

is . . . the best security of its freedom. It is also one of the chief instruments of civilisation . . . it is in the natural and providential order, and indicates a state of greater advancement than the national unity which is the ideal of modern liberalism.

Acton was prepared to admit that 'national custom' might have some limited civilising effect in itself – for example, in accustoming people to exercise civil rights – but 'private liberty' had much the greater civilising effect and strong feelings of nationality, such as the French had, were more likely to reverse than advance the civilising process.[23] The future

---

[21] Taylor, *Decline of Radicalism*, pp. 193–5; quote at 195n.

[22] For condemnations of nationalism in defence of Austria, see Travers Twiss's contributions to *Quarterly Review*, 84 (1848–9), pp. 185–222 and 425–61; Acton prefers Switzerland to Austria or Mexico in 'Nationality' [1862], in *The History of Freedom and Other Essays* (London, 1907), pp. 294–5; Sir Henry Maine also speaks up for Austria in *Popular Government* (London, 1885), pp. 27–8.

[23] Acton, 'Nationality', pp. 289–90. Racial feeling, Acton said, was even more atavistic, 'pertaining more to the animal than to the civilised man': pp. 292–3.

Lord Salisbury, writing in *Bentley's Quarterly Review*, saw nationality in much the same way:

the splitting up of mankind into a multitude of infinitesimal governments, in accordance with their actual differences of dialect or their presumed differences of race, would be to undo the work of civilisation and renounce all the benefits which the slow and painful process of consolidation has procured for mankind . . . It is the agglomeration and not the comminution of states to which civilisation is constantly tending; it is the fusion and not the isolation of races by which the physical and moral excellence of the species is advanced.[24]

His senior colleague Disraeli, backpedalling furiously from the romantic-nationalist stances of his youth, also spoke out against 'this modern new-fangled sentimental principle of nationality' that in the post-1848 period was destabilising European empires, including his own.[25]

These were abstract pronouncements, easy enough to make. In practice, imperial responsibilities might elicit harsher and more pessimistic responses in which the image was not so much of a 'superior race' converting others 'into efficient members of a free community' (as Acton had it),[26] but rather the superior race making its superiority felt by discipline, violence, even extermination. It is the appearance of these latter attitudes after the Sepoy Mutiny of 1857 and in the Governor Eyre Controversy of the late 1860s that causes post-colonial historians to hypothesise a more organic, even biological sense of Englishness displacing the older civilisational perspective.[27] But it is not at all clear that that stronger sense of English nationality was a natural, useful or helpful response to such imperial challenges.[28] Biological racists had long held that the English were physiologically unsuited to colonisation and settlement in tropical climes.[29] Mid-Victorian imperialists who used racial arguments to justify English expansion tended to confine themselves to the temperate zones and to avoid, or to exclude flatly, places like the Caribbean, Africa or

---

[24] [Lord Robert Cecil], 'English Politics and Parties', *Bentley's Quarterly Review*, 1 (1859), p. 22, and similar sentiments in 'The Faction-Fights', *ibid.*, pp. 371–2; see the discussion in *Lord Salisbury on Politics: A Selection from his Articles in the Quarterly Review, 1860–1883*, ed. Paul Smith (Cambridge, 1972), pp. 55–6.

[25] Quoted and discussed by Paul Smith, *Disraeli: A Brief Life* (Cambridge, 1996), pp. 190–1.

[26] Acton, 'Nationality', p. 297. Salisbury again shared Acton's view: he saw colonial peoples 'twining round some robuster stem': Smith, ed., *Lord Salisbury*, p. 55.

[27] Hall, *White, Male and Middle-Class*, pp. 208–9, sees the Governor Eyre Controversy as revealing 'a more aggressive biological racism' which 'encoded an Englishness which celebrated hierarchy and difference'.

[28] By far the best discussion of this question is in Paul B. Rich, *Race and Empire in British Politics*, 2nd edn (Cambridge, 1990), but cf. the almost opposite views given on pp. 13–15 and 16–17. Horsman, *Race*, is confused; his chief source for the prevalence of racial thinking in the 1840s is an (unattributed) article of Mill's, for which see below.

[29] Knox, *Races of Men*, pp. 107–8, 116, 142, 220–4, 268.

India that (so the post-colonial argument suggests) were supposed to be stimulating racial thought.[30] It was also perfectly possible – in fact, quite common – to argue that Negroes were racially distinct without conceding the same distinctions between white stocks, thus separating entirely the race and the nationality questions. It was also possible – again, common – to argue that Negroes or Indians were simply so primitive that they required paternal repression now to make future doses of civilisation possible. Nationality was, after all, an atavism – one which the English had grown out of, other Europeans *should* have grown out of, but which was necessary and even helpful for atavistic peoples. This was Salisbury's view, and that of many pro-Eyre intellectuals at the time of the controversy, who backed a race-conscious approach to the colonies but explicitly repudiated such an understanding of the English.[31]

For even if European and imperial entanglements *had* caused the English to think more racially and nationally in those arenas – whereas, as we have argued, the effects were mixed and as much negative as positive – there remained formidable domestic barriers to thinking this way about the English at home. The civilisational perspective had had the signal virtue of explaining and justifying class distinctions and the persistence of exclusive political institutions. Thinking about the English as a nation instead threatened to collapse these distinctions, and while that might have been attractive to democrats, for the non-democratic majority of the English political and intellectual elite it was a fatal flaw. (Post-colonial analysis tends to emphasise the value of racial thinking for rallying the classes behind the English imperial mission – but this again draws attention to the conceptual gulf between imperial and domestic thought, for rallying the classes was as vital overseas as separating them was at home.)

For English observers unwilling to embrace a full democracy, it was almost impossible to imagine what an organic English nation could be. They were perfectly aware that what was making it possible for their continental contemporaries to accept the nation was the persistence and deference of a peasantry, just the peasantry that England lacked (and that could legitimately be seen as an atavism very gradually on its way out). Peasants not only made nations safe for conservatives, they also provided the stuffing for romantic-nationalist idealisations of the *Volk*: customs, folktales, songs, traditions – in a word, roots. Without these things, it was almost impossible to write a proper *Volksgeschichte* – as Thierry and Michelet did for the French or the Grimm brothers and W. H. Riehl did

---

[30] Sir Charles Wentworth Dilke, *Greater Britain: A Record of Travel in English-Speaking Countries* (1868; 8th edn, London, 1885), pp. 457, 535–47; the same argument is put in J. R. Seeley, *The Expansion of England* (London, 1883), pp. 184–5, 220–8, 240–5, though on a much less racial basis.   [31] Stocking, *Victorian Anthropology*, pp. 234–6.

for the Germans. As J. M. Kemble complained to Jakob Grimm, his projected *Volksgeschichte* of the English would have to be 'more confined,
more strictly bounded, and its contents far less attractive' than Grimm's
Deutsche Rechtsalterthumer, as he lacked documentary material about
popular custom, and had to fall back on legal and administrative records:
the hero of his story was the king, not the freeman.[32]

All of these constraints – the pre-existing strengths of the civilisational
perspective, the warning signals launched by continental nationalism, the
multi-national nature of the United Kingdom and the British Empire,
and above all the difficulty of conceptualising a non-democratic English
nation – seem to me to explain what John Burrow has so amply docu-
mented, the way in which 'the Whig line was held' against romantic
nationalism in mid-Victorian England, 'if only just'.[33] The development
of social-evolutionary thinking in England – the major development in
the historical and political thought of mid-century – was put in the service
of the civilisational perspective, rather than (as with *Darwinismus* in
Germany) deployed to rationalise the nation. The ladder of civilisation,
rather than the branching tree of peoples and nations, remained the dominant metaphor.[34]

How did the civilisational perspective evolve in mid-Victorian conditions? As Burrow and George Stocking have shown us, the Darwinian
lengthening of the timescale and the greater empirical sophistication
about 'primitive' peoples both in the past and in the present gave mid-
Victorian writers far more material for chronological and geographical
comparisons than had been available to the early Victorians, yielding the
'comparative method' so wildly fashionable in England in the 1860s and
1870s. This method was used, for instance by E. B. Tylor and Sir Henry
Maine, not to relativise the idea of civilisation but to demonstrate further
how arduous its attainment was and thus possibly to explain why
England's progress was so lonely. Racial and national consciousness were
now better recognised, but put firmly in the 'primitive' stage of human
development, back towards which it was all too easy to slip. Progress
towards civilisation was possible, but not inevitable, and easily imperiled,
as recent events in Europe showed. England's progress was more
advanced, yet still dependent not on any intrinsic racial or national qualities, but on its precarious institutions that made possible liberty and
prosperity.[35] The Englishman, too, Maine pointed out in *Popular*

---

[32] *Kemble and Grimm, Correspondence*, p. 254.
[33] *Liberal Descent*, p. 241. Burrow is noting here the 'curious fact' that there was no
Carlylean national history.   [34] Burrow, *Evolution and Society*, p. 98.
[35] See esp. the discussion in Stocking, *Victorian Anthropology*, ch. 5; and also Hilton, *Age of
Atonement*, ch. 8, on some optimistic implications of evolutionary thought.

Government (1885), retained atavistic characteristics – appetites for war, hunting, dancing, rhetoric, and party feeling – that made him seem not so distant from the savage, but 'with a newspaper for a totem, instead of a mark on his forehead or arm'. These impulses were held in check, not by the ingrained virtues of a sturdy nation, but by a 'minority of exceptional persons . . . All that has made England famous, and all that has made England wealthy, has been the work of minorities, sometimes very small ones.'[36]

The social-evolutionary adaptation of the civilisational perspective can be found even in one of those works of mid-Victorian political thought that appear most affected by racial and national thinking, Walter Bagehot's *Physics and Politics* (1872). Its title (and for that matter its opening pages) have misled commentators into taking it as clear evidence of the biologising effect of Darwinian thought. Despite Bagehot's evident desire to jump on this particular bandwagon, with his voguish references early on to the 'transmitting nerve element' that finally explains '"the connective tissue" of civilisation', he finds it difficult to deliver on these promises in his exposition.[37] First, he separates off 'the race-making force which, whatever it was, acted in antiquity, and has now wholly, or almost, given over acting'; this accounts for unbridgeable differences between blacks and whites, but not for any finer distinctions among whites, nor even between the English and the Indians, both apparently Aryans.[38] Then he considers 'the nation-making force', which may still be operative, but which produces only 'less marked contrasts . . . the eddies in each race stream', as much a matter of moral and intellectual as of physical variation. Deprived of an essential character, nations can and do change, can and do progress. How this might work puzzles Bagehot: 'The way in which nations change, generation after generation, is exceedingly curious, and the change occasionally happens when it is very hard to account for.' He cannot believe that change works on a nation *en masse*, so 'we are puzzled – at least, I have been puzzled – to conceive how it acts'. He concludes that it must act first on 'some prepared and congenial individuals; in them it is seen to produce attractive results, and then the habits creating those results are copied far and wide'.[39] In the then-current state of biological theory, it was possible to imagine that these characteristics, acquired by imitation, might be heritable, but as Bagehot actually explains it, use-inheritance is unnecessary; he is simply describing the progress of civilisation as one finds it in Maine (a frequent referent for

---

[36] Maine, *Popular Government*, pp. 143–4, 97–8.
[37] Walter Bagehot, *Physics and Politics*, in *The Collected Works of Walter Bagehot*, ed. Norman St John Stevas, 15 vols. (London, 1965–86), VII, pp. 18, 21.
[38] *Ibid.*, pp. 65–7, 78, 120–1.   [39] *Ibid.*, pp. 79–80.

Bagehot), where it lacks any organic element.[40] In Bagehot as in Maine the civilised man is not so far from the savage; his barbaric qualities lie beneath the fragile crust of culture, making possible an unexpected 'atavism' (his word) such as the French Revolution, 'the outbreak of inherited passions long repressed by fixed custom'.[41] Among some nations, progress has proceeded so far as to make possible 'general intellectual freedom' without great risk of degeneration; here Bagehot again considers a racial basis and explicitly rejects it: 'There must be something else besides Aryan descent which is necessary to fit men for discussion and train them for liberty . . . I am not prepared with any simple counter theory . . . what that something is I do not know that any one can in the least explain.'[42] Once it is attained, this higher level of civilisation seems to bring out something in human nature that permits stabilisation: a contemplative spirit, a shift of energies from procreation to intellectual creativity. Civilisation is not so easy or so widespread as the eighteenth century had imagined. But even in Bagehot it still seems widely accessible to a surprising range of peoples, equipped with innate human capacities though mired down in lower stages that only quirkily yield to higher ones.[43]

Cleaving to the civilisational perspective and abjuring nationalism did not mean giving up on patriotism.[44] To the contrary, the lack of an organic vision of the nation gave a stronger motive to glorify those institutions that had put England at the top of the civilisational ladder. Without the integrating force of nationalism, a liberal society's acceptance of exclusive political institutions could only be secured by pious deference to those institutions: in essence, Burke's realisation of the 1790s, now ripe for further development. Bagehot showed his own awareness of this not only in *Physics and Politics*, where the tendency of the mass to imitate their social superiors is the motor of improvement, but also in his best-known work, where deference to established institutions is what makes *The English Constitution* (1867) work. The incredible success of Macaulay's *History of England* in the mid-Victorian decades, binding together elite and popular audiences, undoubtedly stemmed from its blend of the civilisational perspective with a near-romantic story about the heroic role of institutions and statesmen: in Burrow's terms, its mix of 'scientific' and 'vulgar' discourses. Macaulay makes a few Burkean references to the

---

[40] *Ibid.*, p. 100.   [41] *Ibid.*, pp. 104–5.   [42] *Ibid.*, pp. 120–1.   [43] *Ibid.*, pp. 134–44.

[44] There is thus a strong case for retaining the distinction between patriotism and nationalism; cf. Margot C. Finn, *After Chartism: Class and Nation in English Radical Politics, 1848–1874* (Cambridge, 1993), pp. 11, 17–18, and Rohan McWilliam, *Popular Politics in Nineteenth-Century England* (London, 1998), p. 82, which collapse the distinction, contrary (as both grant) to contemporary usage.

'essentially English' quality of English liberty, 'which accords with the peculiarities of our manners and of our insular situation', but like Burke he puts no flesh on these bones, refusing to specify further what the peculiarities of an English people might be, showing no interest in racial or even pre-modern roots, and in general making the institutions – not the people – the hero of the English story.[45]

On the other side of the political divide, Disraeli, despite a few flirtatious references to his own racialist youth, also pinned his rhetoric on individual liberty maintained by deference to institutions. In the famous Manchester and Crystal Palace speeches of 1872, supposedly the starter's pistol for late Victorian nationalism, he stuck carefully to the established Tory line, arguing that whatever the English people *did* have in common was liberty secured by exclusive political institutions. 'It may be said that [England's] achievements are due to the race that inhabited the land, and not to its institutions', he suggested teasingly. 'Gentlemen, in political institutions are the embodied experiences of a race.' These embodied experiences were the 'principles of liberty, of order, of law, and of religion' which 'ought not to be entrusted to individual opinion or to the caprice and passion of multitudes, but should be embodied in a form of permanence and power'. When Disraeli exhorted England to stand behind its 'national' rather than 'cosmopolitan' principles, he meant the task of spreading civilisation (particularly to the Empire) by means of such institutions, a choice which other European peoples had either never had or had abjured.[46] For the mainstream of English politicians and intellectuals, then, falling between Macaulayan whiggism and Disraelian conservatism, patriotism was the acceptable alternative to the dangerously anti-imperial and democratic organicism of 'race' and 'nation'.

III

Not all English political thought falls safely between Macaulay and Disraeli, however. An organic nationalism came most easily to those figures sufficiently alienated from the English mainstream either to break from the civilisational perspective or not to be bothered by the anti-imperial and democratic implications of nationalism. In the former camp lie those who, even without the ballast of a conservative peasantry, struggled to envision a non-democratic English nation. Thomas Carlyle, strongly motivated by disgust with English libertarianism and utilitarianism, came close with his metaphysical belief in an abstracted moral force that could

---

[45] Burrow, *Liberal Descent*, pp. 47–60, 67, 69–70.
[46] *Selected Speeches of the late Earl of Beaconsfield*, ed. T.E. Kebbel, 2 vols. (London, 1882), II, pp. 506, 525, 528–9, 534.

be embodied in a great national hero like Oliver Cromwell. But Carlyle's desperation was so great that he could not really believe in a moral force binding together the whole nation for long – as Mazzini pointed out regretfully:

Nation itself . . . vanishes, or is modified under his hand . . . it is no longer the symbol of a thought, of a special vocation to be followed, indicated by the tradition of the race, by the affinity of tendencies, by the unity of language, by the character of localities; it is something reduced, as much as possible, to the proportions of the *individual*. The nationality of Italy is the glory of having produced Dante and Christopher Columbus; the nationality of Germany that of having given birth to Luther, to Goethe and to others.[47]

Liberal Carlyleans like J. A. Froude and Charles Kingsley, whose fury at their fellow-countrymen was better concealed, were better placed to posit a single spiritual force binding all the English together, though Froude's emphasis on English 'worthies' was still limiting.[48] Kingsley's eccentric, under-studied dissertation on *The Roman and the Teuton* (1862) comes closest of all. It has a quasi-racial base in fashionable Teutonism, a belief in the spiritual continuity of English history, and – what distinguishes it crucially from democratic Teutonism – a theory about the innate taste for hierarchy of the English people, enough to make Kingsley's nationalism safely inegalitarian.[49] Some few followed Kingsley along this twisted path. But the second course – accepting the anti-imperial and democratic implications of nationalism – attracted a more substantial following, and it is among advanced liberals that one finds the strongest form of English nationalism in mid-Victorian thought.

Those democratic implications of 'Germano–Coleridgean' thought, applied to urban England, that appalled English conservatives had a commensurate appeal to advanced liberals. Thinking about the English as a people, or as a nation, was part of John Stuart Mill's 'revolt of the nineteenth century against the eighteenth' – the revolt against an excessively uniform and material understanding of human motive – as well as a democratic impulse. As Mill's was an English-liberal revolt, however, he wished to replace the notion of a self-interested human nature *not* with a variety of human natures, but rather with none at all.[50] His idea of the nation was not a fixed, biological one but rather a product of historical

---

[47] Giuseppe Mazzini, 'The Works of Thomas Carlyle', *British and Foreign Review*, 16 (1844), pp. 274–5. The *British and Foreign Review* was at that time edited by J. M. Kemble.

[48] See the excellent discussion of Froude in Burrow, *Liberal Descent*, esp. pp. 236–42, 251–6.

[49] Charles Kingsley, *The Roman and the Teuton* (Cambridge and London, 1864), esp. pp. 54–5; also 'The Ancien Regime' [1867], in *Historical Lectures and Essays* (London, 1880), esp. pp. 137–8.

[50] J. S. Mill to Charles Dupont-White, 6 April 1860, in *Collected Works of John Stuart Mill*, 33 vols. (Toronto, 1963–91), XV, p. 691.

change, of customs, laws, and physical environment moulding nations into different, plastic forms.[51] Unlike Bagehot, his democratic instincts meant that he had no trouble imagining this process acting on whole peoples at once, and in his immensely influential *System of Logic* (1843) he called the study of 'national (or collective) character' among the most neglected and yet 'by far the most important class of sociological laws'. Mill's was at least in theory a more genuinely popular understanding of the nation than anything whig or conservative thinkers would admit to. A nation's character, he wrote, could be detected

> not so much in the acts of its government . . . but in the current popular maxims, and other marks of the general direction of public opinion; in the character of the persons or writings that are held in permanent esteem or admiration; in laws and institutions, so far as they are the work of the nation itself, or are acknowledged and supported by it; and so forth.[52]

Mill never developed his theory of national character, or applied it specifically to the English. That task was taken up by his acolyte, H. T. Buckle, in the single most developed mid-Victorian work on the English nation, the *History of Civilization in England* (1857–61). The very title indicates Buckle's Millian aspiration to integrate the idea of the nation into the civilisational perspective. Buckle's advanced-liberal version of civilisation defined it as a matter of intellectual rather than moral progress, the extent to which reason or knowledge was freely available.[53] Governments and institutions have some limited effect in hindering or assisting this progress, but most important is the character of the people, as shaped by environment, education, and self-government. The English people have been uniquely suited to civilisation by their insular position in a cool climate, their early access to law and local government, and their series of victories against paternalism won since Elizabeth's day, producing 'that tone of independence, and that lofty bearing, of which our civil and political institutions are the consequence, rather than the cause'.[54] Following Mill, Buckle insisted that race played no role at all in the civilising process, and climate only in its earliest stages, so that, once the process had been started by climatically favoured Europeans, 'the

---

[51] See, for example, his much-quoted attack on 'attributing the diversities of conduct and character to inherent national differences' in the *Principles of Political Economy*, already present in the first edition of 1848: Mill, *Collected Works*, II, p. 319. Even his review of Michelet in 1844, when Mill was still trying to keep an open mind on race (only to be cited by Horsman, *Race*, as evidence of racialism's prevalence in popular discourse in the 1840s), concludes that Michelet 'carried the influence of Race too far'; and thereafter Mill was unequivocal: *ibid.*, XX, pp. 236–7.   [52] *Ibid.*, VII–VIII, pp. 867, 905.

[53] Henry Thomas Buckle, *History of Civilization in England* (1857–61), ed. John M. Robertson (London, 1904), p. 128.   [54] *Ibid.*, pp. 133, 154–9, 352.

heirlooms of mankind' could be transmitted culturally to the less favoured tropical peoples.[55]

Buckle's democratic version of the civilisational perspective was very popular, especially in artisan culture, but its one-dimensional emphasis on intellectual attributes did not satisfy those advanced liberals seeking a meatier appreciation of the English nation – not even Mill.[56] A younger generation, especially, impressed by the achievements of continental nationalities after 1848 and particularly around 1867 seeking a more rhetorically persuasive account of the English nation's political integrity, looked for stronger stuff – and for many in the 1860s and 1870s this took the form of democratic Teutonism. There had been a long plebeian-radical tradition of extolling the Anglo-Saxons' ancient love of liberty and bemoaning its subjection to the Norman yoke; that tradition was, however, fading by the early nineteenth century.[57] What revived it subsequently in different hands was the combination of German-inspired scholarship in Anglo-Saxon language and laws with the democratic impulses of a new generation of advanced-liberal intellectuals.[58] The foundation was laid by J. M. Kemble, whose *Saxons in England* (1849) argued that England's mid-century stability was dependent not upon deference to institutions but upon 'our customs [of] right and justice'.[59] These customs appear in their earliest and purest form among the Teutons, but, as in Buckle, they are accessible to everyone – 'in every age man has had a common nature, a common hope and a common end of being' – and appear to anticipate miraculously laws of political economy that have only recently been discovered and are stealthily making themselves felt across the globe.[60]

---

[55] *Ibid.*, pp. 22, 87, 89, 100–4. Buckle is often falsely labelled a 'geographical determinist' by those who fix on the first rather than on the subsequent stages of his civilisational process: e.g. Greta Jones, *Social Darwinism and English Thought: The Interaction between Biological and Social Theory* (Brighton, 1980), p. 27; but also Stocking, *Victorian Anthropology*, pp. 112–17.

[56] Buckle is still poorly understood; a good, brief introduction to his thought can be found in Bernard Semmel, 'H. T. Buckle: The Liberal Faith and the Science of History', *British Journal of Sociology*, 27 (1976), pp. 370–86. For Mill's verdict, see *Collected Works*, XV, pp. 844–5.

[57] R. J. Smith, *The Gothic Bequest: Medieval Institutions in British Thought, 1688–1863* (Cambridge, 1987).

[58] One can find traces of Teutonism, too, in the purer civilisational perspective: in Guizot, for example, but also in Mill. See Mill's review of 'Guizot's Essays and Lectures on History' [1845], *Collected Works*, XX, pp. 274, 291–2.

[59] John Mitchell Kemble, *The Saxons in England*, 2 vols. (London, 1849), I, pp. v–vi.

[60] *Ibid.*, I, pp. 234, 445, II, pp. 265, 283–4, 341; and n.b. the fascinating final chapter on the place of the poor in commercial societies. However, Kemble could be witheringly racialist in 1848–9 when he saw Slavs and Celts defying what he took to be universal laws of political economy: see *Kemble and Grimm, Correspondence*, pp. 276, 278–9.

Among those young mid-Victorian followers of Mill known as the 'University Liberals', democratic Teutonism was then taken up as an argument for the enfranchisement of a nation that had long been suited to self-government.[61] It reached its highest form in the work of E. A. Freeman. Freeman has been called a 'liberal racist'; it is true that in private he made liberal use of racist epithets, and that in public his writing, more than the other University Liberals, dwelt forcefully upon the specifically Teutonic legacy of the modern English nation. But even Freeman, supposedly at 'the extreme limits of racism', had not cut himself off totally from the civilisational perspective.[62] As a follower of the comparative method, Freeman had to believe that 'Man is in truth ever the same . . . in times and places most remote from one another like events follow upon like causes'.[63] Beyond this, Freeman's profound belief in the Teutonic virtues fuelled his contempt for others' vices *and* his zeal to convert them: as we have noted in his predecessors, the power of his ethnocentrism reined in the temptation of an exclusive racialism. 'Race', Freeman asserted, had no real, physical existence, and was certainly not a basis for national feeling in England.

There is now no practical distinction between the Englishman whose forefathers landed with William, or even between the Englishman whose forefathers sought shelter from Alva or from Lewis the Fourteenth, and the Englishman whose forefathers landed with Hengest. It is for the physiologist to say whether any difference can be traced in their several skulls; for all practical purposes, historical or political, all distinction between these several classes has passed away.[64]

Like other University Liberals, Freeman believed that Teutonic virtue was accessible to all those who found themselves on English shores, including Celts and Jews.[65] What was unusual was his superheated *insis-*

---

[61] Christopher Harvie, *The Lights of Liberalism: University Liberals and the Challenge of Democracy, 1860–86* (London, 1976).

[62] C. J. W. Parker, 'The Failure of Liberal Racialism: The Racial Ideas of E. A. Freeman', *Historical Journal*, 24 (1981), pp. 825–46; MacDougall, *Racial Myth*, pp. 100–1. Freeman's racial consciousness did seem to intensify late in his life, particularly after his involvement in the Bulgarian agitation of 1878 and his visit to America in 1881, but more in private than in public.

[63] E. A. Freeman, *Comparative Politics* (London, 1873), p. 333.

[64] E. A. Freeman, 'Race and Language' [1877], in Michael D. Biddiss, ed., *Images of Race* (Leicester, 1979), p. 222.

[65] On the Jews, David Feldman, *Englishmen and Jews: Social Relations and Political Culture* (New Haven and London, 1994), pp. 73–6; on the Celts, R. F. Foster, *Paddy and Mr Punch: Connections in Irish and English History* (London, 1993), pp. 193, 287–8; on the cross-currents of Celticism and Saxonism which tended to thwart nationalism in Scotland, Colin Kidd, 'Sentiment, Race and Revival: Scottish Identities in the Aftermath of Enlightenment', in Brockliss and Eastwood, eds., *Union of Multiple Identities*, pp. 110–25.

tence on assimilation, on the homogenisation of all stocks into one cohesive English nation. Democracy would only work, he felt, if the whole of the people adhered strictly to those Teutonic standards of right and justice that had been laid down by the ancestors. Because race did not provide an automatic line to national cohesion, national sentiment, 'an artificial doctrine', had to be constructed, tended carefully, and if necessary enforced. Only this way could a nation learn 'liberty'.[66] Freeman was not alone in arguing for the desirability of greater national homogeneity. Famously, Matthew Arnold also called for the suppression of ethnic diversity, though he favoured the adoption of some Celtic characteristics in the mix. As a school inspector with responsibility for Wales, Arnold had more power than most to impose his nationalising vision (which involved suppressing the Welsh language, while incorporating bits of Welshness).[67] At the same time, Arnold felt himself unusual in promoting such a vision and complained bitterly about the inordinate individualism of the English, which left them drifting towards anarchy. 'We have not the notion, so familiar on the Continent and to antiquity, of *the State* – the nation in its collective and corporate character', he wrote in his most celebrated polemic, published in 1869.[68]

By the same token, most of Freeman's advanced-liberal friends found his Teutonism both too zealous and too narrow. There were other, non-compulsory ways of envisioning a democratic English nation that did not require a semi-mystical resort to primitive traits and which recognised a greater diversity of national characteristics. J. R. Green regretted Freeman's very partial view of the English people ('too much of wars and witenagemots, and too little of the life, the tendencies, the sentiments of the people'), and in writing his own *Short History of the English People* (1874) – the nearest approximation to a *Volksgeschichte* the mid-Victorians could manage – he tried to put the political history into a thicker social and religious context.[69] As Kemble had predicted, a rounded picture of the English people could only be obtained by moving beyond philology and ancient charters and stressing more recent developments: in Green's case, a *mélange* of transport and commerce, the spread of vernacular literature, guilds and associations, patriotic leadership and above all

---

[66] Freeman, 'Race and Language', pp. 211, 224, 226–9. See also the sequel to this essay, 'The Southern Slaves' [1877], in Freeman's *Historical Essays*, 3rd ser. (London, 1879), esp. pp. 380–1, and the nuanced discussion in Burrow, *Liberal Descent*, pp. 156–200.

[67] Nicholas Murray, *A Life of Matthew Arnold* (London, 1996), pp. 230–1.

[68] Matthew Arnold, *Culture and Anarchy* (1st edn, 1869; New York, 1983), p. 35.

[69] John Richard Green, *Historical Studies* (London, 1903), pp. 67, 105–6, 108; Asa Briggs, *Saxons, Normans and Victorians* (Hastings and Bexhill, 1966), p. 19. It is significant that Green offered the liberal Carlylean Froude as an exemplar of his preferred social history.

Puritanism. Green's promiscuity was unusual;[70] his demurral from ultra-Teutonism was not.

By the end of our period, the brief liberal fashion for Teutonism had already passed. Other uses for the idea of an English nation proved more pressing than the claims of 'ancient liberty'. Nonconformists followed up Green's hints on Puritanism to put 'high spiritual and moral aims' at the centre of the national identity, inspiring but also transcending mere constitutional arrangements.[71] J. R. Seeley shifted attention, as Burrow says, 'away from Parliament and the constitution towards the nation-state in its external relations'.[72] Seeley shared the advanced-liberal notion of the nation as a crucial vehicle of civilisation, based not on race but on common values and experiences, and more than most liberals saw the potential of the nation-state as the protector of those values.[73] Comparatively unmoved by ancient liberty (which he considered a common European legacy), Seeley saw the Elizabethan age as the crucible of the English people, unleashing the two great tendencies towards democracy ('how liberty might be adapted to the conditions of a nation-state') and overseas expansion.[74] The latter tendency, so far from being rooted deeply in the body or soul of the English people, was made almost an accident in his best-selling *Expansion of England* (1883).

> It is not the blood of the Vikings that makes us rulers of the sea, nor the industrial genius of the Anglo-Saxons that makes us great in manufactures and commerce, but a much more special circumstance, which did not arise till for many centuries we had been agricultural or pastoral, warlike and indifferent to the sea.

The 'special circumstance' was England's fortunate geographical position on the side of Europe pointing to the New World.[75] This comparative indifference to deep-seated national characteristics, or to a rounded picture of the people, puts Seeley rather closer to Buckle than to Freeman or Green, and reminds us that – even among liberals – the drift of thinking about 'nationality' was not always in a romantic, organic direction.[76]

What glued all of these liberals together was their willingness (even eagerness) to conceive, in various ways, of an English nation or people

[70] For instance, in the number of distinct junctures and stimuli he identifies as *the* essential taproot of the English people: J. R. Green, *A Short History of the English People* (London, 1874), pp. 7, 49, 60, 163–4, 449, 542, 587.

[71] Timothy Lang, *The Victorians and the Stuart Heritage* (Cambridge, 1995), p. 211.

[72] Burrow, *Liberal Descent*, p. 296.

[73] J. R. Seeley, *Introduction to Political Science: Two Series of Lectures* (London, 1896), pp. 15–17, 35–6, 69. See also Deborah Wormell, *Sir John Seeley and the Uses of History* (Cambridge, 1980), pp. 14, 36–9, 75–80, 146–7, and Collini, Winch, and Burrow, *That Noble Science*, pp. 227–30.   [74] Seeley, *Expansion of England*, pp. 7–8, 50, 80, 307–8.

[75] *Ibid.*, pp. 87–97 (quote at 87).

[76] Wormell, *Seeley*, pp. 98–103, 123–7. Cf. MacDougall, *Racial Myth*, which lumps together Seeley, Freeman, Kingsley, Froude, and Dilke.

carrying common characteristics – a predilection for liberty and free-thought, a capacity for self-government, Protestant piety, enterprise, expansion. This willingness at least to contemplate a democracy allowed them to develop the idea of 'nation' beyond the fairly weak, institutional form acceptable to whiggish and conservative thinkers. Some took a quasi-racial Teutonist position, tracing predispositions back to the earliest of times; others saw the nation as a product of gradual historical and cultural change, as geography, commerce, the turn of events, the deeds of great men worked on a plastic people. These nation-building forces helped liberals to explain why the English had achieved the heights of civilisation so far in advance of the rest of the world. But few saw those achievements as essentially and eternally distinctive to the English. In this way, most advanced liberals continued to share with conservatives and whigs a fundamental belief in 'civilisation' as a universal human potential.

Famously, the liberals fell out with each other in 1886 over the issue of Irish Home Rule. No simple intellectual principle can explain this division. The civilisational perspective could be (and was) used to justify both Union – necessary to civilise the Irish – and Home Rule – a political recognition that the Irish were in an earlier phase of civilisation. Liberals' strong sense of nationality could be (and was) used to argue both for Union – for the Irish assimilation into the English nation – and for Home Rule – a recognition that the backward, oppressed Irish needed stronger national institutions than the English.[77] The short-term impact of the split – which of course worked to the benefit of Unionism – was to discredit attempts to reconcile nationality and the civilisational perspective. However much racialist and nationalist language was bandied about at the peak of the crisis, in England the upshot was to devalue intellectual attempts to specify national difference (leaving the civilisational perspective with, as Salisbury had seen it, the Irish entwined around the civilising stem of the English); while in Ireland, as Roy Foster has noted, the upshot was to strengthen intellectual nationalism at the expense of the civilisational outlook.[78]

Ireland was not of course the only or even the decisive factor influencing thought about 'race' and 'nation' after 1886: new forms of 'collectivism' (other than democracy) were then being devised that might form the basis for new thinking about nationality; arguments about empire and the relations between white and black peoples also moved

[77] These paradoxes are nicely captured in C. J. Dewey, 'Celtic Agrarian Legislation and the Celtic Revival: Historicist Implications of Gladstone's Irish and Scottish Land Acts 1870–1886', *Past and Present* 64 (August 1974), pp. 56–60, 62; Foster, *Paddy and Mr Punch*, pp. 8–11; Harvie, *Lights of Liberalism*, pp. 218–32.
[78] Foster, *Paddy and Mr Punch*, pp. 8–14.

into a different register; concerns about degeneration put the civilisational perspective as a whole into question. But the debate over Ireland does suggest again that such imperial crises did not have a remorselessly racialising or nationalising effect on English thought. Long after 1886, the civilisational perspective – with its carefully maintained hierarchies based on social and moral rather than racial criteria – retained its prestige, especially among politically dominant conservatives.[79] Excepting a few tentative departures from classical political economy, there were no significant moves before the First World War towards an organic nationalism among conservatives, as Ewen Green has recently shown.[80] When a conservative nationalism finally did emerge, it would in fact borrow many of its ideas from the mid-Victorian liberal nationalists we have been examining, who would thus find their legacy carried on in unexpected ways.[81] Only at that point would the idea of 'nation' – and still a comparatively weak, non-racial, non-organic idea of nation – play a central role in English thought.[82]

---

[79] Reba N. Soffer, *Ethics and Society in England: The Revolution in the Social Sciences, 1870–1914* (Berkeley, 1978).

[80] E. H. H. Green, *The Crisis of Conservatism: The Politics, Economics and Ideology of the British Conservative Party, 1880–1914* (London, 1995), esp. ch. 5.

[81] I make a tentative argument along these lines in 'The Consciousness of Modernity? Liberalism and the English "National Character", 1870–1940', in M. Daunton and B. Rieger, eds., *The Consciousness of Modernity* (forthcoming). Julia Stapleton also suggests that J. F. Stephen's Burkean-liberal thinking on nationality gave a spur to conservative nationalism in the early twentieth century, though I would argue that in his own time Stephen's thinking was idiosyncratic and difficult for either liberals or conservatives to follow. See 'James Fitzjames Stephen: Liberalism, Patriotism, and English Liberty', *Victorian Studies*, 41 (1997–8), pp. 243–63.

[82] See, further, Julia Stapleton's essay in this volume.

11 Political thought and national identity in Britain, 1850–1950

Julia Stapleton

I

Historians continue to find rich pickings in British political thought in the decades enclosing the turn of the nineteenth century. As a result, the forces which invigorated it and the characteristics it assumed have become increasingly clear.[1] A key factor was the growth of government intervention in spheres of society that had been ordered on a largely spontaneous basis hitherto. This provoked much dispute on the merits of such action.[2] Correspondingly, interest in the concept of the state itself was greatly enhanced, particularly the moral purposes of which it was thought to be the highest expression.[3] Political speculation was intensified further by successive extensions of the franchise. These concentrated the minds of political thinkers on the rights and duties associated with citizenship, the social conditions with which its 'spiritual' foundations would best accord, and the role of the state and other organisations in its institutional expression.

However, an additional (although relatively neglected) impetus to political thought derived from the resurgent English/British national consciousness of the mid-nineteenth century onwards.[4] As well as underlying

I would like to thank the following for their very valuable comments on this chapter at various stages in its composition: Stefan Collini, Peter Mandler, Peter Stirk, and William Thomas. Also, I gratefully acknowledge the assistance of ESRC funding.

[1] A recent example is J. Harris, 'Political Thought and the State', in S. J. D. Green and R. C. Whiting, eds., *The Boundaries of the State in Modern Britain* (Cambridge, 1996).

[2] W. H. Greenleaf, *The British Political Tradition*, II: *The Ideological Heritage* (London, 1983), p. 540.

[3] J. Meadowcroft, *Conceptualizing the State: Innovation and Dispute in British Political Thought 1880–1914* (Oxford, 1995), pp. 13–14.

[4] It is important to stress the resurgent rather than nascent character of English national consciousness in this period. See Adrian Hastings, *The Construction of Nationhood: Ethnicity, Religion and Nationalism* (Cambridge, 1997). The following account adheres to the synonymous use of England/Britain that prevailed throughout the nineteenth and much of the twentieth century as well. As J. H. Grainger has remarked, 'The consciousness of Britain was predominantly English.' J. H. Grainger, *Patriotisms: Britain 1900–1940* (London, 1986), p. 53. This is not to deny an enhanced sense of difference within the component nationalities of the 'British' nation, classic evidence of which is A. G. MacDonnell's *England their England* (London, 1933). But, Ireland excepted, the mainstream English culture of Great Britain went largely unchallenged.

the establishment of such key cultural institutions as the National Portrait Gallery (1856), the Oxford English Dictionary (1879), the Dictionary of National Biography (1882), and the Royal College of Music (1883), English nationalism inspired a host of major and minor works across a broad spectrum of political belief. This stimulus is apparent in a variety of ways: in assumptions – sometimes unreflective, sometimes highly self-conscious – about the actual or ideal character of the English people, and the distinctive ways in which their polity had evolved relative to other nations; in concern over the contemporary weakness of traditional English strengths; and in analyses of the changes and resistances to change deemed necessary to preserve English identity in circumstances of increasing international and internal tension. Such questions inevitably stirred great controversy. But the widely divergent assessments of, and aspirations for the English *patria* which were expressed in political thought between 1850 and 1950 conceal a more fundamental and overarching national attachment which – on a similar scale – has been conspicuously absent since. Moreover, while it may be true that political thinkers in Britain were preoccupied with issues that were discussed in other countries too – state intervention, group rights, the imperial state, and so forth – their responses were crucially and consciously shaped by distinctive local influences and national self-conceptions.[5] This chapter emphasises the nuances of British political thought in the light of these attitudes and loyalties.

II

It has been argued that British patriotism, rooted in a love of liberty and justice that transcended a narrow, nationalist agenda, lost much of its early nineteenth-century momentum from the 1840s onwards. No longer the preserve of radicalism, patriotism became the 'nationalised' property of the right. First in Palmerston, then in Disraeli, an atavistic notion of 'England' was invoked in order to shift the language of patriotism towards a Conservative defence of Empire. Suitably deterred, progressives ceased to be motivated by an ideal of 'country' and focused their hopes instead upon cosmopolitanism or working-class solidarity at an international level.[6]

It is certainly true that the fortunes of 'England' in British political

---

[5] The local context of English political thought is, it seems to me, underplayed by Rodney Barker in his *Political Ideas in Modern Britain: In and After the Twentieth Century* (London, 1997), p. 8.

[6] M. Viroli, *For Love of Country: An Essay on Patriotism and Nationalism* (Oxford, 1995), pp. 142–4, 156–7.

thought rose substantially after the middle of the century. But patriotism, in this 'nationalist' form, was neither the exclusive preserve of the right, nor always indifferent or hostile to the welfare of other nations, as will become clear below. In this volume, Peter Mandler emphasises the dominance of the 'civilisation' perspective in English social thought during the mid-Victorian period, and its legacy undoubtedly acted as an inhibiting influence in this respect. Nevertheless, the expression of patriotism was self-consciously and powerfully 'English', for all its focus on institutions and practical achievements, and its understatement relative to nations on the continent. Indeed, these traits became as emblematic of English identity as that of race on the European continent, and were no less suggestive of an homogenous people.[7] Above all, the growth of English national consciousness after 1850 took place in reaction to the perceived *absence* of patriotism of any description among the forces of British radicalism.

This perception was not entirely groundless. The English/British *patria* appeared in much radical discourse on citizenship only as an object of abuse. Such leading lights of radical liberalism as Richard Cobden and John Bright conducted a crusade on behalf of individual liberty in which all aspects of the evolved nation, certainly since the English Civil War, were dismissed as so many evil sources of oppression.[8] Similarly, for John Stuart Mill, displays of Anglophilia such as Ralph Waldo Emerson's in 1849[9] were to be treated as beneath contempt while the mean inheritance of aristocratic rule continued to blight all aspects of English life and character.[10] For all Mill's emphasis on the creative role of nations in human history, his arguments in favour of extending the franchise were judged to

[7] See Peter Mandler's essay in this volume.

[8] John Vincent, *The Formation of the British Liberal Party, 1857–1868* (1966; Harmondsworth, 1972), pp. 28–30. G. R. Searle has recently pointed out that not all radicals were as hostile to patriotism as Cobden and Bright, being prepared to jettison free trade when the defence of national interests required, for example during the Crimean War. However, the priority that was thus given to patriotism lacked the emotional force and self-idealisation that increasingly became characteristic of English nationalism after 1850. *Morality and the Market in Victorian Britain* (Oxford, 1988), ch. 9.

[9] Emerson's remarks are cited in F. A. Hayek, *John Stuart Mill and Harriet Taylor: Their Correspondence and Subsequent Marriage* (London, 1951), p. 301, n. 58.

[10] For Mill's response to Emerson see his letter to Harriet Taylor, dated 14 March 1849, in *Collected Works of John Stuart Mill* (hereafter *CW*), XIV: *The Later Letters, 1849 to 1873*, ed. Francis E. Mineka and Dwight N. Lindley (Toronto, 1972), pp. 15–16. On his criticism of the English aristocracy see J. S. Mill, 'The Spirit of the Age, III [Part 2], *The Examiner*, 13 March 1831, in *CW*, XXII: *Newspaper Writings, 1822–1831*, ed. A. Robson and J. M. Robson (Toronto, 1986), pp. 278–82. His highly negative view of English character is well illustrated in his essay on 'Bentham', *London and Westminster Review* (August, 1838), in *CW*, X: *Essays on Ethics, Religion, and Society*, ed. J. M. Robson (Toronto, 1979), pp. 92–3. On Mill's 'un-English' reputation during his lifetime and immediately after his death, see S. Collini, *Public Moralists: Political Thought and Intellectual Life in Britain, 1850–1930* (Oxford, 1991), p. 320.

be of an *a priori* nature by critics of democracy in the 1860s like Robert Lowe.[11] This triggered a rousing speech on the altogether higher and more real arbiter of the English nation's fate than the abstract right of every citizen to participate in government – 'the great heart of England'.

Mill's essay 'On Liberty' was also considered to be unduly disrespectful of the English nation. For example, the editor of the Unitarian journal *The National Review*, R. H. Hutton, considered that the interpretation which Mill had placed on the growing unity of thought and opinion in England was wholly misguided. As a consequence, his prescriptive theory of liberty had also gone awry. In a review of 'On Liberty', Hutton claimed that Mill had mistaken a decline in sectarianism for the stifling of dissent. Over the last century, however, the sharp distinctions between country gentleman on the one hand, and tradesman and man of letters on the other, and between dissenter and churchman, had been greatly eroded. Similarly, the county map of England no longer corresponded to different shades of religious opinion. The intense political rivalry between Whig and Tory also had no mid-nineteenth-century counterpart.[12] For Hutton, far from this development representing the 'forcible triumph of a single class-creed', as it had done in the United States, its nature was rather that of 'a genuine assimilation of opposite schools of thought'.[13] It had been produced by that clash of opposites which Mill was extolling, but in relation to well-defined groups rather than individuals *per se*. Indeed, for Hutton, the energy and vigour which Mill so admired in individuals were impossible to attain in the absence of pressure exerted by a wider collective ideal. While it was often true that individuals were made to endure the bigotry of majorities, bent on forcing their 'coarser tastes and poor commonplace thoughts on minorities',[14] it was equally the case that societies could suffer from too slack rather than too rigorous a social bond. In the middle of the nineteenth century the stimulus to individuality which was once provided by class and other forms of allegiance had now passed to a homogenous English nation.[15]

Hutton's 'nationalist' misgivings about Mill's conception of liberty were echoed by James Fitzjames Stephen.[16] Stephen complicates Mandler's claim that nationalism was kept at arm's length by mid-Victorian thinkers on account of its 'anti-imperial and democratic connotations'.[17] By contrast, Stephen appealed to English nationhood in

---

[11] Speech by Lowe on the Borough Franchise Bill, 1865, in A. E. Dyson and J. Lovelock, eds., *Education and Democracy* (London, 1975), p. 195.

[12] R. H. Hutton, 'Mill on Liberty', *The National Review*, 8 (1859), in A. Pyle, ed., *Liberty: Contemporary Responses to John Stuart Mill* (Bristol, 1994), pp. 83–4.

[13] *Ibid.*, p. 85.   [14] *Ibid.*, p. 100.   [15] *Ibid.*, pp. 97–8.

[16] The following exposition of Stephen's thought is developed in more detail in J. Stapleton, 'James Fitzjames Stephen: Liberalism, Patriotism, and English Liberty', *Victorian Studies*, 41 (1998), pp. 243–63.   [17] Mandler, '"Race" and "nation"', p. 237.

combating democracy and *defending* empire. Even before his stinging indictment of Mill's liberalism – his *Liberty, Equality, Fraternity* of 1873 – Stephen had identified the chief shortcoming of his master turned adversary[18] as a lamentable want of patriotism. While he found much to admire in the essay 'On Liberty' when reviewing it for *The Saturday Review*, Stephen displayed an optimism about the independent state of opinion among all classes in English society which Mill had emphatically denied. For Stephen, the undiminished capacity of commonplace, as much as distinguished Englishmen to set their imprint upon the world was illustrated in their extraordinary response to the Indian Mutiny. Signalling the manly, muscular conception of liberalism adopted by other liberal intellectuals of his age, he wrote that events in India had provoked feats of 'that desperate courage which is the great constituent element of individuality'.[19] Indeed, to his mind, it was the British Empire which had stirred England's consciousness in recent years. The son of a distinguished colonial administrator – the Right Honourable James Stephen – James Fitzjames Stephen constantly hailed the British empire as an outstanding moral and political feat, particularly its crowning glory in India. Recently returned from his three year tour of duty as the Legal Member of the Viceroy's Council, Stephen proclaimed in his *Liberty, Equality, Fraternity*, 'I do not envy the Englishman whose heart does not beat high as he looks at the scarred and shattered walls of Delhi or at the union jack flying from the fort at Lahore.'[20] The English imperial achievement demanded a more inspiring ethic than Mill's 'abstract' conception of liberty could possibly supply.[21]

Stephen set out the contours of such an ethic in his essay on 'Liberalism' published in 1862, the Burkean, nationalist character of which has been insufficiently emphasised in existing studies of Stephen's thought.[22] The target of this essay moved from Mill's indictment of English society to the wider radical tradition in which his shortcomings were magnified. Stephen's assertion about the nature of liberalism was

---

[18] Stephen had greatly admired the earlier Mill of the *System of Logic* (1843) and the *Principles of Political Economy* (1848), works which were based upon rigorous logical analysis. J. A. Colaiaco, *James Fitzjames Stephen and the Crisis of Victorian Thought* (London, 1983), p. 11.

[19] J. F. Stephen, 'Mr. Mill on Political Liberty', second notice, *The Saturday Review*, 19 February 1859, in Pyle, *Contemporary Responses*, p. 20.

[20] J. F. Stephen, *Liberty, Equality, Fraternity* (1873; Chicago, 1991), p. 113.

[21] Leslie Stephen, *The Life of Sir James Fitzjames Stephen* (London, 1895), p. 317.

[22] The essay merits only a brief quotation in J. Roach, 'Liberalism and the Victorian Intelligentsia' (1957), in P. Stansky, ed., *The Victorian Revolution: Government and Society in Victoria's Britain* (New York, 1973), p. 329; also in K. J. M. Smith, *James Fitzjames Stephen: Portrait of a Victorian Rationalist* (Cambridge, 1988), p. 102. Its patriotic aspect is much underplayed by Colaiaco, *James Fitzjames Stephen*, pp. 7–9. It is not discussed at all in the essay on Stephen by Benjamin Evans Lippincott in *Victorian Critics of Democracy: Carlyle, Ruskin, Arnold, Stephen, Maine, Lecky* (Minneapolis, 1938).

one from which Mill would not have dissented: 'Liberalism . . . ought to mean the opposite of sordidness, vulgarity, and bigotry.'[23] But this sense of liberalism as largeness of mind was signally absent from those who currently identified with the liberal cause in Britain. Prominent among the latter, for example, was the recently enfranchised middle class which, following the lead of the Manchester School, took 'a purely commercial view of politics; which regarded the empire as a heavy burthen, because it did not pay its expenses, and which looked forward to a millennium of small shopkeepers bothered by no taxes or tariffs'.[24] Moreover, that same class remained bent upon subjecting the political establishment of their country to the full force of popular rule. Stephen was resigned to the inevitability of democracy. But the spirit in which a liberal politician should go about the extension of the suffrage was,

to look upon himself as a man charged to introduce to his estate an heir who had attained his majority; he would teach those whom he addressed to see in the institutions of their native land neither a prison to escape from nor a fortress to storm, but a stately and venerable mansion which for eight centuries had been the home of their ancestors, and in which they were now to take their place and play their part.[25]

The ancestral analogies here are striking, defying a recent claim that the similarities between Stephen and Burke are merely 'superficial'.[26] Indeed, Stephen identified very closely with the Burkean Whiggism of Macaulay, who had been a regular visitor to his childhood home.[27]

Clearly, for Stephen, liberalism was inextricably tied to patriotism and the maintenance of traditional English institutions, not least that of a Protestant Church in the face of growing 'ritualist' challenges to its authority. For example, he expressed evident distaste – thinly masked as incomprehension – for such central Roman Catholic practices as that of confession.[28] His antipathy in this regard mirrored the view of a slightly later defendant of Anglicanism, Mandell Creighton, that any attempt to regularise confession within the Church of England would 'show a weakening of the moral fibre of the English character'.[29]

---

[23] J. F. Stephen, 'Liberalism', *The Cornhill Magazine*, 5 (1862), p. 72. Reprinted with notes in J. Stapleton, ed., *Liberalism, Democracy, and the State in Britain, 1862–1891: Five Essays* (Bristol, 1997).   [24] Leslie Stephen, *The Life of Sir James Fitzjames Stephen*, p. 315.

[25] J. F. Stephen, 'Liberalism', *Cornhill Magazine*, p. 75.

[26] M. Francis and J. Morrow, *A History of English Political Thought in the Nineteenth Century* (New York, 1994) p. 264.

[27] J. F. Stephen, 'Lord Macaulay', *The Saturday Review*, 7 January 1860, pp. 9–10.

[28] Stephen, *Liberty, Equality, Fraternity*, pp. 161–2. On Stephen's conception of the (ideal, Protestant) religion upheld by the 'solid, established part of the English nation', see p. 252.

[29] Louise Creighton, *Life and Letters of Mandell Creighton* (London, 1913), p. 365.

The lack of regard for creed and country lay at the root of the conflict between Stephen and so many of his contemporaries, even Thomas Carlyle, with whom his affinities were strongest and who exercised considerable influence upon the writing of *Liberty, Equality, Fraternity*.[30] Stephen's conservatism also distanced him from fellow-adherents of a 'masculine' brand of liberalism – for example, Henry Fawcett. Fawcett regarded liberalism as principally concerned with removing the restrictions upon the unbounded 'energy' which could be found within *all* classes of society. Typically, though, it entailed abolishing the inherited privileges of a landed aristocratic class which severely circumscribed the opportunities of the less fortunate in society for 'manly' independence.[31]

Stephen's liberal imperialism also marked him well off from Mill, despite Mill's instrumental role in reconciling liberalism and imperialism in the mid-nineteenth century.[32] While Stephen applauded the elevation of India to the status of a Crown Colony following the Indian Mutiny of 1857, Mill lamented the passing of the old intermediate body responsible for Indian government, the East India Company. For Stephen, the incorporation of Indian affairs into the mainstream political life of the English nation held great potential for strengthening patriotic loyalties at a time when they seemed much threatened by the clamour for democracy and the misguided popular impulses which underpinned it. By contrast, Mill was more concerned with good government in India than the impingement of a 'wider England' upon the consciousness of citizens at home and, to that effect, argued for the insulation of Indian affairs from political divisions in the metropolis.[33] Moreover, Mill's orientalist sympathies and his concern for the "internal culture" of the native people of India produced a model of imperial rule that was starkly opposed to the authoritarian prescriptions of Stephen.[34] Likewise, Stephen was far more defensive in regard to the misdemeanours of imperial officers in the Indian Mutiny, and guarded in his role in the Jamaica Committee's efforts to prosecute Governor Eyre.[35] Mill, of course, died before the crisis of Home Rule erupted in the 1880s, although remarks he made in *Representative Government* and elsewhere suggest a qualified sympathy for the Irish

---

[30] For Carlyle's influence on Stephen, see S. Heffer, *Moral Desperado: A Life of Thomas Carlyle* (London, 1995), pp. 319, 372. On Stephen's distance from Carlyle, see Colaiaco, *James Fitzjames Stephen*, pp. 14–16; and Smith, *James Fitzjames Stephen*, p. 104.

[31] Collini, *Public Moralists*, pp. 181–2, 193.

[32] See Eileen P. Sullivan, 'Liberalism and Imperialism: J. S. Mill's Defense of the British Empire', *Journal of the History of Ideas*, 44 (1983), pp. 599–618.

[33] See Mill's *Considerations on Representative Government*, in *CW*, XIX, p. 573. On the mutations of Mill's views on India as reflected in, and shaped by, his work in drafting despatches for the East India Company, see Lynn Zastoupil, *John Stuart Mill and India* (Stanford, 1994).   [34] Zastoupil, *John Stuart Mill and India*, pp. 201–6.

[35] Smith, *James Fitzjames Stephen*, p. 137.

cause entailing quite extensive changes in the ownership of land, if not for anything approaching Irish self-government.[36] His old animus against the English aristocracy, Anglo-Irish in this case – with its peculiar hallmark in the monopolisation of land – seems to have been instrumental in shaping such views.[37] But Stephen sided vociferously with Liberal Unionism, and believed that the agrarian grievances should be addressed only once nationalist-inspired agitation had been quelled.[38]

III

Successive proposals for Irish Home Rule helped to force the issue of nationalism in general and English/British identity in particular to the surface of political thought from the 1880s until the outbreak of the First World War. Upholders of the Union typically expressed allegiance to a polity whose inclusiveness was regarded as integral to the liberal values for which it was justly celebrated – diversity, tolerance, and liberty (not least that of Irish loyalists and Ulster Protestants). For the ardent libertarian conservative, Lord Hugh Cecil, the movement for Irish independence was riddled with Jacobinism, reproducing 'some of the worst features of the spirit of French terrorism'. Nationality in any other form than the 'magnification of an amiable local sentiment' was inherently suspect.[39] His fellow-Unionist, A. V. Dicey agreed, notwithstanding the Mazzinian influences of his youth.[40] Certainly, he thought that the English were a model of nationalistic restraint, a virtue which he nonetheless flaunted in a manner bordering on the chauvinism he associated with nationalism elsewhere.[41]

Yet the Unionists held no monopoly over the defence of the United Kingdom's integrity. Both James Bryce and the historian S. R. Gardiner readily embraced Home Rule as a necessary means of consolidating the United Kingdom and appeasing Irish nationalists.[42] This, indeed, explains the late nineteenth-century purchase of the federal ideal more

---

[36] Mill, *Considerations on Representative Government*, pp. 550–1. See also his essay on 'England and Ireland' (1868), in *CW*, VI: *Essays on England, Ireland, and the Empire*, ed. J. M. Robson and J. Hamburger (Toronto, 1982), p. 526; and Sullivan, 'Liberalism and Imperialism', p. 617.   [37] Zastoupil, *John Stuart Mill and India*, p. 187.

[38] Smith, *James Fitzjames Stephen*, p. 153.

[39] Lord Hugh Cecil, *Conservatism* (London, 1912), pp. 240–1. On Cecil's thought more generally, see W. S. Rodner, 'Conservatism, Resistance, and Lord Hugh Cecil', in *History of Political Thought*, 9 (3) (1988), pp. 529–51; and Meadowcroft, *Conceptualizing the State*, ch. 2.

[40] M. Richter, *The Politics of Conscience: T. H. Green and his Age* (London, 1964), pp. 80–1.

[41] A. V. Dicey, *Lectures on the Relation between Law and Public Opinion in England during the Nineteenth Century* (1905; London, 1940), p. 463.

[42] On Gardiner and Home Rule, see Timothy Lang, *The Victorians and the Stuart Heritage: Interpretations of a Discordant Past* (Cambridge, 1995), pp. 155–6.

widely, whatever its disintegrative effect in practice.[43] But Bryce, at least, was an extremely reluctant advocate of Irish Home Rule, sensing all too well the formidable problem posed by Ulster, and his support stopped well short of independence. He certainly gained little confidence from federal solutions to national problems elsewhere; for example, in April 1886, he wrote despairingly to Lord Acton that 'Croatia and Hungary don't get on at all – their case seems nearest to my scheme, so that is unlucky.'[44] The tendency towards separation between England and Ireland must have grieved him all the more because of what H. A. L. Fisher described as his 'full[ness] of the minor loyalties' which 'the corporate tradition in British educational life does so much to promote',[45] and – one might add, certainly Bryce would have so regarded it – to harmonise. Politically, however, as his *Modern Democracies* was to show in 1920, Bryce could not conceal his admiration for the 'English' characteristics of a 'vehement passion for liberty', a 'spirit of individualistic self-reliance and self-help', a 'suspicious attitude towards officials', and a 'spirit of localism', all of which he thought were integral to the establishment of the American republic.[46] This identity with England was notwithstanding deep ancestral roots in Ulster and Scotland and, far from being 'exclusive', co-existed with a generous sympathy for the suffering of oppressed nations like Armenia.[47]

It was not only the threat posed to the Union with Ireland by Gladstone's policies of Home Rule which enhanced simultaneously the sense of, and anxiety about, English national identity. This was reinforced by the growing 'collectivist' character of democracy in Britain, around which so much of the debate about 'citizenship' turned; the loss of imperial face in South Africa; and the rise of protectionism and new association of free trade with social reform.[48] There was no consistent set of

[43] Michael Burgess, *The British Tradition of Federalism* (London, 1995), p. 85.
[44] Quoted in Hugh Tulloch, *Acton* (London, 1988), p. 79.
[45] H. A. L. Fisher, *James Bryce*, 2 vols. (London, 1927), I, p. 337.
[46] James Bryce, *Modern Democracies*, 2 vols. (London, 1921), II, pp. 7–8.
[47] Bryce's Scottish roots, and his exemplification of a 'West British' culture/identity have been played up by Christopher Harvie. See Harvie, *The Rise of Regional Europe* (London, 1994), pp. 42–3; and 'Garron Top to Caer Gybi: Images of the Inland Sea', *Irish Review* (Autumn, 1996), p. 47. On Armenia, see Fisher, *James Bryce*, I, p. 185.
[48] These issues are explored in Christopher Harvie, *The Lights of Liberalism: University Liberals and the Challenge of Democracy, 1860–86* (London, 1976); G.R. Searle, *The Quest for National Efficiency: A Study in British Politics and Political Thought, 1899–1914* (Oxford, 1971); Anthony Howe, 'Towards the "Hungry Forties": Free Trade in Britain, c. 1880–1903', and F. Trentmann, 'The Strange Death of Free Trade: the Erosion of "Liberal Consensus" in Great Britain, c. 1903–1932', both in E. F. Biagini, ed., *Citizenship and Community: Liberals, Radicals and Collective Identities in the British Isles, 1865–1931* (Cambridge, 1996). The way in which 'English national character' became fundamental to Bertrand Russell's opposition to protectionism is discussed in Philip Ironside, *The Social and Political Thought of Bertrand Russell: The Development of an Aristocratic Liberalism* (Cambridge, 1995), pp. 66–7.

attitudes towards these developments.[49] However, the mixed responses they elicited shared one notable feature, namely appeal to an assumed English character which had impressed itself firmly upon national life. This character was either held to have been betrayed by recent policy or to be approaching its apotheosis as a result.

An example of the former is C. H. Pearson's *National Life and Character* of 1893. This work focused upon closing opportunities for emigration with the 'filling up of the world', the tendency of the 'weaker' races to out-number the stronger, and perhaps most worrying of all, the 'loss of the impulse [of Englishmen] to better themselves outside of England'. While these developments had worked to the advantage of patriotism, as many now regarded England as a 'home for life', its disadvantage was the decay of English adventurousness and English inventiveness, and a whole series of measures taken by the state which amounted to 'absolute departures from the time-honoured English principle of leaving every man to do the best for himself, and fare as he may'.[50] The 'lure' of state socialism had encouraged the 'less imaginative' in their ambitions to reconstruct society when their 'cravings' for a better life had been dashed by the only limited migration from the countryside to towns that they were prepared to undertake.[51]

Clearly, on Pearson's analysis, a wedge had been driven between English patriotism and English 'character' by the increased role of the state, the former gaining at the expense of the latter. In his view, the vigour of the English nation was directly proportional to the looseness of its ties to a homeland and, in particular, to the state. This countered the imperi-alist views of Sir John Seeley in the previous decade, for whom 'England' was synonymous with the state, and who was anxious to stress that emi-gration constituted a net gain for the latter rather than a loss.[52] No con-clusions, he argued, could be drawn from the loss of the American colonies since the impulse to their foundation had been religious, an impulse always liable to produce independent statehood; as such, the colonisation of the American seaboard was exceptional in the history of England's overseas expansion.[53] Moreover, whereas for Seeley the build-ing of 'Greater Britain' redounded all to the credit of the state, whose cause it had prosecuted through deft actions of war and diplomacy, Pearson attributed English overseas expansion to the energy of individu-als acting in an entirely private capacity, and whose status as such

[49] Harvie, *The Lights of Liberalism*, pp. 221–2.
[50] Charles Pearson, *National Life and Character: A Forecast* (London, 1894), pp. 110, 103.
[51] *Ibid.*, p. 102.
[52] J. R. Seeley, *The Expansion of England* (1883; London, 1897), pp. 8, 184.
[53] *Ibid.*, pp. 179–80.

remained the bedrock of colonialism. Both Pearson and Seeley shared a heavy sense of English decline. Again though, whereas for Seeley, state-led imperialism constituted the best antidote to troubles emanating chiefly in the party system and in a deep-seated national condition of moral uncertainty,[54] for Pearson, the increasing prominence of the state – both in an imperial and a domestic sense – lay at the root of the current malaise. He wrote, 'No Peterborough or Clive would now be allowed a free hand by his Government. The first impetuous act would provoke a recall by telegram.'[55] This response was loudly echoed in the 'little England' literature of anti-imperialist liberalism which was soon to be intensified by the Boer War. The writings of George Unwin are a case in point.

Unwin became Professor of Economic History at Edinburgh in 1908 and at Manchester in 1910 after rising from humble nonconformist roots in Stockport. A formative influence on his outlook was the years he spent at the turn of the century as secretary to Lord Courtney, a leading scourge of 'jingoism' and protectionism, and a radical of the same mould as his friends and teachers, Fawcett, Mill, and John Elliot Cairnes.[56] Commenting acidly upon Seeley's legacy at the time of the First World War, Unwin wrote, 'The expansion of England in the seventeenth century was an expansion of society and not of the State. Society expanded to escape from the pressure of the State . . . And, as the real expansion has been primarily social, so has been essentially peaceful.'[57] All the belligerence expended in defence of the empire had not prevented the growth of overseas territories by rival powers in the slightest. Like other 'little Englanders' – not least his mentor T. H. Green – Unwin exuded contempt for the 'patriotic imagination' which he held Seeley guilty of attempting to rouse.[58] Yet, like them too, his disdain for the recent rise in patriotic emotions concealed a deep attachment to an alternative projection of England/Britain,[59] one which was starkly contrasted to continental nations like Germany and to which Unwin suspected Seeley of being too

[54] J. R. Seeley, 'Ethics and Religion', in The Society of Ethical Propagandists, ed., *Ethics and Religion* (London, 1900), p. 12; see also D. Wormell, *Sir John Seeley and the Uses of History* (Cambridge, 1980), pp. 138, 131.

[55] Pearson, *National Life and Character*, p. 106.

[56] R. H. Tawney, introductory memoir to *Studies in Economic History: The Collected Papers of George Unwin* (London, 1927), pp. xxvii–xxxv. I have explored Unwin's affinities with the English Pluralists in 'English Pluralism as Cultural Definition: The Social and Political Thought of George Unwin', in *Journal of the History of Ideas*, 52 (1991), pp. 665–84.

[57] George Unwin, Introduction to C. Gill, *National Power and Prosperity* (1916), in *Studies in Economic History*, p. 341.

[58] *Ibid.* On Green's little Englandism, see J. Bryce, *Studies in Contemporary Biography* (London, 1903), p. 97.

[59] On the patriotism of little Englanders, see Grainger, *Patriotisms*, pp. 148–9.

much in thrall.[60] As he argued in his inaugural lecture as Professor of Economic History at Edinburgh in 1908:

> whilst the main feature of British history since the seventeenth century has been the remoulding of a State by a powerful Society, the main feature of German history in the same period has been the remoulding of a Society by a powerful State.[61]

However, positive attitudes towards the English state at the end of the nineteenth century were not always associated with admiration for its external projection of power. In such attitudes a sense of gain rather than loss to the national character in certain recent developments is clearly perceptible. For example, T. H. Green regarded states in their relation to one another as subject to strict moral conditions, a view which was shared by many other British Idealist thinkers too, and not least in relation to the British imperial state.[62] At the same time he defended the state as the focus of a common sense of citizenship. This was an attempt to interpret and justify the growth of government along 'collectivist lines' in philosophical terms, but in an analytical and historical framework that leaned heavily upon the patriotic instinct.[63] For Green, the patriotic bonds essential to statehood based on citizenship were especially exemplified in the cause of Independency or congregationalism championed by Sir Henry Vane during the English Civil War, and with which he regarded Cromwell as a close sympathiser. English Independency, Green maintained, was superior to both the Jesuitry which plagued southern Europe at the time of the Reformation and the Protestantism of the north. The effect of the former was the extinction of all 'public spirit' and the ruin of nations, while that of the latter was the subjection of religion to princely control.[64] Rescuing Cromwell's tarnished image from the nonconformist monopolisation of his legacy – which survived right up until the tercentenary of 1899[65] – Green stressed his 'genuine zeal for the free well-being of the state and nation'.[66] He recognised that the cause of Independency

---

[60] Unwin, Introduction to Gill, *National Power and Prosperity*, p. 342.

[61] Unwin, 'The Aims of Economic History', in *Studies in Economic History*, p. 28.

[62] See D. Boucher, 'British Idealism, the State, and International Relations', *Journal of the History of Ideas*, 55 (1994), pp. 671–94; also John Gibbins, 'Liberalism, Nationalism and the British Idealists', *History of European Ideas*, 15 (4–6) (1992), pp. 491–7. See also J. H. Muirhead, 'What Imperialism Means', *International Journal of Ethics*, reprinted in D. Boucher, ed., *The British Idealists* (Cambridge, 1997), p. 247.

[63] Green insisted on the necessity of patriotism to the maintenance of the state in his *Lectures on the Principles of Political Obligation* (London, 1931), pp. 130–1.

[64] T. H. Green, 'Four Lectures on the English Revolution', in *The Works of T. H. Green*, ed. R. L. Nettleship, 3 vols. (London, 1889), III, p. 282.

[65] Lang, *The Victorians and the Stuart Heritage*, pp. 197–8.

[66] Green, 'Four Lectures on the English Revolution', p. 310.

had throughout been blighted by the 'enthusiasms, mysticisms, and fanaticism' of the Puritans, evils which Cromwell had managed to keep in check but which had quickly surfaced after his death. Indeed, one of Green's followers – John MacCunn – thought fit to elaborate in clear Burkean terms the ground on which his master ultimately censured the radicals of the English Civil War: that of their disrespect for the 'traditions, the habits, the common feelings and interests, even the prejudices which stood rooted in the national character'.[67] Nevertheless, Green concluded his lectures by asserting that the noble impulses and ideals inherent in the 'churches of the sectaries' had themselves left a permanent mark for the better on that national character, thereafter providing 'the great spring of political life in England'.[68] Certainly they had sowed the seeds of the religious ideal of citizenship which he believed his own generation was striving to reap through democracy and social reform alike.

The British Idealists' efforts to give a clear 'English' face to an important historical resource of nineteenth-century radicalism further eroded the antagonism between liberalism and English national culture. By the end of the century even liberal economists upholding a cosmopolitan commitment to free trade were emphasising the strengths of English character which gave Englishmen a special advantage in such a world.[69] In turn, in many and varied ways, liberalism became central to English self-understanding,[70] a position it maintained until the end of the period covered here, and even beyond. In the remainder of this essay the close relationship between liberalism and Englishness will be illustrated. Three episodes will be brought into focus: arguments for the socialist reconstruction of society; the promotion of group rights prior to the First World War; and the resistance to the political extremism of 'foreign' creeds during the interwar period.

IV

The 'collectivist' onslaught against 'individualist' political philosophy at the turn of the century was often based upon an unrecognised debt to its antagonist – as great indeed, as it was always ready to claim from the latter

---

[67] John MacCunn, *Six Radical Thinkers: Bentham, J. S. Mill, Cobden, Carlyle, Mazzini, T. H. Green* (1910: New York, 1964), p. 222.

[68] Green, 'Four Lectures on the English Revolution', p. 364.

[69] See, for example, Alfred Marshall's reflections on the energy, daring, and self-reliance of the English and associated successes in trade and industry, as well as in politics. *Principles of Economics* (1890; 9th edn, London, 1961), annotated by C. W. Guillebaud, Appendix A, pp. 740–1.

[70] D. Smith, 'Englishness and the Liberal Inheritance after 1886', in R. Colls and P. Dodd, eds., *Englishness: Politics and Culture, 1880–1920* (London, 1986), p. 255.

itself.[71] This is apparent in the socialist writings of H. M. Hyndman, on the one hand, and his Fabian rivals, on the other. In particular, both deployed liberal ideals of England to support their respective socialist ends.

Hyndman, founder of the Social Democratic Federation in 1883, combined a deeply ingrained conservatism with Marxism after he converted to socialism in 1880.[72] But his conservatism was of a Tory radical kind, in which lament for the erosion of traditional ties under capitalism contained an ideal of personal independence projected several centuries into the English past. Despite standard socialist calls in *England for All* (1881) for the state to regulate 'that nominal individual freedom which simply strengthens the domination of the few',[73] Hyndman had no hesitation in invoking the historical perspective of Cobbett and other radical conservatives which posited a 'golden-age' of the English labourer. The source of this nostalgia – which so prominent a traditional liberal as Hilaire Belloc was soon to share[74] – lay in the 'freedom' that was universally afforded by the dispersal of landownership. Hyndman's key reference point here was the fifteenth century, after the disappearance of villeinage and before land became concentrated in far fewer hands due to baronial impoverishment following the Wars of the Roses and then the dissolution of the monasteries. In this favoured age, 'the working agriculturist . . . was a well-to-do free man'.[75] Continuing in this vein in his later work, *The Historical Basis of Socialism* (1883), Hyndman elaborated thus:

> It was from this period that the sturdy character of Englishmen as a nation developed, and the nature of the society was such as to encourage the growth of the finest qualities of self-reliance and independence among men.[76]

When Hyndman added the further description of 'vigorous' to his portrait of the English worker's more fortunate predecessors, the resonance of late-nineteenth-century individualism is even more apparent. Indeed, he used the term 'individualism' openly in connection with this period in a subsequent work, adding, in tones that are strongly suggestive of a liberal view of Englishness, that 'A local and national spirit of individual initiative was thus engendered, which was vivifying to all it touched then and rouses our admiration now.'[77]

---

[71] See Sidney Webb's description of the unconsciously collectivist 'Individualist Town Councillor', in *Socialism in England* (1890; London, 1908), pp. 116–17.

[72] M. Bevir, 'H. M. Hyndman: A Rereading and a Reassessment', *History of Political Thought*, 12 (1991), pp. 125–46.

[73] H. M. Hyndman, *The Text-Book of Democracy: England for All* (London, 1881), p. 6.

[74] On Belloc, see V. Feske, *From Belloc to Churchill: Private Scholars, Public Culture, and the Crisis of British Liberalism, 1900–1939* (Chapel Hill, N.C., 1996), ch. 1.

[75] Hyndman, *The Text-Book of Democracy*, p. 10.

[76] H. M. Hyndman, *The Historical Basis of Socialism in England* (London, 1883), p. 22.

[77] H. M. Hyndman, *The Economics of Socialism*, 4th edn (London, 1896), pp. 28–9.

Hyndman was most concerned to impress upon what he called 'the natural leaders of the people' that responsibility for peaceful change, through the 'friendly' auspices of the state, lay largely with them.[78] It was their patriotic duty to put class selfishness behind them and institute a major change in land ownership in the interests of all. It was a challenge that was met with predictable rebuff.[79]

Superficially, nothing could have been more calculated to frustrate Hyndman's nationalist ambitions for socialism than the role of his erstwhile SDF colleague and founder of the Socialist League – William Morris – in disrupting the celebrations of Queen Victoria's Golden Jubilee in 1887. For Morris, her reign was symbolic of the 'bourgeois patriotism' for which he had nothing but contempt.[80] Morris's cultural disaffection on this occasion was more in keeping with the comprehensive alienation from English civilisation evinced by his friend and co-author in the Socialist League, E. Belfort Bax,[81] than Hyndman's hearty patriotism. But it, too, was as much premised upon a vision of the English *patria* as of socialism more widely – one which preceded enclosure and mechanical industry, and which was greatly enriched by art, architecture, and perhaps, above all, the spirit of association. Socialism was a means of reconnecting the future with the medieval past, reversing 400 years of the ravages of commerce such that generations of unborn Englishmen would come to regard their nineteenth-century ancestors as strangers.[82] At another level, Morris's challenge to the dominant liberal projections of 'England' demonstrates the latter's infinite capacity to soften and absorb its more oppositional edges: for the ideal of 'fellowship' which Morris celebrated as the life-blood of medieval society was to become a central construct of Pluralism – broadened out as the mainspring of English historical development more generally.

Even the hard-faced bureaucratic socialism of the Fabians was qualified by an emotional attachment to England, manifested in a concern to return the nation to its 'true' path of historical development before it was blown off course by errant forms of liberalism. For example, the Fabianism of the Webbs was greatly inspired by the example afforded by the pre-1688 institutions of local self-government in England – grounded

---

[78] Hyndman, *The Text-Book of Democracy*, p. 31.

[79] For Mallock's rejection of Hyndman as an outsider, a threat to the 'old culture' of the aristocracy, in which 'centuries of our country's life are embodied', see John Lucas, 'Conservatism and Revolution in the 1880s', in J. Lucas, ed., *Literature and Politics in the Nineteenth Century* (London, 1971), pp. 194–5.

[80] William Morris, *Political Writings: Contributions to Justice and Commonweal, 1883–1890*, ed. N. Salmon (Bristol, 1994), pp. xxii–xxiii.

[81] On Bax, see John Cowley, *The Victorian Encounter with Marx: A Study of E. Belfort Bax* (London, 1992), p. 12.

[82] W. Morris, 'The Hopes of Civilization' (1888), and 'More's Utopia' (1893), in *Political Writings of William Morris*, ed. A. L. Morton (London, 1973), pp. 161–2, 255.

in the principles of custom and mutual obligation – before they were transformed into bastions of oligarchical, capitalist self-interest.[83] In this respect their position on the romantic-utilitarian fault-line was more ambiguous than that which was accorded to them by the Marxist and literary critics who form the subject of Donald Winch's essay in the companion volume, *Polity, Economy, and Society*.[84] Similarly, H. G. Wells, at the peak of his Fabian phase, could write admiringly of the potential of English Whiggism to shape the future of mankind along standardised, denationalised lines. 'The Whig disposition', he wrote, which 'once had some play in India, was certainly to attempt to anglicise the "native", to assimilate his culture, and then to assimilate his political status with that of his temporary ruler.'[85] However, this approach had been superseded by an opposing Rousseauesque type of liberalism: 'sentimental and logical' rather than 'constructive and disciplinary'. The latter had substituted a retrograde and ultimately dangerous policy of cultivating as many independent and dissimilar nationalities as possible. It was even working towards 'the separation and autonomy of detached portions of our own peoples, to disintegrate finally into perfect, because lawless individuals'.[86] Wells was evidently reacting against the 'little Englandism' in the ranks of English liberals, and the continuing vexed question of Ireland's status within the United Kingdom. Nevertheless his use of Whiggism – albeit selective – as a model of progress towards a world state suggests an identity with English culture which belies his more culturally detached scientific cosmopolitanism.

V

The development of liberal paradigms of Englishness continued in the work of Pluralist writers after 1900.[87] They challenged what they conceived as an unwholesome idolatry of the state in the nineteenth century,

[83] J. Stapleton, 'Localism versus Centralism in the Webbs' Political Thought', *History of Political Thought*, XIII (1991), pp. 162–3. See also Feske, *From Belloc to Churchill*, ch. 2.

[84] Donald Winch's essay in *Polity, Economy, and Society*, pp. 243–66.

[85] In fact, the Whig approach to India in the early nineteenth century was divided between Anglicists such as Macaulay, Bentinck, and John Cam Hobhouse and Orientalists such as Thomas Munroe, John Malcolm, Mountstuart Elphinstone, and Charles Metcalfe. See Zastoupil, *John Stuart Mill and India*, pp. 39–40, 56–9.

[86] H. G. Wells, *A Modern Utopia* (1905; London, n.d.), pp. 332–4.

[87] John Burrow has illuminated this relationship in '"The Village Community" and the Uses of History in Late Nineteenth-Century England', in N. McKendrick, ed., *Historical Perspectives: Studies in English Thought and Society in Honour of J. H. Plumb* (London, 1974); and *Whigs and Liberals: Continuity and Change in English Political Thought* (Oxford, 1988), ch. 6. Two recent contributions to Pluralist scholarship are David Nicholls, *The Pluralist State: the Political Ideas of J. N. Figgis and his Contemporaries* (London, 1994); and David Runciman, *Pluralism and the Personality of the State* (Cambridge, 1997).

premised upon an outworn theory of sovereignty.[88] No less discreditable, however, was the individualism of thinkers such as Herbert Spencer, who conceived the bonds of society in terms of the recognition of personal rights. Indeed, Pluralists considered the theory of state sovereignty and political individualism as mutually reinforcing: both stressed the polarities of society in the state and individuals, to the detriment of the rich associational life by which they were bridged. In championing this intermediate territory, Pluralists defended – often aggressively – the 'inherent rights', 'inherent will', and 'spontaneous power of self-development' possessed by groups.

However, such problematic flights into the higher realms of political theory were the – perhaps careless – adjuncts of a more important Pluralist concern. This was to emphasise the unparalleled English talent for forming voluntary societies in pursuit of all manner of purposes. In this guise, Pluralism represented a variation upon a view of England as infinitely diverse which had developed since the 1860s in response to Mill's claim that the country had been engulfed by homogeneity. For example, in the introduction to his translation of part of Otto Von Gierke's *Das deutsche Genossenschaftsrecht*, F. W. Maitland identified in England 'a wealth of group-life . . . richer even than that which has come under Dr Gierke's eye'.[89] This was evident in the existence of Wesleyan chapels, Jewish synagogues, Catholic cathedrals, the Inns of Court, trade unions, the merchant adventurers, Lloyd's Coffee-House, the Stock Exchange, and many other bodies.[90] The reason why this talent for forming societies had passed largely unnoticed was because of its roots in another achievement which was uniquely English: the invention of the Trust under the system of Equity, which had enabled English groups to side-step covertly the odious 'concession' theory of the group under Roman law. Shielded by a 'wall of trustees', English groups were allowed to develop freely, unconstrained by the founding terms to which they would have been rigidly bound by the law of incorporation. Maitland called, therefore, for a radical revision of 'our popular English *Staatslehre*' to become a '*Korporationslehre*' instead.[91]

Sensitivity to the English context of Maitland's Pluralism featured prominently in the writings of J. N. Figgis[92] and Ernest Barker on the subject of groups, even if it was largely lost on younger disciples like

[88] See, for example, H. J. Laski's *Authority in the Modern State* (New Haven, 1917), p. 21.
[89] O. Gierke, *Political Theories of the Middle Age*, transl. and introd. by F. W. Maitland (Cambridge, 1900), p. xxvii.
[90] Some of these examples are drawn from Maitland's paper on 'Trust and Corporation' (1904), extracts of which are in J. Stapleton, ed., *Group Rights: Perspectives since 1900* (Bristol, 1995).   [91] Maitland, Introduction to Gierke, p. xi.
[92] See for example, J. N. Figgis, *Churches in the Modern State* (London, 1913), pp. 47–8.

H. J. Laski and G. D. H. Cole. Indeed, so struck was Barker by the vibrant nature of group life in England, as Maitland had presented it, that he detected a flagrant contradiction in the Pluralist critique of the state: the strength of group culture in Britain suggested that overlordship was manifestly not the normal character of the English state, but something that was held in reserve for extraordinary times of crisis.[93] The English state had effectively turned a blind eye to groups which were shielded by a Trust document. It was only when a searing intra-group dispute brought a voluntary society into the public gaze that the courts had exercised their Roman law right to treat it as if it were incorporated. This had occurred in the Free Church of Scotland case, which was finally decided by the House of Lords in 1904 in favour of a minority group opposed to change and to whom all the property of the church was conceded. But even then, the state – by the Churches (Scotland) Act of 1905 which rescinded the judgement of the House of Lords – had 'provide[d] a remedy for rigidity, after the event, by its power of legislation'.[94] Both English society, and the English state thus provided generous evidence of a liberal political culture and, as such, were the source of much deserved national pride. Whatever the merits of the Pluralist attack upon the state elsewhere in Europe, in England it applied purely to the doctrine and not to the practice of state sovereignty.

VI

The economic depression and political stalemate of interwar Britain fostered considerable disillusion right across the political spectrum. These years were dominated by the 'trench generation' of political thinkers and actors – men such as R. H. Tawney and Oswald Mosley whose experience of the horror of the First World War strengthened their resolve to build society anew in tribute to their lost comrades.[95] When all who were connected with the old world seemed to be dragging their heels, the disaffection of those whom it had presumed to sacrifice turned to bitterness. This is particularly evident in the opening chapter of Tawney's work *Equality* published in 1931 – entitled 'The Religion of Inequality'. Although Tawney could write appreciatively of the 'political genius of Englishmen' immediately after the First World War,[96] his tone became

[93] E. Barker, 'The Discredited State: Thoughts on Politics before the War', *Political Quarterly*, 2 o.s. (1915), in Stapleton, ed., *Group Rights*, p. 81.

[94] E. Barker, Introduction to Otto Gierke, *Natural Law and the Theory of Society, 1500–1800* (Cambridge, 1934), p. lxxix.

[95] On Mosley's 'obligations to his dead comrades', see R. Skidelsky, *Oswald Mosley* (1975; London, 1981), p. 167. See also R. H. Tawney's essay 'A National College of All Souls' (1917), in *The Attack: and Other Papers* (London, 1953).

[96] R. H. Tawney, 'Radical Social Reconstruction', in S. J. Chapman, ed., *Labour and Capital after the War* (London, 1918), p. 98.

increasingly uncompromising. As Grainger has suggested, 'What Tawney invoked was not the long English tradition of trimming, of coming to terms with the adversary, but the zealotry of the Puritan Rebellion and even the dedication of the Russian revolutionaries of 1917.'[97] Nevertheless, despite a sharp leftward turn in British political thought, with consequent shifts of loyalty to Communist Russia,[98] positive ideals of Englishness persisted throughout the interwar period. In particular, they were mobilised and further developed against the 'foreign' extremist creeds of both left and right which appeared to be making dangerous inroads into intellectual opinion at home.

The essence of a wide variety of interwar conceptions of Englishness was an association less with outward achievement than with a distinctively inward and private nation. As noted above, the portrayal of the English in political literature from the 1860s had been one of a hardy, adventurous race, much given to colonial exploration and defence, and to great expenditure of energy in maximising the opportunities which their unique political liberty had afforded.[99] Whether in the realm of politics or commerce, the English nation was considered destined to make an ineradicable impression upon an apparently boundless world. After 1918, however, this image lost much of its appeal. Revulsion from war combined with a weariness of empire to force a retreat of the English imagination to more local, familiar, and domestic contexts.[100] The pride that late nineteenth-century thinkers like Dicey had taken in the absence of English national pride was a theme that became set in a broader view of the 'character' of England. This emphasised the marked introspectiveness, modesty, and quiet pleasure taken by the English in their home environments. In addition, the English were considered a characteristically light-hearted people, yet with a strong propensity to act in accordance with inherited duties. But, beyond that, they were regarded as singularly blessed with a lack of driving ambition and assertiveness (although the 'misunderstanding' to which this could give rise abroad was much lamented by some and brilliantly satirised by others[101]). This may have been a distillation of the attitudes and values of the 'officer class' whose ranks had recently been so heavily depleted and whose memory – it has

[97] J. H. Grainger, *Character and Style in English Politics* (Cambridge, 1969), p. 201.

[98] Neal Wood, *Communism and British Intellectuals* (London, 1959), p. 42.

[99] This is exemplified in the biographies of great imperial figures by G. A. Henty. See, for example, his *With Clive to India: Or the Beginnings of an Empire* (London, 1884), and *With Kitchener in Soudan: A Story of Atbara and Omdurman* (London, 1903).

[100] See Alison Light, *Forever England: Femininity, Literature and Conservatism between the Wars* (London, 1991), p. 86.

[101] See, for example, Sir Alfred Zimmern, 'Our English Burden', in *Spiritual Values and World Affairs*, (Oxford, 1939), p. 136, and A. G. MacDonnell's novel *England their England*, p. 159.

been claimed – was now valorised at all levels of culture.[102] However, it was also a national self-conception which was well tailored to meet the challenge of the supremely activist philosophies underlying totalitarianism, in which political passions were encouraged to run high.

The origins of this national self-portrait are evident in a book published in 1922 – *Soliloquies in England* – and which was greatly taken to heart in the next two decades.[103] The author was the Spanish-American philosopher George Santayana, who acquired a considerable love of England during childhood visits and from his sojourn at Oxford during the war. He captured the mood of retreat which characterised English identity between the wars when he wrote that:

> We should none of us admire England to-day, if we had to admire it only for its conquering commerce, its pompous noblemen, or its parliamentary government. . . . There is, or was, a beautifully healthy England hidden from most foreigners; the England of the countryside and of the poets, domestic, sporting, gallant, boyish, of a sure and delicate heart.[104]

For Santayana, the English were always and everywhere governed by the 'weather in their soul' and never driven by external impulses, a nation which worshipped 'home' – even when, as its members often were, far away – and which was constantly aware of the limitations of 'finitude': the Englishman inhabits the realm of 'terra firma'.[105]

These 'English' themes of home, privacy, and a stolid, down-to-earth nature, were turned to good political account throughout the interwar period. They are central, for example, to the speeches of Stanley Baldwin.[106] Baldwin proved a master of throwing these English characteristics into the sharpest relief, noting, on one occasion, that even the most bitter internal enemies of 'England' were not unmoved by their force. For instance, in discussing the enormous susceptibility of the English to the ties of place, he could not resist mentioning an 'extreme

---

[102] See J. M. Winter, 'British National Identity and the First World War', in Green and Whiting, eds., *The Boundaries of the State in Modern Britain*. On the emergence of an English 'procedural' ideology of 'fair play' and 'balance' at the heart of 'officer class' values, see C. Stray, *Classics Transformed: Schools, Universities, and Society in England, 1830–1960* (Oxford, 1998), pp. 174, 264–5.

[103] George Santayana, *Soliloquies in England: and Later Soliloquies* (London 1922). Santayana's influence is evident in William Ralph Inge's *England* (London, 1926), esp. p. 113; Ernest Barker's concluding essay to *The Character of England* (Oxford, 1947), esp. pp. 551, 567. Santayana's emphasis on England as 'the paradise of individuality, eccentricity, heresy, anomalies, hobbies, and humours' (p. 30), is echoed in Stanley Baldwin's famous address 'On England', in *On England* (London, 1926), and also in G. M. Trevelyan's work. See below.   [104] Santayana, *Soliloquies in England*, p. 3.

[105] *Ibid.*, pp. 30, 34.

[106] On Baldwin's political thought, see Philip Williamson, 'The Doctrinal Politics of Stanley Baldwin', in M. Bentley, ed., *Public and Private Doctrine: Essays in British History presented to Maurice Cowling* (Cambridge, 1993); also his *Stanley Baldwin: Conservative Leadership and National Values* (Cambridge, 1999), esp. chs.8 and 10.

Left Wing Socialist' Member of Parliament who had spoken to him 'almost with tears in his eyes, of the Trent valley, from which his family came'.[107] Baldwin reflected a common attitude towards the empire after 1918 in conceiving it less in terms of power, might, and glory, which had so appealed to Seeley and others at the end of the nineteenth century, than as a simple extension of the Englishman's yearning for rural habitats.[108] Bonds of lineage and tradition were celebrated as the mainspring of empire over authority and the achievement of global supremacy. As such, empire was regarded primarily as a 'spiritual inheritance'.[109] At another level, Baldwin's analysis of the English character underlined its unique stability. In his famous address 'On England' delivered to the Royal Society of St George in 1924 Baldwin remarked that 'the Englishman is made for a time of crisis, and for a time of emergency'. Not inclined to worry overmuch, and being temperamentally unexpressive, the Englishman's nervous system remained 'sound and sane' when that of other peoples was invariably exhausted by perpetual strain.[110]

Baldwin's intention here was not merely to amuse: as in other speeches, he was anxious to warn his compatriots off the superficial attractions of 'foreign' political fare for which – mercifully – they were constitutionally unsuited. To this end, he played up the 'diversified individuality' of the English, their display of the full range of Dickensian characters which matched the deeply variegated nature of the landscape itself, adding that 'we [must] never allow our individuality as Englishmen to be steam-rollered'.[111] It is clear that to Baldwin, the kind of crisis solutions developed abroad would inevitably take that toll.

Baldwin was not alone in linking English individuality with a native imperturbability to which political high-handedness was traditionally alien. His sentiments were echoed by G. M. Trevelyan, whose histories of England are littered with examples of the archetypal 'amateur' Englishman. In the case of the latter, a touch of 'genius' more than compensated for an indifference to intellectual system-building, and the wholesale political reconstruction that invariably accompanied it. As Trevelyan wrote of Caxton, he was 'an early and a noble example of a well-known modern type that has done so much for the world, the individualistic Englishman following out his own "hobbies" with business capacity and trained zeal'.[112]

For Ernest Barker, likewise, there was a constancy and steadiness

---

[107] Stanley Baldwin, 'Country Patriotism', in *This Torch of Freedom* (London, 1935), p. 136.
[108] Stanley Baldwin, 'Empty Spaces and Willing Hands', in *Our Inheritance* (London, 1928), p. 145.   [109] Grainger, *Patriotisms*, pp. 324–5.
[110] Stanley Baldwin, 'On England', p. 3.
[111] *Ibid.*, p. 5; 'The Love of Country Things' (1931), in *This Torch of Freedom*.
[112] G. M. Trevelyan, *Illustrated English Social History*, 4 vols. (1942; Harmondsworth, Penguin, 1964), I, p. 165.

about all things English, qualities which became ever more clear to him as he observed the volatile nature of politics abroad. He shrank, in particular, from the 'eruption' of groups in continental Europe, especially in Germany, where they were apt to become 'great Brocken-spectres, confronting us as we walk.'[113] The three alternatives to 'democracy' which emerged in Russia, Italy, and Germany in the interwar period shared this same group-based feature. Common to all three also was a romanticism (in the case of Soviet communism, a 'romance of tractors and power-stations'[114]), a quality of abstractness to which the solid tradition of politics in England stood starkly opposed. The English temper, Barker maintained, 'is apt to mistrust enunciations of legal and political principle, as being but sounding words and abstract propositions, which may distract attention from the real necessity of actual legal remedies and concrete political institutions'.[115]

A similar message about the basis of English distinctiveness was conveyed to a wide audience by the popular historians of the interwar years: G. M. Trevelyan, H. A. L. Fisher, and Arthur Bryant. All three writers emphasised the limits of England's European involvement in the checking of the various dictators who had emerged there from time to time: Philip II of Spain, Louis XIV and Napoleon, Kaiser Wilhelm II, and now Hitler.[116] In his *Illustrated English Social History* – published in 1942, but written prior to the Second World War – Trevelyan spelt out the nature of the medieval legacy which had determined the separate development of England from continental Europe. He warned, that

unless we become a totalitarian state and forget all our Englishry, there will always be something medieval in our ways of thinking, especially in our idea that people and corporations have rights and liberties which the State ought in some degree to respect, in spite of the legal omnicompetence of Parliament. Conservatism and Liberalism in the broadest sense, are both medieval in origin, and so are trade unions. The men who established our civic liberties in the seventeenth century, appealed to medieval precedents against the 'modernizing' monarchy of the Stuarts.[117]

Despite Trevelyan's mention of trade unions in this characterisation of 'Englishry', the contribution of socialism to the latter is conspicuous by its absence.

Nevertheless, socialism, for its part, was not without its patriots, as the

---

[113] Barker, introduction to Gierke, *Natural Law and the Theory of Society*, p. xvii.
[114] E. Barker, *Reflections on Government* (London, 1942), p. 163.   [115] *Ibid.*, p. 32.
[116] See Philip Bell, 'A Historical Cast of Mind. Some Eminent English Historians and Attitudes to Continental Europe in the Middle of the Twentieth Century', *Journal of European Integration History*, 2 (1996), p. 18.
[117] Trevelyan, *Illustrated English Social History*, I, pp. 191–2.

case of Orwell illustrates. Against the disdain for patriotism in general and England in particular among the left intelligentsia of his time, Orwell insisted that socialist revolution must leave intact 'the unmistakable marks of our own civilisation'.[118] Chief among these was 'a belief in "the law" as something above the State and above the individual'.[119] Even stalwarts of the Communist Party of Great Britain proved susceptible to the lure of 'England' when their Soviet masters demanded that 'communist internationalism' should take precedence over the interests of the British people in 1939. For example, a recent biography of Harry Pollitt stresses, in relation to this episode, that 'It might disturb our cruder notions of both Englishness and Communism, but how very English a phenomenon was Stalinism in the shape that Pollitt gave it.'[120]

The sustained power of the English *patria* in unexpected parts of the political thought of interwar Britain is also illustrated by the writings of E. M. Forster. An associate of Bloomsbury, whose members typically disdained the vulgar, chauvinist emotions connected with their Victorian ancestors, Forster nevertheless rallied to the liberalism which had nourished such attitudes. In an anti-Nazi broadcast of 1940, he emphasised the 'national' character of English culture, 'spring[ing] naturally out of our way of looking at things, and out of the way we have looked at things in the past'.[121] By contrast, in countries like Germany, culture had taken an official, 'governmental' turn for the worse. Being genuinely national, Forster continued, English culture was capable of rising above itself, becoming 'supra-national' and displaying its full potential for generosity and modesty, as when it went to the aid of France.[122]

VII

In some circles, the effect of the Second World War was to amplify these cautionary warnings about the incompatibility between English national culture and an overbearing state. A traditional English resistance to organisation – to 'regimentation', as Forster put it – was widely invoked against the new vogue for 'planning' which emerged from the war. For some, like J. B. Priestley, this image was derived from nostalgia for a pre-1914 world of voluntary communities exemplified in the music-hall culture of cities such as Bradford.[123] For others, like Barker, its source was

---

[118] George Orwell, *The Lion and the Unicorn: Socialism and the English Genius* (1941; London, 1962), p. 85.   [119] *Ibid.*, p. 19.

[120] K. Morgan, *Harry Pollitt* (Manchester, 1993), p. 128.

[121] Forster, 'Three Anti-Nazi Broadcasts' (1940), in *Two Cheers for Democracy* (1951; Harmondsworth, 1965), p. 41.   [122] *Ibid.*, p. 43.

[123] See Chris Waters, 'J. B. Priestley 1894–1984: Englishness and the Politics of Nostalgia', in S. Pedersen and P. Mandler, eds., *After the Victorians: Private Conscience and Public Duty in Modern Britain* (London, 1994), p. 223.

broader. Thus, writing in celebration of the English character in 1945, Barker argued that:

The unseen part of English life is a mass of individual skills, which find a harmony by their own gift of adaptability, and find it in a temper of equanimity and phlegm. There is a nervous tension in planning – a nervous strain on the planner, and a nervous tug at his followers – which hardly accords with our instincts or the general tradition of our life.[124]

Such sentiments continued to be expressed in the next few years, and not simply by those whose political outlook had been shaped by the very different circumstances of the late nineteenth and early twentieth centuries. Prominent among a new generation of political thinkers who utilised long-established beliefs about English political culture and general way of life against the 'rationalist' character of post-war politics was Michael Oakeshott.[125] His thoughts were echoed by polemicists connected with the Society of Individualists – founded by the publisher Ernest Benn – for example, Colm Brogan.[126]

But the debate concerning planning effectively marked the end of the sway which the English *patria* had maintained over British political thought for the best part of a century. Economic and imperial decline hastened the demise of English national consciousness and its centrality to the identity of the United Kingdom more widely. Those, like Enoch Powell, who attempted to detach Englishness from the dual myths of industrial and imperial supremacy, clearly sensed the disadvantages more than the virtues that its characteristically subdued expression would now hold.[127] The idea of an entrenched and homogenous national character and culture – and the seeming political quiescence to which it led – received short shrift from a new generation of professional political scientists, anxious for active and expert government.[128] In so far as it was retained by a burgeoning race relations industry in the 1950s, it was recast

---

[124] E. Barker, ed., *The Character of England* (Oxford, 1947), pp. 554–5.

[125] On the 'English' inspiration behind Oakeshott's political philosophy of, first, anti-rationalism, and then the 'civil condition', see Nevil Johnson, 'Michael Joseph Oakeshott, 1901–1990', *Proceedings of the British Academy*, 80 (1991), pp. 405, 419; and J. L. Auspitz, 'Individuality, Civility and Theory: The Political Imagination of Michael Oakeshott,' *Political Theory*, 4(3) (1976), p. 292.

[126] On the 'Individualist Group's' manifesto which underpinned the Society of Individualists, see D. Abel, *Ernest Benn: Counsel for Liberty* (London, 1960), p. 110. Colm Brogan's books include *Our New Masters* (London, 1947).

[127] Simon Heffer, *Like the Roman: The Life of Enoch Powell* (London, 1998), p. 550.

[128] W. J. M. Mackenzie wrote despairingly in 1955 of Oakeshott's refuge against the dangers of ideological politics in 'nationalism, scepticism, and pessimism'. 'Political Theory and Political Education', in *Explorations in Government: Collected Papers, 1951–1968* (London, 1975), pp. 25–9. It is small wonder that W. H. Greenleaf could write of Oakeshott's patriotism in 1966 that 'feeling of this kind is all too rare nowadays and is likely to be scorned on sight'. *Oakeshott's Philosophical Politics* (London, 1966), p. 84.

in narrow, racial terms.[129] Aside from Powell, custodianship of a version of English national values and national identity that were rooted in history rather than race, common experience, and temperament rather than genetic difference, was henceforth assumed by literary figures like John Betjeman, with a keen popular following. But the rhetoric of Englishness which Betjeman developed was notably devoid of any political content, for all its broadly conservative framework: its main focus was architecture and poetry.

[129] See C. Waters, '"Dark Strangers" in our Midst: Discourses of Race and Nation in Britain, 1947–1963', *Journal of British Studies*, 36 (1997), pp. 207–38.

Contributors

Stefan Collini is Reader in Intellectual History and English Literature in the Faculty of English and a Fellow of Clare Hall, Cambridge. His most recent books are *Matthew Arnold: A Critical Portrait* (1994) and *English Pasts: Essays in History and Culture* (1999). He is currently working on the question of intellectuals in twentieth-century Britain.

Mark Salber Phillips teaches in the Department of History, University of British Columbia. He is the author of a number of studies on historical thought and writing, including *Marco Parenti: A Life in Medici Florence* (1987) and *Society and Sentiment: Genres of Historical Writing in Britain, 1750–1820* (2000).

J. G. A. Pocock is Professor Emeritus of History at Johns Hopkins University, Baltimore. He is the author of *The Ancient Constitution and the Feudal Law* (1957, 1987), *The Machiavellian Moment* (1975), and *Virtue, Commerce and History* (1985). Two volumes of a series entitled *Barbarism and Religion*, centred on Gibbon and his *Decline and Fall*, appeared in 1999.

David Womersley is a Fellow and Tutor in English at Jesus College, Oxford. He is the author of *The Transformation of the Decline and Fall of the Roman Empire* (1988), and is currently completing a further work on Gibbon. He is also preparing a study of Shakespeare's history plays.

Brian Young is a Lecturer in Intellectual History at the University of Sussex. He is the author of *Religion and Enlightenment in Eighteenth-Century England* (1998), and of numerous essays on English intellectual and religious history. He is currently at work on a study of religion, history writing, and empire, beginning with the period immediately before Gibbon's writing career and ending with that in which Macaulay was at work.

Blair Worden is Professor of Early Modern History at the University of Sussex. His books include *The Rump Parliament* (1974) and *The Sound of Virtue: Philip Sidney's Arcadia and Elizabethan Politics* (1996).

William Thomas is a Tutor in Modern History at Christ Church, Oxford. He published a book on the *Philosophic Radicals* in 1979 and a short study of J. S. Mill in the 'Past Masters' series in 1985. He has just completed a book on Macaulay's quarrel with J. W. Croker.

John Drury is Dean of Christ Church, Oxford. He was Lecturer in Religious Studies at Sussex between 1979 and 1981. From 1981 to 1991 he was Dean of King's College, Cambridge. He has written about the New Testament, particularly *The Parables in the Gospels* (1985). His study of Christian paintings in the National Gallery, *Painting the Word*, was published in 1999.

Boyd Hilton is Reader in Modern British History at Cambridge and a Fellow of Trinity College. He is the author of *The Age of Atonement: The Influence of Evangelicalism on Social and Economic Thought, 1785–1865* (1988) and is currently working on the early nineteenth-century volume of *The New Oxford History of England*.

John Burrow is Professor of European Thought, University of Oxford and a Fellow of Balliol College. He is author of *A Liberal Descent. Victorian Historians and the English Past* (1981), and *Whigs and Liberals. Continuity and Change in English Political Thought* (1988). His *Crisis of Reason. European Thought, 1848–1914* is to be published in 2000.

Peter Mandler is Professor of Modern History at London Guildhall University. His most recent books are *After the Victorians: Private Conscience and Public Duty in Modern Britain* (1994, edited with Susan Pedersen) and *The Fall and Rise of the Stately Home* (1997).

Julia Stapleton is Lecturer in Politics at the University of Durham and author of *Englishness and the Study of Politics: The Social and Political Thought of Ernest Barker* (1994).

Acknowledgements

Several individuals and institutions have given valuable help and support to this project. Foremost among these is Rosa Weeks who remained cheerful and resourceful through the challenges presented by contributors and power cuts alike, and who gave up weekends so that a diverse range of not always impeccable electronic missives might be transformed into publisher-ready disks. We are also grateful to Martin van Gelderen who, wearing his several administrative hats, gave practical and tactical assistance. At Cambridge University Press, Richard Fisher was, by turns, encouraging, constructive, and tolerant during the long process separating the initial gleam in the eye from the finished books. We are grateful to the British Academy and the University of Sussex Centre for Literary and Intellectual History for grants to support the colloquium held at Sussex in September 1998. And we are, above all, grateful to the contributors and, especially, our two honorands: not only have all friendships emerged unscathed, if severely tested at times, but also much enjoyment has been had along the way.

Index